IN THE NAME OF ROME

IN THE NAME OF

ROME

THE MEN WHO WON THE
ROMAN EMPIRE

ADRIAN GOLDSWORTHY

WEIDENFELD & NICOLSON

In memory of
Captain William Walker RFA (retired)
'Uncle Bill'
A good friend and a true leader
1933–2002

Weidenfeld & Nicolson
The Orion Publishing Group Ltd
Orion House, 5 Upper Saint Martin's Lane, London WC2H 9EA

British Library Cataloguing-in-Publication Data
A catalogue record for this book is available from the British Library

ISBN 0-297-84666-3

Typography Gwyn Lewis

Printed and bound in Great Britain by Clays Ltd, St Ives plc

CONTENTS

LIST OF MAPS AND DIAGRAMS

PREFACE

'THIS IS THE ONLY PLACE THAT YOU CAN LEARN LEADERSHIP.' IT WAS A
theme to which the Colonel frequently returned in the talks which brought
to a close many of the weekly drill-nights in the Officer Training Corps at
Oxford. After parade, followed by a couple of hours of lectures and training
(about everything from map reading, chemical warfare, first aid and small
unit tactics, to how to write a letter – or later, once I had joined the RA Troop,
tiring but exhilarating practice in taking the light guns into and out of action),
we would file into a large and luxurious auditorium loaned from the (at least
according to legend) fabulously rich University Air Squadron. By this time
most were impatient to be let loose on the Mess, but being both teetotal
and keen on military history I rather enjoyed these sessions. For thirty
minutes or so the Colonel, looking like a properly fed Monty, would talk
about the attributes of a good leader, telling stories of Marlborough, Nelson
and Slim, and on occasions even the more unorthodox methods of Lawrence
and Wingate. Sometimes he would show us a chart or diagram depicting
the skills required to lead, but the assumption was always that leaders learned
not so much from reading, instruction and theory, but from doing. This is
not to say that formal instruction and training is of no value, simply that on
its own it is not enough. Experience is always the best tutor, and of course any
system of training is really just an attempt to impart lessons from the
experience and insights of others.

Leaders matter. So, in their way for and good or ill, does every individual
person involved in any activity or project, but those with greater power and
responsibility to direct an operation inevitably have more influence on events.
I am not a soldier, nor in the solitary existence of a writer am I much called
upon to lead or direct anyone else – a point brought home to me while

writing this book when I gave a talk on Roman styles of leadership to a group of British Army officers. Two years in the Oxford University OTC represents the sum total of my military experience and, although I found it richly rewarding and illuminating, I doubt that it altered my essentially civilian status. It did serve as a useful reminder of how difficult it is to co-ordinate the movements of even a few hundred men, and helped to illustrate how much friction inevitably occurs even on exercise – the whole 'Hurry up and wait' business so familiar to all those who have ever worn uniform. Perhaps even more valuable for the present topic, it provided many illustrations of the difference made by leaders. The best were not always especially visible or even especially vocal, it was just that everything seemed to run smoothly whenever they were in charge. A University Officer Training Corps is filled with young and inexperienced cadets, and inevitably contains a very broad range of talents. A minority were natural leaders, instinctively good at motivating and directing others, while the vast majority had to learn how to do this gradually, inevitably making mistakes along the way. A tiny handful would probably never learn, and in many ways the presence of a bad leader was far more obvious than a good one.

This book is about some of Rome's most successful generals and their victories. Its concern is with establishing what happened during these specific campaigns, battles and sieges, and especially with how the commander went about his task of leading and controlling an army. Roman generals received no formal training before being appointed to high commands, and whatever they had learned up to this point they had learned by experience or informal conversation and study. They were also selected as much – probably more – on the basis of family background and political connections as on any estimate of their ability. In a modern sense they were amateurs, and so by extension unskilled and poor at their job. One of the themes of this book is to reject this assumption, for the standard of Rome's military leaders seems actually to have been good. Although the subjects of this study represent in many ways the pick of the bunch, it will become evident that these men did not act in ways significantly different to other Roman generals. The best commanders simply did the same things better than anyone else. Rome's generals were shaped by practical experience and common sense, two elements which no system of producing leaders or managers should ever neglect.

History concerns the actions and interactions of human beings and as such the study of any aspect of the past tells us something about the nature of humanity and hence helps us to understand our own times. I am sure that lessons can be learnt from studying the campaigns of Roman generals, but that is not the purpose of this book – I have no desire to write something entitled *Management Success the Roman Way*. So many of those who seek to lay down fixed rules for effective leadership give the impression of lacking any of the attributes necessary to exercise it. Much of what a successful general does appears easy and straightforward when written coldly on a page, in the same way that any list of 'principles of war' appears to be little more than common sense. The difficulty lies in implementing these in practice and in how the general gets things done in the field. Thousands could copy the actions and mannerisms of a Caesar or a Napoleon and fail dismally, appearing ridiculous in the process.

I do not intend to spend time in the following chapters dissecting each commander's decisions on campaign, still less putting forward 'better' alternatives of my own devising from the comfort of my office. Nor do I intend to rank the men discussed in order of ability or debate their merits and defects in comparison to famous commanders from other periods. Instead our concern is with such things as what was actually done, why it was done, what it was supposed to achieve, how it was implemented, and what were its consequences in fact. The aim is to understand the past on its own terms, and for an historian that is an end in itself. Once that is done, then those so inclined may usefully add the episodes described to the pool of information which helps each of us to understand how people function in the world around us. Experience, whether personal or vicarious, is of value to leader and follower alike. The hard part is using it well.

I should at this point thank various family members and friends, and in particular Ian Hughes, who read and commented on the manuscript in all of its various stages. I would also like to thank Keith Lowe and the staff at Weidenfeld & Nicolson for putting forward the idea for this book in the first place and seeing it through to publication.

FROM THE BEGINNING:
CHIEFTAIN AND HERO TO POLITICIAN AND GENERAL

> The duty of a general is to ride by the ranks on horseback, show himself to
> those in danger, praise the brave, threaten the cowardly, encourage the lazy,
> fill up gaps, transpose a unit if necessary, bring aid to the wearied, anticipate
> the crisis, the hour and the outcome.[1]

ONASANDER'S SUMMARY OF A GENERAL'S BATTLEFIELD ROLE WAS WRITTEN
in the middle of the first century AD, but reflected a command style which
persisted for at least seven hundred years and was characteristically Roman.
The general was there to direct the fighting and to inspire his soldiers by
making them feel that they were being closely watched and that a conspicuous act of courage would be rewarded as promptly as conspicuous
cowardice would be punished. It was not his job to plunge into the thick of
the fray, sword or spear in hand, fighting at the head of his men and sharing
their dangers. The Romans knew that Alexander the Great had led his
Macedonians to victory in this way time after time, but there was never any
real expectation that their own commanders should emulate such heroics.
Onasander was himself a Greek, and a man without military experience
writing in a genre whose style had been set in the Hellenistic era, but for
all the literary stereotypes contained within his work the figure of the
commander depicted in his *The General* was most decidedly Roman. The
book was written in Rome and dedicated to Quintus Veranius, a Roman
senator who would die while in command of the army in Britain in AD 58.
The Romans proudly boasted that they had copied much of their tactics
and military equipment from their foreign enemies, but their debt to others

was far less when it came to the basic structure of their army and the functions performed by its leaders.

This is a book about generals, and specifically about fifteen of the most successful Roman commanders from the late third century BC to the middle of the sixth century AD. Some of these men are still relatively well known, at least amongst military historians – Scipio Africanus, Pompey and Caesar would all certainly be considered for inclusion amongst the ranks of the ablest commanders in history – while others have been largely forgotten. All, with the possible exception of Julian, were at the very least competent generals who won significant successes even if they ultimately suffered defeat, but most were very talented. Selection has been based on their importance, both in the wider history of Rome and in the development of Roman warfare, and also on the availability of sufficient sources to describe them in any detail. There is only a single subject from each of the second, fourth and sixth centuries AD, and none from the third or fifth centuries, simply because the evidence for these periods is so poor. For the same reason we cannot discuss in detail the campaigns of any Roman commander before the Second Punic War. Yet the spread remains wide, and the individual subjects illustrate well the changes both in the nature of the Roman army and in the relationship between a general in the field and the State.

Rather than survey a man's entire career, each chapter focuses on one or two specific episodes during his campaigns, looking in some detail at how each man interacted with and controlled his army. The main emphasis is always on what the commander did at each stage of an operation and how far this contributed to its outcome. Such an approach, with elements of biography and a concentration on the general's role – on strategy, tactics and their implementation, and on leadership – represents a very traditional style of military history. Inevitably it involves a strong element of narrative and descriptions of the more dramatic elements of wars, of battles and sieges, trumpets and swords. Though popular with a general reader, this sort of history has in recent decades lacked academic respectability. Instead scholars have preferred to look at the broader picture, hoping to perceive deeper economic, social or cultural factors which were held to have a more important influence on the outcome of conflicts than individual decisions or events during a war. To make the topic even less fashionable, this is also essentially a book about aristocrats, since the Romans felt that only the high-born and privileged deserved to be entrusted with high command. Even a 'new man' (*novus homo*) such as Marius, derided for his vulgar origins by the inner élite of the Senate even as he forced his way in to join them, still came only from the margins of the aristocracy and was not in any real sense more representative of the wider population.

By modern standards all Roman commanders were also essentially amateur soldiers. Most spent only part of their career – usually well under half of their adult lives – serving with the army. None received any formal training for command and they were appointed on the basis of political success, which in turn was reliant to a great extent on birth and wealth. Even a man like Belisarius, who did serve as an officer for most of his life, was promoted because of his perceived loyalty to the Emperor Justinian and did not pass through any organized system of training and selection. At no time in Rome's history was there ever anything even vaguely resembling a staff college to educate commanders and their senior subordinates. Works of military theory were common in some periods, but many were little more than drill manuals (often describing the manoeuvres of Hellenistic phalanxes whose tactics had been obsolete for centuries) and all lacked detail. Some Roman generals are supposed to have prepared themselves for high command purely through reading such works, although this was never considered to be the best way to learn. Roman aristocrats were supposed to learn how to lead an army just as they learned how to behave in political life, by watching others and through personal experience in junior capacities.[2]

To modern eyes the selection of generals on the basis of their political influence, under the assumption that they would know enough to be able to pick up the job of a commander as they went along, seems absurdly random and inefficient. It has often been assumed that Roman generals were usually men of extremely limited talents. In the twentieth century Major General J.F.C. Fuller characterized Roman generals as little more than 'drill-masters', while W. Messer declared that they achieved a fairly consistent level of mediocrity. (Perhaps at this point we should remember Moltke's comment that 'in war with its enormous friction, even the mediocre is quite an achievement'.) The undeniable success of the Roman army for so many centuries is often held to have been achieved in spite of its generals, rather than because of them. To many commentators the tactical system of the legions seems designed to take responsibility away from the army commander and instead place much of it in the hands of more junior officers. The most important of these were the centurions, who are seen as highly professional and therefore good at their jobs. Occasionally there appeared men like Scipio or Caesar who were far more talented than the typical aristocratic general, but their skill was largely a reflection of instinctive genius and could not be emulated by others. The subjects of this book could be seen as such aberrations, the tiny minority of genuinely skilful commanders produced by the Roman system along with the vast majority of nonentities and downright incompetents. In much the same way the eighteenth and early nineteenth century British Army's system of purchase and patronage produced the occasional Wellington or Moore amongst such dismal leaders as Whitelocke, Elphinstone and Raglan.[3]

Yet a closer examination of the evidence suggests that most of these assumptions are at best greatly exaggerated and often simply wrong. Far from taking power away from the general, the Roman tactical system concentrated it in his hands. Junior officers such as centurions played a vitally important role, but they fitted into a hierarchy with the army commander at the top and allowed him to have more control of events rather than less. Some commanders were certainly better at their job than others, but the activities of a Scipio, Marius or Caesar on campaign do not appear to have been profoundly different from their contemporaries. The best Roman generals led and controlled their armies in essentially the same way as any other aristocrat, and the difference lay primarily in the skill with which they did so. In most periods the standard of the average Roman commander was actually quite good for all their lack of formal training. Over the centuries the Romans produced their share of incompetents who led the legions to needless disasters, but this has been true of all armies throughout history. It is extremely unlikely that even the most sophisticated modern methods of selecting and preparing officers for high rank will not occasionally throw up an individual who will prove to be utterly unsuited to high command. Others may appear to have every attribute necessary for a successful general, but will fail largely because of factors seemingly beyond their control. Many victorious Roman generals openly boasted that they were lucky, acknowledging that (as Caesar was to write) fortune played even more of a central role in warfare than in other human activities.

Studying the conduct of warfare and the role of the commander may not be fashionable, but that does not mean that it is unimportant or unprofitable. War played a major part in Rome's history, for military success created and for a long time preserved the Empire. Wider factors – attitudes to warfare, and Rome's capacity and willingness to devote enormous human and material resources to waging war – underlay the effectiveness of the Roman military, but did not make its success inevitable. In the Second Punic War such factors allowed the Republic to endure the series of staggering disasters inflicted on it by Hannibal, but the war could not be won until a way was found to defeat the enemy on the battlefield. The events of a campaign, and especially the battles and sieges, were obviously influenced by the wider context, but were still, as the Romans knew, intensely unpredictable. In any battle, and most of all a battle fought primarily with edged weapons, the outcome was never wholly certain and was determined by many factors, morale chief amongst them. Unless the Roman army could defeat its opponents in the field, wars could not be won. Understanding how they did, or did not, do this is never simply a matter of such apparent certainties as resources, ideology, and even equipment and tactics, for it requires a wider appreciation of the behaviour of human beings both as individuals and groups.

All history, including military history, is ultimately about people – their attitudes, emotions, actions and interactions with each other – and this is best achieved by establishing what actually happened before proceeding to explain why it did so. Too heavy a concentration on wider factors can obscure this as easily as the old-fashioned depiction of battles as being fought by symbols on a map where victory goes to the side most purely applying tactics based upon fixed 'principles of war'. The most imaginative tactics were of little value if a commander was unable to get his army – consisting of thousands or maybe tens of thousands of individual soldiers – into the right places at the right time to implement them. The practical business of controlling, manoeuvring and supplying an army occupied far more of a commander's time than the devising of clever strategy or tactics. More than any other single individual, the actions of the general influenced the course of a campaign or battle. For good or ill, what the commander did, or did not do, mattered.

SOURCES

By far the greatest part of our evidence for the careers of Roman generals is derived from the Greek and Latin literary accounts of their actions. At times we are able to supplement this with sculptural or other artistic depictions of commanders, with inscriptions recording achievements, and on rare occasions with excavated traces of the operations of their armies such as the remains of siegeworks. Valuable though such things are, it is only in the written accounts that we are told about what generals actually did and how their armies operated. As we have already noted, the selection of the subjects for the following chapters has owed much to the survival of adequate descriptions of their campaigns. Only a tiny fraction of the works written in antiquity have survived. Many other books are known only by name or from fragments so minute as to be of little value. We are extremely fortunate to have Julius Caesar's own *Commentaries* describing his campaigns in Gaul and the Civil War. Obviously such an account is highly favourable to its author, but the wealth of detail it supplies concerning his activities provides an invaluable picture of a general in the field. Significantly it also highlights those attributes and achievements believed by an audience of contemporary Romans to be most admirable in an army commander. Many, perhaps most, other Roman generals also wrote their *Commentaries* but none of these accounts have survived in any useful form. At best we may find traces of these lost works in the narratives of later historians who drew upon them as a source.

Caesar's operations are understood primarily from his own description of them, which only occasionally is supplemented by information from other authors. The great victories of his contemporary and rival Pompey the Great are only described in any detail by authors who wrote more than a century after his death. Such a gap between the events themselves and our earliest surviving account of them is typical for a good deal of Greek and Roman history. It is all too easy to forget that our most detailed sources for Alexander the Great were written more than 400 years after his reign. Occasionally we are more fortunate and have a work written by an eyewitness of many of the events recounted. Polybius was with Scipio Aemilianus at Carthage in 147–146 BC and may possibly also have been at Numantia, although in fact his description of these operations is in the main only preserved in passages written by others. More directly Josephus was with Titus during the siege of Jerusalem, Ammianus served under Julian the Apostate briefly in Gaul and during the Persian expedition, while Procopius accompanied Belisarius throughout his campaigns. Sometimes other authors refer to similar eyewitness accounts which have been lost, but it was not customary for ancient historians to give the sources for the information they present. In most cases we simply have a narrative written many years after an event whose reliability is usually impossible to prove or disprove.

Many ancient historians open their works with protestations of their intention to be truthful. Yet it was even more important for them to produce a text that was dramatic and highly readable, for history was supposed to entertain as much as, if not more than, it informed. Sometimes personal or political bias led to conscious distortion of the truth, while on other occasions inadequate or non-existent sources were supplemented by invention, often employing traditional rhetorical themes. On other occasions the military ignorance of the author led him to misunderstand his source, as when Livy mistranslated Polybius' description of the Macedonian phalanx lowering its pikes into the fighting position to say that they dropped their pikes and fought with their swords. This is a rare case where the texts of both the original source and a later version have survived, but only seldom do we have this luxury. For some campaigns we have more than one source describing the same events and so may compare their details, but more often we are reliant on a single account. If we reject its testimony then we usually have nothing with which to replace it. Ultimately we can do little more than assess the plausibility of each account and perhaps register varying degrees of scepticism.

POLITICS AND WAR: FROM THE BEGINNING TILL 218 BC

The Romans did not begin to write history until the end of the third century BC, and were virtually ignored by Greek writers until around the same time. It was only following the defeat of Carthage in 201 BC that histories of Rome began to be set down. For times before living memory there were a few formal records of laws, magistrates elected in each year and the celebration of religious festivals, but virtually nothing to set flesh on these bare bones apart from folk memories, poems and songs, most of which celebrated the deeds of the great aristocratic houses. Later this rich oral culture would help inspire the stories Livy and other writers would tell of Rome's earliest days, of Romulus' foundation of the city and the six kings who succeeded him, till the last was expelled and Rome became a Republic. There may well be many faint strands of truth interwoven with romantic invention in such tales, but it is now impossible to separate the two. Instead we shall merely survey the traditions concerning military leadership at Rome.[4]

Traditionally founded in 753 BC, Rome was for centuries only a small community (or probably several small communities which over time co-alesced into one). The warfare waged by the Romans in these years was on a correspondingly small scale, consisting mainly of raiding and cattle rustling with the occasional skirmish-like battle. Most of the Romans' leaders were warrior chieftains in the heroic mould (although the stories about the wisdom and piety of King Numa suggest that other attributes were also felt to be worthy of respect). Such kings and chiefs were leaders because in time of war they fought with conspicuous courage. In many respects they resembled the heroes of Homer's *Iliad*, who fought so that people would say

'Indeed, these are no ignoble men who are lords of Lykia, these kings of ours who feed upon the fat sheep appointed and drink the exquisite sweet wine, since indeed there is strength of valour in them, since they fight in the forefront of the Lykians.'[5]

The revolution which converted Rome from a monarchy into a republic appears to have done little to change the nature of military leadership, for the most prominent figures in the new state were still expected to fight in a conspicuous manner. The heroic ideal was to rush out in front of the other warriors and clash with enemy chieftains, fighting and winning within sight of all. On some occasions such duels could be formally arranged with the enemy, as when the three Horatii brothers fought as champions against the three Curiatii brothers of neighbouring Veii. According to the legend two of the Romans were quickly cut down, but not before they had wounded their opponents. The last Horatius then pretended to flee, drawing the Curiatii into pursuit until they had separated, at which point he turned round and killed each one separately. Returning to Rome amid the acclamations of the army and the rest of his fellow citizens, the victor then killed his own sister for failing to welcome him enthusiastically enough – she had been betrothed to one of the Curiatii. This was just one story of individual heroics – even if its sequel was brutal and used to illustrate the gradual regulation of the behaviour of the men of violence by the wider community. Another involved Horatius Cocles, the man who held off the entire Etruscan army while the bridge across the Tiber was broken down behind him and then swam to safety. Whether or not there is any truth in such tales, they testify to a type of warfare prevalent in many primitive cultures.[6]

A feature of the stories about early Rome was the willingness to accept outsiders into the community, something that was rare elsewhere in the ancient world. Rome steadily grew in size and population, and as it expanded so too did the scale of its wars. The bands of warriors following individual heroic leaders were replaced by a wider levy of all those who could provide themselves with the necessary equipment to fight. In time – we do not understand this process well in the case of Rome or indeed any other Greek or Italian city – the Romans started to fight as hoplites in a tightly formed block or phalanx. Hoplites carried a round, bronze-faced shield some 3 feet in diameter, wore a helmet, cuirass and greaves and fought primarily with a long thrusting spear. The hoplite phalanx gave far fewer opportunities for acts of conspicuous heroism, for the densely packed warriors could see little of what was going on beyond a range of a few feet. As a small number of heroes ceased to dominate battles and the issue was instead decided by many hundreds, sometimes thousands, of hoplites fighting shoulder to shoulder, so the political balance of the community changed. Just as kings and chieftains had justified their authority by their prominence in war, so now the hoplite class demanded influence in the state commensurate with their battlefield role. In time they began annually to elect their own leaders to preside over the state in both peace and war. Most of these men were still drawn from a fairly narrow group of families, descended mainly from the old warrior aristocracy, who did not readily concede power. After a number of experiments with different systems of magistracies, it became established practice to choose by election two consuls to act as the Republic's senior executive officers. The voting took place in an assembly known as the *Comitia Centuriata*, in which citizens voted in groups determined by their function in the army.[7]

The consuls had equal power or *imperium*, for the Romans were afraid to allow supreme authority to any individual, but usually each was given an independent field command. By the fourth century BC few enemies required the attention of Rome's entire military resources under both consuls. It was also an indication of the growing size of the Republic and the increased scale of its wars that in most years war was being fought simultaneously against two enemies. The word *legio* (legion) had originally meant simply 'levy' and referred to the entire force raised by the Republic in time of war. Probably from the early days of the consulship it became normal practice to divide the levy into two and so provide each magistrate with a force to command, and over time 'legion' became the name for the subdivision. Later the number would increase again and the internal organization of each legion become more sophisticated. The Roman Republic continued to grow, defeating the Etruscans, Samnites and most other Italian peoples, before subduing the Greek colonies in Italy by the early third century BC.

Yet in many ways Italy was a military backwater and the Romans along with other Italian peoples somewhat primitive in their methods of warmaking. In the later fifth century BC the Peloponnesian War between Athens and Sparta and their allies had swept aside many of the conventions of hoplite warfare. By the fourth century BC most Greek states were increasingly reliant on small groups of professional soldiers or mercenaries, in place of the traditional phalanx raised when needed from all those citizens able to afford hoplite arms. Armies had become more complex, containing different types of infantry and sometimes cavalry as well, while campaigns lasted longer than in the past and more often involved sieges. Such warfare placed more demands on generals than the simple days of two phalanxes ploughing into each other on an open plain, when the commander had simply taken his place in the front rank to inspire his men.

Though most of these innovations had appeared first in the Greek states, it was to be the barbarian Macedonian kings to the north who created a far more effective army where cavalry and infantry fought in support of each other, which marched quickly to surprise its opponents and was capable of taking walled cities when necessary. Philip II and Alexander overran all of Greece, before the latter crossed to Asia and swept eastwards through Persia and into India. Alexander is supposed to have slept with a copy of the *Iliad* under his pillow and consciously wanted to associate himself with Homer's greatest hero, Achilles. Before a battle Alexander took great care to man-oeuvre and deploy his army so that it could advance and apply co-ordinated pressure all along the enemy's front. Then, at the critical moment he would lead his Companion cavalry in a charge against the most vulnerable part of the opposition's line. In this way he inspired his soldiers to heights of valour, but once the fighting began he could exercise little direct influence on the course of the battle. Instead he trusted his subordinate officers to control the troops in other sectors of the field, although it is notable that he made very little use of reserves, largely because he would have been unable to send the order to commit these troops once the fighting had begun. Alexander was an exceptionally bold leader, paying the price for his command style in a long catalogue of wounds, many received in hand-to-hand combat.[8]

Few of the Successor generals who tore Alexander's empire apart in the decades after his death were quite as reckless, but even so most felt obliged at some stage to lead a charge in person. King Pyrrhus of Epirus, who claimed direct descent from Achilles, was one of the keenest to fight hand to hand and was eventually killed leading his men to storm a city. He was also a thinking soldier who had produced a manual on generalship, which has unfortunately not survived. In battle Plutarch claims that although he '…exposed himself in personal combat and drove back all who encountered him, he kept throughout a complete grasp of the progress of the battle and never lost his presence of mind. He directed the action as though he was watching it from a distance, yet he was everywhere himself, and always managed to be at hand to support his troops wherever the pressure was greatest.'[9] Personal heroism was still considered both appropriate and admirable in an army commander, especially when he was a monarch, but he was also expected to direct his army closely. Alexander's greatest victories had been won over enemies far less effective in close combat than his Macedonians, but his Successors spent much of their time fighting each other and so were usually confronted by armies almost identical in equipment, tactics and doctrine to their own men. With no in-built superiority over the enemy, commanders had to seek some special advantage to ensure victory. The military theory which flourished at this period was greatly concerned with the right conditions in which a commander should fight a battle.

The Romans first came face to face with a modern Hellenistic army when in 280 BC Pyrrhus came to the aid of the Greek city of Tarentum in Southern Italy in its conflict with Rome. After two major defeats, the Romans were finally able to defeat the King of Epirus in 275 at Malventum, but the stubborn resilience of Roman legionaries had more to do with this success than any inspired generalship. In many respects the Roman style of command belonged to an older, simpler era, with far less expectation of prolonged manoeuvring prior to a pitched battle as each side searched for as many little advantages as possible. Yet once the fighting started, the behaviour of the Roman general differed markedly from his Hellenistic counterpart. A magistrate rather than a king, the Roman had no fixed place on the battlefield, no royal bodyguard at whose head he was expected to charge. The consul stationed himself wherever he thought the most important fighting would occur and during the battle moved along behind the fighting line, encouraging and directing the troops. Hellenistic armies rarely made much use of reserves, but the basic formation of the Roman legion kept half to two thirds of its men back from the front line at the start of the battle. It was the general's task to feed in these fresh troops as the situation required.

Rome had certainly not abandoned all heroic traditions and at times generals did engage in combat. Many aristocrats boasted of the number of times they had fought and won single combats, although by the third century BC at the latest they had most likely done this while serving in a junior capacity. At Sentinum in 295 BC one of the two consuls with the army – an exceptionally large force to face a confederation of Samnite, Etruscan and Gallic enemies – performed an archaic ritual when he 'devoted' himself as a sacrifice to the Earth and the gods of the Underworld to save the army of the Roman People. Once he had completed the rites this man, Publius Decius Mus, spurred his horse forward into a lone charge against the Gauls and was swiftly killed. Livy claims that he had formally handed over his command to a subordinate before this ritual suicide (a gesture which was something of a family tradition, for his father had acted in the same way in 340 BC). Sentinum ended in a hard fought and costly Roman victory.[10]

One of the most important attributes of a Roman aristocrat was *virtus*, for which the modern derivative 'virtue' is a poor translation. *Virtus* embraced all the important martial qualities, including not just physical courage and skill at arms, but also the moral courage and other gifts of a commander. A Roman nobleman was expected to be capable of deploying an army in battle order and controlling it during the fighting, paying attention to the small detail of individual units and their commitment to the combat. He was to have the confidence and sense to make appropriate decisions, firmly adhering to them or having the courage to confess an error as appropriate. Most of all he was never to doubt Rome's ultimate victory. Such an ideal permitted a broad range of interpretations. Some men obviously continued to place far greater stress on the aspect of individual heroics, but they were a clear minority by the time of the First Punic War when we can first begin to glimpse something of the behaviour of Rome's commanders in the field. Even those who still aspired to personal deeds of valour did not feel that this absolved them from the direction of their army, for such acts were simply an additional source of glory and did not alter the commander's most important role.[11]

THE CONTEXT OF COMMAND

War and politics were inseparably linked at Rome, and her leaders were expected to guide public life in the Forum or lead an army on campaign as required. Since foreign enemies posed a great and obvious threat to the State's prosperity, and at times even its existence, the defeat of an enemy in war was held to be the greatest achievement for any leader and brought the most glory. Since for many centuries senators provided all of the state's senior magistrates and commanders, the capacity to provide successful military leadership became a central part of the senatorial class's self-image. Later even the most unmilitary of emperors – and we should remember that our word 'emperor' is derived from the Latin *imperator* or general – paraded the successes achieved by their armies and suffered a serious drop in prestige if wars went badly. Until late antiquity the men who commanded Rome's armies followed a career, the *cursus honorum*, which brought them a range of civil and military posts. Governors of a province were expected to administrate and dispense justice or wage war depending upon the situation. However, it is a grave mistake to view the Roman system through modern eyes and to claim that Roman commanders were not really soldiers at all, but politicians, for these men were always both. Military glory helped a man's political career and might in turn lead to further opportunities for command in war. Even men whose talents were more suited either to fighting or politicking had to have at least some minimum proficiency in both if they were to have the chance to show their talents.

Successful generals usually profited financially from their campaigns, but the gains in prestige were in some respects even greater. After a victory in the field, a commander's army would formally hail him as *imperator*. On his return to Rome he could then expect to be granted the right to celebrate a triumph, when he and his troops would process along the Sacra Via, the 'Sacred Way' which led through the heart of the city. The general rode in a four-horse chariot, his face painted red and dressed so that he resembled the old terracotta statues of Jupiter Optimus Maximus. For that day he was treated almost as if he were divine, although a slave stood behind him in the chariot continually whispering to him to remember that he was mortal. A triumph was a great honour, something which the family would continue to commemorate for generations. Many of Rome's greatest buildings were erected or restored by successful generals using the spoils they had won in war, while the family house would be permanently decorated with the wreathed symbols of a triumph. Only a minority of senators won a triumph, but even this group struggled to prove that their triumph was greater than that of anyone else. Inscriptions recording the achievements of commanders tended to go into great detail and most of all sought to quantify success, listing the numbers of enemies killed or enslaved, of cities stormed or warships captured. For a Roman aristocrat it was always important to win victories bigger and better than other senators.

The *cursus honorum* varied in its form and flexibility over the centuries, but always followed an annual political cycle. By the time of the Second Punic War it was supposed to begin with either ten full years or ten campaigns of military service in the cavalry, on the staff of a family member or friend, or as an officer such as a military tribune. After this a man might stand for election for the office of *quaestor*, who had essentially financial responsibilities but might also act as a consul's second in command. Other posts following a year as quaestor, such as tribune of the plebs and aedile, did not have military responsibilities, but by 218 BC the praetorship sometimes involved a field command. However, the most important campaigns were always allocated to the year's consuls. All of these magistracies were held only for twelve months, and an individual was not supposed to be re-elected to the same office before a ten-year interval had elapsed. Magistrates given a military command possessed *imperium*, the power to issue orders to soldiers and dispense justice. The more senior the magistracy, the greater the *imperium* of the individual. Occasionally the Senate chose to extend the command of a consul or praetor for a year at a time, and their rank was then proconsul or propraetor respectively. Elections at Rome were fiercely competitive and many of the 300 or so members of the Senate at any one time had never held any magistracy. The voting system gave disproportionate weight to the wealthier classes in society and tended to favour the members of the oldest and richest of the noble families. A small number of established senatorial families tended to dominate the consulship, with only a small number of other men reaching this post. Yet the Roman political system was not entirely rigid. Though there was always an inner élite of families, the membership of this group altered over the decades as family lines died out or were supplanted by others. It was also always possible for a man whose family had never yet reached high office to gain the consulship.

In a book of this nature it is not possible to describe in detail the development of the Roman army, but equally it is obviously important to provide some indication of the force at the disposal of each general. At the start of our survey the Roman army was recruited from all male citizens who possessed the property to equip themselves for war. The wealthiest served as cavalrymen, since they were able to provide themselves with horse,

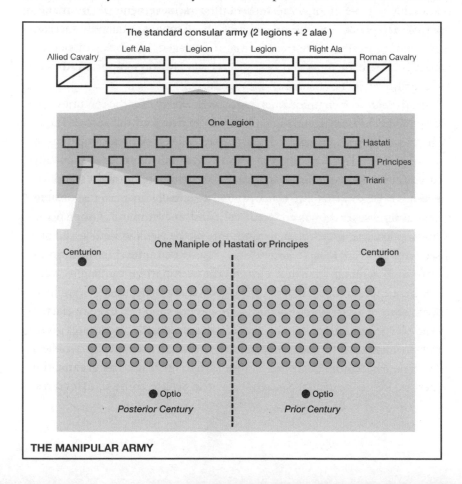

THE MANIPULAR ARMY

armour and weapons. The core of the army was formed by the heavy infantry, most of whom were drawn from the owners of small holdings of land. The poor provided light infantrymen who needed no armour and might also serve as rowers in the fleet. Each legion consisted of these three elements – 300 cavalrymen, 3,000 heavy infantrymen, and 1,200 light infantry (*velites*). The heavy infantry were further divided on the basis of age and military experience into three lines. The youngest 1,200 were known as the *hastati* and fought in the first line. Those in the prime of life were known as the *principes* and were stationed as a second line, while 600 veterans or *triarii* were in the rear.

Each line was composed of ten tactical units or maniples, consisting of two administrative units or centuries each led by a centurion. The centurion of the right-hand century was senior and commanded the entire maniple if both men were present. The maniples of each line were arranged with intervals equal to their frontage between each unit and the next. The gaps were covered by the maniples of the next line so that the legion's formation resembled a chequerboard (*quincunx*). On campaign each Roman legion was supported by a wing or *ala* of Latin or Italian allies, composed of roughly the same number of infantry but up to three times as many cavalry. A consul was normally given two legions and two *alae*. The standard formation placed the legions in the centre with one *ala* on either flank, hence these were usually named the Right and Left *Ala* accordingly. Some of the allied troops – usually one fifth of the infantry and a third of the cavalry – were detached from the *alae* to form the *extraordinarii*, who were placed at the immediate disposal of the army commander. The *extraordinarii* were often used to lead the column during an advance or act as rearguard during a retreat.[12]

Roman soldiers were not professionals, but men who served in the army as a duty to the Republic. The army is often referred to as a militia force, but it is probably better to think of it as a conscript army, for men would often spend several years consecutively with the legions although no one was supposed to be called upon to serve for more than sixteen years. Military service was an interlude to normal life, although one that does not appear to have been generally resented. Once in the army citizens willingly subjected themselves to a system of discipline that was extremely harsh, losing most of their legal rights until they were discharged. Even minor infractions could be punished very harshly, while serious breaches of discipline were punishable by death. The Roman army remained essentially an impermanent force, the legions being demobilized when the Senate decided that they were no longer needed. Although the soldiers might well be called upon to serve the Republic again, they would not do so in the same units and under the same commanders. Each army and legion raised was unique and would gradually increase in efficiency as it underwent training. Legions which saw active service were often very well drilled and disciplined, but as soon as these were disbanded the process would have to begin afresh with new armies. There was therefore an odd mixture of discipline and organization as strict as many professional armies with the impermanence of a continuing cycle of recruitment, training and demobilization before starting again.

Finally it is worth mentioning some of the factors which restricted a general's activity throughout our period. One of the most important was the limit on the speed with which information could be communicated. In all practical respects this was never faster than the pace of a dispatch rider. Instances are recorded of individuals making very long journeys in a short time, and under the Principate the Imperial post was created to provide messengers with fresh horses at regular intervals. It was always easier to convey such messages within the Empire, through settled provinces along well maintained roads. The network of roads constructed by the Romans assisted such communication and the movement of men and supplies in general, but was only really of value within the provinces. Offensive operations beyond the frontiers were usually conducted over a much simpler network of roads and paths. At times the Roman army also devised systems of signalling using flags or more often beacons, but such devices could only convey the simplest of messages and were anyway most suited to an army in fixed positions either along a frontier line or occasionally at a siege.

The most important consequence of this was that a general in the field had at most periods considerable freedom of action, since it was impractical to direct operations in detail from the centre of power at Rome. It was also extremely difficult to control divisions of an army spread over even fairly modest distances, which encouraged commanders to keep their forces concentrated under most circumstances. The ancient world was a world almost without maps, certainly with few if any of sufficient detail and accuracy to assist in the planning of military operations. Commanders could gather information about the landscape from a range of sources – if fighting within a province the quantity and quality of such information was obviously greatly enhanced – but for most practical purposes it was a question of sending someone ahead to look. Generals would often carry out reconnaissance in person, in the same way that they would often personally interrogate prisoners or interview merchants or members of the local population to gather news. The comparatively short range of weaponry, which was still essentially a reflection of human muscle power, was extremely limited and this, combined with the size of armies, ensured that a general could be in a position to see all of his own and the enemy army during a battle. Visibility was only limited by terrain, weather and the capacity of the human eye without the benefit of even such simple optical enhancements as the telescope.

Roman commanders were therefore able to direct operations at a much more immediate and personal level than has been the case in more recent warfare. On campaign and during battle and siege Roman generals were highly active, spending a lot of their time close to the enemy at risk of injury or death from missiles or sudden attackers. Although no longer leaders in the heroic mould of Alexander they were in some ways closer to their men, sharing the hardships of campaign in a way that would be praised as characteristically Roman. Whatever the political and social reality, the ideal persisted of the general as a fellow citizen and fellow soldier (*commiles*), who shared in a common enterprise with the rest of the army.[13]

CHAPTER 1

'THE SHIELD AND SWORD OF ROME'
FABIUS AND MARCELLUS

Quintus Fabius Maximus (c. 275–203 BC)
and Marcus Claudius Marcellus (271–208 BC)

Fabius Maximus when opposed by Hannibal ... decided to avoid taking any
dangerous risks and concern himself only with the defence of Italy, and in this
way earned himself the nickname 'the delayer' and a great reputation as a general.[1]

IN NOVEMBER 218 BC, HANNIBAL CROSSED THE ALPS AND BURST INTO NORTHERN
Italy. The Romans were astounded by the boldness and suddenness of this
attack, so unlike the cautious strategy pursued by Carthage in the First Punic
War. The Second War was sparked by Hannibal's attack on Saguntum, a
Spanish city allied to Rome, and it was in Spain that the Roman Senate had
expected to confront the Carthaginian general. Of the two consuls for 218,
one was to take an army to Spain, whilst his colleague went to Sicily to prepare
for an invasion of North Africa which would threaten Carthage itself.

The strategy was aggressive, direct and characteristically Roman, but
began to unravel almost immediately. Scipio, the consul travelling to Spain,
stopped at Massilia (Marseilles) and discovered that Hannibal and a large
army had recently passed by on its way eastwards. Completely wrong-footed,
the Romans struggled to react to the new situation. Yet for a succession of
commanders Hannibal's invasion seemed like a marvellous opportunity to
win themselves glory by defeating this great enemy. Each displayed great
enthusiasm to close with the Carthaginian army and fight it anywhere and
under any conditions. Scipio hurried back to take command of the legions

GALLI

ALPS

CENOMANI

INSUBRES

LIGURI

ILLYRIA

THE PYRENEES

CELTIBERI

VOLCAE

Massilia

UMBRIA

ETRURIA

R.Ebro

CORSICA

Rome

SAMNIUM

LATIUM

APULIA

CAMPANIA

LUSITANI

R.Tagus

IBERI

R.Baetis

BALEARIC IS.

SARDINA

LIPARI IS.

BRUTT

Gades

New
Carthage

AEGATES IS.

Syracus

MAESULII

MASAESULII

Carthage

0   400 km

THE MEDITERRANEAN WORLD

already in the Po valley campaigning against the Gallic tribes of the region. With his cavalry and light infantry he hastened to make contact with Hannibal, only to be brushed aside with disdainful ease by the numerically superior and more skilful Punic horse near the River Ticinus. In December his recently arrived colleague, Sempronius Longus, eagerly gave battle with their combined armies at Trebia and was utterly defeated, suffering very heavy losses. The following June Flaminius, one of the consuls of 217, following the enemy too closely in an effort to bring them to battle before

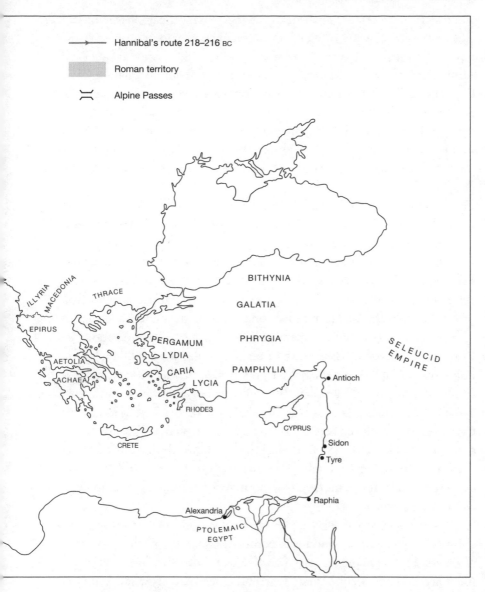

Hannibal's route 218–216 BC

Roman territory

Alpine Passes

ILLYRIA
MACEDONIA
THRACE
EPIRUS
BITHYNIA
GALATIA
PERGAMUM
PHRYGIA
LYDIA
AETOLIA
CARIA
PAMPHYLIA
ACHAEA
LYCIA
Antioch
RHODES
SELEUCID EMPIRE
CYPRUS
CRETE
Sidon
Tyre
Raphia
Alexandria
PTOLEMAIC EGYPT

he was joined by his fellow consul, was ambushed and killed along with 15,000 of his men.[2]

Roman losses in these early operations were appalling, and made all the worse because they came in defeats suffered on Italian soil. The enemy appeared unstoppable, and in some later sources Hannibal assumes the elemental power of a Force of Nature, smashing everything in his path. In truth the Romans were utterly outclassed at this stage of their war. Hannibal was unquestionably one of the ablest commanders of antiquity and commanded an army in every respect superior to the inexperienced legions facing it. It was not really an army of Carthaginians, who provided only its senior officers, but was a mixture of many races – Numidians and Libyans from Africa, Iberians, Celtiberians and Lusitanians from Spain, and in time Gauls, Ligurians and Italians. At its heart were the troops who had campaigned in Spain for many years under the leadership of Hannibal's family, all of them experienced, confident, and highly disciplined. In comparison to this sophisticated fighting force, the legions manoeuvred clumsily, and trusted more to individual courage and stubbornness than superior tactics to win the day.[3]

The ferocity of Hannibal's onslaught shocked Rome and pushed her to the very brink of utter defeat. Yet somehow the Romans endured disaster after catastrophic disaster, any one of which would have been enough to force other contemporary states to capitulate, and in the end went on to win the war. The scale of the achievement was recognized even at the time and highlighted afterwards when it appeared to inaugurate Rome's rapid rise to dominate the Mediterranean world. Later, in the mid second century BC, Polybius, who hoped to explain this sudden rise to a Greek audience, would begin the detailed narrative of his *Universal History* with the Second Punic War. He and later writers were greatly aided in their task because the conflict had inspired the Romans themselves to begin writing prose history. The first, by Fabius Pictor, was in Greek, but in the early second century Cato the Elder produced his *Origines* in Latin. Both men had participated in the war with Hannibal and dealt with the conflict in detail, and, although their works have survived only in fragments, it is at this period that we at last begin to have fuller, more reliable sources for examining the campaigns of Roman commanders.

The two subjects of this chapter were exceptional in many ways. Both enjoyed long periods of continuous command, something which would be rare until the Late Republic. Each had also won high office and military distinction before the Second Punic War, and indeed had grown to manhood and served with distinction during the First Punic War. In 218 Fabius and Marcellus were in their late fifties, rather elderly by Roman standards for a field command. Yet for much of the war they were to lead armies against Hannibal and, if neither was ever able to inflict a decisive defeat upon the Carthaginian, they were able to avoid suffering a similar blow at his hands, which in itself was no mean achievement. Their victories were often small-scale, and nearly always won over Hannibal's allies, gradually weakening his power.

CUNCTATOR (*THE DELAYER*) –
THE DICTATORSHIP OF FABIUS MAXIMUS, 217 BC

'We have been defeated in a great battle,' was the staid, unemotional announcement made in the Forum when news reached Rome of the destruction of Flaminius and his army at Lake Trasimene. In spite of the calm front presented by the urban praetor Marcus Pomponius, Livy tells us that panic and despair began to spread, especially when a few days later the news arrived that a force of 4,000 horsemen, sent by his consular colleague to join Flaminius, had been surrounded and all killed or captured by the enemy. With one army effectively destroyed, the other some distance away and crippled by the loss of its cavalry, there seemed nothing to stop Hannibal from moving directly against the city itself. At this time of crisis the Senate decided to appoint a military dictator, a single magistrate with supreme *imperium*. This was a rarely used expedient, for it violated the basic principle of Roman politics that no one man should hold overwhelming power, and had not been employed for over thirty years. Normally a dictator was nominated by one of the consuls, but since Flaminius was dead and his colleague unable or unwilling to reach Rome, it was decided to select the man by election. Technically, this may have meant that the appointee's title was actually *prodictator*, but, whether or not this was so, his powers were identical to those of any other dictator. The man chosen by the vote of the *Comitia Centuriata*, the assembly of the Roman People organized into groups according to their role in the archaic army, was Quintus Fabius Maximus.[4]

Fabius was 58, a member of one of the patrician clans which had formed Rome's oldest aristocracy. Now they shared their dominant position with a number of wealthy and well established plebeian families, but continued to enjoy distinguished careers. Fabius had already held two consulships in 233 and 228, and the censorship in 230. The name Maximus had been earned by the military achievements of his great-grandfather Quintus Fabius Rullianus (consul 322 and dictator in 315) fighting against the Samnites. The family adopted the name permanently, for the senatorial aristocracy missed no opportunity of publicly celebrating the great deeds of their ancestors and so promoting the electoral success of current and future generations. It was an equally Roman characteristic to give individual senators nicknames, often based on their appearance. In part this was to assist in distinguishing the different members of a family with similar or identical names, but it probably had more to do with the Romans' rather blunt sense of humour. Thanks to a prominent wart on his lip, the young Quintus Fabius Maximus was dubbed

Verrucosus (Spotty). Later accounts describe him as a stolid, cautious child, whose abilities were not at first obvious. Through constant practice as a young adult he became a capable officer and a skilled public speaker, emphasizing the twin dominance of war and politics in the public life of Rome.

There is little detailed information about Fabius' career before the Second Punic War. During his first consulship he campaigned against the Ligurians, a loosely organized and fiercely independent mountain people of Northern Italy. It seems probable that the war was fought in response to raiding against Roman and allied lands in Northern Etruria. Fabius attacked the tribes, defeating them in battle and halting, at least temporarily, their plundering forays. For this success he was awarded a triumph. This experience of campaigning in difficult terrain against an enemy skilled in ambush may well have instilled in Fabius a strong sense of the importance of keeping an army under tight control and only fighting at a time and manner of his own choosing. These were certainly to be the keynotes of his generalship throughout the war with Hannibal.[5]

As dictator Fabius Maximus' first task was to restore some semblance of confidence and normality to Rome itself. Defences were prepared in case Hannibal should mount a direct attack, two new legions were raised and organized, and considerable care was taken to ensure that the Roman field army would be properly supplied. Yet more than anything else, the dictator at first devoted his efforts to religious matters. Flaminius' defeat was publicly blamed on his failure to perform the proper rites before embarking on his campaign. The Sibylline Books – a collection of ancient prophecies – were consulted to ensure that appropriate ceremonies were undertaken and suitable dedications made to regain the gods' favour. As a Greek Polybius found many aspects of Roman religion absurdly superstitious, and believed that many senators cynically viewed such things as a means of controlling the emotions of the ignorant and uneducated poor. Whilst such views were certainly held by men like Caesar and Cicero in the Late Republic, it is not necessarily the case that Fabius and all of his contemporaries shared them. When the Senate spent time discussing such issues it emphasized that public affairs of all types were now to be conducted in a correct and thorough way. From the beginning Fabius made it clear that he expected to be treated in a manner appropriate to the full dignity of his office. He was accompanied by twenty-four attendants or *lictors*, who carried the *fasces*, bundles of rods tied around an axe which symbolized a magistrate's power to dispense corporal and capital punishment. The *imperium* of other magistrates lapsed (or more accurately became subordinate) when a dictator was appointed.

As he went to rendezvous with the surviving consul, Fabius sent a messenger ahead instructing the man to dismiss his own lictors before coming into the dictator's presence.[6]

Having linked up with the consul and taken over command of his army, Fabius had a force of four legions under his command and almost certainly the four allied *alae* which would normally support them. Our sources provide no information about actual numbers, but at normal strength such a force would muster between 30,000 and 40,000 men. This was a strong army by Roman standards, but it was of highly doubtful quality. The consul's army was based around survivors of the defeat at Trebia so that, although they had been in service for more than a year, their experience was mainly of defeat. These legions and *alae* also lacked all or most of their cavalry which had been destroyed in the aftermath of Trasimene. The rest of the army had only been under arms for a matter of weeks and were not yet familiar with each other and their officers. Nor was there much time or opportunity to integrate the two elements of the army into a single body used to operating together. Therefore, however impressive Fabius' field army may have appeared, it was in no respect a match for Hannibal's veteran troops. It was probably also significantly outnumbered by the enemy, and especially at a disadvantage in both the quality and quantity of its cavalry. It is in this context that we must see the campaign waged by the dictator.

As a magistrate with supreme power, a dictator did not have a colleague but a deputy, entitled the Master of Horse (*Magister Equitum*). The title seems to date back to Rome's early history when the strength of the army consisted of the hoplite phalanx so that the dictator led the heavy infantry whilst his subordinate took the cavalry. Law forbade the dictator even to ride a horse on campaign, but Fabius had requested and been granted an exemption to this before leaving Rome. It was impossible for a man on foot to exercise effective command and control over an army of four legions and in this case practicality overrode archaic tradition. Normally a dictator chose his Master of Horse, but in the unusual circumstances of Fabius' election it had been decided to allow the voters also to chose his subordinate. The ballot came out in favour of Marcus Minucius Rufus, who had held the consulship in 221. The two men do not appear to have got along well and Minucius was to display a boldness similar to Scipio, Sempronius and Flaminius.[7]

Hannibal had moved east after Trasimene, crossing the Apennines into Picenum and the rich plains down to the Adriatic shore. Much of his army was in poor health, the men suffering from scurvy and the horses from mange, for the intensive campaigning had denied them sufficient rest to recover from the exertions of the epic march to reach Italy. The lull in the campaign did much to restore the army's fitness, but we cannot be sure how long it lasted. Later in the summer Fabius closed to camp within 6 miles of Hannibal near the town of Aecae (or Arpi according to Livy). The Carthaginian immediately sought a decisive encounter and marched his men out to form up for battle and challenge the Romans to fight. The Roman army remained in camp and, after some hours, Hannibal withdrew, assuring his men that this demonstrated that the Romans were afraid of them. Further attempts to provoke Fabius to battle or to ambush his army failed, for the dictator remained determined to avoid contact. After several days Hannibal marched away, his soldiers devastating the land as they passed through it. That they were able to do this often literally under the watching gaze of the dictator's army, was an enormous blow to Roman pride. The legions were recruited overwhelmingly from farmers, and it was especially depressing for such men to know that they could not prevent an enemy from marauding through the fields of their kindred and allies.

Yet always Fabius shadowed the enemy, staying one or two days' march behind the Punic army and refusing to close. He moved carefully, keeping his army together under close discipline and exploiting their local knowledge of the landscape to move from one favourable position to the next. Whenever possible he kept to high ground, avoiding open plains where the enemy's superior cavalry posed a great danger. Hannibal was never willing to attack Fabius' army when the Romans had the advantage of position. The care taken before the campaign to gather adequate transport animals and supplies of food to support the large Roman army now paid dividends, for it permitted Fabius to move as he wanted rather than continually having to shift position to gather more food and fodder. When foraging parties did have to go out, they were always covered by a strong force formed of cavalry and light infantry to guard against ambush. In the small-scale skirmishing between patrols and outposts of the two armies it was generally the Romans who had the advantage.

Livy and Plutarch both claimed that from the beginning Hannibal was secretly disturbed by Fabius' refusal to be drawn into battle. Certainly, by the standards of the contemporary military theory the dictator was doing the right thing. Much of this literature concerned itself with the circumstances under which a commander should fight a pitched battle. This was to be risked only when the prospects of success were good, and after a general had gained every possible advantage, however minor, for his men. Following the defeats at Trebia and Trasimene the confidence of Hannibal's troops was extremely high. Outnumbered and inexperienced, the dictator's army would almost certainly have suffered defeat in any massed encounter fought on even terms. In these circumstances Fabius, like the good commander of the military manuals, avoided battle, and sought ways to change the odds in his favour. The experience of active campaigning gradually improved the efficiency of the Roman army; the small victories won in skirmishes helped to boost morale, and, very, very slowly, began to wear down the enemy. It would take a long time to recover from the early defeats and build an army capable of confronting Hannibal without enjoying overwhelming advantages of position, but Fabius started the process.[8]

The dictator's strategy made perfect sense by the standards of contemporary military theory, although we cannot know whether Fabius was aware of this or was simply acting in a way he considered to be appropriate to the situation. Rome still had an essentially impermanent militia army, rather than the professional forces fielded by other large states. Knowledge of military theory does not yet appear to have been widespread amongst the senators who provided the army commanders and as a result Roman methods of making war often lacked subtlety, relying instead on aggression and brute force. These attitudes had characterized Ticinus, Trebia and Trasimene, but even these defeats do not appear to have done much to dampen the Roman élite's instinctive urge to attack the enemy as soon as possible. Fabius' cautious shadowing of the Punic army was deeply unpopular with the army and especially its senior officers, most notably the Master of Horse. As the campaign progressed his opposition to the strategy became increasingly vocal. Fabius was nicknamed Hannibal's *paedogogus*, after the slave who accompanied a Roman schoolboy, carrying his books and other paraphernalia. [9]

Hannibal, having drifted steadily westwards, then drove into Campania and plundered the *ager Falernus* (Falernian Plain), a fertile area whose wine would later win the praise of the poet Horace. Marauding through this area, he hoped either to spur the Romans into risking a battle or to demonstrate to Rome's allies that she was no longer strong enough to protect them. It is possible that the Carthaginian already had hopes of persuading the Campanians to defect. In spite of the urgings of Minucius and his other officers, Fabius kept to the high ground which surrounds the Campanian plain, observing the enemy and refusing to be drawn. However, Livy tells us that one patrol consisting of 400 allied cavalry led by Lucius Hostilius Mancinus disobeyed orders and were nearly all killed or captured in the ensuing skirmish.[10]

Fabius felt that at last the enemy had made a mistake. He guessed that Hannibal would withdraw by the same pass that he had used to enter the plain and managed to occupy the place before the enemy. Late in the day a detachment of 4,000 men set up camp in the pass itself, whilst the main army camped on a hill overlooking it. It was a very strong position and Fabius hoped that, should the enemy try to force the pass, he would be able to inflict considerable losses upon them, and at the very least prevent them from carrying off the great quantity of plunder which they had gathered during their raiding. Hannibal's army was cut off from its original base in Spain and from its allies in Cisalpine Gaul, and, lacking a port, was not in effective communication with Carthage. Even a minor defeat could seriously damage him, shattering the impression of invincibility created by his early victories and discouraging any of Rome's allies from defecting. The rival armies were camped some 2 miles apart. Livy claims that Hannibal launched a direct attack on the pass, but was repulsed, although the more reliable Polybius does not mention this. All of our sources are agreed on what happened next, for it became one of the classic ploys or stratagems of the ancient world.

Hannibal instructed Hasdrubal, the officer responsible for overseeing the army's supply train amongst other things, to gather a great quantity of dry wood. These faggots were then tied to the horns of 2,000 plough oxen taken from the great herd of captured cattle. During the night, servants were ordered to light these torches and then drive the cattle up through the pass. With them went his experienced light infantrymen, who were tasked with keeping the herd together. In the meantime, the remainder of the army, who had earlier been given specific orders to eat and rest, formed up into a march column headed by the best of the close order infantry – most probably the Libyans. The Roman force in the pass, mistaking the fires for the main column, came down the slope to attack, but the confused skirmish was broken up when many of the panicking cattle stampeded through the middle. With the pass now open the Carthaginian army was able to march through unopposed. Fabius and the main Roman force did nothing, waiting in camp for daylight. It was unclear from the mass of torches and the noise of fighting precisely what was going on, and the dictator utterly refused to risk battle without a clear knowledge of the situation, in case he was lured into a trap. Fighting at night was rare in the ancient world, especially for large armies, as it was very difficult for leaders to control their men and easy for troops to get lost or fall into confusion and panic. It is probable that Fabius realized that his own army was likely to be at a great disadvantage in such circumstances when faced with Hannibal's better trained and more experienced soldiers. By the time the sun rose on the next day, Hannibal's main force, along with the bulk of its baggage train, was through the pass. The Carthaginian was even able to send back a force of Spanish foot to extricate the light infantrymen, killing around 1,000 Romans in the process.[11]

The escape of the Carthaginian army reflected once again its high quality and the genius of its commander, but it was a major humiliation for Fabius. It was now near the end of the summer and Hannibal began to look for a suitable place to take up winter quarters. The Roman army followed him as he went east again, but Fabius was required in Rome to oversee some religious rites and for a while the army came under the command of Minucius. Hannibal stormed and sacked the town of Gerunium in Luceria, and then began to send out large detachments of men to gather provisions, intending to find sufficient supplies to maintain the army throughout the winter. Whilst much of his army was dispersed in this way, and its commander disinclined to fight a serious action as a result, the Master of Horse attacked and won a large-scale skirmish outside the town. Exaggerated reports of this action were brought to a Rome starved of any good news for the last two years. In a wave of popular enthusiasm, which was allegedly opposed by all but one of the Senate, Minucius was granted equal power to the dictator, effectively a return to the normal situation of having two consuls of equal authority rather than a single supreme magistrate.

On his return Fabius and Minucius divided the army into two equal parts and camped separately, the dictator having apparently refused a suggestion that they hold command of the whole force on alternate days. A short while afterwards, Minucius was lured into an ambush by Hannibal. Only the arrival of Fabius' men to cover their retreat prevented the defeat from degenerating into yet another disaster. The Master of Horse led his men into Fabius' camp, and there greeted the dictator not simply as commander, but as father. It was a very emotive gesture by Roman standards, for fathers possessed massive powers over their children and it was almost inconceivable for a son to oppose his father politically. This brief experiment with two commanders being abandoned, the remainder of the campaigning season passed without major fighting. At the end of his sixth month of office, Fabius laid down the dictatorship and returned to Rome. He had granted the Romans a breathing space to recover and rebuild their forces. In the next year one of the largest armies ever fielded by the Republic would serve under the command of the consuls. In the event, it marched to an even greater disaster than any which had preceded it.[12]

A HERO OF THE OLD SCHOOL – MARCUS CLAUDIUS MARCELLUS

On 2 August 216 BC almost 50,000 Roman and allied soldiers were slaughtered on the narrow plain north of the little ruined town of Cannae. Fabius' efforts had been wasted, but the defeat was not inevitable and certainly not anticipated by the Romans. Nor should we automatically accept the later tradition of Livy and others who declared that the former dictator had wanted the consuls of 216 to pursue his own strategy of avoiding battle. Once again, in a time of crisis the Romans appointed a military dictator, Marcus Junius Pera, who began the slow process of rebuilding Rome's strength. Hannibal did not march against Rome after Cannae, something which the Romans never quite understood, and, although there were moments of panic, his failure to do so allowed them time to recover mentally and revert to their normal belief that a war could only ever end in eventual victory. Yet the situation was still extremely bleak, for much of Southern Italy had defected to the Carthaginians by the end of the year.[13]

The consuls elected for 215 were Lucius Postumius Albinus and Tiberius Sempronius Gracchus. However, a few months after Cannae the former was ambushed and killed along with most of his army in Cisalpine Gaul in another dreadful blow to Roman confidence. The man elected to replace him was Marcus Claudius Marcellus but, when he took up office on 15 March, bad omens were held to have declared the vote invalid. Fabius Maximus may well have been behind this, for after a rapidly held election he received the vacant magistracy. Part of the objection may have been that both Marcellus and Gracchus were plebeians, when it was normal for one of the two consuls each year to be a patrician. Yet it really is very difficult to understand precisely what was going on behind the scenes. One of the most striking things about the Second Punic War is the degree to which normal politics went on at Rome even at times of appalling crisis, as senators scrambled for the opportunity to play a distinguished role in the fighting. It is possible that Fabius felt that Marcellus was too aggressive a general for the current circumstances, but since he anyway received a field command as proconsul this seems unlikely. When Fabius presided over the elections for the next year, he demanded that the people think again when two inexperienced men began to head the polls. In the event he was re-elected with Marcellus as his colleague, although to what extent this was a matter of choice is impossible to know.[14]

Marcellus was 57 in 214 BC, and had already been consul in 222 and praetor in 224 and 216. As a youth he had fought in Sicily during the First

Punic War, winning many decorations as well as a reputation for individual acts of heroism. Amongst these honours was at least one civic crown (*corona civica*), Rome's highest decoration, presented by one citizen to another as an admission that the recipient had saved his life. This was given to him by his brother, Otacilius. In many ways Marcellus resembled Achilles, Hector and the other aristocratic warriors of Homer's *Iliad*, or Rome's early heroes, in his boldness, aggression and the relish he took in single combat. It was an old-fashioned style of fighting, associated more with tribal war bands than regular armies, but continued to characterize his approach to warfare even when he reached high command. In 222 he and his consular colleague, Gnaeus Cornelius Scipio, launched a joint invasion of the territory of the Insubres in Cisalpine Gaul. The tribe had suffered a serious defeat at the hands of Flaminius in the previous year, but Marcellus and Scipio were so eager to fight a campaign that they had persuaded the Senate to turn away some Gallic envoys intent on negotiating a surrender. The consuls advanced and besieged the hilltop town (*oppidum*) of Acerrae. In response the Insubres, along with allied or mercenary warriors from north of the Alps known as Gaesatae, surrounded Clastidium, a village allied to Rome. Leaving Scipio with the main force, Marcellus took two thirds of their combined cavalry and 600 light infantrymen to meet the new threat. What then occurred could have come straight out of Homer, and was taken as a subject by the poet Naevius, though our account comes from a later source.[15]

When the Romans approached Clastidium the Gauls came out to meet them, led by a certain King Britomarus. Our sources claim that there were 10,000 of them, but this may well be an exaggeration. The horsemen in a Gallic army, as in the legions at this time, consisted of the wealthier, more aristocratic members of the tribe, able to afford a horse and suitable equipment. Gallic cavalry were in general well mounted – the Romans were later to copy many aspects of horse harness and training from the Gauls – and extremely brave, if unsophisticated tactically. Such men had to justify their honoured position in society by conspicuous displays of courage in war. With Britomarus at their head, standing out as was proper for a king in his lavishly gilded and silvered cuirass, the tribal horsemen rushed to engage the outnumbered Romans. Marcellus was equally keen to engage, but Plutarch tells us that during the advance his horse shied and began to turn away. Thinking quickly, the consul pretended that he had deliberately turned his mount to pray to the sun, so that his men would not be discouraged. Putting a positive slant on what appeared to be a bad omen in such a way was another of the attributes of the good general of military theory.

Marcellus is supposed to have vowed to dedicate the most impressive panoply amongst the enemy to Jupiter Feretrius if the god would grant Rome victory. Then, deciding that Britomarus himself wore the finest equipment, the Roman consul spurred ahead of his men to reach the king. The two leaders met between the rival lines. Marcellus drove his spear into the Gaul's body, knocking him from his horse, and then finished him off with a second and a third blow, before dismounting to strip the corpse. If Plutarch is to be believed the two sides did not close whilst this was going on. Then the Roman horse charged home and, after a hard fight, defeated the Gauls.[16]

By the time Marcellus rejoined Scipio, Acerrae had fallen and the Romans had moved against Mediolanum (modern Milan), the greatest town of the Insubres, which eventually fell after some hard fighting. On his return to Rome, Marcellus crowned his triumph by dedicating the *spolia opima* in the temple of Jupiter Feretrius on the Capitol. He was only the third man in Rome's history to be awarded this honour, granted to a general who had killed the enemy leader in single combat before a battle. Romulus was supposed to have been the first and established the tradition that the commander performing this rite should carry the spoils of the defeated enemy suspended from an oak branch.[17]

In spite of his age, Marcellus held an almost unbroken series of field commands from the very beginning of the Second Punic War. He was the first Roman commander to come into contact with the main Carthaginian army in the months after Cannae. The actions he fought in late 216 and 215 outside the town of Nola were probably very small in scale, little more than large skirmishes, but they came at a time when Rome was desperate for the slightest military success. This region is very rugged, with few open areas large enough to permit armies to deploy into formal battle lines. Livy's account of the fighting is dramatic, but even he doubted that the casualties in some of these engagements were as heavy as some of his sources claimed. Marcellus led his troops in his usual aggressive manner, but his willingness to attack the enemy should not hide the care he took to do so in the most favourable circumstances possible. Hannibal was unable to outwit and surprise him, as he had so easily baffled other Roman commanders. In this sense the cautious Fabius' and bold Marcellus' command styles were very similar, for both men kept their armies under tight control. On the march the men were not allowed to stray from their units, and the column moved behind a screen of outposts along a route which had already been carefully reconnoitred by patrols, sometimes led by the commander himself. The sites for temporary camps were chosen with care and engagements begun only when the general chose to fight.

Such precautions may appear obvious, almost trivial, but had in the past been frequently ignored by Roman armies. The willingness of Roman citizens to serve in organized units under strict military law should not blind us to the essentially impermanent nature of the legions. The clumsiness with which Roman armies manoeuvred in the initial campaigns of the war was typical for this period, as was the frequency with which they were ambushed or collided unexpectedly with an enemy column. Prolonged service, especially successful campaigning, steadily increased a Roman army's military efficiency, but it took a considerable time to achieve basic competence and years for them to reach similar standards to professional troops. Their considerable past experience of campaigning, combined with natural ability, set Marcellus and Fabius apart from the majority of contemporary Roman commanders, and made their style of command much closer to the Hellenistic ideal.[18]

As far as we can tell, the two men were able to co-operate effectively whenever this was necessary. It should be noted that Fabius' reluctance to confront Hannibal in battle was not extended to smaller detachments of the Punic army and, most especially, to the Italian communities who had defected to the enemy. Fabius continued to avoid battle with an army which he did not believe he had the capability to defeat, but consistently attacked that enemy indirectly, hoping gradually to weaken him. Both Fabius and Marcellus also took great care to preserve the loyalty of Rome's allies, especially when these appeared to be wavering. A similar story is told about both men winning over a distinguished allied soldier who, discontented by what he felt was a lack of recognition of his services, was planning to defect. In 214 the two consuls combined to recapture the town of Casilinum, captured by Hannibal in the previous year. The siege at first went badly, and Livy claims that it was Marcellus' determination to persevere that prevented a Roman withdrawal, but there is no hint of a major rift between the two men. Both consistently displayed the ideal behaviour of the Roman aristocrat, by refusing ever to contemplate the possibility that Rome could lose the war. Hannibal is said to have been exasperated by the enthusiasm with which Marcellus would renew an action, even when he had suffered a reverse on the previous day. The lost account of the Greek philosopher Posidonius reported that, because of their differing approaches to war, Marcellus and Fabius were dubbed the 'Sword and Shield of Rome'. Whatever their differences of temperament, and perhaps of political ambitions, this does highlight their essentially complementary and co-operative relationship when it came to fighting the Carthaginians.[19]

Marcellus' greatest achievement of the Second Punic War was the capture of Syracuse in Sicily after a long siege. An early attempt at direct assault having failed, due in part at least to the array of ingenious siege engines used by the defenders and designed by the geometrician Archimedes who was a native of Syracuse, the Romans resorted to blockade. In the end, a surprise attack allowed the Romans to take the outer ring of fortifications in 212, and during the next year the remainder of the city was captured betrayed to the Romans, or surrendered. Rivals in the Senate, claiming that the Sicilian campaign was incomplete, managed to deny him a triumph for this achievement, and Marcellus instead celebrated an ovation, riding on horseback instead of in a chariot as he led the possession. The spoils brought back from Syracuse included great quantities of Hellenistic art, up until that point a rarity at Rome.

In 209, during his fifth consulship and his last field command, Fabius Maximus recaptured the city of Tarentum through a similar mixture of stealth and treachery on the part of some of the garrison. Marcellus held a fourth consulship in 210, during which he seems to have won a marginal victory over Hannibal at Numistro, and a fifth term in 208. Moving once again into close contact with the Carthaginian in the hope of forcing a battle, he and his consular colleague personally led 220 cavalry to reconnoitre a hill between the two camps. The patrol rode into a trap, for Hannibal had deliberately concealed men on the high ground suspecting that the Romans would try to occupy it. Marcellus died fighting hand to hand. The other consul and Marcellus' son escaped, though both were wounded, the former mortally. The loss of both consuls was a dreadful blow to Roman pride, but, whilst Marcellus was at long last outwitted by the Punic general, he had not led his entire army to defeat and destruction. Polybius, who believed that it was not a deliberate ambush but a chance encounter with Numidian foragers, was highly critical of a general who risked his own life by leading such a patrol. Yet, as we shall see, many Roman commanders chose to take this chance for the sake of gaining a personal view of an important position.[20]

It was the generation of men who reached maturity during the First Punic War, men like Fabius and Marcellus, who managed to steer Rome through the crisis of the Second War. Yet, in the last years of this conflict, it was a younger generation who would actually win the Roman victory. These were men like Caius Claudius Nero who contributed more than anyone else to the defeat of Hannibal's brother Hasdrubal and a new invading army at Metaurus in 207. The greatest of these new commanders, and also the youngest, was Publius Cornelius Scipio.

CHAPTER 2

A ROMAN HANNIBAL: SCIPIO AFRICANUS

Publius Cornelius Scipio Africanus (c.236–184 BC)

My mother bore a general (*imperator*), not a warrior (*bellator*).[1]

ONE OF THE MOST STRIKING ASPECTS OF THE SECOND PUNIC WAR WAS THE willingness of the Roman Senate to dispatch armies to fight in several theatres simultaneously, and the persistence with which these campaigns were prosecuted even when Hannibal was on the loose in Italy and the issue of the war very much in doubt. Over time, the efforts of Fabius, Marcellus and others in Italy denied the Carthaginian victory, but the sum of their achievements was still essentially to prevent Rome from losing the conflict. Campaigns in Spain, Sicily and Macedonia prevented more than a trickle of reinforcements and supplies from reaching Hannibal's army, and so supported the Roman war effort against him. Yet in the end it was these theatres which proved decisive, for Roman victories in Spain and Sicily made possible the invasion of Africa, which in turn led to the recall of Hannibal and, ultimately, the capitulation of Carthage.

The burden of maintaining a war on so many separate fronts was made possible by the great resources of the Roman Republic, although these were stretched almost to breaking point. Roman society was geared to warfare in a way that Carthage was not, but this should not lead us to understate the broader strategic vision and grim determination with which the Senate oversaw the conflict. They also adopted a pragmatic approach to political convention, permitting the multiple consulships of veterans like Marcellus and Fabius. In 210 BC they granted proconsular *imperium* and command of the war in Spain to the 27-year-old Publius Cornelius Scipio. There was no precedent for such a responsible position being given to so young a man, but the choice soon proved to have been exceedingly good. It was Scipio who drove the Carthaginians from Spain, and then took an army across to Africa where he won victory after victory, finally defeating Hannibal himself at Zama in 202 BC.

It is easy with hindsight to underestimate just how startling a reversal of fortune Scipio's campaigns brought about. In 211 BC the Roman armies in Spain, which until now had enjoyed steady success, were almost annihilated. A remnant managed to cling to a small patch of land north of the River Ebro, fighting off Punic attempts to dislodge them. Scipio brought only modest reinforcements, bringing his total forces roughly up to the strength of a consular army, and was faced by three Carthaginian armies of a similar or larger size. Yet, within the space of four campaigning seasons, he had driven the Carthaginians entirely from the peninsula. Later, in Africa, he would outwit and outmanoeuvre significantly larger Punic armies, demonstrating the same sort of superiority over them which Hannibal had shown over the Roman commanders who had first faced him in Italy. He adopted the name Africanus, as a permanent reminder that he was the man who had ended the war with Carthage.

The Second Punic War dominated Scipio's life. He was 17 when it began, and took part in the first action of the Italian campaign at Ticinus. Later he was probably at Trebia, possibly at Trasimene, and certainly at Cannae. Like all aristocrats of his generation he underwent longer periods of more arduous military service than any Romans either before or afterwards. If not killed, or crippled by wounds or disease, these men gained at an early age far more military experience than most senators had had in a lifetime. Nearly all became capable officers, and many proved exceptionally gifted. Scipio stood out even amongst his peers. By the time that the war ended he was only in his mid thirties, and yet had spent much of his life on campaign, commanding an army for eight years, fighting and winning five major battles, as well as countless smaller engagements and sieges. The catalogue of his achievements dwarfed those of any other senator, yet, although he had already held the office in 205, he was still technically too young to be consul. The Republic, which had been glad enough of his services during the Second Punic War, struggled to find a place for him once it had finished, for its political system was supposed to prevent any one individual from gaining too much power or influence. Under normal circumstances he could expect another thirty or so years of active public life, but the world of the early second century BC presented no opportunities to equal, let alone surpass his earlier deeds. In the end he was forced out of politics into an embittered retirement, dying a disappointed man at a comparatively young age.

SCIPIO'S EARLY LIFE AND CHARACTER

Sensitive, intelligent and charismatic, Scipio had the boundless self-confidence of a patrician who knew from childhood that he was destined to play a prominent role in Rome's public life. Some of the stories about his early life have much in common with the tales told about Hellenistic princes and kings. Later, a myth identical to one associated with Alexander the Great even grew up hinting at divine parentage, claiming that his mother had been discovered lying with an enormous snake. Scipio was certainly an openly pious man, who when he was young developed the habit of going before dawn to sit in solitary silence in the Temple of Jupiter on the Capitol.[2] Later he would openly claim that his plans were sometimes guided by dreams sent by the gods. Polybius, a rational Greek who felt that the Romans were inclined towards excessive superstition, argued that Scipio did not actually believe his own claims, but understood that the less sophisticated were readily swayed by such things. The historian lived in the household of Africanus' grandson by adoption, Scipio Aemilianus, and so had access to family traditions and lore. He also met the elderly Laelius, who had been Africanus' close friend. Yet it is not easy to know whether he correctly understood Africanus, or mistakenly ascribed to him the attitudes of his own, more cynical age. Scipio certainly had a genius for theatrical gestures and his true views may well have been complex, and neither simply manipulative nor wholly sincere.[3]

Scipio's father, also called Publius, was consul in 218 and, like many sons, he accompanied his father on campaign as a tent-companion or *contubernalis*. The practice was seen as a good way for young aristocrats to gain early military experience. Most of the consul's army went on to Spain under the command of his older brother Cnaeus (Marcellus' colleague as consul in 222), but Scipio returned to Italy with his father when the latter discovered that Hannibal was moving to cross the Alps. In November 218, the consul led his cavalry and light infantry (*velites*) across the River Ticinus to locate the enemy position and discover his strength and intentions. Encountering a numerically larger and better trained force of Punic cavalry led by Hannibal himself, the Romans were routed. The consul was wounded and family tradition maintained that he had been saved from death only by the intervention of his son. According to Polybius, the young Publius had been given command of a picked troop of horsemen and stationed at the rear out of harm's way. Seeing his father isolated with just a few bodyguards and threatened by numbers of enemy cavalry, Scipio urged his troop to ride to the rescue. The men refused, and it was only after he had spurred his horse forward in a lone charge that they were shamed into following. Pliny the Elder, writing in the first century AD, claimed that the consul subsequently offered his son the *corona civica*, but that Scipio refused. However, Livy mentions another version of the story given in the lost history of Coelius: that the consul's rescuer was in fact a Ligurian slave, although he says that most authorities credited Scipio with the deed.[4]

When the elder Scipio recovered from his wound he went as a proconsul to join his brother Cnaeus in Spain. His son remained in Italy, and in 216 was a military tribune in the Second Legion, one of eight such units mustered under the joint command of the year's consuls, Lucius Aemilius Paullus and Caius Terentius Varro. Scipio was married to – or would soon marry, the chronology is uncertain – Paullus' daughter, Aemilia, so that in one sense this was another instance of the common practice of young aristocrats gaining military experience in an army led by a relative. However, a very high proportion of Rome's aristocracy volunteered for service in this year, joining the great army which was intended to confront and overwhelm the enemy who had humiliated the Republic. The result was not what the Romans had anticipated, for at Cannae Hannibal's outnumbered army surrounded and all but annihilated the massive Roman force. Casualties were appalling, and especially high amongst the senatorial families. Paullus was killed, as were over eighty senators, including Minucius Rufus, Fabius' *Magister Equitum*, and more than half of the military tribunes. Scipio survived, and was one of four tribunes who found themselves with the largest body of fugitives at the nearby town of Canusium.

Although one of the other tribunes was Fabius Maximus' son and would himself be elected to the consulship in 213, command devolved upon the two youngest men, Scipio and Appius Claudius. The latter had been aedile recently, but it was their continued confidence and sheer force of personality, rather than any great experience, which caused the others to follow their lead. The scale of the holocaust engendered panic in many of the survivors. One group of young noblemen, including the sons of distinguished magistrates, were openly speaking of abandoning the doomed Republic and fleeing abroad. Scipio went with a few reliable soldiers to the quarters – presumably a house in the town – of their leader Quintus Caecilius Metellus, where the deserters were behaving in a typically Roman way and holding a council (*consilium*) to discuss what to do. Bursting into the room, the 20-year-old tribune stood sword in hand and swore a solemn oath to Jupiter Optimus Maximus, inviting dreadful retribution on himself and his family should he break it. The oath declared that not only would he never desert the Republic, but that he would not permit anyone else to do so and would kill them if necessary. One by one, he made each of his stunned audience swear the same oath. Over the next few days more stragglers came into the town, so that, by the time the surviving consul came to take charge, there was a force of over 10,000 men mustered there. It was a pitiful remnant of the 86,000 strong force which had marched out to battle on the morning of 2 August, but it was a beginning.[5]

In the aftermath of Cannae Scipio had personified the *virtus* expected of a Roman aristocrat, and especially a member of such a distinguished family, faced with adversity. His behaviour was all the more noticeable when other members of his class began to waver. The Romans accepted that they would sometimes suffer defeats, but refused to concede that these could ever be final. All citizens, and especially the high-born, were expected to fight bravely, but, as long as they had done so, there was no shame in having been defeated. A leader faced with defeat and disaster was not expected to die fighting, unless there was no way out, nor to commit suicide. Instead he was to begin to rebuild the army's strength, salvaging as many men as possible from the chaos of a lost battle, and preparing for the next encounter with the enemy. For there would always be a next time, and eventually Rome would win. This was the spirit linking Fabius and Marcellus, in spite of their radically different approaches to facing Hannibal, for neither man ever openly questioned the assumption that Rome would keep fighting or that she might not eventually win. *Virtus* meant that any setbacks, however appalling, must be endured and the war continued until ultimate victory was achieved. When Varro, the consul widely blamed for the disaster at Cannae, returned to Rome, he was formally greeted by the Senate and thanked for 'not having despaired of the Republic'.[6]

In 213 Scipio was elected to the post of *curule aedile*, but little else is known about his career after 216. It is probable that he underwent further military service given the high levels of mobilization in these years. However, it is not until he was appointed to the Spanish command in 210 that our sources once again describe his activity. In the previous year his uncle and father had both been killed, when the defection of their Celtiberian allies left the Roman armies in Spain dangerously exposed and massively outnumbered. A remnant of the army rallied under the leadership of an equestrian officer named Lucius Marcius and managed to cling on to a corner of north-eastern Spain, but most of Rome's allies defected to the enemy. The Senate sent Caius Claudius Nero to take command and he seems to have won some-small scale actions, before returning to Italy within the year. There appears to have been considerable uncertainty over the choice of a successor. Many of the more ambitious and distinguished Roman commanders – and it should not be forgotten that the casualties incurred in the war so far did mean that there were fewer distinguished men left alive and fit for service – had no enthusiasm for a posting to Spain. The situation in the peninsula was bad, the resources likely to be committed there modest. From 218–211 Cnaeus and Publius Scipio had repeatedly complained to the Senate that they were not given sufficient men or funds to defeat the enemy. Unable to reach a consensus on a suitable commander, Livy claims that the Senate had recourse to deciding the issue by election and so convened the *Comitia Centuriata*. At first no candidates came forward, until suddenly Scipio announced his desire to stand and was elected unanimously. However, his youth – he was in his mid twenties – and inexperience began to make many citizens wonder if they had acted unwisely and it was only after Scipio had made a speech that they were reassured. Livy's narrative is extremely strange, for there is no evidence of the Romans ever acting in a similar manner on another occasion, so that many scholars have rejected this version of events. One suggestion is that the Senate had already decided to choose Scipio and then held a public vote to grant some official legitimacy to what was a highly unorthodox appointment. Whatever the actual details, Publius Cornelius Scipio was dispatched to command in Spain as a proconsul.[7]

THE CAPTURE OF NEW CARTHAGE, 209 BC

Scipio landed at Emporion – a Greek colony in Spain which had been allied to the Romans from before the war – with some 10,000 or so reinforcements, which brought the total Roman strength in the province to 28,000 infantry and 3,000 cavalry. There were three Carthaginian field armies in the peninsula, each one equal or superior to this force, and commanded respectively by Hannibal's brothers Hasdrubal and Mago, and Hasdrubal son of Gisgo. Yet the young Roman commander was supremely confident. Before he left Rome he had come to the conclusion that the disaster of 211 had not been the result of any Carthaginian brilliance. His father and uncle had recruited 20,000 Celtiberian allies for their final campaign. Emboldened by this great increase in strength, they split their forces into two and operated independently. When the Celtiberians proved unreliable and deserted en masse, each of the brothers had been attacked separately and overwhelmed by sheer weight of numbers. Scipio determined not to repeat the same mistake, and went to Spain determined to act aggressively rather than simply remaining on the defensive and clinging to the small region still controlled by Rome.[8]

Polybius had read and referred to a letter written by Scipio to King Philip V of Macedon, in which he explained how he planned this first operation in Spain. In 210 Rome was at war with Macedonia, a conflict which ended in 205 but was renewed almost as soon as the Second Punic War was complete, so this correspondence must date to the beginning of the next century. It may well have been written in 190, when Scipio accompanied his brother on campaign in Asia Minor and their army received aid and support from Philip V, who had been defeated in 197 and was now Rome's ally. It is more than likely, then, that this source was written twenty years after the events it described and quite possibly reflects the assurance of hindsight, so that it must be treated with the same caution as the recollections of more recent commanders. Nevertheless this is the first time that we have even a hint at what a Roman general was actually thinking when he planned a campaign.[9]

Once in Spain, Scipio began to gather more information about the enemy's strength and dispositions. The reports were encouraging. The three Punic armies had separated and were operating some distance apart. Hasdrubal Gisgo was in Lusitania (roughly equivalent to modern-day Portugal) near the mouth of the River Tagus. Hasdrubal Barca was engaged in the siege of a town of the Carpetani in central Spain, whilst his brother Mago was probably stationed in the extreme south-west of the peninsula, although an apparent contradiction in Polybius' text makes it a little hard to locate his position precisely.[10] Now that the Romans' capacity for offensive action in Spain appeared virtually destroyed, there was no good reason for the Carthaginians to keep their strength concentrated, greatly increasing the on-going problem of keeping their troops supplied. The move was hastened by friction between the three generals and also the growing need to suppress rebellions amongst the tribes allied to or subject to Carthage. Punic rule appears to have grown much harsher and more exploitative once the fear of defections to Rome was removed. There was now little love for Carthage amongst the tribes, but for the moment there remained respect for Punic military might. When Roman fortunes began to revive many would seek alliance with Rome and provide Scipio with valuable contingents of troops, although he held firmly to his original resolve of not becoming over-reliant on their aid.

Scipio had decided to launch an offensive, and one of the Punic field armies offered an obvious target for this. His own army was strong enough to face and defeat any one of these forces so long as he was able to give battle in reasonably favourable circumstances. Yet ensuring that it did so would take careful manoeuvring and, most probably, time. The formal battles of this period rarely occurred without days or weeks of delay once the armies had closed. When one side occupied a strong position and refused to leave it, few commanders would risk an attack. Even Hannibal, for all his genius, was unable to lure Fabius Maximus into battle and unwilling to fight on ground chosen by the Roman. However bitter the disputes between the Carthaginian generals may have been, they would most certainly not wait passively for Scipio to defeat each of them in turn. Therefore, as soon as the Roman presence was discovered, messengers would be dispatched summoning aid. If Scipio could not fight and win his battle within a couple of weeks of closing with the enemy – and the expectation of reinforcement would doubtless deter his Punic counterpart from risking a battle – then he would find himself seriously outnumbered and facing a disaster similar to the ones which had overwhelmed his father and uncle.

Therefore, instead of singling out one of the Punic field armies and seeking a decisive battle, Scipio resolved to strike at the enemy's most important base in Spain, the city of New Carthage (modern Cartagena). Founded by Hannibal's father Hamilcar as the seat of government for the Punic province in Spain, and the base from which he had begun his epic march to Italy in 218, New Carthage was a strong symbol of Punic, and especially Barcid, pride. Virtually all Carthaginian colonies included a harbour, but the one at New Carthage was bigger and better provided than any other in Spain. Apart from the records and treasury of the provincial government, the city contained hostages taken from the noble families of many Spanish communities. There were also considerable stores of food and military equipment, as well as the factories and skilled labour force to produce more of the latter. All in all, New Carthage was an attractive target, one whose capture would strike a massive moral blow to the enemy as well as weakening his war-making capacity whilst greatly enhancing that of the Romans.

Each of the Carthaginian field armies was at least ten days' march away from the city, and its garrison of trained soldiers was comparatively small. Yet New Carthage was still a fortified city and one defended on one side by the sea and on another by a salt lake, so that it could only be approached from the land across a narrow isthmus. Fortified places rarely fell to direct assault in this period. Sieges were more successful, although still uncertain, but a siege would take months and Scipio would have at best a few weeks before one or more of the enemy armies arrived. Quicker results came from treachery, but there was no prospect of that. Scipio did, however, receive a piece of information which was to prove vital. He had sought out fishermen and sailors from the allied city of Tarraco (Tarragona), men who regularly sailed along the coast as far as New Carthage. This in itself was an indication of the care with which the Roman general was preparing his campaign. These men told him that the lake to the north of the city could be forded at a certain place, and that the water level dropped even further in the evening. What the fishermen could not tell him was how his men could fight their way over the north wall of the city once they had waded across to it.

As he spent the winter visiting his troops, overseeing their training, and touring Rome's few remaining allies, Scipio resolved on attacking the city, but as yet confided only in his close friend and senior subordinate, Laelius. Openly he praised his troops, scorned the Carthaginians' achievements in the last two campaigns and spoke of the opportunity for bold action against them in the spring. He took particular care to praise and honour Lucius Marcius, the equestrian who had risen through sheer force of personality to command the survivors of the Roman armies after the disaster in 211, but had then upset the Senate by styling himself as 'propraetor' in his letters to them. At the beginning of the campaigning season he concentrated his forces near the mouth of the River Ebro. Only 3,000 foot and 500 horse were to be left behind to defend the area still loyal to Rome. The main force of 25,000 infantry and 2,500 cavalry advanced across the river under Scipio's direct command. A squadron of thirty-five war galleys, many of them undermanned, sailed under Laelius to rendezvous with the army at New Carthage.[11]

The details of the first phase of the operation are a little obscure. Polybius tells us that Scipio arrived outside New Carthage on the seventh day of a rapid march. The text implies, although unlike Livy it does not explicitly state, that they had begun at the Ebro. Elsewhere he informs us that the distance from New Carthage to the Ebro was 2,600 *stades* or 312 miles, which would imply an average speed of some 45 miles a day. This would be remarkably fast, especially for an army with baggage, and it may be that the figure is either wrong or describes only the last phase of the approach from some nearer spot. Yet the march probably was rapid by the standards of the day and went smoothly, army and fleet meeting outside the enemy stronghold as planned. It is not known at what point Scipio revealed their objective to his senior officers.[12]

New Carthage lay on a headland with the lake to the north and the bay which formed its natural harbour to the south. A canal connected the two. The city was surrounded by a curtain wall some 2.5 miles in circumference – a detail which Polybius tells us he had confirmed himself when he visited the place – and included five hills, one of which was topped by the citadel. The garrison commander, another Mago, had 1,000 regular troops, backed by a levy of male townsfolk, some 2,000 of whom were reasonably well equipped and confident. Scipio camped on the high ground at the end of the narrow neck of land facing towards the main gate. He ordered the construction of an earth rampart fronted by a ditch from one side of the isthmus to the other at the rear of his camp, but deliberately left unfortified the front nearest the city. It was an expression of confidence, but not a great risk, since the high ground would give his men a clear advantage against any sally. Scipio prepared for the assault, telling his men of the importance of the city,

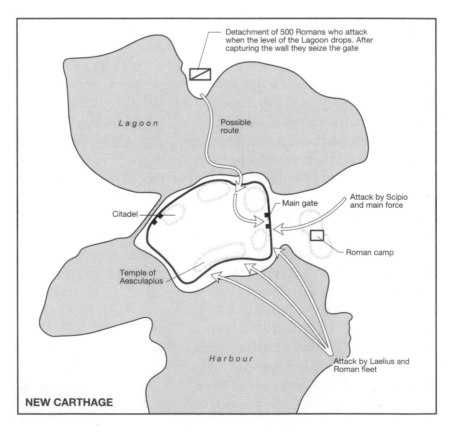

Detachment of 500 Romans who attack when the level of the Lagoon drops. After capturing the wall they seize the gate

Lagoon

Possible route

Citadel

Main gate

Attack by Scipio and main force

Roman camp

Temple of Aesculapius

Attack by Laelius and Roman fleet

Harbour

NEW CARTHAGE

and promising lavish rewards to the brave, most notably the mural crown (*corona muralis*) to the first man over the walls. He also proclaimed that Neptune had appeared to him a dream, the sea god promising that when the time was right he would come to their aid. Polybius once again viewed this as a cynical ploy.[13]

The attack began at the third hour on the next day. It went in from two directions, Laelius' ships rowing into the harbour and assaulting from the sea, whilst a storming party of 2,000 soldiers supported by ladder-bearers attacked from their camp. Mago had divided his regulars between the citadel and another hill, topped by a temple to the god of healing, Aesculapius, and facing towards the harbour. The best part of the levy were posted ready to attack from the main gate, whilst the remainder were distributed around the walls and provided with a good supply of missiles to hurl at the enemy. Almost as soon as Scipio sounded the trumpet call which sent the main storming party into the attack, Mago ordered the armed civilians to sally out from the main gate, hoping to break up the impetus of the Roman assault before it had even reached the city wall.

A striking feature of many ancient sieges was the willingness of the defender to leave the security of his fortifications and fight in the open. It was an expression of confidence, intended to intimidate the besieger, and served the practical purpose of delaying the real assault. On such a narrow frontage it was difficult for the Romans to bring their greater numbers into play immediately, and there was certainly no question of the Carthaginians being outflanked. In the initial confrontation 2,000 defenders faced a similar number of Romans. Probably deliberately, as he hoped to inflict heavy casualties on the boldest of the defenders, Scipio had held his men back close to the camp so that the fighting lines clashed about a quarter of a mile from the city walls.

The Carthaginians may have lacked training, but they displayed considerable enthusiasm and at first the combat seemed even. To the noise of the fighting was added the cheering of the defenders on the walls and the unengaged Roman troops as they urged on their sides. Yet Scipio had the bulk of his army formed and waiting in reserve only a short distance from the fighting line, and gradually fed in more and more fresh troops. Mago had few reserves to send to the aid of his men, and those few had to leave the city by the single gate and had much further to go before they could join the combat. The Carthaginians began to be driven back, and as the pressure increased eventually they collapsed into rout. The vast majority of casualties in ancient battles were inflicted at this moment, when one side fled from close contact and was pursued by an exultant and vengeful enemy. The sally which had begun so well ended in chaos as a mob of fugitives fled for the sanctuary of the single gate. The panic spread to many of those watching from the top of the wall, and for a while it seemed that the Romans might break into the city, intermingled with the routers.

Scipio had been supervising the battle from an elevated position in front of his camp on the high ground. Seeing the defenders' confusion, he sent men and ladder parties to escalade the city wall. The general went with them, but he was no Marcellus, charging sword in hand at the head of his troops. Polybius tells us that

> Scipio took part in the battle, but consulted his safety as far as possible; for he had with him three men carrying large shields, who holding these close covered the surface exposed to the wall and thus afforded him protection. So that passing along the side of his line on higher ground he contributed greatly to the success of the day, for he could both see what was going on and being seen by all his men inspired the combatants with greater spirit.[14]

Staying close to the fighting without getting directly involved, Scipio performed the two roles which were to characterize the Roman style of command for many centuries. As a general he paid attention to the large and small details of the battle, intervening even in minor tactical decisions when necessary, but always maintaining a sense of the wider battle. As a leader, and a leader who had promised great rewards to the brave, he acted as a witness to his men's behaviour. Polybius elsewhere emphasized that the rewards lavished on those who performed conspicuous acts of bravery, and the punishments inflicted on the cowardly, were major factors in maintaining the Roman army's fighting spirit and aggression. Roman soldiers fought better when they believed that their individual behaviour was being observed by their commanders. In the first century BC the historian Sallust praised the warlike spirit of past generations, claiming that 'the greatest competition for glory was between themselves; each man strove to be the first to kill an enemy, to scale an enemy wall, and most of all to be seen performing such a feat.'[15] This desire for an audience to watch and praise brave deeds was a survival of the old heroic ethos which would have been familiar to Homer's warriors. It was the spirit which had inspired the conduct of Marcellus and many Roman generals before him, but which Scipio deliberately set himself outside. As Polybius said, he had already proved his physical courage at Ticinus and Cannae, and had rightly decided that there were more important things for a general to do. Thus he concentrated on directing the battle, doing this from close quarters because this gave him the best opportunity of judging how things were going, but taking care to minimize the risk to himself.

Taking a high and defended wall by escalade was never an easy task. In the initial chaos following the rout of the Carthaginian sally, the Romans were able to reach the foot of the wall and set up their ladders, but the wall was the highest and strongest part of the city's defences and a few defenders remained. Some ladders broke apart under the weight of the soldiers climbing them, others were pushed away by the Carthaginians. It is possible that other ladders were too short, for it was always extremely difficult for the attackers to calculate the necessary length before an attack. At Syracuse, Marcellus' men had used a period of negotiation to count the number of courses of stone in one section of the city's walls. Multiplying this by their estimate of the size of an individual stone, they had successfully calculated the height and constructed their ladders accordingly.[16]

A barrage of missiles greeted the soldiers trying to climb this wall and the men of the fleet attacking from the sea. In time, many of the defenders who had panicked were rallied and returned to join their comrades on the wall. Every Roman attempt to break into the city was thwarted and their casualties mounted. After some time, Scipio judged that his men were too weary to continue and called off the attacks, withdrawing the soldiers to their camp where they rested and re-formed. Mago and his defenders were elated, feeling that they had beaten off the enemy's main attack, and could only look on in dismay when, later in the day, the Romans renewed their assault. Fresh ladders were brought forward in even greater quantity than before and the legionaries attacked with redoubled enthusiasm. Yet, even though the defenders had largely exhausted their ready supply of missiles, the Romans were still unable to fight their way over the wall.

It was now late in the day and the tide in the lagoon was beginning to drop. During the lull Scipio had prepared a fresh unit of 500 picked men to ford across and assault the wall from a new direction. He went with the soldiers to the edge of the lagoon and encouraged them to step boldly into the ebbing water, but, holding to his resolve to direct the battle and not get directly involved, he did not lead the attack. Guides, presumably some of the fishermen from Tarraco, took the party into the lake and showed them the route across. They reached the wall without difficulty and found it unguarded and not especially high, for attack from such a direction was considered unlikely and the defenders had all been drawn away to oppose the other attacks. Setting their ladders against it, they climbed to the top and began to march along the walkway towards the main gate. The few defenders encountered were easily killed or driven off, the long body-shield and short stabbing sword of the Roman legionaries being especially well suited to fighting in such a confined space.

Some of the main attacking force had seen their comrades rushing across an apparently deep lake, and witnessing such an apparent miracle had remembered Scipio's claim that Neptune would aid them. With renewed enthusiasm they pressed against the walls. One party raised their shields over their heads to form a *testudo* and advanced to the gate, men in the front rank bearing axes to chop through its timbers. In the meantime, the 500 attacked the defenders of this position from behind. Panic was almost immediate and the defence collapsed. Romans hacked at the gate from both sides until it was shattered, whilst more and more men were able to swarm up the ladders and across the wall. Perhaps because of a general slackening in the enthusiasm of the Carthaginians or maybe solely through their own efforts, at about the same time Laelius' sailors also scaled the wall near the harbour.

The Romans were through the main circuit of defences, but that did not mean that their victory was certain. Mago's regulars seem to have played little role in the defence and remained in control of the citadel. Ancient cities tended to be crowded, with very narrow streets running amongst a maze of buildings. Once inside, it was very difficult for the leaders of an attacking army to control their troops or respond to any new threat. If a defender was able to rally enough men or possessed still formed reserves, then it was more than possible that the attackers would be driven out once again. Scipio entered the city through the main gate almost as soon as this had been cleared. From outside he could neither see what was going on nor do anything to influence the course of events. Most of his army poured into the narrow streets and alleys, with orders to kill everyone they met, but not to begin looting until instructed by signal. Polybius tells us that this was the normal Roman practice, and suspected that it was intended to terrify, 'so that when towns are taken by the Romans one may often see not only the corpses of human beings, but dogs cut in half, and the dismembered limbs of animals, and on this occasion such scenes were very many owing to the numbers of those in the place.'[17] The Roman sack of a city was extremely brutal, and the roots of these customs probably date back to the early predatory warfare of the archaic period. Massacre was intended to give the defenders no chance to rally and return to the fight. Plundering was restricted and regulated so that all of the Roman army would benefit equally, and this assurance helped to keep the various sections of the attacking force at their appointed task.

Whilst much of the army dispersed to spread fear and slaughter through-out the city, Scipio kept a body of fresh troops formed up and under his tight personal control. After passing through the main gateway they followed the principal road into the open marketplace. From there he dispatched one detachment against one of the hills which still seemed to be defended, and led the main force of 1,000 against the Carthaginian mercenaries holding the citadel. After a brief resistance, Mago surrendered. Once the citadel was secure, and all formal resistance over, the trumpet was sounded to turn the men from slaughter to pillage. Each maniple was supposed systematically to plunder an area, all of the spoils being taken back to the marketplace, the whole process being supervised by the tribunes. Scipio and his 1,000 men occupied the citadel throughout the night, whilst other troops were on guard in the camp. When the booty was auctioned off – largely to the Roman traders and businessmen who accompanied any Roman field army, but possibly also to some locals – the profits were distributed to the entire army, each man receiving a share in proportion to his rank. Perhaps even more important than this financial reward was the parade at which those who had distinguished themselves were decorated and publicly lauded by their commander. At one stage a dispute between the fleet and the legions over who had been first to reach the top of the city walls threatened almost to spill over into violence, until Scipio declared that the rival claimants, Sextus Digitius from the navy and the centurion Quintus Trebellius of the Fourth Legion, had reached the top at the same moment and gave each man the corona muralis.[18]

The capture of the city was a remarkable achievement, especially as the first operation of a new commander with no experience of leading a force of this size. Its boldness was characteristically Roman, but the careful planning and preparation which had underlain his rapid drive into enemy territory were symptoms of greater military sophistication than had been shown in most earlier campaigns. There has been some scholarly debate over the precise nature of the natural phenomenon which permitted his men to cross the lagoon, in part because our sources are somewhat contradictory in this respect. The main controversy concerns whether the phenomenon was a daily occurrence or the occasional result of the wind blowing from a certain direction. If it was the latter, then it is suggested that Scipio was relying on fortune. If it was a regular and predictable occurrence, as our most reliable source Polybius clearly believed, then some have wondered why the Romans did not attack from this direction at the same time as they launched their first assault. Such a view misunderstands the difficulty of capturing a line of fortifications by escalade. Though the wall facing the lagoon was lower than elsewhere, it is unlikely that the attack would have succeeded if it had been held by even a small number of defenders. The Roman attacks were intended to draw the Carthaginians' attention away from this vulnerable spot, and therefore needed to be delivered in full force, in spite of the high cost in casualties. There was always the slight chance that they would succeed on their own, as the fleet's attack may actually have done. More importantly, Scipio gambled on these gaining and holding Mago's attention so that the attack from the lake was likely to be successful.

New Carthage's capture utterly changed the balance of power in Spain. In practical terms Scipio gained considerable military resources, ranging from artillery to another eighteen warships to add to the fleet, their crews made up of captured slaves who were promised their freedom if they served faithfully. Much of the population was set free, but 2,000 artisans were declared public slaves and set to produce weapons and equipment for the Roman army, and these men were also given the promise of freedom when victory was achieved. About 300 hostages from the noble families of Spain also fell into Roman hands. The stories of Scipio's honourable treatment of these people, most especially the noblewomen amongst them, echo the tales of Alexander the Great's capture of ladies of the Persian royal household. The women were placed under his personal protection and, in spite of the young Roman's reputation as a womanizer, not molested in any way. One story claimed that the legionaries found an especially beautiful girl and brought her to their commander, but that, after thanking them, he refused to take advantage of the situation and restored her to her parents. Livy tells an even more romantic version in which the girl was returned to her betrothed, Scipio personally assuring the young aristocrat that her virtue was intact. The restoration of the hostages to their families set in course a round of diplomacy which would prompt an increasing number of tribes to ally with Rome.[19]

New Carthage gave Scipio a base in southern Spain and brought him more resources than he could expect to receive from Italy. The war effort in the peninsula was from now onwards to a great extent self-sustaining. Although the number of his Roman and Italian troops remained essentially the same, these were well clothed, equipped and fed and, as the commander imposed a rigorous training programme on them in the months after the capture of New Carthage, highly disciplined. However many allied soldiers were acquired, the core of the army remained the two legions and *alae* and it was these who would play the critical role in all his subsequent successes.

THE BATTLE OF ILIPA, 206 BC

In 208 Scipio led his highly trained army against Hasdrubal Barca. It is a little difficult to tell from our sources whether the resultant action at Baecula was a full-scale battle, but what is clear is that the Roman and Italian troops out-manoeuvred their opponents. Scipio's victory may have been marginal, and Hasdrubal was soon to begin his journey to join his brother in Italy, but it may be that the Romans inflicted serious losses upon him and made that expedition much more difficult. Hasdrubal left Spain, removing one of the Punic field armies from the peninsula and further shifting the balance of power in Rome's favour. Although he reached Italy, he rapidly discovered that the Romans were far better prepared than had been the case in 218. The new Carthaginian invasion was rapidly confronted by superior numbers of well-trained and led Roman troops and utterly defeated at Metaurus in 207. Hannibal only became aware of his brother's arrival when enemy horsemen hurled Hasdrubal's severed head into his camp. As these events were occurring in Italy, Scipio achieved a series of minor victories in Spain, but his main offensive failed to draw Hasdrubal Gisgo into a pitched battle.[20]

By 206 Hasdrubal had become a lot more confident. Joining forces with Mago Barca, they together fielded an army of 70,000 infantry (although Livy gives the figure as only 50,000), 4,000–4,500 cavalry, some of them the superb Numidian light horse led by Prince Masinissa, and thirty-two elephants. This represented the bulk of the mercenaries in Spain, supported by many less disciplined and skilful contingents provided by Carthage's allies and subjects. There was little time for the Punic commanders to integrate these elements into a cohesive whole, so this great host would manoeuvre clumsily, but its sheer size was daunting. Scipio was able to lead against it 45,000 infantry and 3,000 cavalry. He was therefore somewhat outnumbered, possibly by a very large margin. Even worse, only around half of the foot were his superbly drilled and confident legions and *alae* and the remainder the very allies on whom he was resolved never to rely. The Roman army, just as much as the Carthaginian, was not a united and coherent force used to operating together. When he advanced to camp near the enemy outside Ilipa – not far from modern-day Seville – the Roman general was faced with the problem of how to make use of the diverse troops at his command.[21]

As the Roman column began to construct its camp, Mago and Masinissa led the bulk of the Punic cavalry in an attack intended to disrupt and dismay the newly arrived enemy. It was normal practice for Roman armies to post pickets of formed troops to cover a camp both during and after construction, but in this case Scipio had taken the precaution of stationing his cavalry in the dead ground behind a hill. The sudden Roman counter-attack panicked the leading Carthaginian horsemen, some of whom – probably the Numidians who rode bare-backed – were unseated. A more protracted combat developed with the formed squadrons supporting the Punic attack, but these were gradually forced back as units of legionaries advanced from the camp. Close formation infantry provided stable shelter behind which horsemen could rest and re-form before advancing once more, and were very difficult for enemy cavalry to break on their own. Such support gave cavalry formations the stability which they inherently lacked. Cavalry combats were whirling affairs as squadrons charged, pursued, lost their formation and were in turn beaten back and chased themselves. Gradually, the Carthaginians found that they were re-forming nearer and nearer to their own camp as the Roman foot soldiers pressed forward to hold gains made by their cavalry. In the end the pressure grew too great, and the Punic horsemen fled back to their camp.[22]

This seems to have been the first of several skirmishes fought between elements of the two armies in the days before the actual battle. Such encounters were common precursors to a massed encounter and success or failure in this small-scale fighting was seen as an indication of the relative courage and prowess of the two sides. A few days may have been occupied in this skirmishing, before Hasdrubal decided to deploy his entire army and offer battle to the enemy. The Punic camp was on high ground and, fairly late in the day, the Carthaginians marched to the edge of the plain below before forming their line. The deployment was conventional, with the best infantry, Libyan spearmen and perhaps some formations of citizens from the Punic colonies in Spain, were placed in the centre. Hasdrubal divided his Spaniards on either flank and placed the cavalry, with elephants to their front, on the wings. Scipio swiftly matched the enemy's confident gesture and deployed his own army, placing the Romans in the centre and the Spanish on either side of them, with the cavalry facing their enemy counterparts. As the dust clouds thrown up by so many marching feet began to settle, the two armies stood and watched each other. For all their initial confidence, neither commander wished to push his men forward and force a battle. After some hours, with the sun beginning to set, Hasdrubal gave the order for his men to return to camp. Observing this, Scipio did the same.

Over the following days this became almost a routine. At a late hour, which in itself suggested no great enthusiasm for battle, Hasdrubal led his army onto the edge of the plain. The Romans would then match the move, both armies deploying in the same formation as on the first day. Then the armies would stand and wait, until near the end of the day, first the Carthaginians and then the Romans returned to their respective camps. As we have seen, such delays were common before the battles of this period, but at first neither side appeared to be gaining any significant advantage from these displays of confidence. There was perhaps a marginal benefit in morale to Hasdrubal from initiating the challenge each day, but he had so far done nothing to build upon this.

The effort involved in deploying armies of this size into battle order should not be underestimated, for it was a process which must have taken hours. Most armies deployed using the processional method. As soon as the troops left their camp – or in the case of the Romans, whose camps were deliberately designed with space between the tent lines and wall, inside the camp – they were marshalled into a column. In the lead was the unit which would take station on the extreme right flank of the battle line. Following this was the unit which would take station to its left, and so on until the rear of the column was formed by the troops who would compose the extreme left of the line. Once formed into this order, the army column marched to the point where the left of the battle line would take station, before wheeling to the right and processing along the eventual line's frontage. When the leading unit reached its position on the extreme right it halted and changed from open marching order into tighter battle formation facing towards the enemy. Behind it, the other units of the army performed the same man-oeuvre until each was in its appointed place. The Roman method differed only in the respect that the troops were formed into three columns, one cor-responding to each of the three lines in the *triplex acies*. All of this required a good deal of supervision by senior officers to ensure that everyone ended up in the right place. Most armies sent out cavalry and light troops to cover the main column as it moved into position if there appeared to be any threat of enemy attack. The processional method was slow, particularly with large armies, but effective, especially since no army had yet developed drills which would allow it to deploy any more speedily. The biggest weakness of this system was its rigidity. A commander needed to decide on what his battle order was to be before forming the column up. Once this had been done, it was virtually impossible to alter it in any significant way. Most armies usually took up the same battle order, for each unit's familiarity with its place in the line eased the entire process.

Scipio's tactics at Ilipa need to be understood within the context of this system. After several days of matching Hasdrubal's challenge without either commander actually committing their forces to battle, Scipio decided to force an encounter on the next day. Written orders were issued, probably in the early hours of the morning, for the troops to rise and breakfast early. Just before dawn he dispatched his cavalry and light troops to attack the Carthaginian pickets. The remainder of his army prepared to deploy, but this time Scipio altered his formation. On this day his Spanish allies would take up position in the centre of his line, whilst his best troops were divided between the two flanks, quite probably with one legion and one *ala* on either side. Once his troops had formed, he advanced more boldly than in the preceding days and did not halt until he was midway across the open plain. Whilst our sources do not state this explicitly, it is certain that the Roman general must have discussed this change with his senior officers, so that they were able to form the army's columns accordingly. This most likely occurred at the *consilium* which a Roman commander normally held before a major action. Although sometimes translated as 'council of war', these were not normally forums for debate, but a gathering (rather like an 'O' Group in the British Army) at which the general's plan was explained. In this case Scipio must surely also have explained the complex manoeuvres with which he had decided to open the battle.

When Hasdrubal's outposts came under attack from the Roman cavalry and light troops, the Carthaginians responded quickly. Behind this attack, the main Roman force was visible as it marched out to deploy, although it is doubtful that at this distance – judging from later events it was probably at least a mile – that the Punic general could see more than vague masses of men and great clouds of dust. Responding quickly to this challenge, Hasdrubal issued orders for his men to arm themselves and prepare to deploy. He may have felt that this sudden display of Roman confidence was intended to restore their spirits after days of responding to Carthaginian challenges. If Hasdrubal was to maintain any moral advantage then he had to respond to this Roman move and could not allow Scipio the chance of telling his men that the enemy were afraid of them and did not dare to meet their advance. Therefore the Punic commander had no hesitation in ordering the army to form up in the same order they had adopted on each of the previous days. They did this in haste, and most of his men had no opportunity to eat anything. Yet, even at this stage, it remained possible that no battle would result, and that the two armies would once again stand and stare at each other for most of the day.

The Punic cavalry and light infantry went out first, confronting their Roman counterparts and engaging in a whirling combat without clear result.

The main Carthaginian army marched out and formed line at the edge of the plain beneath the hill on which they had camped. Scipio's men were about half a mile away, much closer than they had come in the past. At this distance Hasdrubal was at last able to see that the legions were not in their usual place in the centre, but were on the wings facing his weaker troops. This did mean that his best foot opposed the Romans' Spanish allies, which may have been some consolation, for if it came to a head-on clash between the battle lines then his Libyans ought to beat these poorly drilled and less heavily equipped troops. Though he was perhaps disconcerted by the change,

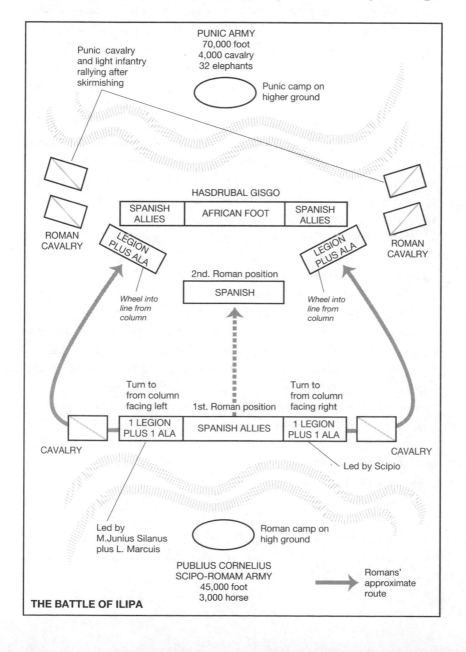

PUNIC ARMY
70,000 foot
4,000 cavalry
32 elephants

Punic cavalry and light infantry rallying after skirmishing

Punic camp on higher ground

HASDRUBAL GISGO

| SPANISH ALLIES | AFRICAN FOOT | SPANISH ALLIES |

ROMAN CAVALRY

LEGION PLUS ALA

LEGION PLUS ALA

ROMAN CAVALRY

2nd. Roman position

SPANISH

Wheel into line from column

Wheel into line from column

Turn to from column facing left

1st. Roman position

Turn to from column facing right

CAVALRY

| 1 LEGION PLUS 1 ALA | SPANISH ALLIES | 1 LEGION PLUS 1 ALA |

CAVALRY

Led by Scipio

Led by M.Junius Silanus plus L. Marcuis

Roman camp on high ground

PUBLIUS CORNELIUS SCIPO-ROMAM ARMY
45,000 foot
3,000 horse

Romans' approximate route

THE BATTLE OF ILIPA

it is not obvious how this benefited his opponent. It would also now have been virtually impossible for him to change his own deployment to conform to that of the enemy. If he tried to shift large contingents around, this would only create confusion which the nearby and fully prepared enemy would surely exploit by launching an immediate attack.

There followed another of those lulls so typical of the battles of this period. Scipio advanced no further and the Carthaginians remained stationary at the edge of the plain. The cavalry and light infantry continued to skirmish with each other, but with both sides so closely supported by their main lines, it was relatively easy for groups under pressure to retire and reform behind the close order foot. After some time, all retired through the intervals between the units in their respective main lines and were sent to the wings. Eventually Scipio resumed the advance, but gave orders for the Spaniards in his centre to move slowly, whilst the wings began a complex series of manoeuvres which, as at Baecula, demonstrated the exceptionally high standard of their drill. Scipio himself commanded the troops on the right wing, whilst Lucius Marcius and Marcus Junius Silanus the propraetor controlled the left. Livy claims that Scipio sent an order to these officers telling them to copy his manoeuvres, but, whilst an instruction or signal to begin these may have been sent, it would seem likely that the officers were already aware of what was expected from them.

Scipio's men on the right wing began by each individual maniple in three lines turning or wheeling to the right, so that they once again formed three columns. The three maniples which formed the heads of the columns then wheeled to the left and marched straight at the enemy line, the units behind following on. The movements of the left wing were a mirror image of these manoeuvres. Columns with a narrow frontage will move much faster than lines with a broad frontage, for it is much easier for the men to keep in ranks as they encounter fewer obstacles, and need to stop less often to restore order. Therefore the three columns closed with the enemy very quickly, leaving the slow-moving Spanish in the centre well behind. At only a comparatively short distance from the Punic line, Scipio wheeled his three columns to the right once again (whilst the left wing made the opposite manoeuvre), and led them along until they formed into a battle line which overlapped the enemy flank.

Hasdrubal and the Carthaginian army seem to have watched mesmerized as the Roman columns came towards them. Missiles from the Roman light infantry and cavalry drove off the elephants, some of whom stampeded through the Punic troops to their rear, spreading confusion. The Roman and Italian troops then attacked Hasdrubal's Spanish allies on either wing. For a while the latter managed to hold their own, but gradually they were forced back. The Romans, who had eaten and been able to prepare for battle carefully, displayed greater endurance, no doubt helped by the normal tactics of feeding fresh troops into the fighting line from the maniples of *principes* and *triarii*. Slowly, they began to force the Spaniards back. After a while the retreat turned into a rout. Throughout this combat there was no serious fighting in the centre. Scipio's allied contingents were deliberately held back, but by their very presence pinned the Libyans in place, for they could not go to the aid of their own wings without exposing themselves to attack from the Roman centre. When the Punic flanks gave way, the rest of the army fled with them. Hasdrubal tried in vain to stop the rout. For a while he managed to form a shaky line on the lower slopes of the high ground in front of his camp, whilst the Romans paused at the foot of the hill, quite possibly a sign that Scipio was keeping his men under tight control. When the Roman advance began once again, the flimsy Punic line collapsed and fled back to the safety of the camp. Our sources maintain that, had it not been for a sudden and violent thunderstorm, the Romans would easily have overrun the enemy position. During the night, Hasdrubal's allies began to desert. He fled with the reliable sections of his army, but most of these were captured or killed in the subsequent Roman pursuit. Hasdrubal himself escaped, to fight with no more success against Scipio during the African campaign.[23]

AFRICANUS

Ilipa effectively ended the Carthaginian presence in Spain, for in the following months their remaining enclaves were mopped up with little difficulty. Before he left Spain, Scipio had to deal with mutiny amongst his own troops and a rebellion by some of his former allies, but he had already turned his attention to the invasion of Africa. He returned to Rome and the consulship – for which he was still technically too young – for 205, after which he managed to secure himself the province of Sicily as a base and permission to invade the enemy's homeland. Support for this was not unanimous. Fabius Maximus, nearing the end of his life, opposed the move, in part through jealousy of the popular fame of the maverick commander from Spain. He also appears to have feared that an unsuccessful invasion of Africa might cause a revival of the Carthaginian war effort, as it had in 255. There were further problems when one of Scipio's subordinates, a man named Pleminius, became involved in a scandal whilst acting as military governor of the city of Locri. This officer not only plundered the place he was supposed to protect, but managed to turn the tribunes under his command against him, even resorting to having them publicly flogged. When Scipio first intervened he showed loyalty to his own man, and supported Pleminius, who promptly threw off all restraint and executed the tribunes. Eventually the Locrians managed to send a deputation to Rome, leading the Senate to place the man under arrest.

Scipio's rivals in the Senate attempted at this point to give his command to another magistrate, but were thwarted by his continued popularity with most Roman citizens. Their trust proved well founded, as Scipio demonstrated the same ability and skill in the new campaign as he had shown in Spain. In the first place he took care to prepare thoroughly before launching the expedition from Sicily, so that when he did finally sail it was at the head of a superbly trained army backed by ample logistic support. In North Africa he consistently outwitted his opponents, attacking with ruthless efficiency at the critical moment. The first two armies sent against him were destroyed in their camps by a surprise night attack. As at New Carthage, Scipio had taken great care to gather intelligence about the enemy's strength and positions before the onslaught. During a period of negotiations he had attached centurions and other officers disguised as slaves to the following of his embassies. On one occasion one of the centurions is supposed to have been publicly beaten to maintain the subterfuge. Eventually, the Carthaginians were forced to recall Hannibal from Italy to face the invader. The two great generals met at Zama in battle that was not marked by especially subtle manoeuvring on either side. In the end, the Romans prevailed in the resultant slogging match, helped considerably by their numerical superiority in cavalry.[24]

Scipio returned to celebrate a spectacular triumph, taking the name Africanus as a permanent memorial to his achievement. He was still only in his early thirties and yet had achieved far more than most Roman senators managed in a lifetime. Although he continued to remain active in public life, it was hard to see how his subsequent career could possibly match, let alone surpass, what he had already done. He was elected to a second consulship in 194 and led an army against the Gallic tribes of Northern Italy, but was not engaged in heavy fighting. In 190 his younger brother Lucius became consul and, once Africanus announced that he would go with him as a senior subordinate or *legatus*, was given the command against the Seleucid Empire of Antiochus III. Scipio's presence was considered especially appropriate because Hannibal, now an exile from his native Carthage, had taken refuge at Antiochus' court and was expected to receive an important command. In the event the Carthaginian was placed in charge of part of the Seleucid fleet, whilst Scipio was ill and so missed the decisive land battle at Magnesia. It may be that the sickness was invented or exaggerated to ensure that Lucius gained full credit for his victory. There were also rumours of a deal with Antiochus to ensure the safe return of Africanus' son who had been taken prisoner. Yet on their return from this war, scandal was once again to beset Scipio and his brother. Both were prosecuted on charges of misappropriating state funds during the campaign. Scipio's response reflected the immense self-confidence which had marked his campaigns, but also revealed his modest political skills. In court he tore up his brother's accounts from the war against the Seleucids instead of reading them out. On another occasion his trial was convened on the anniversary of the battle of Zama, so Scipio suddenly proclaimed his intention to sacrifice and give thanks to the gods in the temples on the Capitol. Everyone apart from the prosecutors and their attendants followed him, but in spite of the crowd's enthusiasm the charges against him did not go away. In the end he left Rome and its politics and went to live out the last few years of his life in a country villa. It was a disappointing end for a man who had achieved so much in the service of the Republic.[25]

Livy had read an account which claimed that Scipio, as a member of a senatorial deputation sent to Ephesus in 193, met and conversed with Hannibal. During one of their encounters:

> Africanus asked who, in Hannibal's opinion, was the greatest general of all time. Hannibal replied, 'Alexander...because with a small force he routed armies of countless numbers, and because he traversed the remotest lands....' Asked whom he placed second, Hannibal said: 'Pyrrhus. He was the first to teach the art of laying out a camp. Besides that, no one has ever shown nicer judgement in choosing his ground, or in disposing his forces. He also had the art of winning men to his side....' When Africanus followed up by asking whom he ranked third, Hannibal unhesitatingly chose himself. Scipio burst out laughing at this, and said: 'What would you be saying if you had defeated me?'
>
> 'In that case,' replied Hannibal, 'I should certainly put myself before Alexander and before Pyrrhus – in fact before all other generals!' This reply, with its elaborate Punic subtlety...affected Scipio deeply, because Hannibal had set him apart from the general run of commanders, as one whose worth was beyond calculation.[26]

The story may well be apocryphal, but such a judgement was certainly not undeserved.

CHAPTER 3

THE CONQUEROR OF MACEDONIA:
AEMILIUS PAULLUS

Lucius Aemilius Paullus (c. 228 – c. 160 BC)

For my part, I shall do my duty as a general; I shall see to it that you are
given the chance of a successful action. It is no duty of yours to ask what is
going to happen; your duty is, when the signal is given, to play your full part
as fighting men.[1]

ALTHOUGH SCIPIO ACHIEVED LITTLE AFTER 201 AND ENDED HIS LIFE IN BITTER
retirement, the early second century BC was a time of great opportunity for
most senators of his generation, who would come to dominate Roman
public life for several decades. The heavy casualties amongst the Senate in
the early disasters inflicted by Hannibal accelerated the rise to prominence
of men who had reached adulthood during the war, and also severely reduced
the number of distinguished elder statesmen whose *auctoritas* ensured them
a significant role in debates. These men, whether descendants of established
families, or equestrians whose gallantry had won them admission to senatorial rank, had spent many years on campaign. When in time they reached
high magistracies and were themselves given command of the Republic's
armies, they led forces composed at all ranks of a very high proportion of
Punic War veterans. The combination proved lethally effective and for a
while the legions consistently displayed the same level of discipline and
tactical skill which had won victories at Metaurus, Ilipa and Zama.

There was no shortage of opportunities for both commanders and
armies to demonstrate their prowess. Warfare was almost constant in
the Spanish provinces and Cisalpine Gaul. Such fighting required the

overwhelming bulk of Rome's military resources, but was overshadowed by the more dramatic, if less common, wars fought against the great Hellenistic powers of the eastern Mediterranean. Alexander the Great had died in 323 BC without a clear adult heir, and his vast empire had swiftly been torn apart as his commanders fought each other for power, shaping the Greek world into which Rome would intervene. Eventually three great dynasties had emerged, the Seleucids in Syria, the Ptolemies in Egypt and the Antigonids in Macedonia itself. Smaller kingdoms, such as Pergamum and Bithynia in Asia Minor, were able to exist in the disputed border zones between these powers. Greece itself still contained some important independent cities, notably Athens, but many others had been incorporated with varying degrees of enthusiasm into the Aetolian or Achaean Leagues. The communities of the Greek world, whilst sharing a common language and culture, at no period showed any great enthusiasm for political unification, and their fierce sense of independence was only usually overcome by force or the need for aid against a stronger enemy. During disputes between cities, and often enough between rival factions within the same city, it was common to seek diplomatic and military aid from stronger outside forces. Hellenistic kings made frequent use of such appeals to intervene in areas allied to their rivals, and their propaganda routinely declared that they were fighting for the freedom of the Greeks.

Rome had had some diplomatic contact with the Hellenistic world long before there was any direct military involvement, and in 273 BC formed a treaty of friendship with Ptolemy II. In 229 and 219 the Republic fought wars in Illyria on the Adriatic coast, campaigning against the piratical rulers of the region. The creation of what was effectively a Roman protectorate on the Illyrian coast was not welcomed by Philip V of Macedon, who viewed the area as within his own sphere of influence. Hannibal's invasion of Italy and the string of devastating defeats he inflicted on the Romans offered the king an opportunity of expelling the intruders and in 215 he allied with Carthage against Rome. The result was the First Macedonian War, as the Romans somehow found sufficient troops and resources to open a new theatre of operations in Illyria and Greece. The conflict was not one of large, set-piece battles, but was instead characterized by raid, ambush, and attacks on strongholds and cities. Much of the actual fighting was done by the allies of the two sides and, when Rome's important local ally, the Aetolian League, concluded a separate peace with Philip V in 206, the Romans lacked the strength to continue the struggle effectively. A year later, hostilities formally ended with the Peace of Phoinike, which preserved Rome's allies in Illyria but also permitted the king to retain many of the cities which he had captured during the war.

Such a treaty, with concessions granted to both sides in proportion to their relative strength at the cessation of hostilities, was the normal way of ending a war in the Hellenistic world. The intervention of a neutral third party, in this case Epirus, to open negotiations with the combatants and promote the agreement of peace terms, was also common. Indeed, both Pyrrhus and Hannibal had evidently expected the Republic to concede defeat and seek just such a negotiated peace after they had smashed the legions in battle. Yet the Romans had not reacted as any other contemporary state would have done in the face of such catastrophes, for their whole under-standing of warfare was different. A Roman war ended when the Republic dictated peace terms to an utterly defeated and subject people. The will-ingness to negotiate with Macedonia as with an equal reflected the Senate's preoccupation with winning the struggle with Carthage. It did nothing to diminish the Romans' bitterness at the king's unprovoked attack at a time when Hannibal had driven them to the very brink of utter defeat.[2]

In 200, less than a year after the defeat of the Carthaginians, Rome responded to an appeal from Athens for aid against Philip V by declaring war. Victory in the Second Punic War had come at an enormous cost to Rome and her allies in Italy. The number of casualties had been immense, and much of the adult male population had been called upon to undergo excep-tionally long periods of service. Paying, feeding and often equipping unprece-dented numbers of legions had drained the Republic's treasury. For nearly a decade the rival armies had campaigned across Southern Italy, consuming or destroying crops and herds, burning settlements and massacring or enslav-ing the population. In the worst affected regions it would be some consid-erable time before agriculture could begin to recover, but throughout all Italy there was a sense of exhaustion and the need for a period of peace and recovery. This spirit prompted the *Comitia Centuriata* to reject the consul Publius Suplicius Galba's motion 'that it is the Will and Command of the Roman people that war should be declared on Philip, King of Macedon, and on the Macedonians under his rule, because of wrongs inflicted on the allies of the Roman people, and the acts of war committed against them.'[3] Such a reluctance to go to war was exceptionally rare at Rome. Before a second meeting, Galba addressed the citizens, explaining that Philip V was a proven enemy and emphasizing just how easy it would be for a Macedonian fleet to land an army on the shores of Italy. He raised the spectre of appease-ment, claiming that, had the Romans stood up to Hannibal and his family in Spain, the invasion of Italy would never have occurred. His reasoning clearly struck a chord with his audience, for this time the vote was overwhelmingly in favour of war.

The Second Macedonian War (200–197 BC) at first followed a similar pattern to the First, with most of the fighting occurring on a very small scale. In both conflicts Philip V displayed a considerable talent for the leadership of small columns, frequently leading charges spear in hand in the best tradition of Alexander the Great. In 199 he fortified the valley where the River Aous ran between mountains, adding strongpoints mounting artillery to an already formidable position. The Roman commander camped within 5 miles, but did not attempt to force his way through the line. The following year one of the new consuls, Titus Quinctius Flamininus, succeeded to the Macedonian command. He was only 30 and had won election to such high office when well below the legal age largely through the reputation he had won fighting against Hannibal. After Flamininus had demonstrated against the line without result, a local ally sent a guide who led a Roman force to outflank the position. The Macedonians suffered some loss, but were able to draw off the bulk of their army unscathed. Little else was achieved by the end of the campaigning season. In the winter Flamininus opened negotiations with the king, and it seemed for a while as if once again war between Rome and Macedon would be concluded with another Hellenistic-style treaty like the Peace of Phoinike. The consul was nervous that one of the two consuls for 197 would be sent to replace him, and hoped to gain credit for ending the war even if it were through negotiation rather than victory. However, Flamininus soon received letters from friends in the Senate who informed him that due to a crisis in Cisalpine Gaul, both of the new consuls were to be sent to the area and his own command would be extended. He immediately broke off the talks, resuming operations at the beginning of spring, and it was as a proconsul that he met and defeated the main Macedonian army at Cynoscephalae.[4]

This time the treaty concluding the conflict was more typically Roman, for it made it clear that the defeated state was, and should always be, inferior to Rome. Philip V gave up all the cities subject or allied to him in Greece and Asia Minor, and was in future not to make war outside Macedonia without Rome's express approval. The king was to pay Rome 1,000 talents of silver as reparations, and also to hand over all Roman prisoners, whilst paying to ransom his own men. The Macedonian fleet was reduced to a handful of warships, sufficient for little more than a ceremonial role. The treaty did not please the Aetolian League, which had once again fought as Rome's ally.

This dissatisfaction, coupled with a fear that Roman influence in Greece had now become too strong, led them in 193 to implore the Seleucid king Antiochus III to liberate the Greeks from foreign oppression. In the event, very few other cities chose to welcome the Seleucid expeditionary force and both the Achaean League and Philip V supported Rome. In 191 Antiochus' army was dislodged from the Pass of Thermopylae, made famous by Leonidas and his Spartans in 480 BC. The Romans under Marcus Acilius Glabrio, just like Xerxes' Persians centuries before, had found a path around the pass and were able to take the enemy from both sides. The war was then shifted to Asia Minor and culminated in the defeat of a huge Seleucid army at Magnesia by Lucius Scipio. Once again the treaty concluding the war severely restricted Antiochus' war-making capacity, reducing his fleet to a token force and banning him from keeping war elephants. Again as with Philip V, the king was not allowed to make war or form an alliance with communities outside his realm.[5]

Scipio's successor in the Asian command, Gnaeus Manlius Vulso, arrived to find the war already won and, after an unsuccessful attempt to provoke Antiochus into renewing hostilities, commenced a campaign against the Galatian tribes of Asia Minor. These were the descendants of Gauls who had migrated to the region in the early third century BC, and since then often extorted money from their neighbours under threat of violence. They were also frequently to be found serving as mercenaries or allies with the Seleucid kings, and on this basis Vulso justified his actions. In a swift campaign fought in the mountains the three tribes were defeated, but the consul faced strong opposition in the Senate on his return to Rome. Accused of starting an un-authorized war for his personal glory and profit, Vulso came close not only to losing the right to a triumph, but also to prosecution and the probable end of his political career. In the end his friends amongst the Senate, augmented by a good few senators bribed with the plunder from his campaign, pre-vented this from happening and his triumphal procession proved to be one of the most spectacular ever seen. Although the outcome was different, this political attack on a magistrate who had achieved spectacular success was similar in many ways to the assault on Africanus and his brother. Flamininus avoided such direct attacks himself, but suffered the humiliation of having his brother Quintus expelled from the Senate as unfit to be a member of this body. The latter had held a naval command during the Second Macedonian War and done his job competently enough, but had subsequently become involved in a scandal when it was alleged that he had ordered the execution of a prisoner during a banquet simply to indulge a male prostitute with whom he was in love. Each of the commanders who won a major campaign in the Eastern Mediterranean gained massive wealth and prestige. None were able to use this to achieve a dominant position in political life back in Rome for any length of time.[6]

THE THIRD MACEDONIAN WAR, 172–168 BC

Philip V had aided the Romans in their wars against the Aetolians and the Seleucids, his enthusiasm doubtless increased by the knowledge that it was not in his interest to permit either of these to increase their power in Greece. The Romans had always expected allies, even recently defeated allies, to support their next round of war-making. The legions which won Cynoscephalae, Thermopylae and Magnesia were fed to a great extent with grain supplied by Carthage in its new capacity as a faithful ally of Rome. Yet over time, the Macedonian king began to resent the restrictions imposed upon him in 197 and gradually sought to rebuild his power, looking especially to the Thracian tribes on his north-eastern border, since his activity in Greece was heavily restricted. When Philip V died in 179, he was succeeded by his son Perseus who continued his policies. Perseus was widely believed to have arranged the murder of Demetrius, his younger and more popular brother who had spent time as a hostage in Rome and was considered to be pro-Roman. The Senate's suspicions of the new king seemed confirmed when he allied himself with an extremely warlike Germanic tribe, the Bastarnae, and showed a willingness to aid democratic factions in the cities of Greece. Macedonia was no longer behaving as a subordinate ally should and came to be seen as a threat, although whether this view was realistic is harder to say. Attacks on Roman allies provided the classic justification for the declaration of war against Perseus in 172 BC.[7]

The conflict was to prove almost the last gasp of the generation of Romans which had fought and defeated Hannibal. When the army destined to serve in Macedonia was enrolled the presiding consul sought out as many veteran officers and soldiers as possible. Livy tells us that a dispute arose when twenty-three former senior centurions were enrolled as ordinary centurions. The spokesman of the group, one Spurius Ligustinus, is said to have made a speech recounting his long and distinguished service and was eventually given the post of senior centurion of the *triarii* of *Legio I*. The others agreed to accept whatever rank was given to them, and it is notable that the Senate had decreed that no citizen below the age of 51 was to be granted an exemption from service should the consul and tribunes choose to conscript them. The army sent to Macedonia was experienced, if in some cases a little elderly, and may well have included a number of men who, like Ligustinus, had served in the area before. It was a standard two-legion consular army, as indeed were the forces which had defeated Philip V and Antiochus the Great. In this case, though, the legions were exceptionally large, with 6,000 infantry and 300 cavalry apiece. With the addition of allies it mustered 37,000 foot and 2,000 horse.[8]

To oppose them, Perseus is said to have fielded an army of 39,000 infantry and 4,000 cavalry at the start of the war. Like the armies of all the Hellenistic kingdoms, its organization, equipment and tactics were derived from the forces with which Philip II and Alexander had overrun first Greece and then the Persian Empire. Whilst some allied and mercenary contingents were employed, the bulk of the army consisted of full-time professional soldiers recruited from the citizen body. The regiments of the phalanx, which altogether made up just over half of the infantry of the army, were entirely recruited from citizens. In a pitched battle, though probably not in raids and sieges, these men fought in dense blocks as pikemen.

The pike itself, or *sarissa*, seems to have become a little longer than in Alexander's day and measured some 21 feet in length. The butt consisted of a heavy bronze counterweight, which allowed the soldier to balance the weapon and still have two thirds of its length projecting ahead of him. Since both hands were needed to wield the *sarissa*, a circular shield was suspended on a strap from the shoulder. Additional protection was provided by a bronze helmet, a cuirass – usually of stiffened linen – and in some cases greaves. Each soldier normally carried a sword, but this was very much a secondary weapon and the strength of the phalanx relied on massed pikes. Each soldier occupied a frontage and depth of 3 feet in battle order. (There was an even tighter formation, known as 'locked shields' (*synaspismos*) where each man was allocated a frontage of only 18 inches, but this was purely defensive, since it was impossible for the phalanx to move when formed in this way.)

The great length of the *sarissa* meant that the spearheads of the first five ranks projected at intervals of some 3 feet or so in front of the formation. As long as the phalanx remained in good order, it was exceptionally difficult for any enemy attacking from the front to get past this hedge of spear points and wound the pikemen themselves. However, the *sarissa* was an unwieldy weapon and the restrictions of the formation meant that it was difficult for individual pikemen to aim strong thrusts at an opponent. In a frontal confrontation a well-ordered phalanx would win a combat more by its staying power than its capacity for killing the enemy and actively breaking up their formation.

The phalanx had become the dominant arm in the Successor armies. The other contingents of infantry, which usually included a good number of skirmishers and missile-armed troops, played a supporting role. So did the cavalry, and it was in this respect that the tactical doctrine of later Hellenistic armies differed radically from the days of Alexander the Great. In his major battles the phalanx acted as a pinning force, advancing to engage the enemy and applying steady pressure against his centre. Then, at the right moment and in the critical spot – usually where the enemy had been forced to overextend himself – the decisive charge was delivered by the close order Companion cavalry, led by the Royal Squadron which in turn was led by Alexander himself. This method had proved brutally effective at Issus and Gaugamela against Darius' Persians. It was less easy for Successor generals to achieve the same result when fighting against other Macedonian-style armies with an identical tactical doctrine and more solid formations of troops. More importantly, the break-up of Alexander's empire divided the manpower and resources of the old kingdom of Macedonia. Successor kings preferred whenever possible to recruit the bulk of their army from the descendants of 'true' Macedonians, drawing far too deeply on a resource depleted by war and colonization. One result of this was that it was difficult to recover in the short term from serious losses in battle, making these highly professional armies somewhat brittle. Limited resources of men, and even more limited supplies of suitable horses, made it difficult for any of the kingdoms to muster large numbers of cavalry. Alexander had about 7,000 cavalry and 40,000 infantry at Gaugamela, a ratio of roughly one to six. This was very high, even if it did not quite rival Hannibal's one to four at Cannae. Successor armies rarely managed much more than a ratio of one to ten. Fewer in numbers, Hellenistic cavalry in the later third and second centuries BC were also generally inferior in manoeuvrability, discipline and sheer aggression when compared to Philip II and Alexander's horsemen.

Many Successor generals experimented with a range of unusual or exotic weapons, such as elephants and scythed chariots, hoping to gain an advantage over other Hellenistic armies which were almost identical to their own. Occasionally these methods succeeded spectacularly, but few were reliable enough to provide a consistent advantage and they were anyway swiftly copied by opponents. Superficially, Hellenistic armies from this period contained a wide diversity of troop types, but in reality they were not as well balanced as their predecessors who had served under Alexander, resembling more the bludgeon than the rapier. Alexander had made little use of reserves, instead deploying his army to deliver a co-ordinated sequence of attacks which combined to shatter the enemy. His practice of personally leading the main cavalry charge ensured that he had no opportunity to issue orders summoning contingents in reserve to join the fighting. Most Successor commanders chose to lead their armies in a similar way, greatly restricting their capacity to issue orders or respond to a changing situation once the battle had begun. It continued to be very rare for any sizeable contingent of a Hellenistic army to begin the battle in reserve and not as part of the main fighting line.

Lacking sufficient high-quality cavalry, and unable to rely on exotic weapons, the phalanx assumed ever greater importance as the army's main strength. To increase its chances of grinding down the enemy – especially when that enemy was another pike phalanx – there was a tendency to employ very deep formations. Most phalanxes were at least sixteen ranks deep, whilst the Seleucid pikemen at Magnesia formed in thirty-two ranks. Deeper formations had greater staying power in combat – simply because it was so difficult for the men in the front ranks to run away – and looked intimidating, even if their actual fighting power was no greater than a shallower formation of similar frontage. If by the time of the wars with Rome Hellenistic armies had become clumsy and bludgeon-like, they could still in the right circumstances deliver a very heavy attack on an enemy to their front. Yet the circumstances needed to be just right, for a phalanx required flat, open land if it were not to fall into disorder, and its flanks needed to be kept secure because the pikemen themselves could not easily respond to a threat from any direction apart from the front.[9]

Roman armies had first encountered a Hellenistic army and commander in 280 BC, when King Pyrrhus of Epirus had joined the city of Tarentum in its war with Rome. Pyrrhus was considered to be the ablest commander of his generation and led an army somewhat closer to the Alexandrian model. He defeated the legions at Heraclea in 280 and Asculum the following year, but was eventually beaten at Malventum in 275 BC. Each of these battles was extremely hard fought with heavy casualties on both sides, as the grinding power of the phalanx was faced by the native stubbornness and *triplex acies* system which allowed the Romans to feed fresh troops into their fighting line. Pyrrhus' initial victories had been assisted by his small corps of war elephants, creatures which the Romans found unfamiliar and terrifying. Curiously enough, in the Third Macedonian War Perseus had no access to supplies of elephants, whereas the Roman force included a number of these beasts supplied by their Numidian allies. A more important difference between the war with Pyrrhus and the conflicts of the second century BC was the quality of the Roman armies. Many of the legions of this period, composed of and led by veterans of the war with Hannibal, were as well drilled and confident as any professional soldiers. The Macedonian and Syrian wars were not fought by inexperienced militia on the one hand and hardened professionals on the other. Indeed, if anything, the Macedonian and Seleucid soldiers had less battle experience than most legionaries at this time.

At the beginning of the war this did not especially matter, for as in the earlier campaigns against Philip V, there were no pitched battles and instead the armies spent their time in raids, surprise attacks and sieges. Perseus lacked his father's flair in this type of fighting, but still managed to win a cavalry skirmish near Larissa in 171 against the consul Publius Licinius Crassus. Neither Crassus nor his successor Aulus Hostilius Mancinus displayed much ability and the actions of the forces under their command were poorly co-ordinated and lacking in purpose. Perhaps some of the centurions and tribunes appointed to the legions were now too elderly for active service, or maybe the consuls, aware of the need to achieve fame in a single campaigning season before they were replaced, did not spend enough time training the army before beginning operations. Decades of military success may well have made the Romans overconfident. Both Crassus and Mancinus reached the consulship at the normal age, and were too young to remember the darkest days of the Hannibalic War. Crassus' colleague, Caius Cassius Longinus, had hoped to receive the Macedonian command and had been bitterly disappointed when the lot gave him the province of Illyria instead. Once in his province he had mustered his army at the colony of Aquileia, gathered supplies sufficient for thirty days and begun to march overland to Macedonia, planning to win the victory himself. By chance the Senate heard of this unauthorized expedition and rapidly dispatched commissioners to recall their errant consul.[10]

In 169 Quintus Marcius Philippus was the consul sent to take charge of the army in Macedonia. Livy describes him as 'more than 60 years old and grossly overweight', but emphasizes that in spite of this he was as active as a Roman general should be in encouraging and controlling his soldiers.[11] Philippus was older and more experienced than Crassus or Mancinus, although his first consulship in 186 had been marred by a defeat suffered at the hands of the Ligurians. He had also been one of the two senior envoys sent to Perseus before the declaration of war in 172. By falsely encouraging the king to believe that the Senate might be willing to come to terms, the ambassadors had delayed the start of hostilities and so given the Republic more time to prepare for war. Although most senators approved of this deception, several of the more senior members had claimed that it was out of keeping with the Romans' traditionally open way of waging war, which relied more on courage than trickery.

By the time Philippus assumed command of the army in Thessaly, Perseus had gone over to the defensive, fortifying the passes and key positions on the borders of Macedonia itself. Within nine days of his arrival, the consul made a very bold attempt to break through this chain of fortifications. The army had to march through extremely difficult, mountainous terrain, where the war elephants became a positive hindrance. Fortunately for the Romans, a lethargic reaction by Perseus allowed them to reach the coastal plain. Dium, Heracleum and a number of other cities capitulated or were stormed, but the Roman army was exhausted by its difficult march and its supply lines were insecure. Philippus failed to force a decisive battle, and the campaigning season ended with the Roman and Macedonian armies camped a few miles apart on either side of the River Elpeüs, which flowed down from a valley on the side of Mount Olympus, the traditional home of the Greek gods. Philippus was heavily criticized by a senatorial commission and the state of the war became a subject for widespread and ardent debate both publicly and privately at Rome.

AEMILIUS PAULLUS AND THE BATTLE OF PYDNA, 22 JUNE 168 BC

Dissatisfaction with events in Macedonia resulted in the consular provinces for 168 being allocated much earlier than usual, so that the new command er would have more time to prepare. The lot fell to Lucius Aemilius Paullus, a result which is supposed to have been greeted with great enthusiasm by the people. As praetor with proconsular authority he had governed Further Spain from 191 to 189 BC, campaigning against the Lusitanian tribes. Although he suffered an early defeat at a place called Lycho, Paullus later enjoyed considerable success and was awarded a formal thanksgiving or supplication at Rome, and may just possibly have celebrated a triumph. After several unsuccessful electoral campaigns he won his first consulship in 182 BC and was sent to Liguria. Once again the campaign began badly, and for a while he found himself besieged in his camp, but, after breaking out, he defeated the enemy and this time was definitely granted a triumph. Whatever his abilities as a commander, Paullus does not seem to have been especially popular with the electorate, and he was unable to fulfil his ambition of holding a second consulship until 168 BC, by which time he was about 60 years old. Probably the same desire for experienced magistrates which had permitted Philippus' success in the previous year also worked in Paullus' favour. The latter had especially strong connections with the Hannibalic War. His father was the consul killed at Cannae, whilst his sister had married Scipio Africanus. Paullus himself had four sons, and the two older boys were both adopted by other leading families who lacked male heirs. The eldest became Quintus Fabius Maximus Aemilianus, whilst the other was taken in by Africanus' son to become Publius Cornelius Scipio Aemilianus. Both were in their late teens and would serve with their true father in Macedonia.[12]

Paullus was not given a new army to take to his province, but a supplementary levy of 7,000 Roman infantry and 200 cavalry and 7,000 Latin foot and 400 horse to bring the legions in Macedonia back up to full strength and to provide additional forces as garrison units. Other reinforcements were sent to the smaller armies operating in the Adriatic theatre. Care was also taken with his officers. A senatorial decree was passed by which only men who had held a magistracy were to be appointed as military tribunes. Paullus was then allowed to pick which of these men would fill the twelve posts in his legions. Before leaving Rome he made a speech in the Forum, which was aimed mainly at the banquet-table strategists who were so eager to dissect each rumour and report from the war. Paullus offered to pay the expenses of any of these worthies who wished to accompany him on campaign, and forcibly suggested that anyone who declined the opportunity should in future restrict his conversation to the business of the city itself. Such bluntness appears to have been characteristic of the man, and may explain why, in spite of the widespread respect in which he was held, the consul was never a popular man.[13]

Paullus arrived at the army's camp outside Phila in early June. The camp was badly placed and the first problem to confront him was the poor supply of locally available water. Leading the army's water-carriers (utrarii) onto the beach area – the camp was little more than a quarter of a mile from the sea – he set them to digging wells. Almost immediately an underground stream was discovered which was able to provide ample supplies of fresh water. Paullus' next action was to take the tribunes and senior centurions to reconnoitre the enemy position on the line of the Elpeüs, seeking the easiest crossing points across the dried-up river bed and assessing the strength of the Macedonian defences. These were formidable, for Perseus had devoted considerable effort to fortifying the line between the slopes of Mount Olympus and the sea. To assist in the labour, civilians had been called out from the nearest towns, with even the women being ordered to carry food supplies to the camp. Artillery of various sizes was installed in the chain of forts. The reliance placed on fixed lines of defences by Philip V at Aous, Antiochus the Great at Thermopylae, and Perseus at the Elpeüs is strikingly at contrast to the campaigns of Alexander the Great. Then it was the Persians who depended on the advantage of defending a river line at Granicus and Issus, or who specially prepared the battlefield at Gaugamela. Alexander had interpreted this as a sign that the enemy lacked confidence and, just as he was later to do at the Hydaspes in India, successfully attacked each position. It was another sign of the poor quality of later Hellenistic armies, and the over-caution of their commanders, who tried to take as few chances as possible.

The arrival of a new commander – or indeed a new manager/leader in any environment – inevitably involves a period of difficult transition for the troops under his command. Many things, even down to minor aspects of daily routine, were and are often changed to suit the preferences of the new man, upsetting officers and men used to alternative practices. Paullus straight away issued a new set of standing orders, of which Livy highlights three main points. The commander emphasized tight discipline on the march. Instead of issuing an order by signal directly to a column which most probably stretched for many miles, the consul would first issue a warning order to a military tribune, who would quietly pass it on to the senior centurion of the legion, who would in turn brief his subordinates. Given clear forewarning of the commanders' intention, the army could then respond smoothly to the order, avoiding the danger of misinterpretation and conflicting actions by different units. Secondly, sentries were forbidden to carry shields, for Paullus was aware of the old soldier's trick of propping *pilum* against the long legionary *scutum* and dozing off whilst leaning on this support. Finally, the outposts which were always stationed in front of the army's camp were now to be replaced twice, instead of once a day, so that the troops were less likely to grow weary in the heat and so become vulnerable to a sudden attack.

The consul also took the opportunity to address the troops, once again emphasizing discipline and obedience. It was not the job of soldiers or junior officers to discuss the campaign or question orders. They must rely on him to do his job as a commander and then fight bravely when the time came. As far as Paullus was concerned, a Roman soldier 'should concern himself with the following: his body, to keep it as strong and as nimble as possible; the good condition of his weapons; and the readiness of his food-supply [made from rations issued uncooked] for unexpected orders.'[14] Our sources claim that the consul's style of command immediately invigorated recent recruit and veteran alike, the latter relieved when they recognized that things were now being done properly. However, Paullus seems to have spent little more than three or four days in training and preparation, so it is possible that they exaggerated the difference made by the general and that discipline and morale had already been improving under Philippus. Polybius, on whom all of our surviving sources relied heavily, was obviously especially well disposed to the father of his patron Scipio Aemilianus. Even so, it is more than possible that Paullus was able to inject a new sense of purpose into the army in this short time.[15]

After this brief period of preparation, the Roman army advanced a few miles from Phila to camp on the south bank of the Elpeüs. The land forces were supported by a naval squadron under the praetor Cnaeus Octavius. News of the defeat of one of Perseus' most important allies in Illyria heartened the Romans and correspondingly discouraged the Macedonians, but did nothing to assist them with their own immediate problem of overcoming the enemy line of fortifications. Paullus responded to this in a thoroughly Roman way, by summoning his senior officers to a *consilium*. Livy tells us that some of the younger men favoured a direct assault, but that the consul judged that this would be costly and had no guarantee of success. Others suggested Octavius should be sent with the fleet to raid the coastline of Macedonia in the rear of the king, and hopefully draw off some or all of his army. Paullus made no public announcement of a decision at the *consilium* and, after he had dismissed his officers, summoned two local merchants familiar with the passes through the mountains. These informed him that the actual routes were not too difficult, but that Perseus had stationed detachments guarding them. The consul resolved to send a column through the mountains guided by the traders, hoping that a fast-moving force could make use of the cover of darkness to surprise the enemy. As a deception, he gave orders for Octavius to bring the fleet to Heracleum and gather sufficient supplies to feed 1,000 men for ten days. A force of soldiers commanded by the tribune Publius Cornelius Scipio Nasica and Paullus' own son, Fabius Maximus, was also to march to Heracleum. Perseus was certain to become aware of this activity and so draw the conclusion that a raiding force was about to embark for an attack on the coast further north. The size of the detachment is uncertain. Livy says that it numbered 5,000 men, but according to Plutarch, who referred to a letter written by Scipio Nasica himself, there were 3,000 picked Italians – perhaps the *extraordinarii* – and the left *ala* numbering about 5,000, supported by 120 cavalry and 200

Cretan and Thracian infantry. Nasica was from a different branch of the Scipionic family to Africanus, but was married to the latter's eldest daughter.

It was only after Nasica's column had reached Heracleum and the men eaten their evening meal that he revealed to his officers their true task. During the night they marched again, turning back inland towards the mountains. The guides were instructed to take them on a route which would bring them to the pass at Pythium on the third day of their journey. The next morning Paullus formed his army up in battle order and sent his *velites* forward to engage the Macedonian outposts. The skirmish continued without significant advantage being gained by either side until Paullus recalled his men at midday. On the following day he repeated the exercise and this time the Romans forced their way – or were lured – further forward and came within range of the Macedonian artillery, which inflicted a number of casualties. Paullus did not attack on the third day, but made a show of examining another section of the river, as if looking for an alternative crossing point.

In the meantime Nasica had reached Pythium and attacked just before dawn. His letter claimed that one of the Cretans had deserted and warned Perseus of his approach, leading the king to dispatch a strong force to garrison the pass. This seems unlikely, since Livy states that guards were already in place, but it may be that a reinforcement was sent. Whatever the details, the Romans achieved surprise and in a vicious skirmish killed or drove off the enemy. Nasica claimed that he was himself attacked by a Thracian mercenary fighting for the Macedonians and killed the man with a spear thrust to the chest. Having captured the position, the Roman column descended by the Petra Pass onto the plain near Dium. As soon as Perseus discovered this force to his rear, he withdrew from the line of the Elpeüs and retired towards Pydna. Paullus crossed the river unopposed, joined forces with Nasica and followed him.[16]

Perseus was in a difficult position. Now that the enemy had reached the heartland of his kingdom, his prestige would suffer severely if he did not meet them in battle. In a similar way Antiochus had been forced to choose between giving battle or enduring the humiliation of retreating without fighting in the face of an invader. Therefore, Perseus deployed his army outside Pydna on 21 June and offered battle to the approaching enemy in an open plain which suited his phalanx. The evident determination with which the Macedonians were waiting to be attacked surprised Paullus. His own men were tired from a long march along dusty roads under the hot sun, but much of the army, and especially some of the officers, were eager to fight immediately. Only Nasica put his feelings into words, urging the consul to attack immediately and so prevent Perseus from withdrawing. According to Livy, Paullus replied that 'from the many vicissitudes of war I have learned when to fight and when to refuse battle. There is not time to instruct you while we are standing ready for battle as to the reasons why it is better to be inactive today. You shall ask for my reasoning at another time; now you will be satisfied to take the word of an experienced commander.'[17]

The consul ordered the marching columns to deploy into battle order, the tribunes supervising the process and urging the men to make haste. The general himself rode around encouraging the troops. Once the *triplex acies* were formed, however, he did not order an advance, but simply waited. Gradually, fatigue and thirst eroded the legionaries' ardour for an immediate battle, and some of the tired soldiers could be seen doing what Paullus had forbidden his sentries to do and propping themselves up on their shields. Feeling that his men would now understand his reason for hesitating, the consul gave orders for the senior centurions to mark out the army's camp. This was probably on the lower slopes of Mount Olympus to the west of the Macedonian position.[18]

Perseus' army was relatively fresh and certainly fully prepared for battle. The Romans were tired and their formation hastily put together and doubtless more than a little ragged. The king had not seized the opportunity of attacking immediately, but was still close enough to take advantage of any disorder as the Romans withdrew to set up camp. Therefore Paullus took great care that his army withdrew carefully and in good order. Once the lines of the camp had been marked out and the baggage piled, the *triarii* were marched back to begin its construction. Later, the middle line formed by the *principes* moved to join them in their labour. Then the front line, the *hastati*, turned to the right and, led by the maniple which had formed the extreme right of the line, processed back to camp. The cavalry and *velites* continued to face the enemy, covering this withdrawal, and did not join the rest of the army until the ditch and rampart surrounding the camp was complete. An attack uphill against such a fortified position was unlikely to result in success, especially since it would draw the phalanx onto unsuitable ground. Perseus had probably missed an opportunity by not forcing a battle. He contented himself with the moral victory gained when the enemy withdrew to camp before he gave the order to his own men to do likewise. Hasdrubal had derived similar comfort from Scipio's actions before Ilipa.[19]

At this period Rome's official calendar was several months ahead of our calendar, making that day 4 September, whereas by our calendar it was only 21 June. That night there was a lunar eclipse, a powerful omen to both

Romans and Macedonians. Livy tells us that the tribune Caius Sulpicius Gallus – who had already been praetor and would reach the consulship in 166 – had sufficient knowledge to predict and explain the phenomenon to the soldiers, so that there was less panic in the Roman camp than in that of the enemy. Even so, as the moon at last reappeared, Paullus acted in the proper fashion for a Roman magistrate and sacrificed eleven heifers. At dawn he ordered the sacrifice of oxen to Heracles. Twenty of the beasts were examined without producing favourable omens, before the twenty-first ox suggested that victory would be won by the side which remained on the defensive. These rituals took some time and it was not until the third hour of the day that the consul summoned his officers to a *consilium*.

Paullus explained in some detail his reasons for not fighting a battle on the previous day. Apart from the exhaustion of the soldiers after their long march and the raggedness of the Romans' battle line in comparison with the enemy, he stressed the importance of constructing a defended camp. If they had fought a battle straight from the line of march, about a quarter of their entire strength, probably the *triarii*, would have had to be left to protect the army's baggage train, further reducing their forces in the face of an enemy who anyway outnumbered them. It also seemed extremely unlikely that the Macedonians were planning to retreat in the night, escaping battle and forcing the Romans into a long-drawn-out and arduous campaign of manoeuvre. If Perseus did not intend to join battle, Paullus felt that he would not have waited outside Pydna or formed his army into battle order on the previous day.

The consul announced that he planned to fight a battle in this place, but that he would do so only when the moment was right. Not all of his officers were convinced, but the consul's insistence that subordinates were there to obey orders without question ensured that none made any comment. Neither he nor Perseus planned to fight a battle on that day, anticipating the usual period of waiting as each sought to gain any slight advantage. The Romans sent out men to gather wood for the cooking fires and fodder for the horses. Both armies stationed outposts of formed troops in front of their respective camps, but the bulk of the troops remained in the tent lines.[20]

The Romans' outposts consisted entirely of allied troops. Furthest forward, not far from the shallow stream separating the two camps, were two Italian cohorts, the Paeligni and Marrucini, and two *turmae* of Samnite cavalry, all under the command of Marcus Sergius Silus. Closer to the Roman camp was another force led by Caius Cluvius consisting of one Italian cohort of Vestini and two Latin cohorts, from the colonies of Firmum and Cremona respectively, supported again by two *turmae*, in this case Latins from Placentia and Aesernia. Livy says that both Silus and Cluvius were *legati*, senior subordinates of the consul who held delegated *imperium*. Presumably the troops were relieved at noon in accordance with Paullus' standing orders, so these contingents may have been the second ones to perform the task on that day. Our sources do not describe the composition of the Macedonian outposts in comparable detail, but these seem to have included a band of 800 Thracians. There is no report of any bouts of skirmishing or occasional single combats between the two sets of outposts during the day, as so often seems to have occurred in similar circumstances. Men, mostly slaves, from both forces went forward to draw water from the stream.

Late in the day, Livy says at about the ninth hour, some Roman slaves lost control of a pack animal – probably a mule – which bolted across the stream. Three Italian soldiers gave chase through the knee-deep water and killed one of two Thracians who had grabbed hold of the beast. The surviving Thracian's comrades soon came to his aid and the fighting escalated, sucking in first the troops stationed as outposts and then the main armies. Plutarch says that a band of Ligurian auxiliaries were amongst the first Roman troops to be committed – although he does not say whether they also had formed part of the outposts – and that Nasica rode forward to join the skirmish at an early stage. He also mentions a tradition which claimed that Paullus had deliberately ordered the release of a horse into the enemy camp in the hope of provoking a battle, but this seems extremely unlikely and the most plausible version is that the battle began accidentally. Paullus is said to have realized the inevitability of an action and gone around the camp encouraging the soldiers.[21]

Both sides deployed in considerably more haste than was usual, but the Macedonians appear to have responded more quickly and heavy fighting soon developed a mere quarter of a mile from the rampart of the Roman camp. In their haste to advance neither side at first appears to have formed a single, properly organized fighting line. Instead each unit marched out of camp, changed into battle formation and advanced. Plutarch, who provides the fullest account of the actual battle, says that the Macedonian mercenaries and light troops first reached the fighting, and were then joined on their right by the most élite division of the phalanx, the royal guards or *agema*. These were followed from the camp by the remainder of the phalanx, divided into the 'Bronze Shields' (*Chalcaspides*) on the left and 'White Shields' (*Leucaspides*) on the right. Thus the army was effectively deploying in reverse order from left to right, rather than the other way round, each unit going straight into the attack rather than waiting to move to its proper position. Last to leave the camp were more mercenaries, including probably both Gauls and Cretans. These were eventually to form the army's right wing, but it seems likely that these never got into position. Certainly none of our sources mention any significant fighting on this side of the battle. For a while the Macedonians advanced in a loose echelon of units, a more coherent battle line only developing when they began to meet stiffer Roman resistance.[22]

In later years Paullus admitted that the sight of the Macedonian phalanx with its serried ranks of spear points bearing down on his men was the most terrifying thing he had ever seen in his life. A general who prized order and careful planning in all operations was inevitably unhappy when a battle began in such a confused way. Nevertheless he concealed both his fear and his frustration as he went around the army encouraging his soldiers. Plutarch notes that he was wearing neither body armour nor helmet, to show his disdain for the enemy. The consul personally led the First Legion into position in the right centre of the Roman line, roughly opposite the 'Bronze Shields'. Lucius Postumius Albinus, who had been consul in 173 BC and was presumably serving as a *legatus* or perhaps a tribune, followed with the Second Legion and eventually took post to Paullus' left and squared up against the 'White Shields'. Other officers led one or both of the allied *alae*, along with the elephants, into place on the right of the legions.[23]

The first encounter between a body of formed troops and a part of the Macedonian phalanx occurred when the Paeligni, and probably with them the Marrucini, clashed with the *agema*. The Macedonians were in good order and the Italians found it difficult to dodge the rows of *sarissa* points and get close enough to attack the pikemen themselves. The *agema* consisted of some 3,000 men and was supported by mercenary units to its left, so that the Italians probably lacked the numbers to threaten the vulnerable flanks of the formation. In an effort to break the stalemate, Salvius, the cohort's commander, grabbed the unit's standard and hurled it into the enemy ranks. The Paeligni surged forward to recapture the precious standard and a short but brutal combat developed as they struggled to hack their way into the enemy formation. Some men tried to cut off the *sarissa* points or deflect them with their swords, others took the blows on their shields, whilst a few grabbed the enemy weapons and tried to shove them out of the way. Some Macedonians were killed, but the remainder kept their formation and the phalanx remained unbroken. As Italian casualties began to mount, the Paeligni drew back and withdrew up slope towards their camp. Plutarch says

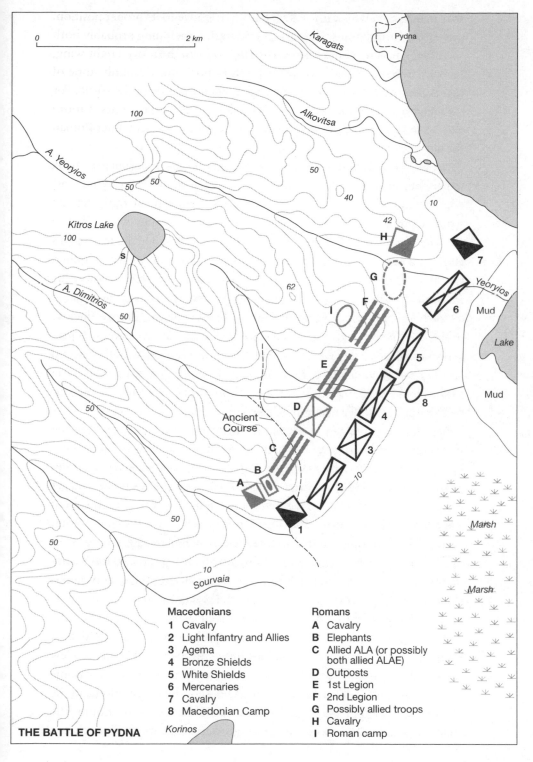

0   2 km

Karagats

Pydna

Alkovitsa

A. Yeoryios

100

50

50   50

40

10

Kitros Lake

100

50

42

H

7

S

A. Dimitrios

50

62

G

F

I

Yeoryios

6

Mud

E

5

Lake

Mud

D

8

Ancient
Course

C

4

3

B

A

2

10

1

50

50

Marsh

10

Sourvaia

Marsh

Macedonians
1   Cavalry
2   Light Infantry and Allies
3   Agema
4   Bronze Shields
5   White Shields
6   Mercenaries
7   Cavalry
8   Macedonian Camp

Romans
A   Cavalry
B   Elephants
C   Allied ALA (or possibly
     both allied ALAE)
D   Outposts
E   1st Legion
F   2nd Legion
G   Possibly allied troops
H   Cavalry
I   Roman camp

THE BATTLE OF PYDNA

Korinos

that according to a fiercely pro-Macedonian source written by Posidonius the Italians' retreat caused the consul to tear his tunic in frustration.[24]

The same Posidonius also presented a far more flattering version of Perseus' behaviour than that given by our other sources. Polybius stated that the king galloped back to the city of Pydna at the start of the battle, claiming that he needed to perform a sacrifice to Heracles, and hence took no part in the fighting. According to Posidonius, Perseus had been kicked the day before, presumably by a horse, and this injury at first forced him to keep out of the battle. However, in spite of his pain, Perseus is then supposed to have mounted himself on a pack animal and charged into the thick of the combat, and was struck by a javelin which tore his tunic without actually wounding him.[25]

The First Legion arrived first and seems to have brought the Macedonian attack to a standstill. As the Second Legion moved into position things began to turn the Romans' way. On the right flank, the war elephants caused considerable disorder amongst the enemy. Earlier in the campaign Perseus had formed a special anti-elephant unit, but the novel weapons and spiked armour of these soldiers proved utterly ineffective. The king had also tried to train the army's cavalry horses to become used to the strange appearance, noise and smell of the great beasts, but this too had failed. Already thrown into confusion by the elephants, most of the Macedonian left wing was swept away by the attacking allied *ala*. In the centre the phalanx had broken up into its constituent units. Even in Alexander's day this had tended to happen whenever the phalanx advanced over any distance, for it was and is extremely difficult to march across even the flattest of plains in formation without deviating to one side or the other. The Roman system of maintaining wide intervals between maniples was in part intended to prevent such fluctuations from causing two units to merge. Macedonian doctrine required narrower gaps between units, but there was a natural tendency for sections of the line to bunch up and others to spread out during the advance. Broken or uneven ground exacerbated the problem and it is possible that at Pydna the slope leading up to the Roman camp contributed to the break-up of the phalanx. However, the main reason for the problem was the lack of time to deploy the army properly before the battle began. If the Macedonians could have kept the advance going, never reducing the pressure on the Romans, it is possible that they would have won in spite of this. Once both legions were in place and the phalanx became stalled, the essentially inflexible nature of this formation put it at a major disadvantage.[26]

On one side was a single line of individual blocks of pikemen, each at least sixteen ranks deep. Behind this line there were no reserves, and the blocks themselves had little capacity for manoeuvre. Facing them was a line of maniples, perhaps half that depth, intervals roughly equivalent to each unit's frontage separating it from those on either side. Covering these gaps were the maniples of the *principes*, and behind them the *triarii*. The Macedonians could only fight effectively against an enemy to their front, and even this was dependent on their keeping together and presenting an unbroken wall of *sarissa* points to the enemy. Each maniple was led by a centurion – the commander of the right-hand century having seniority if both men were present – and the *triplex acies* formation gave it the space to act as a single unit.

With the fighting lines stabilized, the centurions began to lead their men into the gaps in the enemy line to strike at the unprotected flanks and even rear of the pike blocks. Plutarch tells us that Paullus gave orders for this to occur, first speaking to the tribunes and senior subordinates who then passed the instructions on to the junior officers. This is probably true, for we must expect Paullus, like any other Roman commander, to have been willing to intervene in the small tactical decisions of a battle. However, altogether the legions will have occupied a frontage of a mile or so, and it would have taken too much time for each local attack to be ordered by the general. The Roman army had a significantly higher proportion of officers to men than the Macedonians. A legion had six tribunes and sixty centurions, twenty in each line, apart from any *legati* or other members of the general's staff sent to that sector of the line. The initiative for many of the local attacks probably came from these men, and even perhaps on occasions from ordinary soldiers, for the Romans were always keen to encourage individual boldness.[27]

Gradually, small groups of Romans infiltrated the Macedonian line. A legionary was primarily a swordsman, who could if required fight effectively as an individual. A Macedonian equipped with a 21 foot *sarissa* could only fight as part of a group. Once the Romans began to attack each knot of pikemen from the flanks the battle became very one-sided. Some Macedonians dropped their cumbersome weapons and drew their side arms, but the men were poorly trained and badly equipped for this sort of work. The legionaries carried the 'Spanish sword' (*gladius hispaniensis*), a well balanced, cut and thrust weapon, with a tempered steel blade. A thrust from such a sword was often fatal, a cut horribly disfiguring. Livy describes how appalled Philip V's soldiers had been in the First Macedonian War when they first saw the corpses of men killed with the Spanish sword. At Pydna, the Macedonian pikemen were slaughtered whilst inflicting little or no loss on the enemy. By the end of the day some 20,000 Macedonians had fallen and another 6,000 had been taken prisoner. The *agema* was virtually wiped out. As the phalanx collapsed into rout, the Macedonian cavalry rode away from the battlefield. Many of these troops had not actually fought and their units were still intact. Perseus fled with them to his capital Pella, but broke away from the horsemen when they were overtaken by an angry mob of fugitives from the rest of the army.

The battle lasted for no more than an hour, an unusually short time for a major engagement, and cost the Romans about 100 dead and a larger number of wounded. For a while Paullus feared that his son, Scipio Aemilianus, was amongst the fallen and was disconsolate until the boy returned, having become separated during the pursuit with a couple of companions. The son of Cato the Elder, who would subsequently marry Paullus' daughter Aemilia and was then serving as a cavalryman, had also distinguished himself during the fighting. At one point he is said to have lost his sword. Wandering the battlefield he gathered a group of friends and together they attacked a group of the enemy, routed them, and finally discovered the weapon buried under a pile of corpses. Both Paullus and Cato's own stern father praised him for an action in keeping with the behaviour of a true Roman.[28]

The Roman victory at Pydna owed much to the flexibility of the Roman tactical system. Its accidental start prevented either commander from employing any sophisticated tactics. At best they could inspire their men – although in Perseus' case he may not even have attempted to do this – and help them to deploy into some sort of fighting line. In the confused situation which developed, the legions were better able to respond to each local problem. Similar factors had proved decisive at Cynoscephalae and Magnesia. At Cynoscephalae, the two armies had bumped unexpectedly into each other when they had approached the pass of that name from opposite directions. Each side followed the normal procedure of wheeling their march column to the right to form a battle line. In such a situation the right flanks of both the Roman and the Macedonian armies were at the head of the column and so moved into position and changed into battle order first. The right flank of each army then attacked and routed the enemy left, which was still unprepared for battle. The Romans were in their usual *triplex acies*, Philip V's infantry in a single deep phalanx without reserve lines. An unnamed tribune took twenty maniples from the *principes* and *triarii* of the Roman right and led them round to attack the king's victorious troops. The phalanx could not respond to this new threat and was routed.

At Magnesia the armies were properly deployed and expecting battle.

Antiochus III led a cavalry charge in the best traditions of Alexander and punched a hole through the Roman line, taking his men on to attack the enemy camp. There were no reserves to exploit his success. The Romans did have reserves, and these, along with the men stationed to guard the camp, defeated the king's cavalry. When the Romans broke through the Seleucids' main line and infiltrated the immensely deep phalanx, the latter could do nothing to plug the gaps and were overwhelmed. In these battles, as at Pydna, the victory was achieved at a very low cost, even by the standards of the ancient world.

After Cynoscephalae, Magnesia and Pydna, Philip V, Antiochus the Great and Perseus respectively conceded defeat in the war and accepted the peace terms imposed on them by the Roman Republic. In 168 the Senate decided that the kingdom of Macedonia would cease to exist, and divided the land into four autonomous regions. Perseus was taken back to Rome to walk in Paullus' triumphal procession and spent the rest of his life as a prisoner. However, for a while it seemed that the consul would be denied the honour of a triumph. Paullus was an efficient commander, but never seems to have had the knack of gaining the affection of his troops. Some sections of the army felt that they had not received sufficient reward for the campaign, in terms of both praise and, especially, plunder. This was in spite of a senatorially approved act of brigandage after Pydna, when Paullus had taken the troops to plunder the city of Epirus. Led by the tribune Servius Sulpicius Galba, many soldiers lobbied for the consul to be denied a triumph and it was only after a struggle that the majority of the Senate approved the granting of the honour. Many were persuaded in this by the ageing Punic War veteran and former consul Marcus Servilius Pulex Geminus, a man said to have killed twenty-three enemies in single combat.[29]

Ultimately Paullus was granted the right to a triumph and led an especially spectacular celebration spread over three days and watched all along the Sacred Way through the heart of Rome by crowds sitting on specially erected seating. On the first day 250 wagons carried statues and other art works looted during the war. On the second day the carts carried captured weapons, armour and other military equipment, emphasizing the different panoplies of the foreign allies and mercenaries serving with Perseus as well as the native Macedonian gear. Much of the equipment was arranged to look like the heaped debris of battle. In other wagons the 'arms and armour were somewhat loosely arranged, so that as they were carried along they struck against one another and gave out a harsh and fearsome sound, and even though they had belonged to the losers in the war their appearance was not without its terrors'.[30] Following after the carts were the silver coins and the treasure captured from the enemy, displayed in 750 boxes, each carried by a team of four men.

Finally, on the third day came the main procession, led by trumpeters playing the calls and fanfares sounded in battle. Behind the musicians were 120 sacrificial oxen, their horns gilded and their heads decorated, accompanied by youths carrying the necessary libations. Then once again the wealth of the defeated enemy was stressed, for seventy-seven containers each holding three talents of gold coins and a collection of Perseus' most precious vessels were carried through the streets. The king's chariot, empty save for his arms and armour and his royal diadem, was led behind his possessions. Then came his young children, two boys and a girl, with their nurses and many other domestic slaves. It was a pathetic sight and many of the watching Romans, who as a race were rarely inclined to conceal their emotions, were moved to tears. Perseus walked behind them with his own attendants and courtiers. His plea to be spared the humiliation of being paraded through the city had received a brusque response from Paullus, who implied that the king could always avoid this fate by committing suicide.

Then, after the symbols and spoils of his victory, came Paullus himself,

> mounted on a magnificently decorated chariot. He would have made a remarkable sight even without all these trappings of power; he wore a cloak dyed with purple and shot through with gold, and held in his right hand a spray of laurel. Every single soldier likewise carried laurel. The army marched behind their commander's chariot in their units and divisions, with the men singing partly traditional songs with an element of humour in them, and partly hymns of victory and praise for Aemilius' achievements. No one could keep their eyes off him; he was an object of universal admiration… [31]

Plutarch's description gives some sense of the splendour of a Roman triumph, but for Paullus there was little need for the slave to whisper in his ear reminders of his mortality. His 14-year-old son fell sick and died five days before the ceremonies began. Three days after the parade, the same fate befell the boy's 12-year-old brother. Only the two eldest sons survived and both of these had been adopted into other families and taken their names.

'CAPTURED GREECE ENSLAVED THE FIERCE CAPTOR'

Before he left Greece, Paullus had spent some time touring the country, sightseeing and doing his best to win over the hearts and minds of the population. At Amphipolis he staged a determinedly Hellenic festival of drama, poetry and sport, summoning performers, athletes and famous race-horses from throughout the Greek world. The influential guests were treated to lavish feasts. Some expressed surprise that this large-scale entertainment could have been so successfully staged at such short notice, to which Paullus dryly commented that a 'man who knew how to conquer in war could also arrange a banquet and organize games'.[32] During a visit to the famous oracle at Delphi, the consul saw a bare plinth which was to have mounted a statue to Perseus. Paullus commissioned a monument to his own victory instead, some of which has survived to the present day. He was not the first Roman magistrate to become involved in the cultural life of Greece. Flamininus had remained in Greece for several years after the Second Macedonian War, and from the beginning showed a deep love for all things Hellenic. At the Isthmian Games in 196 BC when he had proclaimed the 'Freedom of the Greeks', his speech – delivered in Greek – had been greeted with rapturous applause. The honours lavished by Hellenic communities on Roman generals, whether through fear or genuine respect, mirrored those conventionally granted to kings. This encouraged a belief that any Roman senator, and especially a prominent and successful general, was at the very least the equal of any foreign monarch. Flamininus and Paullus and the other men who triumphed in the eastern Mediterranean gained prestige far greater than the vast majority of senators. This prestige and their wealth could have unbalanced Roman political life, and it was in part to prevent this that other senators attacked them with such fervour on their return to Rome.

It is hard to gauge to what extent Roman aristocrats were aware of Greek culture in the third century BC. Rome had interacted with and eventually conquered the many Hellenic colonies in Italy and later Sicily. The spoils of war in particular yielded art works and slaves which were brought back to Rome. By the time of the Second Punic War there were Roman senators such as Fabius Pictor whose Greek and knowledge of literature were of a sufficiently high standard to permit them to write the first works of Roman prose history. Whilst preparing the invasion of Africa from his base in Sicily, Scipio Africanus and his youthful staff dressed in Greek fashion and took a delight in such characteristically Hellenic institutions as the gymnasium. This love affair with Greek language and culture would seize the Roman aristocracy and persist for centuries. In the early second century BC it offered yet another arena in which senators could compete to show their superiority, as each strove to demonstrate greater awareness of all things Greek.

By the middle of the century, the vast majority of educated Romans were bilingual, for Greek was the language of true civilization, just as French was spoken by virtually all the aristocracies of eighteenth-century Europe. Only a few voices publicly resisted this trend. The most famous of these was Marcus Porcius Cato, the man who had led one of the outflanking columns at Thermopylae and whose son distinguished himself at Pydna. When serving as an ambassador in Greece, Cato refused to address the locals in their own language, and insisted in delivering his speech in Latin. This was not through ignorance, for he clearly possessed an extensive knowledge of Hellenic literature – Polybius recalled an incident where Cato had made a joking allusion to Homer's *Odyssey*. Throughout his career Cato derided the aristocrats who aped the noblemen of Greece, and instead stressed the superiority of Rome's own simple, but virtuous traditions. As Scipio's quaestor in 205 BC, he had publicly criticized the consul and his friends for their behaviour in Sicily. Later he would write the first history in the Latin language, one of a broad range of works he wrote or translated into Latin.

Unlike the senators who collected Greek art and copied Hellenic fashions of dress, decoration and dining, Cato portrayed himself as an old-fashioned Roman, living a frugal life of service to the Republic. He was a 'new man' who could not rely on the achievements of his ancestors or a well-established family reputation and so had to work hard to create a reputation. This meant that he missed no opportunity to display a clear set of views and characteristics, gradually building up a 'public image' – virtually a brand name – to match those of the established families. Thus, in a real sense, Cato used the spread of culture as a means of competing with other senators just as much as those men did who embraced the new ideas.

CHAPTER 4

'SMALL WARS':

SCIPIO AEMILIANUS AND THE FALL OF NUMANTIA

Publius Cornelius Scipio Aemilianus Africanus Numantinus (185/4–129 BC)

It is foolish to incur danger for small results. He must be considered a reckless general who would fight before there is any need, while a good one takes risks only in cases of necessity.[1]

THE WARS FOUGHT AGAINST THE GREAT HELLENISTIC POWERS WERE IMPORTANT, intensely dramatic, and highly lucrative to the victors, but they were also comparatively rare events. Throughout the second century BC the bulk of Rome's war effort was devoted to campaigns against the tribal peoples of Spain, Northern Italy and Southern Gaul, and, to a lesser extent, Illyria and Thrace. These campaigns were fought against peoples with – to the Greeks and Romans at least – obscure and uncouth names, who fielded armies of brave, but often ill-disciplined and poorly equipped warriors. Politically they were divided into many tribes, which in turn were often enough split between the followers of various chieftains. The defeat of one tribe or clan did not necessarily mean that their neighbours would capitulate, in the way that a single decisive battle ended each of the wars with Macedonia and the Seleucids. Therefore warfare in these provinces tended to consist of lots of individual campaigns to defeat each community or leader in turn.

A triumph over the Arevaci or Boii did not provide the same prestige as one over a famous kingdom such as Macedonia, nor was it likely to enrich an army and commander on a comparable scale. Frequent warfare in the Spanish and Gallic provinces meant that victories won in these theatres were common. Senators eager to gain the maximum advantage from such a success liked to claim that this was the first time a particular people had been encountered by a Roman army, along with the familiar catalogues of numbers – men killed and captured and towns and villages stormed. Concerned that triumphs were being won too often and too easily, the Senate decided that a minimum of 5,000 enemies needed to have been killed in battle before a magistrate could claim the honour. The details of this measure are obscure, though it probably occurred at some point during the second century BC, and it is impossible to know just how rigorously it was implemented.

Such restrictions should not lead us to the conclusion that all Roman campaigns against tribal opponents were one-sided affairs or in any way 'cheap' victories. A few were, but the majority were difficult operations against an enemy who was brave, often numerous, and well used to exploiting the natural strength of their homeland. Battles against Gauls, Ligurians and the various Spanish peoples were usually hard-fought encounters and Roman success was never inevitable. Many generals suffered heavy defeats at the hands of these tribesmen. Gauls had sacked Rome in 390 BC and threatened it again in 225 BC, until sheer good fortune rather than design had allowed both of that year's consuls to attack their army, one from either side, at Telamon. In 216 the appalling catastrophe of Cannae only in part obscured a disaster in the Po valley where the tribes had ambushed and all but wiped out an army of two legions and two *alae*. Among the dead was the Roman commander, the praetor Lucius Postumius Albinus, a highly experienced man who had already held two consulships and had just been elected in his absence to a third term for the following year. This was probably the most spectacular Roman defeat in this region, although it was certainly not the only one. Reverses in the Spanish peninsula tended to be on a smaller scale, but were even more frequent.[2]

A properly trained, supplied and competently led Roman army could under most circumstances be expected to prevail over tribal opponents. At the start of the second century BC these conditions usually applied, since all ranks were composed predominantly of veterans of the Hannibalic war. In these years the legions on the frontiers in Northern Italy and the Spanish provinces demonstrated the same high levels of discipline, confidence and tactical flexibility which had smashed the professional armies of the Hellenistic powers. Often enough they were composed of the same men, for most of the officers and soldiers who fought at Cynoscephalae and Magnesia had already served in one of the western provinces. Aemilius Paullus, for instance, had led armies in Spain and Liguria before taking up command in the Pydna campaign. Cato, the man who subsequently led the outflanking column at Thermopylae in 191 and whose son distinguished himself at Pydna, had been sent as consul in 195 to Nearer Spain. After a period of training and small-scale operations intended to give the troops practical experience and build up their confidence, he fought a pitched battle with the main Iberian army outside the city of Emporion. A night march went undetected by the Spaniards and brought the Roman army to a position with the enemy between them and their own camp, for Cato was determined that his men should have no chance of survival other than through victory.

The Iberians were jostled into a hasty deployment, as the battle developed at a time and in the fashion chosen by the Roman commander. Throughout the fighting Cato made careful use of his reserves, sending two cohorts – probably of the *extraordinarii* – to feint against the enemy rear, and breaking the stalemate between the main battle lines by adding the weight of fresh units to the Roman attack. Finally, he brought up the Second Legion, which had to this point played no part in the fighting, to storm the Spanish camp. The Roman commander was also ready to intervene personally in the action, moving to rally his troops when the retreat of some cavalry caused a panic on his right, and physically grabbing and stopping some of the soldiers as they fled. Later he led the Second Legion in its advance, and made sure that the men moved in good order and did not let their enthusiasm get out of control. Cato rode up and down in front of the line, striking with a hunting spear at any legionary who broke formation and ordering the nearest centurion or tribune to mark the man down for future punishment.[3]

In the first quarter of the second century BC the resistance of the tribes of Cisalpine Gaul was permanently broken. South of the Po, the Boii lost much of their land to Roman colonists and were virtually destroyed as a significant political unit. Further north peoples like the Cenomani and Insubres fared better and over time their aristocrats gained citizenship and were absorbed into the Roman system. The Ligurians were a mountain people, with a loose social organization and few leaders recognized outside their own villages. Primarily pastoralists, their flocks were vulnerable to attack at the very beginning of spring before they moved away from the winter pastures to higher and more dispersed grazing areas. Yet campaigning in such difficult terrain was always a risky business, whilst the defeat of one village rarely did much to persuade others to stop raiding the nearest Roman colonies and allied communities. Fighting continued to the middle of the century and it was only after extensive transplantation of the population to settlements in Southern Italy that the Ligurians were pacified. In Spain warfare was almost constant until in 177 the consul Tiberius Sempronius Gracchus employed a mixture of military force and skilful diplomacy to establish a peace that would last for more than twenty years.[4]

By the time that Gracchus' settlement broke down in the 150s, the Roman army had declined. The Second Punic War generation was either dead or too elderly for active service and much of its accumulated experience had been forgotten. The impermanence of the militia system made it difficult to preserve knowledge in any institutional way and the problem was exacerbated by the comparative infrequency of warfare in the second quarter of the century. By 157 BC the Senate was especially eager to send an expedition to Dalmatia because it was feared that prolonged peace might make the men of Italy effeminate.[5] Inexperience was compounded by complacency as many persuaded themselves that Rome's long run of successful warfare had occurred inevitably and not as the product of careful preparation and training. The performance of Roman armies in the field throughout the remainder of the century was often dismal. At a time when very few commanders performed creditably, Scipio Aemilianus' considerable ability stood out in even higher relief than it might otherwise have done.

EARLY LIFE AND THE THIRD PUNIC WAR

The adoption of an heir or heirs to continue the family name was common amongst the senatorial aristocracy and an adopted son was considered no different from an actual son. That he became in every legal and emotional sense a member of a new family did not exclude the preservation of a strong link with his blood family. Although adopted at an early age by Africanus' son, Scipio Aemilianus spent most of his early life in the household of Aemilius Paullus and, as we have seen, served with him in Macedonia and rode with him in his subsequent triumph. The second son, as a youth Scipio showed no particular signs of exceptional promise and, like his father, he was cautious and somewhat reserved. Unlike most young men embarking on a public career, he did not practise forensic oratory and seek to make a name for himself as a legal advocate. Instead he preferred sports and military training, preparing himself to fight for the Republic in war. At Pydna he fought well, if a little overenthusiastically, and during the months in Greece following the victory discovered what would prove to be a lifelong love of hunting as he, along with his older brother and their friends, went on many expeditions in Perseus' wide estates. Paullus permitted his sons to take very little from the king's treasures, but did allow them to take their pick of his extensive library. Greek literature and culture would play a major part in Scipio's life, his interests encouraged and fostered by a long friendship with Polybius, who arrived in Rome as a hostage in the aftermath of the war.

In time Scipio and his circle of friends, which included Laelius, the son of Africanus' old confederate, would be seen as representatives of the best sort of philhellenism. They were true Romans, possessed of all the traditional *virtus* expected from a member of a senatorial family, but had added to this a sophistication and wisdom derived from a knowledge of all that was good about Greek culture. Cicero would present his philosophical discussion of the nature of the Roman State, *De Re Publica*, as an imagined debate between Scipio, Laelius and their associates in 129 BC. Scipio was a rational man, educated in both Greek and Roman traditions and interested in philosophy, and none of the stories about him contain any of the elements of mysticism associated with Africanus.[6]

The series of conflicts which was to end with Scipio Aemilianus' destruction of Numantia began in 153 BC. A Celtiberian tribe, the Belli, determined to enlarge their main city of Segeda by expanding its circuit walls and bringing in, willing or not, the population from neighbouring communities. Reluctant to permit the emergence of such a large stronghold well placed to raid into the province of Nearer Spain, the Senate dispatched the consul Quintus Fulvius Nobilior with a strong consular army of some 30,000 men to move against the tribe. The fortifications of Segeda were still incomplete when the Roman force began to advance, so the Belli abandoned the work and fled to the territory of the neighbouring Arevaci, whose main city was Numantia. Uniting with their Celtiberian kindred under an elected leader, the combined army ambushed Nobilior and inflicted heavy losses on the Roman column before being driven off. The consul moved on to assault Numantia itself, but the attack ended in disaster when one of the Romans' war elephants was struck on the head by a stone and panicked. Soon all ten elephants were stampeding to the rear, trampling any troops who got in their way. The Celtiberians exploited the disorder to counterattack and completed the Roman rout. In 152 Nobilior was succeeded by Marcus Claudius Marcellus, grandson of 'the Sword of Rome' and now holding his third consulship. The more experienced commander captured a few minor towns and, by granting them favourable terms, encouraged the Arevaci and Belli to seek peace. Like Flamininus in 198, Marcellus was eager to gain the credit for ending the war before his year of office expired and the Senate sent out a man to succeed him. Therefore he encouraged the Celtiberian ambassadors in their belief that the Senate might grant them the same terms as had been given to them by Gracchus decades before.[7]

Although delegations from the tribes had arrived in Rome and it was still uncertain whether or not the war was over, the Senate resolved that Lucius Licinius Lucullus, one of the new consuls for 151, should anyway go to Nearer Spain with a new army. Recruiting this army proved unexpectedly difficult as, for once, Roman citizens of all classes were reluctant to serve in the legions. Rumours of the ferocity of the Celtiberians had been encouraged by Nobilior and his officers on their return to Rome and the current war was seen as likely to be arduous and bring little reward. Few men came forward on the day appointed for the levy and there were complaints that in recent years this had fallen too heavily on a small section of the population, as new commanders tended to prefer experienced men. Therefore, the levy was conducted by lot. Few young senators had put their names forward for election or appointment to the rank of tribune, posts which were usually hotly contested as good opportunities for gaining a reputation for courage and ability. Lucullus also appears to have been having trouble finding men to serve as his senior subordinates or *legati* (representatives). A number of young senators are supposed to have feigned illness to excuse their cowardice. According to Polybius, it was only when the 33-year-old Scipio Aemilianus made a public statement of his willingness to serve in either capacity that others were shamed into volunteering. The historian probably exaggerated his friend and patron's influence, but nevertheless the incident certainly earned him a degree of popularity. It is uncertain whether Scipio went to Spain as a legate or as a tribune, but the latter seems more probable.[8]

Lucullus' Spanish campaign was to be shrouded in controversy. By the time he reached his province a peace had been concluded with the Arevaci. Most magistrates were eager to win glory before their term of office expired, but Lucullus had especially strong reasons for desiring a successful and lucrative war to pay off his large personal debts. Therefore he led his army against another Celtiberian tribe, the Vaccaei, attacking several of their towns under the pretext that they had been supplying the Arevaci with food. Whether or not the campaign was justified on strategic grounds, the performance of the army was undistinguished and Lucullus' own actions provoked outrage at Rome. At Cauca he accepted the surrender of the city but, once he had brought large numbers of his troops within its walls, ordered the massacre of the entire adult male population. On the whole the Romans were willing to accept the need for savagery in war when it achieved a useful purpose, but disapproved of any act which struck against Rome's reputation for good faith (*fides*) in its relations with other states.

To make matters worse, a similar atrocity was carried out by the praetor Servius Sulpicius Galba in Further Spain at almost the same time. A large number of Lusitanians and their families had surrendered to Galba after he had promised to provide them with land on which to settle – a practice which had proved very successful in Liguria. Instead, Galba divided the tribesmen into three groups, disarmed them, and then ordered his soldiers to slaughter them all. The new brutality of Roman war-making in Spain can perhaps be seen as the sign of a generation of tougher commanders determined to provide a permanent solution to the military problems posed by warlike tribes. More probably it was a product of desperation as the declining quality of Roman armies made it more difficult, especially for inexperienced commanders, to win a clear military victory. For all the outrage produced by the behaviour of Lucullus and Galba, neither man was actually punished on his return to Rome. Although brought to trial, Galba secured his acquittal through a mixture of massive bribery and emotional showmanship, bringing his weeping children into court to move the jury to pity.[9]

Only a little is known about Scipio Aemilianus' part in the campaign. When the Romans advanced on the town of Intercatia, a large and splendidly armoured Celtiberian warrior repeatedly rode between the two armies offering to meet any Roman in single combat. Eventually, Scipio went forward to meet him, displaying something of the same impetuous spirit he had shown at Pydna. His career was nearly cut short when the enemy champion wounded his horse and he was thrown, but, landing on his feet, he continued the fight and in the end prevailed. Later he acted as guarantor of Roman good faith when the townsfolk wanted to surrender but were reluctant to trust Lucullus.[10]

In 149 the Romans deliberately provoked a war with Carthage with the intention of destroying a city which was now beginning once again to prosper. In spite of this cynical premeditation, they proved woefully unprepared for actually fighting the war. The expeditionary force sent to Africa was poorly led and badly trained, so that the war opened with a catalogue of failure and incompetence. Scipio was serving as a tribune in the Fourth Legion,[11] and repeatedly demonstrated the leadership, skill and courage that was so lacking in the rest of the army. His own troops were kept under tight control and on several occasions managed to prevent botched operations from descending into total disaster. A growing reputation, combined with a strong sense amongst the electorate that it was appropriate to send a grandson of Scipio Africanus to defeat Carthage, resulted in his election to the consulship in 147. The fact that Aemilianus was about 36 or 37 and so below the minimum legal age for holding this office provided another similarity with his illustrious ancestor and strengthened the feeling that this was the right thing to do. Scipio had originally been standing for the more junior post of aedile, but was chosen as consul by the *Comitia Centuriata*. After some opposition, the law which stipulated minimum ages for each magistracy, the *lex Villia annalis*, was annulled and re-enacted at the beginning of the next year. Intervention by one of the tribunes of the plebs then ensured that Scipio, rather than his consular colleague, was given Africa as his province.

The election of Aemilianus and his appointment to the African command were certainly irregular, though far less so than the career of his ancestor by adoption during the Second Punic War. In both cases the choice proved a happy one for the Republic. Once in Africa Scipio Aemilianus set about restoring the army's discipline and morale and ensuring that from now on the troops were properly supplied, something which neither of his predecessors had managed. The operations of the army were marked by the same careful preparation, close supervision and controlled boldness which he had displayed in more junior roles. First the Carthaginian forces outside the city were defeated or persuaded to defect, and then a series of assaults launched on Carthage itself. After considerable feats of engineering and much bitter fighting in the narrow streets of the city's quarters, Carthage was captured. Its people were moved and the city itself formally slighted. Scipio wept and quoted a passage from the *Iliad* foretelling the destruction of Troy. According to Polybius he wondered whether the same fate would one day engulf his own homeland. In spite of these melancholy thoughts, he returned to Rome to celebrate a triumph which, like that of his own father decades before, was more lavish than any earlier procession.

THE SIEGE OF NUMANTIA

Before the end of the Third Punic War, a serious conflict had broken out in Further Spain. One of the few survivors of Galba's massacre was a certain Viriathus. In the aftermath he gathered a band of warriors and by 147 was strong enough to ambush the army of the praetor Caius Vetilius. The Romans suffered heavy losses – 4,000 according to Appian – and Vetilius himself was captured and promptly killed by a warrior who did not recognize him and doubted that such an elderly and fat prisoner would be worth anything. Viriathus' power grew rapidly after this success, as more and more communities decided that it was better to pay him tribute than to be raided by his warriors. In 145 Scipio's older brother Fabius Maximus Aemilianus went as consul and campaigned against the Lusitanian leader. He had a newly recruited army under his command and his reluctance to attempt a complex or bold operation with such troops meant that he achieved little more than a few minor victories during his year of office. In 142 his brother by adoption, Fabius Maximus Servilianus, had more success, taking several strongholds loyal to Viriathus. His methods were brutal, but at first effective, until he was defeated in a major battle and offered the bandit leader extremely generous peace terms, by which he would become a 'Friend of the Roman People'. In 140 his actual brother, Quintus Servilius Caepio, gained the consulship and was sent to replace him in Further Spain. Caepio swiftly broke the treaty, but the Romans only achieved victory after bribing some of Viriathus' senior chieftains to murder him in his sleep.[12]

Viriathus' success had encouraged the Arevaci to renew their own war against Rome in 143. The first army sent against them was led by the consul Quintus Caecilius Metellus. He attacked suddenly, driving into the tribes' territory before they had carried out the harvest. Most of the Arevaci surrendered and, after handing over considerable tribute, they were once more restored to allied status. Only Numantia and a few smaller walled towns continued to hold out by the time that Metellus was replaced by Quintus Pompeius Aulus, a 'new man' eager to win glory. At his disposal was a strong consular army of some 30,000 infantry and 2,000 cavalry, most of whom were now in their sixth year of continuous service and were therefore very experienced by the standards of these decades. Pompeius won a few minor victories, but suffered rather more small-scale defeats. He decided to maintain a blockade of Numantia throughout the winter months, in spite of the fact that his experienced troops had been discharged and replaced by new recruits. Unused to campaigning, the newly arrived legionaries suffered badly in the cold Spanish winter. However, the blockade did put pressure on the Numantines, who accepted Pompeius' offer of peace. Appian claims that he was so eager to gain credit for finishing the war that he secretly promised the Celtiberians very favourable terms. Amidst bitter recriminations at Rome, the Senate rejected the new settlement and in 137 the consul Caius Hostilius Mancinus was sent against Numantia.

The campaign was a long catalogue of disasters. After losing several skirmishes outside Numantia, the consul panicked at a rumour that neighbouring tribes were planning to join the Numantines. A confused night-time retreat brought the Roman column to the site of one of Nobilior's camps from the 153 campaign. They were surrounded by Celtiberian warriors, who firmly controlled all escape routes. Mancinus surrendered, the details of the truce being negotiated by his quaestor Tiberius Sempronius Gracchus, son of the man who had brought peace to Spain decades before. The terms were humiliating, for although the army was permitted to leave, the soldiers were forced to leave all their baggage behind. The treaty saved more than 20,000 lives but was not the way that a Roman war was supposed to end. Men who led armies to disaster, but stubbornly refused to admit defeat, often received praise. A commander who admitted that he had been beaten and negotiated with the enemy from this weak position was treated with contempt. On receiving a report of the campaign, the Senate immediately rejected the peace terms. Mancinus was held responsible and taken back to Numantia. There, naked and bound, he was deposited outside the walls for the Celtiberians to treat as they pleased. In the event they did not want him, and Mancinus was allowed to return to Rome where he commissioned a statue of himself, naked and in chains, which he proudly displayed in his house as a reminder of his willingness to sacrifice himself for the good of the Republic. He was never again to be granted a command in the field. His successor in the command did little better, failing to take Pallantia after a long siege and being forced into a disordered and costly retreat.[13]

In 134 Scipio Aemilianus was elected to a second consulship and given the province of Nearer Spain. A decade had passed since he had first held the senior magistracy and he was by now old enough to be eligible without any need to suspend the law, but recent legislation had banned men from holding a second term as consul. However, it seems certain that the recent disasters in Spain created a strong feeling that Rome's most distinguished commander should be sent against the Celtiberians and once again law was suspended on his behalf. Scipio did not raise a new army for the campaign, taking only a contingent of 4,000 volunteers to reinforce the troops already in the province. Included amongst these were 500 of his own clients, a unit known as the 'squadron of friends'. At a higher level there was also to be a strong family element to this campaign. Fabius Maximus Aemilianus accompanied the consul as his senior legate, and the latter's son, Fabius Maximus Buteo, was given the task of organizing and transporting the volunteers to the province after the two brothers hurried on to Spain. It is probable that Polybius went with them, although it is uncertain whether or not he wrote an account of this campaign amongst the lost sections of his *History*. The tribune Publius Rutilius Rufus certainly did produce a detailed narrative of the army's operations which was used by Appian, but has not itself survived. All the sources for the Numantine War seem to have been highly favourable to Scipio, which probably reflects his skilful handling of publicity.[14]

On arrival in the province Scipio discovered a demoralized and undisciplined army. Virtually his first act was to order the expulsion from the camp of the horde of prostitutes, merchants, diviners and soothsayers. From now on, he ordered the soldiers to eat only their simple ration, and forbade them from supplementing this with locally purchased delicacies. No Roman army at any period could function without a significant number of slaves (*lixae*), who relieved the fighting soldiers from such tasks as foraging, drawing water and supervising the baggage train, but Scipio reduced their numbers to an absolute minimum. The vast majority of personal slaves, whose only task was to cook or assist in their master's grooming, were barred from the camp. Officers in particular were inclined to take a large part of their private household with them on campaign in order to ensure a degree of comfort and, when this trend went unchecked, the extra mouths to feed and the non-essential personal baggage seriously encumbered a campaigning army. Scipio ruthlessly purged the train of all unnecessary loads, cutting the number of pack animals, and especially wagons, which were permitted to march with the column and selling off the rest. In the camp itself a fixed routine was introduced and rigorously maintained. The general granted very few exemptions to any of his new rules and set a strong personal lead. When he banned all ranks from sleeping on camp beds – probably in part to reduce the amount of equipment being carried in the train – Scipio was the first to sleep on a simple straw palliasse. He deliberately made himself inaccessible to petitioners, seeking obedience from his men rather than affection. According to Appian:

> He often said that those generals who were severe and strict in the observance of the law were serviceable to their own men, while those who were easy-going and bountiful were useful only to the enemy. The soldiers of the latter…were joyous but insubordinate, while those of the former, although downcast, were obedient and ready for all emergencies.[15]

His inspections were frequent, extremely thorough and often critical. On these occasions it was not unknown for him to smash any vessel he considered too luxurious for active service. One soldier who had an especially well decorated shield provoked the barbed comment that it was no wonder he lavished such attention on it when he evidently 'placed more faith in this than his sword'. Rank was no defence against the consul's scathing and public denunciations and the tribune Caius Memmius came in for particular criticism. At one point Scipio announced that at least Memmius 'would only be useless to him for a short time, but that he would remain useless to himself and the Republic forever'.[16]

Alongside these disciplinary measures, Scipio put the army through an intensive period of training, which was made as realistic as possible. A lot of time was spent marching, the troops carrying rations for several days and formed into three parallel columns which could readily be transformed into battle order. The baggage train was kept in between the columns to protect it from sudden attack. Always the emphasis was on very tight march discipline and both units and individuals were forbidden to move away from their assigned place. In past campaigns many of his soldiers had provided themselves with mules or donkeys and ridden at their leisure, but Scipio banned this and demanded that all infantrymen should march on their own two feet. Once again he set a personal example, marching with his officers and eating ration bread as he went, and moving around the army to observe each section. Particular attention was paid to men who had difficulty keeping up, and cavalrymen were ordered to dismount and allow the weary to ride until they had recovered. Scipio also tried to take care of the army's beasts of burden, and when he discovered any pack mules which had been overburdened, he had infantrymen carry part of the loads. At the end of each day's march the army constructed a temporary camp as if in enemy territory. The procedure was always the same. The units which had formed the vanguard for that day took up positions around the chosen campsite and remained in formation and under arms to act as a covering force. Every other part of the army had its allotted task, marking out the camp with its tent lines and roads, or excavating the ditch and building the defensive rampart. There were many similarities between Scipio's training programme and his father's standing orders during the Third Macedonian War. Both reflected best practice learnt over many campaigns by the militia army.[17]

Scipio supplemented his Roman and Italian troops with strong contingents of local allies. According to Appian this raised the number of soldiers under his command to 60,000. Once the consul decided that the soldiers were ready, he advanced on Numantia, the army moving with the same discipline and caution which he had enforced during training. Instead of attacking the Celtiberian stronghold directly, he bypassed it and ravaged the fields of the neighbouring Vaccaei, cutting the Numantines off from this source of supply. It was a region in which he had served under Lucullus and, in recompense for the atrocity committed by that general, Scipio issued an

official proclamation permitting any of the surviving inhabitants of Cauca
to return to and rebuild their community.

Outside Pallantia a force of cavalry under the command of Rutilius
Rufus pursued a retreating enemy over-eagerly and was lured into an
ambush. Scipio personally led more horsemen to the rescue and, by alter-
nately attacking and retiring on each flank, managed to cover the retreat of
Rufus' men and escape himself. In many ways the action was reminiscent
of his skilful leadership of his legion's cavalry whilst serving as a tribune in
the Third Punic War. On another occasion he discovered that the Celtiberians
had laid an ambush for his army at the point where the route they were following crossed a river. Scipio instead took the army in a night march over
an alternative, and much more difficult route. Training paid off as the soldiers
accomplished this arduous journey, in spite of shortages of water which
became all the more pressing as the hot summer sun rose on the next day.
The army escaped with the loss of a few cavalry mounts and pack animals.
Soon afterwards the cavalry screening a Roman raiding party was attacked
whilst the main force was plundering a village. Scipio had a trumpet call
sounded to recall the plunderers and, when he felt that as many as were
likely to arrive quickly had done so, formed them into units. With just under
1,000 men, he went to the aid of the Roman cavalry. After a while the
Celtiberians were driven back, permitting the Romans to withdraw.[18]

Scipio had done much to deprive the Numantines of aid and support
from the other Celtiberian communities. He had also tested the army's
training in actual operations and given the soldiers the encouragement of
some minor victories. Now it was time to turn against Numantia itself. Scipio
split the army into two and camped both divisions near the town, retaining
command of one himself and placing the other under his brother. Soon
after the Romans arrived, the Numantines left the protection of their fortifications and came out, challenging the Romans to battle. There were no
more than 8,000 warriors facing the much larger Roman army and it may
well be that they were expecting to contest the approaches to the town walls
as Mago's men had done at New Carthage rather than to fight a pitched
battle. Scipio had no intention of risking either a battle or a direct assault.
The overwhelming bulk of his army consisted of men who were used to
being defeated by the Celtiberians. Storming a well defended city was always
an extremely difficult operation and even a minor check might result in
widespread demoralization, destroying all of his efforts to rebuild the army.
One of Scipio's maxims was that a wise commander should never take an
avoidable risk. It is probable that from the beginning of the campaign he

planned to blockade Numantia into submission, so, ignoring the Numantines' challenge, he set his army to constructing a line of fortifications surrounding the town.

Traces of Scipio's siege works around Numantia survived above ground and were excavated in the early twentieth century by the German archaeologist Schulten. Although unfortunately there has been no extensive modern work on the site to confirm some of his conclusions, there is certainly a reasonably close correspondence between the remains and Appian's description of the siege. Scipio's men constructed seven forts, which were then joined together with a ditch and rampart. The latter eventually stretched for 6 miles or so, and was built of stone 8 feet wide and 10 feet high, and strengthened by wooden towers at 100-foot intervals. The forts also had stone walls and soon acquired large numbers of internal stone buildings, allowing the troops to live in reasonably healthy and comfortable conditions during the long siege. Interestingly enough, these temporary camps, and indeed other Republican camps discovered in Spain, have walls which exploit the natural contours of the ground, unlike the ideal marching camp described by Polybius, which was supposed to be constructed on a perfectly flat plain. At first there was a gap in the circuit at Numantia where it was broken by the River Durius (modern Duero) and the Numantines were able to bring in supplies and send out men by boat. To counter this, Scipio ordered a tower built on either bank and had a boom, the timbers studded with knife blades and spearheads, put across the river.[19]

The Roman army was organized into divisions, each of which was allotted a specific task in the construction of the siege lines. Scipio and Fabius kept reserve troops under arms ready to come to the aid of any division under attack, who were to signal their need by raising a red flag in daytime or lighting a beacon at night. Once the lines were completed the organization was extended so that around 30,000 men were divided between the sections of wall. Many catapults and *ballistae* were installed in the towers, whilst slingers and archers were attached to each individual century to increase its firepower.[20] Another 20,000 men were placed to move up and reinforce each sector whenever there was an attack, with the remaining 10,000 kept back as a reserve which could be sent anywhere. Any signal was to be repeated by each tower in turn so that it might more swiftly reach the commander and bring aid.

The strength of the walls and the effectiveness of Scipio's organization was proved when each Celtiberian attack was repulsed. One Celtiberian nobleman, named Rhetogenes Caraunius, managed with a few friends to climb the wall one dark night. After killing the sentries, they used a folding wooden bridge to bring their horses across and rode around to other communities in their tribe, hoping to persuade them to raise an army and break the siege. Some of the younger warriors at the town of Lutia were sympathetic, but the town elders sent a warning to Scipio, who rushed with a force of light troops to the spot, surrounding the town and threatening to sack the place if the culprits were not immediately handed over to him. The Celtiberians swiftly complied with his demands. Scipio ordered that the 400 prisoners should have their hands cut off as a dreadful warning of the penalty for resisting Rome, and then hurried back to Numantia.

By this time the Numantines were running desperately short of food and decided to send ambassadors to Scipio requesting peace terms. His only response was to demand unconditional surrender, and Appian claims that this so enraged the tribesmen that the ambassadors were lynched on their return to the town. As things grew worse it was claimed that there were outbreaks of cannibalism, but in the end the defenders were forced to capitulate. Some committed suicide to avoid this disgrace. The remainder, emaciated and filthy, marched out and laid down their arms. Scipio kept fifty to march in his triumph and sold the others as slaves. Numantia itself was razed to the ground and the remains visible there today date to a later period when it became a Roman settlement.

Scipio returned to celebrate his second triumph and, if this lacked the spectacle of the procession commemorating the destruction of Carthage, there was considerable relief that the war with the Celtiberians was finally over. For a while he was extremely popular, but during his absence on campaign Roman politics had turned increasingly bitter and violent and he was soon to become involved in controversy. In 133 Tiberius Sempronius Gracchus – the man who had negotiated the surrender of Mancinus' army – had been elected a tribune of the people and had used this post to pass a law calling for a widespread redistribution of publicly owned land throughout Italy. Much of this had been incorporated into large estates owned by the wealthy and Gracchus' intention was to take this land and grant it to poorer citizens, in this way making them eligible for military service and so swelling Rome's reserves of military manpower. He faced widespread opposition from other senators, both because many were landowners and also because all feared that Gracchus would win himself so many clients (citizens indebted to him and therefore likely to support him with their vote) by this act that he would be difficult to oppose in any future election. Fears that he was aiming at permanent personal power – the one thing which the Republican constitution was supposed to prevent – seemed confirmed when he announced his intention to stand for a second consecutive tribunate. In an apparently spontaneous riot, Gracchus was lynched by a band of senators led by his cousin, Scipio Nasica (son of the man who had served at Pydna).

Scipio Aemilianus was in Spain when this occurred and his own attitude to these events is unclear. Gracchus' mother was Cornelia, daughter of Africanus and he himself was married to Tiberius' sister, although the marriage had proved childless and there was little affection between the couple. In addition, his associate Laelius had proposed a similar piece of legislation during his consulship in 140, but had backed down in the face of such strong opposition, earning himself the nickname 'the Wise' (*Sapiens*) in the process. On his return to Rome he accepted appeals to champion the cause of Italian noblemen who complained that the Commission established to enforce the Gracchan Land Law was treating them too harshly. This willingness to speak up for allied peoples angered many of Gracchus' supporters in Rome, especially amongst those who hoped to escape from their poverty by being sent to colonize public land. In 129 Scipio was found dead in his house. He had not been ill and there was no trace of injury on the corpse. Soon, rumours abounded that he had been poisoned, perhaps by his wife Sempronia, or his mother-in-law and aunt, Cornelia. The truth will never be known.[21]

CHAPTER 5

'A PERSON DEVOTED TO WAR':
CAIUS MARIUS

Caius Marius (157–86 BC)

And there is nothing a Roman soldier enjoys more than the sight of his commanding officer openly eating the same bread as him, or lying on a plain straw mattress, or lending a hand to dig a ditch or raise a palisade. What they admire in a leader is the willingness to share the danger and the hardship, rather than the ability to win them honour and wealth, and they are more fond of officers who are prepared to make efforts alongside them than they are of those who let them take things easy.[1]

ROMAN COMMANDERS WERE ARISTOCRATS, AND THIS WAS ESPECIALLY TRUE of the generals we have so far discussed. Fabius Maximus, Scipio Africanus, Aemilius Paullus and Scipio Aemilianus were all from patrician families – the last both by birth and adoption – and so members of Rome's oldest ruling élite. By the third century BC the patricians had lost their monopoly of high office and a number of plebeian families had forced their way into the small privileged group which, generation after generation, dominated the Republic's highest magistracies. Some patrician lines died out or dwindled to obscurity, whilst others, such as the Julii, continued to enjoy modest success, but remained largely on the fringes of real power. Four patrician clans, the Aemilii, Fabii, Cornelii and Claudii, were consistently strong, and provided a disproportionately high percentage of consuls. The greatest plebeian families rivalled them in wealth and influence, and shared a common ideology. Any successful leader must be confident, but the self-assurance and refusal to listen to criticism of Fabius Maximus, Paullus and the Scipios

– and to a lesser extent Marcellus – owed much to their distinguished birth and patrician outlook. From his earliest youth each man knew that it was both his right and his duty to serve the Republic in a distinguished capacity, earning fame, honours and wealth in the process. A youth born into one of the dominant senatorial families was almost assured a reasonably success-ful political career regardless of personal ability. All the men we have studied had exceptional military talent, and at least some political ability. This, combined with their family background, not a little luck, and the opportun-ities presented by real or apparent crisis facing Rome, granted each man an exceptionally distinguished series of magistracies and field commands.

In spite of the dominance of the *nobiles*, in every generation there were always a few 'new men' who managed to reach the consulship. Such a rise was never easy, though perhaps not so difficult as successful 'new men' were inclined to claim, but always possible. When Caius Marius was elected consul for 107 BC, there was little to single him out as markedly different from any other *novus homo*. Some episodes in his career to this date had been contro-versial, but this was also true of many other senators, and it was only at this point that Marius began to shatter many conventions. His consulship proved to be the first of seven, more than any senator had ever held before. It was not simply the number which was unprecedented, but the nature, for five were held in consecutive years between 104 and 100, whilst the seventh he seized, as he had taken Rome itself, with armed force in 86. Marius was one of the key figures in the civil war which erupted in 88, the first in a long cycle of internal conflicts which would eventually destroy the Republican system of government. Roman politics and society had changed profoundly by the end of the first century. So had the fundamental nature of the Roman army, which had evolved from the traditional militia composed of a cross section of the propertied classes into a semi-professional force recruited primarily from the very poor. Marius' career, and the disorder of his times, was a symptom of these changes.

MARIUS' EARLY LIFE AND THE NUMIDIAN QUESTION

Plutarch claims that Marius' parents laboured with their own hands to work their small farm near the village of Ceraetae outside the town of Arpinum.[2] Tales of the poverty of 'new men' were common, adding to the drama of their subsequent political success, but must be taken with a pinch of salt. Only equestrians could seek election to any important magistracy at Rome, and membership of this Order required very substantial property. Members of senatorial families began their lives as equestrians, until political success led the censors to enrol them in the Senate, but these formed a small minority of the Order, most of whom chose not to enter politics. Evidently senators considered most ordinary equestrians as their social inferiors, but this snobbery should not blind us to the fact that the latter were people of considerable wealth and status, close to the top of Roman society, if not quite at its pinnacle. Marius' family were doubtless part of the local aristocracy at Arpinum with considerable influence and power in the town, however rustic and obscure they may have appeared to the *nobiles*. His education may have been a little conservative by the standards of the day, Plutarch claiming that he had lacked much knowledge of Greek literature and culture and rarely, if ever, used the language. Yet in most respects Marius, like all other 'new men', differed little from the sons of senators in his attitudes and ambitions.[3]

Marius began his military service in the Celtiberian war and may have served there for several years before the arrival of Scipio Aemilianus. He readily accepted the stricter discipline imposed by the new commander and one story tells of the good impression he made during one of Scipio's frequent inspections of his army's weapons, equipment and baggage. On another occasion he is said to have fought and won a single combat whilst the consul was watching, a feat which won him decorations and other marks of favour. Marius was 23 years old and probably a tribune by this time, just as Scipio had been when he won fame in a similar encounter. Such displays of bravado were evidently not considered inappropriate for officers of this rank, even if army commanders and their most senior subordinates no longer took such risks.[4]

It was common for ambitious young men who lacked inherited reputation, wealth and influence to be supported in their careers by powerful families. Marius and his parents were clients of the Caecilii Metelli, plebeian *nobiles* who enjoyed frequent success. In 119 Lucius Caecilius Metellus Delmaticus was elected consul and seems to have assisted Marius in his successful campaign to become a tribune of the plebs. This was the office through which the Gracchi had pushed their programmes of reform, but a man of Marius' obscure background could not hope to emulate such projects. He carried through some minor bills, one of which altered electoral procedure and brought him into direct conflict with his patron, an incident which won the tribune some reputation for independence and courage. Even so, few would have guessed at his future fame, for he failed to win election to the office of aedile, and only just scraped into the praetorship for 115. Charged with bribing the electorate, Marius was just as narrowly acquitted. Sent as governor to Further Spain, he carried out some minor operations to suppress banditry, but had no opportunity to win great fame or wealth. Around this time he married into the Julii Caesares, an ancient patrician family who were no longer especially prominent and only managed to produce a single consul in the entire second century. It was a good match, but scarcely guaranteed significant political advancement. It is more than probable that Marius unsuccessfully sought the consulship on one or more occasions in the following years and it may have seemed that his career had run its course, until a military crisis in Numidia offered him a fresh opportunity of attracting the public eye.[5]

Scipio's invasion of Africa in 204 BC had been greatly aided by the defection to the Romans of the Numidian Prince Masinissa, who was subsequently established in an enlarged kingdom as a reward for his support. After the Second Punic War, Numidia proved useful to Rome as a check on the renewal of Carthaginian power. Both Masinissa, who died in the early stages of the Third Punic War, and his son Micipsa loyally provided grain, troops and elephants whenever requested by the Romans. Micipsa's nephew Jugurtha took a contingent of elephants and infantry skirmishers to aid Scipio Aemilianus in the Numantia campaign, where he won a high reputation for skill and courage. In 118 the king died, bequeathing his kingdom jointly to Jugurtha, whom he had adopted, and his own sons Adherbal and Hiempsal. The latter was swiftly killed on the orders of his cousin. Adherbal fled to Rome, and the Senate decreed that the kingdom should be divided equally between the two rivals, but the truce was soon broken by Jugurtha. Dynastic struggles of this nature had never been uncommon amongst the Numidian and Moorish royal houses, and it was just such a dispute which had first prompted Masinissa to seek aid from Scipio. However, in 112 Adherbal was besieged in Cirta, whose population included a substantial number of Roman and Italian businessmen. These formed the main strength of the defence and, after the city's capitulation, were massacred by Jugurtha's men.

Rome was outraged by this news. Much of the fury may have come from the equestrian heads of the great business companies which had interests in the region and agents amongst the dead, but there does seem to have been widespread anger from all sections of the population. This was further roused by the tribune-elect Caius Memmius – quite possibly the same man who had provoked Aemilianus' scorn at Numantia – until the Senate decided to send the consul Lucius Calpurnius Bestia with an army to North Africa. Jugurtha was persuaded to come to Rome, where he indulged in widespread and blatant bribery of influential senators and even arranged the murder of another member of his family who was in exile there. As he left Rome, he is supposed to have declared it 'a city up for sale and likely to perish if it finds a buyer!' Popular fury redoubled, and much of it was directed at the perceived incompetence and corruption of the Senate.

Worse was to come in 110 when Bestia's successor Spurius Postumius Albinus led a spiritless attack on Jugurtha before leading his ill-disciplined army back to winter quarters and placing his brother Aulus in command. Politicking at Rome, where two tribunes wished to prolong their year of office and held up all magisterial elections, led to Aulus Postumius Albinus' being left in command for far longer than had been expected. Deciding to make the most of this, he advanced on the stronghold at Suthul which contained Jugurtha's main treasury. The Numidian king feigned a willingness to negotiate once more and secretly began to bribe the centurions and other officers in the Roman army. Then he launched a sudden night attack on Postumius' camp. The result was panic and rout, as a number of legionaries, an entire cohort of Ligurian infantry and two *turmae* of Thracian cavalry deserted en masse, whilst the senior centurion (*primus pilus*) of the Third Legion allowed the enemy to come through the section of fortifications which he was supposed to be defending. Resistance was both feeble and short-lived as a mob of fugitives fled from the camp to a nearby hill, leaving the Numidians to plunder the tents.

The next day Jugurtha surrounded Aulus and his men and offered to make a treaty ending the war. In return for acknowledging him as the rightful king of Numidia, he would allow the Romans to depart freely, once they had undergone the symbolic humiliation of walking under a yoke of spears. The precise origins of this archaic ritual are unknown, but it clearly implied a loss of warrior status. Nor is it certain whether it was widely practised outside Italy, or chosen on occasions by Rome's enemies precisely because they knew of its significance to the Romans. As at Numantia the treaty was immediately repudiated by the Senate. This did little to still the public outcry against the incompetence and corruption which had caused this disaster.[6]

In 109 the consul Quintus Caecilius Metellus, the younger brother of Delmaticus, was sent to take command of the war against Jugurtha, taking drafts of replacements for the legions already in Africa rather than raising an entirely new force. Marius' rift with the Metelli had evidently not been irreparable, for he and Publius Rutilius Rufus accompanied Quintus as his senior legates. With two old hands from Numantia on his staff, it was probably unsurprising that many of Scipio Aemilianus' methods were soon being employed to knock the legions into shape. Albinus' troops had spent the last months in ill-disciplined idleness, not bothering to fortify or lay out their camp properly and shifting it only when forced to by lack of locally available forage or because the stench of their own waste became overpowering. Soldiers and camp slaves marauded and plundered at will. Metellus imposed a set of regulations very close to those of Aemilianus. Traders and other unnecessary hangers-on were expelled, and soldiers forbidden to buy food – many had been in the practice of selling their ration of grain to purchase ready baked white bread rather than eating wholemeal loaves they had prepared themselves. The ordinary soldiers were barred from keeping their own slaves or pack animals. From now on the army broke camp every day, and marched to a new position where it constructed a marching camp as if in hostile territory. Just as Scipio had done, Metellus and his legates set an example on the march, moving around the columns to ensure that units and individuals kept their positions and were always properly equipped and ready.[7]

When Metellus considered that his army was ready, he advanced against Jugurtha. At first the king avoided battle, so the Romans turned their attention to his towns, capturing several small strongholds and the capital at Cirta. Such losses seriously dented Jugurtha's prestige, prompting him to attack the Roman army as it marched across open country near the River Muthul. In a confused whirling fight, during which the fast-moving enemy broke the columns up into several sections, the Numidians were eventually driven off with heavy loss, most of their war elephants being killed or captured. The Romans had also suffered heavy casualties and Metellus rested the army for a while, allowing the men to recover and tending to the wounded. Parades were held to decorate all those who had distinguished themselves in the recent fighting. After four days they began once again to ravage the most fertile areas of Numidia and to threaten its towns and strongholds. Storming fortified towns was never easy, and Metellus was forced to withdraw from Zama after a siege which had involved very heavy fighting. An attempt was made to dispose of Jugurtha in the same way that the Romans had defeated Viriathus, by bribing some of his own leaders to murder him, but this time the plot was discovered and failed.

It is difficult to see what else Metellus could have done with the resources at his disposal, but there was growing discontent at Rome about the time it was taking to wreak revenge on Jugurtha. In 108 Marius sought permission to return to Rome and announce his candidacy for the consulship. Sallust tells us that he was encouraged in his ambitions by a soothsayer at Utica who had prophesied that he would have a most distinguished career. Throughout his life Marius appears to have had a strong sense of his personal destiny, and took encouragement from various omens. The general's response was scornful, suggesting that Marius should wait until he could stand with Metellus' own son, a lad only in his early twenties and currently serving on his father's staff. Marius continued to serve as legate, but from this point on lost no opportunity to belittle his commander. Both with the army and when he met some of the many Roman traders and businessmen in the province of Africa, he accused Metellus of needlessly prolonging the war to gain more glory and plunder for himself. A stream of letters went back from such men to their connections at Rome, criticizing the commander and lavishing praise on his legate.

A further opportunity to attack his old patron was offered when the garrison of the town of Vaga was massacred by a sudden rebellion of the populace who had decided to defect to Jugurtha and only the commander, a certain Titus Turpilius Silanus, was spared. The town was swiftly recaptured, but Marius was part of the court set up to investigate Silanus' conduct and successfully recommended his execution, in spite of the fact that he too was a client of the Metelli. Eventually Metellus relented and permitted his disloyal and troublesome legate to return to Rome.

Marius' electoral campaign was both swift and highly successful. Although our sources are inclined to depict his chief support as coming from the poorer sections of society, we need to remember that Rome's electoral system gave a disproportionate influence to the wealthier citizens and many equestrians favoured his candidature. So did a fair number of senators, but other members of the House were incensed at the intemperate speeches the new consul-elect made attacking the *nobiles*. An experienced soldier, Marius contrasted himself with the soft aristocrats who tried to learn about war from books:

> Now, compare me, fellow citizens, a new man, with those arrogant nobles. What they know only from hearsay or reading, I have seen with my own eyes or done with my own hands – what they have learned from books I have actually done during my military service. Work it out for yourself whether words or deeds are worth more. They hold my humble origins in contempt – I scorn their worthlessness; I am reproached for the chance of birth – they for their infamous conduct. Personally, I believe that all men have one nature, and that the bravest are the best born. And if now the fathers of Albinus and Bestia were asked whether they would prefer to have me or those men as their offspring, what do you reckon they would reply, if not that they wished to have the best children?

> If they [the *nobiles*] justly look down on me, then let them also despise
> their own ancestors, whose nobility began with courage, as did my own...[8]

The words are those of Sallust, for it was conventional for a Greek or Roman historian to invent speeches appropriate for the events and the characters they described, but they may well be a genuine reflection of Marius' tone and attitude in 107. However much he enraged the *nobiles* with such outspoken criticism, his speeches delighted the mass of the population. Marius had already decided that he wished to replace Metellus in the African command, and publicly he promised to bring the war to a rapid conclusion. Normally the Senate alone decided which provinces would be allocated to the new magistrates and which governors' commands were to be prorogued, but a tribune brought a bill before the Popular Assembly (*Concilium Plebis*) granting Marius command in the war with Jugurtha. Metellus refused to meet his replacement, leaving Rutilius Rufus to hand over the army to the consul.

Marius did not win a swift victory in Numidia in spite of all his boasting. His popularity does not appear to have suffered because of this, and ensured that his command was extended, but it took three years to end the war. His strategy differed in no way from that followed by Metellus, the Romans concentrating on taking Jugurtha's strongholds one by one since they could not force him into a decisive battle. Luck often favoured the Romans, as when a Ligurian auxiliary out looking for edible snails discovered a concealed pathway leading up to a weak spot in the defences of a fortress near the River Mulaccha. Marius, who had been on the point of abandoning the siege, was able to use this information to storm the place. Yet in spite of repeated successes, Jugurtha himself always eluded the Romans and never wavered in his determination to continue the struggle. Finally Marius resorted to treachery, persuading Jugurtha's ally King Bocchus of Mauretania to betray him to the Romans in late 105 BC. The operation was organized and led by his quaestor, Lucius Cornelius Sulla, who managed to retain a good deal of the credit. Nevertheless, Marius returned to celebrate a triumph on 1 January 104, entering on the same day into a second consulship to which he had been elected during his absence. This was highly irregular, but Italy was now threatened by a massive migration of barbarian tribes, who had already swept aside a number of Roman armies, and there was a strong feeling that the Republic's most popular general must be sent against them.[9]

'MARIUS' MULES'

Neither Metellus nor Marius had been allowed to raise a new army for the African campaign, and they took with them only drafts of troops to bring the forces already in the province up to strength. In 107 Marius broke with precedent by accepting volunteers from outside the classes whose wealth made them eligible for military service. These men were the *proletarii* or 'head count' (*capite censi*), listed in the census simply as numbers because they lacked significant property. In the past the *capite censi* had only been summoned for military service at times of extreme crisis, such as in the darkest days of the Second Punic War, though it is possible that they served more often as rowers in the fleet. Traditionally the army had drawn its strength from men of property, and chiefly from farmers. Such men had a stake in the Republic and were therefore expected to fight all the harder to preserve it. However, by the late second century this duty had become burdensome. Sallust tells us that Marius' opponents in the Senate hoped that even the levying of troops to bring the African army up to strength would dampen popular enthusiasm for the new consul. Taking willing volunteers from outside the normal recruiting base avoided this and provided plenty of keen recruits encouraged by his speeches and the promise of glory and plunder.

Marius' action in 107 has sometimes been seen as a major reform, the moment when the Roman army effectively changed from being a citizen's militia to a professional force recruited predominantly from the very poor. From now on legionaries saw the army as a career and means of escaping poverty, rather than as a duty which came as an interruption to normal life. Under the traditional system legions had been renumbered each year, but with the rise of the professional soldier the legions became increasingly permanent and over time acquired a stronger sense of identity and tradition. Marius contributed to this trend when he issued each of his legions with a silver eagle as its standard. In the past each legion had possessed five standards – an eagle, a bull, a horse, a wolf and a boar. Since recruitment was no longer based on wealth, the old divisions based on class and age ceased to have any real significance. *Velites* are last mentioned during Metellus' campaign in 109, and Roman citizen cavalrymen seem also to have disappeared around the same time, so that the legion no longer had integral light infantry or cavalry. The names *hastati*, *principes* and *triarii* – the latter usually under their alternative title of *pili* – were preserved in the army's ceremony and administration, but real distinctions between the lines vanished along with their tactical significance. All legionaries were now heavy infantrymen, uniformly equipped with helmet, mail or scale cuirass, *scutum*, sword and *pilum*.

The century remained the basic administrative sub-unit of the legion and seems to have had a paper-strength of eighty men. The maniple was replaced as the most important tactical unit by the larger cohort, which consisted of three maniples, one from each of the old lines, and numbered 480 men. There were ten cohorts in a legion. In battle the legion still frequently formed in three lines, usually with four cohorts in the first line, and three each in the second and third. However, since all the troops were identically equipped and the cohorts all organized the same, it did not have to fight in this formation and had far more tactical flexibility than the manipular legion. The cohort legion might equally deploy in two or four lines, although a single line of cohorts was rarely employed and was probably considered too weak.

Most scholars now play down the significance of the Marian reform in the transition from a militia to a professional army, preferring to see this as a much more gradual process. Certainly from the time of the Second Punic War there had been periodic reductions in the minimum level of property which qualified a citizen for military service. Spurius Ligustinus – the spokesman of the group of disgruntled former senior centurions enrolled in the levy in 172 BC – farmed a plot of land too small to make him eligible for service and repeatedly volunteered during his twenty-two years with the legions. It is hard to know how common this was before Marius, although we ought to remember that Ligustinus spent all but three years as a centurion and is thus an example of a semi-professional officer rather than a professional soldier. It is equally difficult to know how large a proportion of the citizen population remained ineligible for legionary service in spite of the lowering of the property qualification for service.[10]

What is certain is that the role of the army had changed significantly since the early days of the militia system. When campaigns had been fought against Rome's Italian neighbours, it had been possible for a man to be enrolled in a legion, serve in a campaign and still return home in time for the harvest. As the Republic's power expanded, wars were fought further and further away and lasted for longer periods. By the late second century BC there was a need for the army to provide permanent garrisons in Spain, Transalpine Gaul and Macedonia, whether or not a war was actually being fought. Long years of continuous military service were a difficult burden for the owner of a small farm, which might easily fall into ruin during his absence. At the same time overseas expansion had massively enriched Rome's élite, who bought up large tracts of Italian land to form grand estates worked by a labour force of slaves, cheaply available as one of the products of the same conquests. More Roman wars led to more citizens being dragged away from their smallholdings for years on end, causing many to fall into debt and sell their property, which was promptly swallowed up into the great estates or *latifundia*. Each time this happened the number of men eligible for army service dropped.

We do not possess sufficient reliable statistics even to estimate the extent to which Rome's reserves of military manpower were declining in this period. Our sources may have exaggerated the problem, but make it clear that there was widespread concern amongst contemporaries about this. This issue lay at the heart of Tiberius Gracchus' reform programme in 133, when he attempted to redistribute publicly owned land to increase the number of yeoman farmers who had traditionally formed the heart of the legions. Concerns about dwindling supplies of manpower may well have been reinforced by the poor showing made by Roman armies in so many of the campaigns since the middle of the century. The decline in the quality of Roman soldiers was at least as serious as their diminishing numbers.

Enthusiasm for legionary service may well have declined by the late second century BC, though we only hear of this in spectacular cases such as 151 BC or can infer it from the Senate's hope that Marius would lose support once he began to recruit soldiers. Even if service did not lead to financial ruin and destitution, it may well have been resented. The levying (*dilectus*) of an army was carried out entirely under the control of the responsible magistrate and it was sometimes felt that these drew too heavily on certain individuals, as each new army wanted as many experienced soldiers as possible. The maximum term of conscripted rather than voluntary service was sixteen years – a substantial part of a man's life. In 123 Caius Gracchus had renewed the old law which stated that no one younger than 17 could be forced to join the army, which suggests that some aspects of proper procedure were often ignored.

The obligation of all citizens who possessed sufficient property to undergo military service when required by the State was never formally abolished. Armies were levied after Marius, but it is unclear to what extent the process employed resembled the traditional *dilectus*. It seems unlikely that any attention was paid to the old property classes. In the first century BC and throughout the remainder of Rome's history, conscription was always hugely unpopular. Marius may not have been the first to recruit volunteers from the *proletarii*, but he was the first to do this openly. From 107 onwards the vast majority of legionaries were recruited from the poor – whenever possible from the rural poor who were considered to be better material than their urban counterparts. No longer was the army a cross section of the Roman people under arms.

The army Marius commanded in Numidia was a mixture of his new drafts of replacements drawn mainly from the *proletarii* and the existing troops raised under more traditional methods. On arrival in the province he spent some time integrating the two by a programme of training and gave the troops a series of easy successes as he ravaged a fertile but poorly defended region of Numidia. Throughout his campaigns Marius insisted that his soldiers remained at a high state of readiness, always following the standard procedures which he had set down. Yet he was no martinet and the discipline in his legions was not considered harsh by Roman standards. Sallust tells us that Marius preferred to control his soldiers more through appealing to 'their sense of shame than through punishment'.

Much was demanded from the soldiers. Just as he had whilst serving as Metellus' legate, Marius continued to lay great importance on the army marching with as small a baggage train as possible. Luxuries were not permitted and the legionary was expected to carry all of his kit on his own back, for they were barred from keeping slaves or pack animals to take the burden. Marius may have introduced, or more probably standardized, the practice of each man suspending his leather pack from a pole which was carried over the shoulder, quite possibly tied to the *pilum*. This method allowed the pack to be dropped quickly. So burdened were the legionaries that they were nicknamed 'Marius' mules'. The general always set a strong personal example, closely supervising and sharing in all of the army's activities on campaign, eating the same ration as the ordinary soldiers and living in the same conditions. It was his custom to inspect personally the sentries guarding the camp, not because he did not trust his subordinate officers to perform this task properly, but so that the soldiers would know that he was not resting whilst they were on duty. He was never slow to speak directly to men of any rank, whether to criticize and punish or to praise and reward. He was respected as a tough, but fair commander.[11]

The African army was demobilized after the defeat of Jugurtha and for the war against the northern barbarians Marius took command of the army raised by Rutilius Rufus during his consulship in 105. He is said to have preferred to do this because he felt that these legions were better trained than his own men. Some of the African troops had been serving continuously since the beginning of the war and the more recent recruits, having won the glory and plunder which Marius had promised them, may well have not been too keen on a further arduous campaign. Rufus' men were probably also drawn predominantly from the poorest citizens and he had brought in gladiatorial trainers to teach them weapons handling. These techniques, which involved the recruit learning to fence first against a 6-foot post and then an actual opponent, would become standard in the army for many centuries. At first the soldier employed a wooden sword and wicker shield, both heavier than the standard issue items, to build up his strength. Traditionally it was assumed that any citizen qualified for military service would be taught to handle weapons – themselves family property and often probably handed down from generation to generation – as a youth by his father. Now the soldier was issued equipment by the State which also trained him in their use. It was another sign of the shift to a professional army.[12]

Rufus' men may have been better trained and disciplined than the African army, and had certainly been raised and prepared with a view to facing the Cimbri and Teutones, whose tactics differed markedly from the Numidian way of fighting. However, Marius led these men in exactly the same way that he had commanded the legions in Africa. He maintained a continuous training programme, with regular route marches and a strong emphasis on physical fitness. As in Africa, the soldiers were expected to carry and prepare their own ration. Marius drove them hard, rewarding good conduct and punishing bad with equal impartiality. One incident involved his nephew Caius Lusius, who was serving as an officer, perhaps a tribune, in the army. This man tried repeatedly to seduce one of the soldiers under his command, but was always rebuffed. When finally, he summoned the legionary to his tent and attacked him, the latter, one Trebonius, drew his sword and killed him. Put on trial for the murder of his superior officer, Trebonius' story was backed by the testimony of his comrades. Marius not only dismissed the charge, but personally presented Trebonius with the *corona civica* for defending his honour so staunchly. Polybius mentions that homosexual activity in the camp was punishable by death, and this law continued when the army became professional. Apart from a widespread and deep Roman and Italian repugnance for homosexuality – which, if never quite universal, was markedly harsher than Hellenic attitudes – the main reason for this strictness was the fear that such relationships might subvert the military hierarchy as had occurred in this case. More immediately, condoning the killing of not just an officer, but a relative, provided a clear object lesson that discipline applied to all without exception.[13]

THE NORTHERN MENACE

In 104 BC it seemed to most Romans that it was only a matter of time before the northern barbarians swept over the Alps and threatened Italy and Rome itself as no foe had done since Hannibal. These tribes, chiefly the Cimbri and Teutones, but including a number of other groups such as the Ambrones and Tigurini, were not mere raiders, but migrants, seeking land on which to settle. Estimates of their numbers in the ancient sources – Plutarch says that there were 300,000 warriors and many more women and children – are almost certainly wild exaggerations, but very large numbers of warriors and their families were clearly on the move. They did not travel in a single vast column – which would have made it impossible for them to find sufficient food and fodder for their basic needs – but in many lesser groups, so that even the individual tribes were spread over a wide area. The Romans were not certain where the tribes had come from, other than somewhere beyond the Rhine and perhaps near the Elbe, whether they were Gallic or Germanic, or why they had begun their migration. The cause of this mass movement may have been simple overpopulation in the tribes' home territories, civil war, pressure from external foes, or a combination of all three. Just how well Greek and Roman commentators understood the relationships between the various tribal peoples they encountered remains highly uncertain. The Cimbri and Teutones were most probably Germans, although archaeologists have generally found it difficult to confirm the clear distinctions between Gallic and Germanic tribes maintained in our Greek and Roman sources. Differences in the style and shape of artefacts suggest rather different boundaries, but of course may not automatically reflect variations in language, race and culture. As the German tribes passed through lands occupied by Gallic peoples, large numbers of Gauls seem to have joined them.[14]

In 113 BC some of the Teutones drifted into Noricum. Although the main purpose of the migration was a search for land, this did not prevent many groups of warriors from engaging in some enthusiastic plundering as they passed. Noricum was not a Roman province, but bordered on Illyricum and the Alps and its people were allied to Rome. The consul Cnaeus Papirius Carbo advanced with an army against the Teutones. The tribesmen sent ambassadors, explaining that they had been unaware of the alliance and had no wish to come into conflict with Rome. Carbo gave a conciliatory reply, but launched a surprise attack on the Germans' camp before the ambassadors returned. In spite of this deception the warriors responded vigorously and the Roman army was defeated with very heavy losses. Afterwards this band moved westwards into Gaul.[15] Four years later a group of migrants, who included the Tigurini – a subdivision of the Helvetii who lived in what is now Switzerland – approached the province of Transalpine Gaul (modern-day Provence) and defeated an army led by another consul, Marcus Junius Silanus. Following this success they asked the Senate for land on which to settle, but when this appeal was rejected did not mount an invasion, although the Tigurini raided the Roman province.

In 107 the Tigurini ambushed and killed the consul Lucius Cassius Longinus along with much of his army. The survivors surrendered and were sent under the yoke. These disturbances and the blows to Roman prestige prompted a rebellion amongst one of the tribes in Transalpine Gaul, but this was swiftly suppressed by Quintus Servilius Caepio. As part of this operation Caepio plundered the shrine of the Tectosages at Tolosa, where considerable amounts – some sources said over 100,000 pounds each of gold and silver – had been thrown into the sacred lake. Scandal erupted when this vast haul of treasure vanished on its way back to Italy. In 105 Caepio as proconsul was joined by the consul Cnaeus Mallius Maximus, for the Cimbri and Teutones had returned to threaten the Rhône frontier. Together the two men controlled one of the largest Roman forces ever to take the field when they met the invaders at Arausio (Orange). Bickering between the commanders contributed to a disaster where the casualties may well have rivalled those of Cannae.[16]

Five consular armies had been badly defeated by the northern barbarians and there seemed nothing to stop them from pushing on into Italy and sacking Rome just as the Gauls had done centuries before. The string of defeats was worse than anything the Romans had suffered for a hundred years. For the last time in their history, the nervous Romans openly carried out a human sacrifice, burying alive a Gallic and a Greek couple in the Forum Boarium just as they had done after Cannae. After the shameful conduct of Bestia and Albinus in Numidia, the events in the north prompted even more criticism of the *nobiles*. Silanus, Popillius (the legate in charge of the survivors of Cassius' army who had surrendered in 107), Mallius and Caepio were all prosecuted, the last both for incompetence and on a charge of having stolen the Tolosa loot. The disillusion with the established aristocracy combined with the rarity of successful commanders led to the popular demand that Marius should take charge and thus to his second consulship.

The movements of the tribes continued to be as erratic as ever, for after Arausio the bulk of the Cimbri and Teutones wandered westwards and tried unsuccessfully to cross into Spain. In 104 Marius and his army had no one to fight, but everyone knew that the threat remained and that the Romans had done nothing to deter it. Determined that only Marius was fit to stop the anticipated invasion and encouraged by the story of his stern impartiality in the case of Lusius and Trebonius, the *Comitia Centuriata* once again elected him consul. At another time his command might have been prorogued, but the Senate did not normally make such decisions until after the elections and Marius' supporters may well not have wanted to rely on their doing this. It is also true that proconsuls and propraetors were rarer in these decades than they had been earlier in the century. This third term was followed by a fourth, as once again the enemy failed to materialize, and it was only then, in 101, that the tribes finally launched their invasion.[17]

Little is known about the forces under Marius' command, but they most probably consisted of a strong consular army of two legions and two *alae*, these units anything up to 6,000 strong and supported by substantial contingents of auxiliaries, some 30,000–35,000 men all told. These had taken up and fortified a strong position on the banks of the River Rhône, where Marius had massed immense quantities of supplies. During the long wait for the enemy, he had set his soldiers to the construction of a canal to the sea, greatly improving communications and facilitating this gathering of provisions. The consul was determined that he should not be forced either to fight a battle or to move his position through shortage of food. Further to the east, the main passes into Cisalpine Gaul were guarded by his colleague, Quintus Lutatius Catulus, with a weaker consular army of just over 20,000 men. The Romans were aware that the tribes had split, the Teutones and Ambrones heading towards Marius, while the greater part of the Cimbri swung back into Noricum and were threatening the Alps. Reports of enemy movements came to the Roman commanders from the many Gallic tribes allied to Rome, or at least hostile to the arrival of great numbers of migrants. Sulla, the man who had captured Jugurtha, served Marius as a legate in 104 and a tribune in 103, during which time he was involved in several diplomatic missions with the Gauls, for instance persuading the Marsi into an alliance. Rather more unorthodox were the exploits of Quintus Sertorius, an officer who had been wounded at Arausio and only escaped by swimming the Rhône. Disguised as a tribesman – he had some rudimentary knowledge of the language – he infiltrated the enemy camp and provided a detailed report on their numbers and intentions.[18]

When the Teutones and Ambrones approached the Roman camp on the Rhône, the sight confronting the legionaries was a daunting one.

According to Plutarch, 'their numbers were limitless, they were hideous to look at, and their speech and war-cries were unique'.[19] Elsewhere he describes the barbarians as they came out to battle, the cavalry

> wearing helmets made to look like the gaping jaws of fearsome wild beasts or the heads of fantastic creatures which, topped with feathered crests, made the wearers look taller. They were also equipped with iron breastplates, and white shields which gleamed in the light. For throwing, each man had a javelin sharpened at both ends, and for fighting at close quarters they wielded large, heavy swords.[20]

All seemed to be big, heavily muscled men, with pale skin, fair hair and blue eyes. Descriptions of the Cimbri and Teutones were heavily influenced by the literary and artistic stereotype of the wild northern barbarian; strong but lacking in stamina; brave but without discipline. Though exaggerated, there was more than a little truth in the topos and tribal armies were usually clumsy forces. Tactics were simple, and ultimately relied on a headlong charge. This was a terrifying thing, and at times could swiftly sweep away an opponent – especially a nervous opponent – but if it was halted the tribesmen would tend to lose their enthusiasm and eventually give way.

The migrating tribes had been travelling and fighting together for years on end and it is probable that they had become somewhat more efficient than most tribal armies raised to defend their own territory or to launch a brief raid. Nevertheless the warriors were essentially individual fighters, all – and especially the noblemen and the well-equipped men of their followings – eager to win personal glory by conspicuously heroic acts. They were also supremely confident, despising the enemy whom they had routed in all previous encounters. These victories, even if they had been won over badly trained and even more poorly led Roman armies, inevitably had the opposite effect on Catulus' and Marius' men as they waited to meet the invasion. Rumour doubtless magnified the numbers and ferocity of the enemy and added to the legionaries' nervousness. Soldiers who entered a battle in a such a mood were extremely unlikely to stop a wild, screaming charge of terrifying, and up to this point invincible, warriors.[21]

Marius was aware of the mood of his soldiers, and for this reason declined the enemy's offer of battle when the tribes arrived and camped near his army. For several days the Teutones formed up on the plain between the two camps and issued boastful challenges. Such displays were a central part of intertribal warfare as they have been in so many other heroic warrior societies. One warrior hoping to win great fame shouted out that he wished

Marius to come forth and meet him in single combat. The consul suggested that the man should go and hang himself if he was so eager to die. When the German persisted, Marius sent out a diminutive and elderly gladiator, announcing that if the enemy champion would first defeat this man, he might then go out himself. This mockery of the Germans' code of honour – for a proud warrior required an appropriately distinguished opponent – was markedly different to Marcellus' willingness to match such overtly heroic behaviour.

Marius also kept his men under very strict control, stopping any from going out as units or individuals to meet the enemy. He wanted his men to see the barbarians at close quarters and get used to their appearance and the noises they made, rightly believing that this would make the enemy seem less terrifying. After a while his soldiers began to chafe at their commander's refusal to join battle. The Teutones ravaged the surrounding landscape and even launched an attack on the Roman camp in their efforts to force Marius to fight. The attack was easily repulsed and the tribes decided to advance past the static enemy and push on to the Alpine passes. It is quite probable that remaining in one place for such a long time had caused them to run short of food and fodder. Yelling out to the Roman soldiers to ask if they had any messages for their wives, as the Teutones would soon be visiting them, the barbarians passed on. Plutarch says that it took six days for them all to pass the camp, implying that this was because of their vast numbers, but, if there is any truth in this story, it more probably reflects the loose march discipline of the tribes.[22]

Marius waited for the enemy to pass and then left camp to follow them. For the next few days he shadowed them, keeping close without actually coming into contact, and carefully choosing his campsites so that they were protected by the terrain against attack. He had already announced to his soldiers that he had every intention of fighting, but was determined to wait for the right moment and place to ensure their victory. Marius very publicly included in his entourage a Syrian woman named Martha who had won popular fame as a prophetess. Rumour said that his wife Julia had encountered the woman at a gladiatorial fight, where she had successfully predicted the outcome of each encounter in the arena. Now she was carried on the march in a litter. Other omens predicting the army's success were widely reported. As with Scipio Africanus' claim to have been inspired by Neptune before the attack on New Carthage, even our sources were unsure as to whether the general actually believed in these signs or was simply manipulating his men's mood.[23]

Eventually, when the Teutones had reached Aquae Sextiae (Aix-en-Provence), Marius judged that the moment had at last arrived. As usual the Romans camped near the enemy in a strong position. In this case, however, the site had the major disadvantage of lacking an adequate source of fresh water. Frontinus blamed the advance party which always preceded the main column and marked out the shape of the next camp for this poor choice. Marius declared that this would give the men even more incentive to defeat the barbarians who were camped near the river and adjacent hot springs. However, his first priority was to ensure that the new camp was properly fortified and he set the grumbling legionaries to this task. The army's slaves (and even though Marius had reduced these to an absolute minimum, substantial numbers were still essential for such tasks as supervising the baggage train and looking after the draught and pack animals; some of these – *galearii* – wore helmets and rudimentary uniform and carried basic weapons) headed down to the river to draw water. The Germans were not expecting to fight that day, for the Romans had been following them for some time without displaying any inclination to seek battle, and were widely dispersed, many of them bathing in the springs.

A skirmish developed as the nearest warriors clashed with the Romans' slaves, the noise attracting growing numbers of Germans. The Ambrones were probably camped nearest to the disturbance, for after a while a substantial body of their warriors formed up and drove back the slaves. Plutarch claims that there were 30,000 of them, but this seems highly unlikely. They were met first by Ligurian auxiliaries – quite possibly posted to cover the construction of the Roman camp – and afterwards by other troops as Marius reluctantly reinforced the combat. The tribesmen became split into two bodies as only some managed to cross the river, and were then defeated separately. The Romans overran part of the enemy encampment, where even some of the women attacked them.[24]

The fight had not been planned or desired by Marius, but had occurred accidentally. The result was a Roman success, and a useful encouragement to the army who had now proved that they could defeat the feared enemy. Yet the engagement also meant that there had been no time to complete proper defences around the Roman camp. The army spent a nervous night listening to laments for the fallen being chanted by the enemy, and Marius all the while nervous of a sudden attack. Frontinus claims that he ordered a small party of men to go near to the tribal encampment and disturb their rest with sudden shouts. Plutarch makes no mention of this, and claims that there was no fighting on the following day as the Teutones needed time to muster their forces, which again may be an indication that they tended to move dispersed over a wide area. On the following night Marius picked out a detachment of 3,000 men under the command of Marcus Claudius Marcellus and sent them under cover of darkness to conceal themselves in some woods on high ground behind the enemy position. Frontinus says that the force consisted of both horse and foot and was accompanied by many of the army's slaves leading pack animals draped with saddlecloths so that from a distance they appeared to be cavalry. If this is true, then it must have been even more difficult for Marcellus to lead his party into position without either getting lost or being discovered. Once there he was out of communication with Marius, and his orders were to launch an attack on the enemy rear once battle had been joined. It was left to Marcellus' discretion to choose the precise moment.[25]

Early the next morning, Marius led his army out of camp and deployed in battle order on the slope in front. He sent his cavalry down into the plain, a gesture which swiftly had the desired result of provoking the Teutones into attacking. Officers rode around the Roman army, repeating the commander's orders that the men were to remain where they were and wait for the enemy to advance up the hill. Only when they were close, within effective range of some 15 yards or so, were the legionaries to hurl their *pila*, draw their swords and charge. Marius himself was in the front rank, determined to put into practice his own instructions and relying on his own skill at arms and fitness. This is one of the very few occasions when a Roman general chose to take a part in the fighting from the start of an action, for in such a position he could do little to control the battle. Yet the gesture was a powerful one, showing the soldiers that their commander was sharing every danger with them. For all their rigorous training and the encouragement of the defeat of the Ambrones, the legions were still facing a numerous and confident enemy and might collapse under the shock of the enemy charge. The need to stiffen his men's nerve in every possible way probably contributed to Marius' decision to lead in this way. He is not recorded as doing the same thing in any other battle, either before or after Aquae Sextiae.

The Germans attacked up the slope, the ground making it difficult for their bands to keep together and present a continuous wall of shields to the enemy. In the earlier engagement Plutarch described the Ambrones rhythmically clashing their weapons against shields and chanting their name as they advanced. The legions waited until they were close and then launched a volley of *pila*. The heavy throwing spears were given added force by being thrown from uphill and punched through shields, the slim shank sliding easily through the hole to reach and wound the man behind. Some tribesmen were killed or disabled, others whose shields had been pierced by a *pilum* which remained fixed in place had to discard them and fight unprotected. Impetus had gone from the charge and the close formation had been broken up. Then the legionaries charged, using their heavy shields to strike and unbalance the enemy, and so open the way for a thrust with their short swords. The Germans were first halted and then gradually driven back. The slope favoured the Romans, but when the Teutones withdrew to the plain, this advantage was lost and the tribesmen tried to re-establish a solid fighting line. It was then that Marcellus led his men into an attack against their rear. The new threat caused a panic and in a short time the army collapsed into rout. It is said that 100,000 prisoners were taken, along with a large amount of plunder. The Teutones and Ambrones were destroyed as a threat to Italy. As the army celebrated, news arrived that Marius had once again been elected consul. He decided to defer his triumph until the Cimbri had also been defeated.[26]

The news was not all good, for in the meantime the Cimbri had reached Italy. Catulus' men, not so carefully prepared for their encounter with the enemy, had panicked at the sight of the fierce barbarians, and had abandoned their positions in flight. The consul, realizing that nothing could stop them, had seized a standard and ridden to the head of the mob, stating that in this way the shame of the incident would fall on him for having led them, rather than on the soldiers. In spite of this failure, he was made proconsul and his command extended into the next year, for Marius' colleague was needed in Sicily to suppress a serious slave rebellion. The two Roman armies united and eventually encountered the Cimbri at Vercellae. Accounts of this action are not good, for there was subsequently to be considerable bickering between Marius' and Catulus' men over who had contributed most to the victory. The leaders of the Cimbri continued to wage war in an heroic manner which seemed archaic to the Romans. King Boeorix with a small troop of followers rode up to the Roman camp and issued a formal challenge to meet the legions at a time and place of their choosing. Marius was now more confident in his men's ability to defeat the enemy and, after stating that it was not the Romans' custom to let their enemy decide their course of action for them, accepted the offer. In a single day of fighting fought under the hot sun and in clouds of dust thrown up by so many tens of thousands of feet and hoofs, the Cimbri were cut to pieces. Some of the fleeing enemy committed suicide. Others were killed by their own wives, who then killed their children and finally themselves. Even so, vast numbers of prisoners were taken to be sold as slaves. Both Marius and Catulus celebrated a triumph.[27]

THE LATER YEARS – MARIUS IN POLITICS AND CIVIL WAR

Although the war was over, Marius was still determined to win another term as consul. He had clearly needed considerable political skill to launch his career in the first place, and in particular to exploit popular agitation and win election as consul for 107, but in later life his touch was less sure. Perhaps years as a general, where he could command and was not required to persuade, left him unprepared for public life in Rome itself, or maybe the mood had simply changed. His methods had certainly made him many enemies in the Senate. His fame won him a sixth consulship in 100, but he had trouble securing many of his aims, most notably a programme to settle many of his discharged soldiers on land in Transalpine Gaul, Sicily and Greece. Many of the veterans of Numidia had already received plots of land in North Africa. In the past Marius had been generous in grants of citizenship to allied soldiers who had fought well, and his desire to include these in his settlement programme was not welcomed by many at Rome.

In the end Marius allied himself with the radical tribune Lucius Appuleius Saturninus, a demagogue who frequently resorted to mob violence, and even – it was rumoured – assassination, to defeat his opponents. For a while Marius' veterans supported the tribune, resulting in a full-scale riot in the Forum. Then Saturninus went too far, arranging for the murder of the former tribune Memmius, leading to a break with Marius. The Senate passed its ultimate decree (the *senatus consultum ultimum*), which effectively suspended normal law and called on the magistrates to employ any means necessary to protect the Republic. This had last been used to justify the violent suppression of Caius Gracchus and his followers, and now it gave legality to similar use of force against Saturninus. Marius surrounded the tribune and persuaded him and his followers to surrender, but they were lynched before any decision could be made about their fate.[28]

After 100 BC Marius for a long time played little part in political life. For a decade Rome lurched towards a confrontation with many of her Italian allies who felt that they were not sharing sufficiently in the profits of an empire which their soldiers had helped to win. In 90 BC this developed into an open rebellion, the Social War, fought on a massive scale between armies that were identical in tactics, equipment and military doctrine. For a while things went badly for Rome, but eventually she won, as much by generous grants of citizenship to all those allies who had remained loyal, or quickly surrendered, as through the use of force. In the years after the war the franchise was extended to virtually the entire free population south of the River Po. Within a few decades Cisalpine Gaul was also included. Marius held an important command in the first year of the war, fighting with competence and skill though he failed to win a major victory. His health was poor and may have prevented his taking a prominent role in the later stages of the conflict.

One of the commanders who did distinguish himself was Sulla, who as the war was ending won election to the consulship in 88. Although a member of the patrician Cornelii, Sulla's family had decayed into obscurity and his rise had been almost as difficult as if he had been a 'new man'. In the eastern Mediterranean King Mithridates VI of Pontus had sought to expand his power while the Romans were weakened by the war in Italy. Over-aggressive Roman diplomacy convinced the king that war was inevitable, and led to his invasion of the province of Asia in 88, where he ordered the massacre of all Roman businessmen. The figure of 80,000 Romans and Italians killed in this episode is doubtless an exaggeration, but the number could well have been substantial. The reaction at Rome was similar to that which greeted the news of the fall of Cirta. Sulla was given the war with Mithridates as his province.

For some reason Marius was obsessed with taking this command for himself. In the 90s he had visited Asia as a private citizen and had evidently reached the conclusion that war with Pontus was only a matter of time. Marius was now 69, which was very elderly for a field command. Yet something, perhaps the knowledge that only recent military success had kept him at the centre of public life and certainly a rivalry with Sulla who had tried to steal his glory in Numidia, made him willing to go to any lengths to be sent against Mithridates. Once again he allied himself with a tribune, Publius Sulpicius Rufus, who used the Popular Assembly to bypass the Senate's decision and pass a law granting Marius the eastern command as proconsul. Sulla was outraged, seeing the opportunity for renewing the fortunes of his line being sacrificed to the vanity of another man. The six legions which he had raised for the war were nervous that Marius would take other troops instead – wars in the eastern Mediterranean were by now synonymous with easy victories and rich plunder. The consul paraded his troops and made a speech explaining his grievances. Then he marched his legions against Rome to 'free her from her tyrants'. Never before had a Roman army shown itself willing to use violent force to support its commander in a dispute with his political rivals. All save one of the senatorial officers with the army immediately disassociated themselves from the decision and left the army.[29]

Rome was easily occupied, for Sulla's opponents had no troops to oppose him. Sulpicius was killed, but Marius fled, eventually escaping to Africa. His health was poor and his sanity sometimes questionable. He is supposed sometimes to have hallucinated that he was actually leading an army against Pontus, bellowing out commands and making signals to imaginary troops. In the meantime Sulla led his army east to fight Mithridates, a conflict which lasted for several years. Marius was eventually able to rally sufficient supporters, many of them from the colonies established for his veterans, to return to Italy and seize Rome in 87. His arrival in the city was savage, his followers a rabble who murdered and looted without restraint. Without bothering with the formality of an actual election, Marius and his ally Cinna declared themselves consuls for the following year. However, age and illness finally took their toll and Marius died suddenly no more than a couple of weeks into this, his seventh term of office.[30]

Marius in his later years was a selfish, vindictive, and at times also pathetic figure, who plunged the Republic into the first of the civil wars which would in time destroy it. Little seemed left of the genuine talent which had won him his unprecedented string of consulships and brought him victory over the Cimbri and Teutones. If with hindsight it seems inevitable that the Roman Republic would triumph over a few migrating barbarian tribes, few Romans can have felt such confidence at the time and Marius seemed genuinely the hero and saviour of Italy. His achievement was considerable, ending the run of shattering defeats which the Cimbri and their allies had inflicted on the legions. Perhaps it is better to end this chapter not with the civil war, but with an incident from the Social War, which encapsulates the proper attitude for a 'good general'. Plutarch says that on one occasion Marius had taken up a very strong position and was blockaded by the enemy who tried to make him risk a battle. 'Pompaedius Silo, the most impressive and powerful of his opponents, said to him, "If you are a great commander, Marius, come out and fight." To this Marius replied, "If you are a great commander, make me fight even though I don't want to."'[31]

CHAPTER 6

GENERAL IN EXILE:
SERTORIUS AND THE CIVIL WAR

Quintus Sertorius (c. 125–72 BC)

In the open field he was as bold as any commander of his time, while for any campaign which required secrecy of movement or a sudden initiative in seizing strong positions or crossing rivers, or of operations which demanded speed, the deception of the enemy, or, if necessary, the invention of falsehoods, he possessed a skill which amounted to genius.[1]

'NEW MAN' AND ARISTOCRAT ALIKE, ROMAN SENATORS WERE FIERCELY competitive. Public life was a scramble for office and the opportunity to win fame and glory, where the ideal was to outshine the achievements not only of contemporaries but also of past generations. Even when not actually holding a magistracy or canvassing for election, senators strove always to advertise their successes and virtues, and missed no opportunity of adding to the number of those indebted to them for some favour. Some stressed their Hellenic sophistication, others such as Cato and Marius, their supposedly old-fashioned 'Italian' simplicity. Altars were dedicated and temples or other monuments built to commemorate achievements, and family events such as weddings and funerals became public occasions. Gladiatorial fights were first staged as part of funeral ceremonies, and whatever religious or sacrificial element they may originally have had, they soon became primarily a form of entertainment. Spectacular and exciting gladiatorial games drew large crowds who would be suitably impressed and grateful to the family who had staged and funded the event. Politics had always been competitive, but by the first century BC senators were forced to spend ever greater sums of money to stand any chance of success. The wealth lavished on buildings and games continued to rise, as each politician struggled to surpass his rivals. From 133 BC onwards, there was always the chance that such rivalry would culminate in violence. Sulla's decision to march on Rome in 88 led to nearly two decades of civil war and disturbance. An attempted coup in 63 was followed by years of mob violence in the 50s, and finally in 49 another bout of civil war which would not end until 31 when Caesar's adopted son Octavian defeated his last serious rival.

The Roman political élite was not unique in its competitiveness and desire to excel. The aristocracies of most Greek cities – and indeed of the overwhelming majority of other communities in the Mediterranean world – were just as eager to win personal dominance and often unscrupulous in their methods of achieving this. Roman senators were highly unusual in channelling their ambitions within fairly narrow, and universally recognized, boundaries. The internal disorder and revolution which plagued the public lives of most city states were absent from Rome until the last century of the Republic. Even then, during civil wars of extreme savagery when the severed heads of fellow citizens were displayed in the Forum, the Roman aristocracy continued to place some limits on what means were acceptable to overcome their rivals. A common figure in the history of the ancient world is the aristocratic exile – the deposed king or tyrant, or the general forced out when he was perceived to be becoming too powerful – at the court of a foreign power, usually a king. Such men readily accepted foreign troops to go back and seize power by force in their homeland – as the tyrant Pisistratus had done at Athens – or actively fought against their own city on their new protector's behalf, like Alcibiades.

Rome's entire history contains only a tiny handful of individuals whose careers in any way followed this pattern. The fifth-century BC, and semi-mythical, Caius Marcius Coriolanus probably comes closest, for when banished from Rome he took service with the hostile Volscians and led their army with great success. In the story he came close to capturing Rome itself, and was only stopped from completing his victory by the intervention of his mother. The moral of the tale was quintessentially Roman. However important it was for an individual to win fame and add to his own and his family's reputation, this should always be subordinated to the good of the Republic. The same belief in the superiority of Rome that made senators by the second century BC hold themselves the equals of any king ensured that no disappointed Roman politician sought the aid of a foreign power. Senators wanted success, but that success only counted if it was achieved at Rome. No senator defected to Pyrrhus or Hannibal even when their final victory seemed imminent, nor did Scipio Africanus' bitterness at the ingratitude of the State cause him to take service with a foreign king.

The outbreak of civil war did not significantly change this attitude, since both sides invariably claimed that they were fighting to restore the true Republic. Use was often made of non-Roman troops, but these were always presented as auxiliaries or allies serving from their obligations to Rome and never as independent powers intervening for their own benefit. Yet the circumstances of Roman fighting Roman did create many highly unorthodox careers, none more so than that of Quintus Sertorius, who demonstrated a talent for leading irregular forces and waging a type of guerrilla warfare against conventional Roman armies. Exiled from Sulla's Rome, he won his most famous victories and lived out the last years of his life in Spain, but never deviated from the attitudes of his class or thought of himself as anything other than a Roman senator and general.

EARLY CAREER AND THE CIVIL WAR

Sertorius was another 'new man', his family part of the local aristocracy in the Sabine city of Nussa. He was probably the first of his line to seek public office at Rome, for which he had been groomed from an early age, and certainly none of his ancestors had held an important Roman magistracy. A gifted orator and with some learning in law, he began to gain a reputation in the courts before embarking with enthusiasm on a period of military service. As mentioned in the last chapter, he managed to survive the disaster at Arausio in 105, swimming the Rhône in spite of his wounds and still managing to bring away his personal weapons. For the remainder of the war with the Cimbri and Teutones he served under Marius, winning both decorations and promotion on numerous occasions, most notably for going in disguise to spy on the enemy. A few years later in 97 he went as a military tribune to Spain, further adding to his reputation for courage and coolness when the troops he was wintering with at the Celtiberian town of Castulo were suddenly attacked by the population. The Roman soldiers there were poorly disciplined, neglectful of their duty and given to drunkenness. Plutarch does not say whether other Roman officers were present and another in command, but implies that Sertorius was not responsible for the troops' condition which would suggest that there was someone else in overall charge. It was perhaps because of this experience that in later years Sertorius would make it a rule never to billet soldiers in towns, ordering them instead to construct proper camps outside, even in winter, and live under strict military discipline.

The Roman garrison's behaviour may have provoked the Celtiberians to rebellion and certainly encouraged their expectation of success. Assistance was sought from the neighbouring Oretani, and on a given night their warriors were admitted into the city. Surprise was complete and many of the legionaries were slaughtered in their billets. Sertorius and a few companions managed to break out of the town, and he swiftly rallied as many other fugitives as he could find. Discovering a gate which the enemy had left both open and unguarded, Sertorius posted a detachment to seal off this means of exit and led the rest of his men back into the streets. Taking control of all the key positions in the town he then ordered his men to kill every Celtiberian male old enough to bear arms. Near disaster had been turned into victory, but Sertorius was not yet content and decided to punish the Oretani immediately. Ordering his men to dress in Spanish tunics taken from the dead, he marched them to the latter's town. The ploy worked and the Romans found the unsuspecting enemy waiting with open gates and cheering crowds to greet what they believed to be their returning raiding party. Many of those caught outside were swiftly killed and the town immediately surrendered. Most of its population was sold into slavery. Such deceptions were not uncommon. In 109 Metellus had retaken Vaga by putting some Numidian allied cavalry at the head of his column. The townsfolk, who had earlier massacred the Roman garrison, mistook these for Jugurtha's own troops and had let them in before they discovered their mistake. However, similar ploys did not always work and could be risky. On one occasion Hannibal had tried to use a force of Roman deserters posing as ordinary legionaries to capture a city in Italy, but the deception was revealed and the deserters ambushed and killed.[2]

Sertorius' exploits in Spain helped him to win election to the quaestorship, and during the Social War he was tasked with raising, training and leading troops, although his precise rank is unclear. Roman commanders and senior subordinates were expected to lead and direct their soldiers from just behind the fighting line, a style of leadership which inevitably involved considerable risk of wounding or death. Sertorius led in an especially bold fashion, inspiring his men with his contempt for the enemy and trusting to his personal skill at arms to protect himself from any attack. His methods brought him considerable battlefield success, although at the cost of a wound which permanently blinded him in one eye. Plutarch tells us that he was proud of this disfigurement, claiming that he was fortunate in having a symbol of valour which was always visible, unlike a medal which could only be worn occasionally. Proof of his growing fame was given when he attended the theatre at Rome and the crowd greeted him with enthusiastic cheers. Encouraged by this, Sertorius sought election to the post of tribune of the plebs for 88, but was publicly opposed by Sulla, then consul elect, and was defeated. The source for this opposition is unclear, but it led to a permanent breach between the two men. In the turmoil after Sulla had marched his legions on Rome and then departed to fight the eastern war, Sertorius sided with Cinna, who in turn allied himself to Marius.

The occupation of Rome by Cinna's and Marius' partisans was brutal in the extreme. Sertorius stood out amongst the leaders of this group by not indulging his personal hatreds and in his efforts to restrain others from their atrocities. Marius had recruited a gang of thugs from among the slaves of men he had executed and granted them licence to murder, rape and steal from anyone out of favour with the new regime. In the end, with Cinna's support, it was Sertorius who dealt with these so-called *Bardyaei*, surrounding them whilst they were asleep with a body of disciplined soldiers and killing them all, mostly with missiles. With Marius' sudden death, the worst of the excesses were over, and in 83 Sertorius became praetor, in time to take part in the war against the returning Sulla. Cinna had been lynched when some legions mutinied in the previous year, and supreme command devolved on a number of individuals, distinguished solely by their lack of any discernible military talent. Sertorius was placed in the unenviable position of having his advice ignored, but finding that the accuracy of his predictions concerning the inevitable disaster awaiting the chosen courses of action made him widely resented. It is doubtful that he felt much reluctance to go out to his province in Spain later in the year. However, Sulla's overwhelming victory in Italy freed his legions to stamp out any survivals of the Marian cause elsewhere, and Sertorius was soon expelled from his province. For a while he wandered around the western Mediterranean, meeting mainly with defeat and failure, until he managed to overcome a Sullan army in Mauretania. This success was followed by a direct appeal from a deputation of Lusitanians to return to the Spanish peninsula and rid them of an oppressive governor. From then on, his fortunes improved dramatically.[3]

THE WAR IN SPAIN, 80–72 BC

These Lusitanians were most probably representatives of the highly Romanized and settled communities, rather than from the wilder groups on or beyond the margins of the Roman province. Although Sertorius was to draw much of his strength from the indigenous peoples of Spain, the conflict was always fought as part of the civil war and not an attempt to win independence from Rome. His armies also included some troops originally raised in Italy, as well as contingents formed from the Roman settlers in the peninsula. In the beginning, his forces were not numerous, and Plutarch tells us that at first they numbered 2,600 legionaries, some 700 Libyans he had acquired during his time in North Africa, 4,000 Lusitanian lightly equipped infantry (or *caetrati* – the name was derived from the small round shields which they carried), and about 700 mixed cavalry. The whole force was supported at first by no more than twenty cities. He also possessed, or was to acquire, a small navy with which to support operations on land. Taken as a whole, his resources were dwarfed by those of Sulla's generals in Spain, who altogether are said to have disposed more than 120,000 infantry, 6,000 cavalry and 2,000 skirmishers. Yet from the beginning Sertorius' operations met with success after success, and his opponents failed to co-ordinate their war effort effectively. In the first year he defeated the governors of both the Spanish provinces, and in the next his troops defeated and killed the replacement governor of Nearer Spain, one Lucius Domitius. The new proconsul of Further Spain was Quintus Caeclius Metellus Pius, son of the man who had campaigned against Jugurtha. He suffered several reverses, and one of his legates was badly defeated and killed, as he tried to deny the coastal areas of Lusitania to Sertorius.[4]

With each success Sertorius' power grew. Though doubtless short of money and all the things necessary to support his campaigns, he always treated the provincials fairly and generously, and insisted that his troops and officers did the same. He took particular care of the local aristocracies, usually granting freedom and restoring their property to those who had opposed him once they capitulated. At Osca (possibly modern-day Huesca) he established and paid for a school for the sons of the wealthy and influential, where the pupils dressed in togas and received a properly Roman education. That these children served also as hostages for their good faith did not reduce the enthusiasm of the Spanish aristocracy for this open declaration of willingness to admit their families into the élite of the Roman province. For Sertorius always declared himself to be a properly appointed magistrate of the Roman Republic. From the many exiles who fled to him from an Italy dominated by Sulla's supporters he formed a 'Senate', and each year held elections to appoint magistrates.[5]

In spite of its mixed composition, Sertorius also imposed Roman standards of discipline throughout his army. All of his troops were organized into cohorts. Most were equipped in Roman fashion, but all were well trained and drilled both as individuals and as formations. Soldiers were encouraged to use highly decorated arms and armour, both to discourage their loss and to increase the men's pride in themselves. They were expected to obey orders and misbehaviour was punished harshly. In an incident reminiscent of the Bardyaei, Sertorius is said to have executed an entire detachment of Romans who had gained a reputation for extreme brutality in their treatment of the local civilians. In at least one case he did exploit the native military tradition, taking a personal bodyguard of Celtiberians. These men were bound to their leader with a solemn oath, so that they were not supposed to outlive him if he were killed, in return for which he provided them with weapons, food and the chance to win glory. The practice was reasonably common amongst the tribes of Spain, as well as Gaul and Germany, and provided some chieftains with fanatically loyal bands of followers. It seems to have been quite normal for warriors to bind themselves to chieftains of other tribes, so the transferral of the same relationship to a Roman commander was not in that sense unusual. Julius Caesar would later have a similar guard of 900 German and Gallic cavalry.[6]

At times his forces were augmented by contingents of allied Spanish warriors who had not had time to undergo proper training, forcing the commander to devise ways of restraining their enthusiasm to fight in unfavourable circumstances. One object lesson is preserved in several accounts. Sertorius is supposed to have brought out two horses, one healthy and the other small and in a poor condition. He then ordered one of his strongest men to pull the tail off the small horse, whilst at the same time instructing a tiny soldier to removed the big horse's tail one hair at a time. Eventually, after much fruitless effort, the strong soldier was forced to give up his attempt, whilst his smaller colleague slowly completed his task. Sertorius declared that this showed how even the most dangerous opponent could be defeated if gradually worn down in small skirmishes, for continuous pressure is more effective than mere brute force.[7]

Just as Marius had paraded his soothsayer and Africanus had told his soldiers of the messages given to him by the gods in his dreams, Sertorius added a mystical element to his leadership. At some point a hunter had presented him with a young doe, which the general fed with his own hand until it became completely tame. After a while he began to claim that the animal had been sent to him by the goddess Diana, and that it brought him messages. Sometimes he would announce news brought to him by scouts or messengers as if they came from the fawn, which was also decorated with garlands of victory whenever he heard of a success won by other detachments of his army. Our sources believed that such methods greatly impressed the superstitious Spaniards.[8]

The sources for Sertorius' campaigns are meagre, and do not permit the reconstruction of a detailed narrative of the war in Spain, still less permit analysis of individual actions. Instead they provide us with a broad overview, and many stories of his skill as a leader and wiliness as a general. On the whole the surviving accounts present an unfavourable portrait of Metellus, who is depicted as an elderly and lethargic leader. More complex is their portrayal of Cnaeus Pompey, who was appointed by the Senate to govern Nearer Spain in 77 BC, and was already renowned as one of the Republic's most successful commanders and later as Caesar's opponent in the Civil War. Pompey's highly unorthodox career is the subject of the next chapter, but at this point it is worth emphasizing that at 29 he was very young for a Roman general. Desire to contrast his youthful energy with Metellus' aged caution may well have encouraged our sources to treat the latter in a less favourable way. Sertorius is said to have nicknamed Pompey 'Sulla's pupil'. Metellus he had even more scornfully dubbed 'that old woman'.[9]

Around the same time Sertorius had himself received some reinforcement from Italy. In 78 one of the consuls, Marcus Aemilius Lepidus, had led a rebellion against the Senate, rallying many disaffected Marians to his cause. He had been defeated, but some of his supporters led by Marcus Perperna Vento escaped to Spain. Perperna came from an established, if not notably pre-eminent family, and had pride greatly in excess of his actual capacity, for his military record was an unbroken string of defeats, several of them inflicted by Pompey. At first he disdained to place himself and his men under the command of a new man like Sertorius, but eventually the issue was decided for him when his army heard that Pompey was on his way to Spain and forced him to join the successful general. Pompey was unable to move against Sertorius until 76, for he was forced to fight some of the local tribes as he marched through the province of Transalpine Gaul. In commemoration of victories won en route to his new command, he would later erect a triumphal monument in the Pyrenees.[10]

In 77 Sertorius and his quaestor Lucius Hirtuleius had inflicted several defeats on Metellus, thwarting his attempt to capture the main town of the Langobritae. Not only did they manage to smuggle water into the town in spite of the enemy blockade, but they also brought out a large number of non-combatants. Soon Metellus' legions were running out of supplies and, after a foraging party was ambushed and nearly destroyed, he was forced to withdraw. Before this operation Sertorius had even invited Metellus to face him in a single combat, an idea for which the latter's soldiers showed considerable enthusiasm, their morale having dropped to a low ebb. Pompey's arrival did much to reinvigorate both army and commander. Sertorius decided to take the measure of his new opponent before risking a pitched battle, and gave strict instructions to his subordinates to avoid a major action with the main army of either Metellus or Pompey. Two of Pompey's legates leading small detachments were defeated individually, but the young general advanced with great confidence when he learned that Sertorius himself was besieging the city of Lauron (probably somewhere near modern Valencia).

Orosius – a very late source who must be treated with considerable caution – claims that Pompey had 30,000 foot and 1,000 horse, and was opposed by Sertorius with twice as many infantry and 6,000 cavalry, but such a great numerical advantage seems unlikely. A race for control of high ground dominating the town was won by Sertorius, but then Pompey closed in behind him, apparently trapping his opponent between his own legions and the town. His confidence is said to have been so great that he sent messengers to the townsfolk inviting them to climb onto their walls and watch as he smashed the enemy. It was only then that he discovered that Sertorius had left 6,000 men in his old camp on high ground which was now behind Pompey's position. If he deployed his army for a full attack on Sertorius' main force then he would himself be taken in the rear. Instead of ending the war in a swift victory, Pompey was forced to watch impotently as Sertorius prosecuted the siege, for he felt that to withdraw altogether would be an open admission of the superiority of the enemy.

This was only the beginning of the lesson which Sertorius had decided to teach 'Sulla's pupil' at Lauron. During the siege there were only two areas from which Pompey's army could draw forage and firewood. One was only a short distance from his camp, but this was continually being raided by Sertorius' light infantry. After a while, Pompey decided that his foraging parties should switch their attention to the other, more distant, area, which his opponent had deliberately left unmolested. The time required to travel to the area, gather forage, and return ensured that any expedition in this direction could not complete its task in a single day. Yet at first this did not appear to be a serious risk, as there continued to be no sign of any enemy activity in this area. Finally, when Pompey's men had become complacent, Sertorius decided to ambush an expedition which he had observed leaving the opposing camp. He sent out Octavius Graecinus with a strong force of ten cohorts armed as legionaries – we do not know whether these troops were Spanish or Roman or a mixture of both – and ten cohorts of Spanish light infantry *caetrati*, supported by 2,000 cavalry commanded by Tarquitius Priscus.

They moved by night, avoiding detection by Pompey's main force, and took up a position along the route which they knew the convoy would have to take on its return journey. These officers amply rewarded the trust Sertorius had invested in them, making a careful reconnaissance of the ground before leading their troops into position. The ambush force was concealed in a wood with the *caetrati* in front and the heavy infantry in close support. The cavalry were stationed in the rear to prevent a neighing horse from revealing the position. The whole force then waited for dawn, but it was not until the third hour that the Pompeian convoy began to lumber along the path in front of them. March discipline was poor, and many of the men who should have been acting as escort had wandered off to forage or loot. The sudden attack of the *caetrati* – fighting in a way which was traditional for many of the Spanish peoples – threw the whole column into confusion, many isolated individuals being cut down. Pompey's officers then began to react and tried to rally the escorts and form a rough fighting line, but before this was complete the Sertorian close order cohorts had emerged from the woodland and charged. The Pompeians fled, their rout harried by Priscus and his 2,000 horsemen.

In any period of history, broken infantry have been at the mercy of well-handled cavalry. Priscus certainly seems to have known his trade. He had detached 250 men and sent them riding by another pass to emerge ahead of the fugitives and cut them off from the sanctuary of Pompey's main camp. News of the ambush had prompted Pompey to send a legion under the command of Decimus Laelius to the convoy's rescue. Priscus' cavalry seemed to give way before this new force, wheeling off to the right, but their officers kept them under tight control and took them round to threaten the legion's rear. Soon Laelius was under attack from Octavius and the main force in front, and from Priscus in the rear. As the situation worsened Pompey rapidly got his entire army on the move in the hope of mounting a rescue. As they moved out of camp so did Sertorius' main force, which deployed in battle order on the opposite hillside. If Pompey advanced to aid Laelius, then he would be exposed to a massive attack from the rear and would most probably suffer a catastrophic defeat. He was therefore forced to look on as the ambush mopped up both the convoy and most of Laelius' command. Frontinus, our main source for this episode, refers to a lost passage of Livy which claimed that Pompey suffered some 10,000 casualties in this engagement.[11]

Once the population of Lauron realized that their visible ally was unable to aid them, they surrendered to Sertorius. He permitted the population to go free, but razed the town itself to the ground in an effort to complete Pompey's humiliation. It was an extremely disappointing end to Pompey's first campaign in the peninsula, a bitter blow to a man who liked to style himself as a second Alexander the Great, but who may now have realized that he was for the first time facing a commander of real ability. Perhaps his only consolation came from Sertorius' reluctance to fight a massed battle with him.

Things got off to a better start for Pompey in 75, for this time he came into contact with a force led by Sertorius' subordinates, including the inept Perperna, and swiftly defeated them. Although he had planned to join forces with Metellus before confronting Sertorius himself, this easy victory seems to have led to overconfidence and a reluctance to share the credit for winning the war. Pompey hurried on to attack the main enemy army which was encamped near the River Sucro. Sertorius, knowing that Metellus was approaching and preferring to fight a single opponent rather than wait for the two to unite, this time accepted his challenge to battle. Both Pompey and Sertorius stationed themselves at the beginning of the fighting with the troops on the right flank – which was often held to be the place of honour – and left subordinates in charge of the rest of the line. After a while reports reached Sertorius that Pompey's men were driving back the left wing of his army. Quickly he rode to that part of the field and set about restoring the situation, rallying units in flight and leading up those reserve troops which had remained steady.

His presence injected a fresh impetus into his men, who stopped the enemy and then counter-attacked, driving them back in rout. In the chaos Pompey himself was wounded in the thigh and almost captured, but managed to escape on foot when his pursuers were distracted by the expensive trappings on his horse's harness and began to squabble over this plunder. However, in his absence, Sertorius' own right flank had been routed by Pompey's legate Afranius. As was often the case in ancient battles, these troops made no effort to exploit the breakthrough by rolling up the rest of the enemy line, but simply kept on going to attack and loot

Sertorius' camp. Later in the day Sertorius was able to form up sufficient troops to attack the scattered enemy and inflict heavy losses on them, whilst also retaking the encampment. On the following day Metellus' legions arrived, dissuading Sertorius from joining battle again. He is supposed to have exclaimed that he would have finished off 'that boy' if that 'old woman' had not come up.[12]

With their armies united, Metellus and Pompey were too strong for Sertorius to attack, but their very numbers presented serious problems when it came to keeping the troops supplied. As they operated in the plains around Saguntum, they found their foraging parties continually under attack and in the end were forced to accept battle on Sertorius' terms. He had been joined by Perperna, augmenting the strength of his forces. Additional encouragement to the men's, and especially the Spaniards', morale came when his white doe, which had gone missing, was found again and restored to health. The ensuing action was fought near the River Turia, and Metellus' and Pompey's legions may have been caught separately. Sertorius defeated Pompey again, driving his troops back and killing his legate and brother-in-law, Memmius. Metellus also came under heavy pressure and was himself wounded by a javelin. Surrounded by a group of his men, he was carried to safety, and if anything the incident seemed to stiffen the resolve of his men. Sertorius' troops were probably tired, and may well have fallen into disorder during their successful advance, for they were now driven back and only their commander's skill prevented a complete rout. On the following day he seems to have launched a surprise attack on Metellus' camp and, although this was driven off, it did slow the enemy's pursuit.

Yet Metellus and Pompey still scented victory, and eagerly followed the enemy as he withdrew back into the mountains. Sertorius halted when he reached the town of Clunia. Believing that they had cornered him at last, his two opponents began a blockade, but Sertorius had in fact dispatched messengers to allied communities instructing them to raise reinforcements and send them to him as soon as possible. When the large force approached, he attacked and broke through the blockade to join them. Rather than engaging the enemy's main force, Sertorius began to attack their supply lines, raiding widely and ambushing any isolated detachments. The two generals were soon forced to withdraw back to the coastal regions, but even there maritime raiders harassed the coast and intercepted convoys of ships bringing supplies. There were few enough of these to begin with, for the Senate in Rome had sent little assistance to its commanders in Spain since the beginning of the war.

Although Sertorius was always faced with the problem of mounting a war effort funded only by the revenue gained from control of parts of the peninsula, and had no ready access to supplies of fresh Roman, rather than local, recruits, his enemies were not much better off. In the winter of 75–74, Pompey wrote to the Senate complaining of their lack of support, and saying that supplies and money barely sufficient for a single year's campaigning had had to last him for three. His own funds, which he had freely spent to maintain the army, were exhausted, and the legions were now on the brink of starvation, with their pay hugely in arrears. The historian Sallust gives a version of the letter which ends with Pompey threatening to bring his army back to Italy. Whether or not this was so explicit or merely implied in the original, the desired result was achieved and a reinforcement of two legions along with considerable funds was swiftly dispatched to his aid.[13]

At about the same time Sertorius received an embassy from Mithridates of Pontus. Defeated by Sulla and forced to make peace in 85, a number of incidents, most notably the Roman annexation of Bithynia, had convinced the king that only the defeat of Rome could prevent the steady erosion of his power. Therefore he offered Sertorius an alliance, promising to send warships and money in return for Roman military advisers to retrain his army in the methods of the legions, and acknowledgement of his rightful claim to territories including the provinces of Asia and Bithynia. Sertorius put the matter before his Senate, most of whom were inclined to agree, since the loss of lands which were not under their control seemed a small price to pay for aid. His own attitude was different and once again emphasized that he saw himself first and foremost as a servant of the Republic, for he granted Mithridates the right to everything except Asia, which was an old and well-established Roman province. On hearing this reply, Mithridates is supposed to have wondered what sort of terms would be demanded by Sertorius had he actually been in control of Rome and not penned into a distant corner of Spain. Nevertheless the treaty was confirmed and forty galleys and the great sum of 3,000 talents of silver duly sent by the king.[14]

In the next years Metellus and Pompey again co-operated during the campaigning season, but their strategy was now far more methodical and consisted of the systematic capture of strongholds loyal to the enemy. At times Sertorius was able to thwart their attacks, replacing the timber fortifications which Pompey had burned at Pallantia before his arrival and then moving on to defeat an enemy force outside Calagurris, inflicting 3,000 casualties. Fortunes were mixed, but the final defeat of Sertorius seemed no nearer. Metellus was desperate enough to have a huge price put on his enemy's head, promising not only land and wealth but the right for any exile to return to Rome if they killed Sertorius.[15]

Yet if Sertorius was not losing the war, it was by now clear that he could not win it. Only in Spain, under his command, were there any Romans who still fought against the Senate established by Sulla during his dictatorship. Sulla had retired to private life in 79 and died less than a year later. Most of his enemies were dead, and the Senate which he had enlarged with his partisans had guided the Republic for long enough to convince virtually every citizen of its legitimacy. Certainly, as the years passed the chances of Sertorius and his senate being recognized as the rightful leaders of the Republic dwindled to nothing. With Sulla gone the main reason for the war had vanished for, like all of Rome's civil wars, the causes of this conflict were the personal rivalries of individual politicians. Even if the Senate was slow in bringing its full resources of waging war to bear against the rebels in Spain, there was no longer any doubt that it would eventually win. Sertorius seems to have realized this, and Plutarch tells us that after several of his victories he sent envoys to Metellus and Pompey offering to lay down his arms. His only condition was that he be permitted to return home to Rome and live there in retirement as a private citizen. These offers were always refused. The same drive for absolute victory which made the Romans so difficult to defeat in foreign wars ensured that their internal struggles were always waged to the death. Compromises and settlements between enemies were very rare and never proved permanent. It was perhaps a growing sense of despair which prompted Sertorius to abandon his previously frugal habits and give himself over to drunkenness and womanizing.

Sertorius fought on, but the same sense of futility pervaded the Romans with his army. There was growing resentment of the fact that he kept a bodyguard of Celtiberians, and rumours that he did not trust his own countrymen. Perperna carried on a concerted whispering campaign to subvert the authority of his commander. The Roman officers with the army became increasingly brutal in their treatment of the natives, in spite of Sertorius' realization of the need to maintain loyalty. Such behaviour prompted rebellions, after which he felt forced to inflict savage punishment on the communities. A number of the boys attending his school were executed in response to acts of disloyalty by their parents. Over time the just administration of the provincials degenerated into despotism and the goodwill developed over the years rapidly vanished. Deserters, both Roman and Spanish, began to defect in some numbers to the enemy. The Romans may have been encouraged by legislation passed at Rome to grant pardons to Lepidus' former supporters if they gave in. Perperna had no intention of surrender and wanted instead to seize supreme command for himself. In 72 he entertained Sertorius and some of his bodyguard at a feast and, once they were drunk, ordered soldiers to kill them all. Though his ambition raged unchecked, Perperna's skill as a leader had not increased and he was quickly defeated by Pompey, who thus brought the war to an end.[16]

Sertorius was a tragic, rather romantic, figure who had the misfortune to commit himself to the losing side in a civil war. By the standards of the Roman political élite he was a decent and extremely capable man. Although a 'new man', he should under normal circumstances have had a highly successful career. His gifts as a leader, administrator and commander were of the highest order – Frontinus recounts far more of his stratagems than of those of any but a handful of other Roman generals – and shine through in spite of the meagre sources for his campaigns.

CHAPTER 7

A ROMAN ALEXANDER:
POMPEY THE GREAT

Cnaeus Pompeius Magnus (c.106–48 BC)

> But it is as relevant to the glory of the Roman Empire as of one man to mention
> at this point all the names and triumphs of Pompey the Great, for they equalled
> in brilliance the exploits of Alexander the Great and virtually of Hercules
> himself.[1]

FROM THE EARLIEST DAYS OF THE REPUBLIC, ROMAN ARMIES WERE LED BY
elected magistrates or men granted pro-magisterial *imperium* by the Senate.
The decision to give the Spanish command to Scipio Africanus in 210 was
exceptional given his youth, but was made legal by a vote in the *Comitia
Centuriata*. It was an extreme example of the flexibility of Rome's political
system which permitted the relaxation of the normal regulations governing office-holding at times of crisis. The multiple consulships of Marcellus and
Fabius Maximus, and the election of Africanus and Aemilianus to the senior
magistracy when they were technically too young, were other instances of
this willingness to bend the rules in the interests of winning a war. Yet, once
the victory was won, public life rapidly returned to normal, and such careers
became impossible, at least until the next emergency.

Even then it was only for a handful of gifted and popular individuals
that the conventional pattern of office-holding could be altered. Marius' run
of five consecutive consulships was unprecedented, but essentially confirmed the principle that magistrates and thus commanders were chosen
by the electorate, even if the latter were normally not expected to select the
same individual repeatedly. No other senator was able to copy Marius and

win election as consul even in two consecutive years, at least until the conditions of civil war effectively ended open elections. In this one respect – that simply because one man was given an extraordinary career it did not mean that all senators could expect to emulate him – Pompey the Great's run of commands conformed to the spirit of the emergency measures which had granted early responsibility to Scipio. In every other important way his career was a radical subversion of the traditions of public life, for he ignored the *cursus honorum* and took his own path to fame.[2]

It began when the 23-year-old Pompey raised an army to fight in the Civil War. He had no authority to do this, for he held no rank or office and was simply a private citizen. In 210 Scipio had at least held the aedileship and was probably a member of the Senate, which Pompey most certainly was not, whilst Africanus' command was formally conferred on him by the Senate and People of Rome. Pompey acted entirely on his own initiative, equipping his army and paying his soldiers from his personal fortune. Once the force existed, neither it nor its commander could be ignored. For more than a decade Pompey was employed first by Sulla and then by the Senate in a series of campaigns, culminating in the war with Sertorius. At no point during these years did he show any desire to embark on a more conventional career, preferring the greater responsibilities which he had assumed by his actions. In 70 BC he joined the Senate and became consul simultaneously, having already been awarded two triumphs. Still only 36, he remained active and was given even more spectacular commands in subsequent years. After such an unorthodox career, it is all the more surprising that Pompey ended his life as the apparent champion of the establishment against the maverick Julius Caesar.

AN UNELECTED GENERAL

Pompey was not a 'new man' – his father Cnaeus Pompeius Strabo had been quaestor in 104, praetor in 92 and consul in 89 – but nor was his family part of the well-established plebeian aristocracy, although they were certainly extremely wealthy, with extensive estates in Picenum. Like Marius, Pompey began life with only two names, for Strabo or 'squinty' was merely a nickname at the expense of his father's appearance. Strabo played a distinguished role in the Social War, taking Asculum by siege during his consulship. Although his ability was widely respected, he was never a popular man, either with his soldiers or other senators, and the distribution of the spoils of Asculum reinforced his reputation for greed. When the Civil War broke out in 88 BC, Pompeius Strabo had no close connection with the leaders on either side, and his attitude was for a long time ambivalent. The Senate, presumably with Sulla's support, had decided to replace Strabo with the other consul for 88, Quintus Pompeius Rufus, who may have been a distant relation. Rufus was delayed in setting out, and only with the army for just over a day before he was murdered by a mob of soldiers. Strabo was widely believed to have orchestrated the lynching and immediately resumed command of the army. In the following year he eventually sided against Cinna and Marius, but following an indecisive battle he died suddenly. One tradition maintained that he had been struck by lightning during a storm, another that he had fallen prey to a disease which had spread through the camp, but it is possible that his death had not been natural. Such was his unpopularity that his funeral procession was mobbed and the corpse desecrated.[3]

The teenage Pompey had served with his father's staff since 89. Little is known about his activities during the campaign, but he did thwart an attempt by one of Cinna's partisans to assassinate Strabo. In the confused aftermath of this failed attempt, the camp fell into uproar, and it was the 18-year-old Pompey who did most to rally the men and restore order. According to Plutarch he tearfully begged the soldiers to calm down and obey orders and, when a crowd of soldiers had begun to flee from the camp, he threw himself down in the gateway and defied the fugitives to trample over him. The youth was considerably more popular than his father, and most of the soldiers were shamed into returning to their tents. After Strabo's death, Pompey returned to Rome where he was prosecuted for the misappropriation of much of the plunder taken from Asculum. Eventually it emerged that one of his father's freedmen was chiefly responsible, but Pompey's acquittal had as much to do with the skill of his advocates, his own good looks, confident bearing and ready answers, and, most especially, a secret betrothal to the judge's daughter, Antistia. Word of this quickly spread, so that when the verdict was finally announced the watching crowd immediately bawled out the wedding-cry *'Talassio!'* – a slightly crude Roman equivalent of 'You may now kiss the bride.' The atmosphere in Rome was very tense in the years when it was uncertain whether Sulla would return, and the city was an especially uncomfortable place for a man whose father had fought against the current regime. Pompey soon retired to the family estate in Picenum and remained there for some time.[4]

By 84 Cinna began more urgent preparations to meet Sulla's invasion. Pompey decided to join his army, but was treated with considerable suspicion and soon returned to Picenum. Shortly afterwards Cinna was murdered during a mutiny by some of his own soldiers and supreme command assumed by the consul Cnaeus Papirius Carbo. In 83 news arrived that Sulla was at last en route to Italy, and Pompey resolved not to risk another rebuff from the Marians and to switch his allegiance to the returning proconsul. Quite a number of young aristocrats, especially those who had lost relatives in Marius' and Cinna's purges, would similarly join Sulla after he had landed at Brundisium, but Pompey was determined to stand out and not to arrive empty-handed. Cautiously at first, the 23-year-old began to recruit troops in Picenum. His own popularity, and doubtless a general reluctance to upset the wealthiest local landowner, ensured an enthusiastic response both from communities and individuals. Carbo's agents were unable to stop the flood of recruits and were soon forced to flee. In a short time Pompey was able to organize some cavalry and an entire legion, appointing centurions and organizing it into cohorts in the proper way, and using his personal fortune to buy the necessary equipment and to pay the legionaries' wages. He also purchased food and the transport needed for the army to carry its supplies. In time a further two legions would be raised and financed in the same manner. Everything was done carefully and in the approved manner, save for the essential detail that Pompey had no legal authority to raise any troops at all.

When he was ready Pompey began to march south to join Sulla. Several enemy armies attempted to intercept him, but the forces opposing Sulla were, as ever, dogged by divided and incompetent leadership. It should also be remembered that whilst Carbo and his allies had raised an enormous number of troops – Appian claims some 250 cohorts – the vast majority of these were as raw and untrained as Pompey's men. Threatened by three forces, each as large or larger than his own, Pompey gathered his legion together and attacked the nearest enemy, which included a contingent of Gallic auxiliary cavalry. The young, self-appointed general began the action when he personally led his cavalry into the attack. Singling out the leader of the Gallic horsemen who came out to meet him, Pompey spurred ahead and struck their leader down, just as Marcellus had once killed Britomarus. The death of their chief panicked the Gauls, who fled to the rear, spreading confusion amongst the rest of the army, which in turn dissolved into rout.

This was the first of several victories which Pompey would win before he had even reached Sulla and his main army. The welcome he received exceeded even his own hopes, for the proconsul dismounted to greet the young general, hailing him as *imperator*, the appellation traditionally awarded only to a victorious commander. Pompey became one of Sulla's most trusted senior subordinates, and the latter never failed to rise from his seat or to bare his head as a mark of respect whenever his young ally appeared, honours which he notably failed to extend to many more distinguished men.[5]

Neither side in the war was paying much respect to precedent and law, for Carbo had himself elected consul again for 82, taking Marius' son, who was not yet 30, as his colleague. In the spring Pompey was sent to Cisalpine Gaul to assist another of Sulla's men, the proconsul Metellus with whom he would later serve in Spain. The two men won a number of victories in Northern Italy while Sulla himself took Rome. Some of Carbo's Samnite allies lured him away and almost retook the city, but he managed to return in time to win a narrow victory at the battle of the Colline Gate. At one point during the fighting Sulla had ridden to his left wing, which was coming under heavy pressure, and was singled out as a target by two of the enemy. Intent on controlling the battle, he failed to notice the threat and could well have been killed had his groom not been more alert and whipped the general's white horse forward to avoid the javelins thrown at him. The Roman style of command exposed the general to considerable danger, even when he stayed out of the actual fighting.[6]

His hold on Rome now firmly established, Sulla had himself made *dictator rei publicae constituendae* (dictator to restore the Republic), reviving the old supreme magistracy, but placing no six-month limit on its powers. The vengeance he wrought on his enemies was no less brutal than that of Marius and Cinna, but was in many ways far more organized. Samnite prisoners taken at the Colline Gate had been massacred en masse, but in Rome itself Sulla followed a more formal process and posted lists of names in the Forum. The men named in these documents were 'proscribed', immediately losing all their rights as citizens and making it lawful for anyone to kill them. The corpse, or most often the dead man's severed head, had to be brought to the authorities as proof of death and many of these gruesome trophies soon decorated the Forum and other public spaces of Rome. Most of the victims' property went to Sulla and the Treasury, but the dictator was generous in distributing such profits amongst his supporters and many of these became extremely rich. Later there would be many rumours of names being added to the proscription lists simply to satisfy personal hatreds or through sheer avarice.

The chief casualties of the proscriptions fell amongst senators and equestrians, because of both their political significance and their wealth. Afterwards Sulla enrolled many new members into the Senate, doubling its previous size to around 600. Over the next year or so he introduced a programme of legislation, reducing the power of the tribunes of the plebs and making this office less attractive to the ambitious by forbidding them to hold any further magistracies. The courts were reformed and the traditional restrictions on office holding and the activities of magistrates and governors either re-stated or strengthened. Sulla's reform programme as dictator was the most comprehensive until Julius Caesar gained the same office following his own victory in a later civil war.

Yet on balance what is most striking is how little Sulla sought to change the basic nature of the Republic. For all the viciousness with which the leaders in Rome's internal struggles fought each other, these conflicts rarely had any significant ideological basis. Men fought to seize power or to prevent it passing to a hated rival. Though some revolutionaries made promises of grants of land or abolition of all standing debts in order to win support, no one seems to have planned to change the way the Republic worked in any of its fundamentals. The chief aim was always for a leader and his associates to supplant those who currently dominated the State. Sulla won such a victory, and the cornerstone of his reforms was to pack the Senate with his partisans.

Although the Civil War was virtually over in Italy, Marian sympathizers continued the struggle in some of the provinces. Sulla sent Pompey to Sicily in the autumn of 82 and for the first time he was granted some official power when the Senate gave him propraetorian *imperium*. The campaign did not take long, for the Marian propraetor Perperna swiftly fled, but it was completed by the capture and execution of Carbo himself. Pompey incurred some opprobrium from the manner in which he treated the enemy leader, although the latter won only scorn through his failure to meet execution with the courage expected of a Roman aristocrat. There were other stories of the young commander relishing the licence derived from almost unrestricted power, but on the whole Pompey was believed to have behaved with more restraint than many of Sulla's men.[7]

After Sicily he was sent to Africa, leading a massive invasion force of six legions. His forces landed at Utica just outside Carthage, which was now a Roman colony. Soon afterwards a group of soldiers dug up a hoard of Punic coins and the rumour swiftly ran through the camp that during the war with Rome many wealthy Carthaginians had buried their valuables for security. For several days all discipline collapsed as the legionaries went into a frenzy of treasure-hunting. It was an indication of the questionable discipline of many of the legions raised amidst the confusion of civil war. Their commander realized that nothing could be done to restore order and simply wandered through the surrounding plain, laughing at the furiously toiling legionaries. No more gold was discovered and in the end the men gave up their quest. Pompey announced that their self-imposed fatigue was punishment enough and at last moved the army against the enemy. A confused fight developed during a rainstorm, with Pompey's men gaining the advantage, but being unable to exploit it. In the aftermath of this action the young commander was almost killed when he failed to answer the challenge of a nervous sentry – a risk which has been not uncommon throughout history and was always especially great with hastily raised troops. A decisive victory was won soon afterwards and Pompey made a point of fighting the battle bareheaded to avoid becoming a target for any more of his own men. He rounded off the African campaign by an enormous hunting expedition, declaring that even the animals ought to have a display of Roman power and skill.[8]

A dispatch arrived from Sulla instructing Pompey to remain in the province with a single legion and send the remainder of the army back to Italy. His soldiers saw this as a slight to their beloved commander and demanded that he lead them personally back to Italy. Pompey mounted the tribunal which was always built in a camp occupied for any time, and tried unsuccessfully to restore discipline. After a while he gave up and, tears streaming down his face, retired to his tent, but he was promptly hauled back onto the platform. Only after he had sworn an oath to kill himself if the legionaries did not give up their demands did the uproar finally subside, and even so he did actually accompany the troops back to Italy.

At first Sulla feared a renewal of civil war, but reports soon made it clear that Pompey's loyalty had not changed. The dictator greeted his young protégé warmly, bestowing on him the title Magnus – 'the Great' – although Plutarch claims that Pompey himself did not employ the name for several years. Sulla may have been a little reluctant to grant the young commander the triumph he requested, but in the end relented. Pompey's plans were grandiose, and probably betray a measure of immaturity, for he wanted to ride in a chariot drawn by elephants and was only thwarted in this ambition by the discovery that such a team could not fit under one of the main gateways on the processional route. A further problem came when the still unruly soldiers decided that they had not been given a sufficiently generous share of the booty and threatened to disrupt the parade. To counter this Pompey threatened to forgo the triumph altogether and deny them the honour of marching in procession through the city. The threat worked and this time the unrest quickly subsided. In the end the ceremony went well, but it was less the splendour of the occasion than the fact that Pompey had achieved it whilst he was still in his mid twenties and had never held a magistracy that would be remembered. Scipio Africanus had not received a triumph after his victory in Spain.[9]

POLITICS AND WAR

Pompey chose not to become a senator, although it seems certain that Sulla would willingly have enrolled him in his Senate. It would have been difficult for him now to begin the traditional *cursus* and seek such junior posts as quaestor or aedile, and so instead he preferred to remain outside conventional politics. This certainly did not mean that he lacked ambition to become a dominant figure in the Republic, but simply that he was pursuing this aim in his own unique way. His marriage to Antistia had been contracted for an immediate political advantage and in 82 the dictator decided that a similar bond was necessary to tie the young Pompey to him. The latter was instructed to divorce Antistia and marry Sulla's stepdaughter Aemilia, who was already pregnant by her current husband. The blow was especially harsh for Antistia, whose father had been murdered because of his connection to Pompey and whose mother had committed suicide soon afterwards. However, marriage alliances were a traditional part of Roman political life and it was only in the degree of cynicism that this differed from many aristocratic weddings. The initiative came from Sulla, but Pompey appears to have displayed little reluctance to comply, for the match was certainly advantageous to both parties. The marriage proved to be of brief duration, for Aemilia died shortly afterwards in childbirth. Senators rarely remained single for long, and in 80 he wedded Mucia, a member of the distinguished Mucii Scaevolae family, and thus made another useful political connection.

For senators marriage was most often a matter of political expediency and greater affection was often bestowed on mistresses than on wives. Plutarch tells us that Pompey for a while carried on an affair with the courtesan Flora, whose beauty was such that she was used as a model for a portrait which Metellus Pius had placed in the Temple of Castor and Pollux – an early example of a practice which became common in the Renaissance. Flora is said to have boasted that the young general's passion for her was so great that she could always show his toothmarks after they had made love. Yet even in this case, Pompey revealed the ambition of a politician who most of all wanted others placed in his debt, for eventually he passed Flora on to a friend of his who was also in love with her, but whom she had rebuffed on his behalf. His sacrifice was considered all the greater because he was still believed to be in love with her.

At times the young Pompey's behaviour was more akin to that of a Hellenistic prince than a Roman aristocrat. He was widely considered to be extremely handsome, with a ready smile and knack of winning affection. Many likened him to the youthful Alexander, a comparison which is said to have pleased him deeply. Although he held no formal power and remained outside the Senate, he nevertheless wielded considerable influence. In late 79 he threw his support behind the electoral campaign of Marcus Aemilius Lepidus, who as a result won the consulship for the next year instead of Sulla's preferred candidate. The latter may already have resigned as dictator and would soon retire to his country villa. His health was failing and he had only a few more months left to live, but malicious tongues claimed that he gave himself over to debauchery. Lepidus had openly proclaimed his intention of repealing much of Sulla's legislation, especially his curbing of the power of the tribunate.

Pompey's judgement of men's character was often poor and his confidence in his own ability to control their behaviour misplaced. The reasons for his support of Lepidus are unclear, but the decision was soon to prove a serious error. When Sulla fell prey to a disease which, according to our sources who go into gruesome detail, caused his flesh to rot and his body to be covered in lice-infested sores, Lepidus tried to prevent his receiving the public funeral so important to senators. Pompey, whether through lingering affection for his former leader or through bitter memories of the mistreatment of his father's corpse, was one of those who ensured that the funeral was carried out properly and not disturbed. Sulla's ashes were interred in the Campus Martius, in a monument bearing an inscription of his own devising which declared that no man had ever done more good for his friends or more harm to his enemies.

Within a few months of taking office Lepidus was at the head of an army in open revolt against the Senate. Whatever link there had been between the two men had disappeared, for Pompey had not joined the rebellious consul and showed no reluctance to answer the call of a desperate Senate to march against him. He quickly raised several legions – once again largely from his home turf of Picenum and bearing most of the cost himself – and in a short campaign suppressed the rising. He captured and executed Lepidus' senior legate, Marcus Junius Brutus (the father of the man who would lead the conspiracy against Julius Caesar in 44). Lepidus fled to

Sardinia where he fell into despondency and died shortly afterwards. It was said that he was more depressed by discovery of his wife's repeated infidelity than by the failure of his revolution. Many of the rebels, including Perperna, fled to Spain, where they would eventually join Sertorius. Italy was once again at peace, but Pompey showed a marked reluctance to disband his legions and return to private life. Lucius Marcius Phillipus, one of his oldest allies in the Senate, suggested that the victorious young commander should be sent to assist Metellus Pius in Spain. His case was greatly strengthened when both of the men elected consul for the next year failed to display any enthusiasm for taking up this command themselves. In the end the Senate accepted that they had little option other than to grant the province of Nearer Spain and proconsular *imperium* to the 28-year-old Pompey, for this offered the best chance of defeating Sertorius. Phillipus quipped that Pompey was not being sent as a proconsul (*pro consule*), but 'instead of both consuls' (*pro consulibus*).[10]

As we have seen, in Spain Pompey found himself up against a much tougher opponent than any he had faced in his earlier campaigns. 'Sulla's pupil' was taught several sharp lessons by the Marian commander, especially in their early encounters. Yet Pompey learned from his experiences and consistently displayed his own superiority over any of Sertorius' subordinates. In the end he and Metellus gradually forced their opponent back into a smaller and smaller section of the peninsula. Sertorius' victories became less frequent, whilst he continued to suffer losses which he was unable to replace and his supporters, both Roman and Spanish, began to waver in their allegiance. The struggle in Spain was a grim war of attrition, waged with little mercy on either side. Excavations in Valencia have revealed a burnt level dating to the time when the town was captured by Pompey's men. Within it were a number of skeletons. Some had died from wounds evidently inflicted during the fighting, but at least one – an older man who may well have been an officer – had been tortured and was found with a *pilum* thrust up his rectum. The war in Spain was long and caused much devastation and disruption to the settled life of the provinces. After its conclusion Pompey devoted considerable effort to reorganizing the province, founding such towns as Pompaelo (modern Pamplona) to encourage some of the more unruly hill tribes into a more settled and peaceful existence. It was not until 71 that he finally took his army back to Italy.[11]

SPARTACUS, THE GLADIATOR TURNED GENERAL

Although free of civil strife since the defeat of Lepidus, Italy was not at peace. In 73 a group of some eighty or so gladiators had escaped from a gladiatorial school in Capua and taken refuge on the slopes of Mount Vesuvius. Raiding the local area they were joined by many runaway slaves until their leader, Spartacus, found himself in command of a substantial and ever growing army. Little is known about this remarkable man, save that he was Thracian. Various sources claim that he had fought against the Romans and been captured, or that he had served as an auxiliary with the legions. Both might be true, although perhaps the second claim is a little more doubtful, as the Romans were fond of declaring that their most dangerous opponents were always those whom they had trained themselves, just as Jugurtha had learned how to fight when serving with Aemilianus at Numantia.

Whatever the truth of his origins, he displayed a genius for tactics, leadership and organization, turning his disparate mob of German, Thracian, Gallic and many other nationalities of slaves into a formidable army. The Romans first sent small forces against the slaves, but these were defeated. Then they mustered full-size armies under consular commanders only to have these just as thoroughly trounced by Spartacus, who with each victory captured more weapons and armour to equip his forces. In time the slaves established workshops to manufacture military equipment, trading the plunder they took from wealthy country estates for iron, bronze and tin. When both the consuls of 72 had been defeated, the Senate entrusted the main command against the slaves to Marcus Licinius Crassus, who had been praetor in the previous year. Crassus was another man who had sided with Sulla during the Civil War – both his father and older brother had been killed in the Marian purges. He served Sulla well, if not as spectacularly as Pompey, and commanded one of the wings of the army at the battle of the Colline Gate. A grateful dictator granted a good deal of property confiscated from the victims of the proscriptions to Crassus, who rapidly converted this into an enormous fortune through shrewd investments and business activity.

Crassus began his command in the Servile War by ordering the legions which had been routed under his predecessors to suffer the archaic punishment of decimation. One out of every ten soldiers was chosen by lot to be beaten to death by his colleagues. The surviving 90 per cent of the legions suffered a more symbolic punishment, being issued with a ration of barley instead of wheat and – at least in some cases – forced to lay out their tents outside the walls of the army's camp. Such a brutal measure was an indication of the prevalent fear of the slaves as well as Crassus' ruthless determination to succeed. To these two legions he added a further six of newly raised troops. The praetor defeated a group which had broken away from Spartacus' main army, and then built an immense line of fortifications hemming the rest of the slaves into the toe of Italy. Spartacus managed to break out, but was finally brought to battle in 71 and defeated after a very hard fight. At the start of the action the former gladiator had slit his own horse's throat – the animal had been captured from a defeated Roman commander and was of great value – to demonstrate to his men that he would not run away but would fight and die with them. The gesture was reminiscent of Marius' decision to place himself in the front rank at Aquae Sextiae.

Plutarch claims that Spartacus was cut down as he tried to reach Crassus himself, having already killed two centurions who met him together. Most of the slaves were killed, but 6,000 adult male prisoners were taken. Crassus had them all crucified at regular intervals all along the Appian Way from Rome to Capua as a ghastly demonstration of the fate awaiting slaves who rebelled. With a society that relied so heavily on slavery, the thought that the slaves might turn on their outnumbered masters was one of the Romans' darkest fears. Yet precisely because Spartacus had proved so formidable an opponent when alive, the threat he had posed was played down after his death. Crassus was denied a triumph and had to make do with the lesser honour of an ovation.[12]

When Pompey's army returned to Italy he happened to run into and annihilate a group of several thousand slaves who had escaped Spartacus' defeat. Showing a rather petty jealousy given the scale of his own achievements and the second triumph which he was soon to celebrate, Pompey claimed to have been the man who completed the Servile War. This only fuelled an existing animosity between the two men which dated back to Crassus' jealousy of the more prominent place given to the other by Sulla. Pompey was now 35 and had decided at long last to enter formal politics by seeking the consulship. Crassus, who was eight or nine years older and whose career since the Civil War had been largely conventional, was also keen to seek the senior magistracy. Both men kept their armies not far from Rome under the pretext of waiting to march in their triumph and ovation respectively. Perhaps this was a barely veiled threat, perhaps it reflected each man's suspicion of the other, but at some point in the last months of 71 the two successful commanders buried their personal animosity and announced a join electoral campaign. The Senate swiftly realized that such a combination could not be opposed and permitted Pompey to stand whilst still below the legal age set down in Sulla's law and both men to stand *in absentia*, since neither was permitted to enter the city until the day of their triumph and ovation. Pompey's popularity and Crassus' money, combined with their genuine achievements and, possibly, fear of their armies, resulted in a landslide victory. On 29 December 71 BC Pompey rode in triumph along the Sacra Via, entered into his consulship and became a senator all on the same day.[13]

There was one last act in Pompey's transition to something approaching a legitimate place in Roman public life – a piece of political theatre of the type loved by the Romans. It was traditional for the censors elected every five years to make a formal record of any equestrians who had come to the end of their military service, recording details of their actions and formally praising or condemning their behaviour. By the first century BC this was a fairly archaic practice, since equestrians no longer provided cavalry for the legions and only a proportion chose to serve as tribunes or other officers, but diminishing relevance rarely caused the Romans to abandon traditional ceremonies. As the censors were engaged in this task a rumour spread that Pompey was approaching, accompanied by the twelve lictors which marked him out as a consul and leading a horse which symbolized the old military role of an *eques*. The consul ordered his lictors to clear a path for him to the censors, but such was the shock of the latter that it took them a moment to frame the traditional words enquiring whether a man had fulfilled his duty to the Republic. Pompey replied in a voice which carried to the watching crowd that he had served whenever the State had asked him to and had always done so under his own command. Amidst tumultuous cheering and applause, the censors formally escorted the consul back to his house as a mark of respect.[14]

THE PIRATES

The alliance between Pompey and Crassus did not last long, and their consulship was marked by a good deal of bickering. Pompey fulfilled his electoral promise to restore the power of the tribunate, removing the restrictions which Sulla had placed on this office. Since both consuls had just completed a successful war, neither showed any desire to take a province after their year of office was over. Pompey had now added political legitimacy to his wealth and prestige and was content for the moment with a position as one of the most prominent members of the Senate. He was soon to find, just as Scipio Africanus had done more than a century before, that a youth spent in the field and at the head of an army provided a poor schooling for the rough and tumble of Roman politics.

At the beginning of his consulship, he had asked Marcus Terentius Varro – descendant of the man who had lost the battle of Cannae and a noted polymath who wrote numerous and wide-ranging studies – to prepare him a manual explaining senatorial procedure and conventions. Now that he could no longer command obedience or defeat opponents in battle, Pompey found it difficult to get what he wanted by turning his prestige and wealth into real political influence. Crassus used his money with great skill, granting loans to the many senators who struggled to afford the high costs of a political career, and over time placed the overwhelming majority of the Senate in his debt. Pompey lacked the experience and instinct to do the same. His oratory was undistinguished and as time went by he spent less and less time in the Senate and rarely acted on behalf of anyone in the courts. He seems to have been very sensitive to criticism and hostility and preferred to avoid any damage to his prestige by staying out of public life. Yet after a few years he began to become frustrated that his great deeds did not seem to have brought him the permanent pre-eminence which he felt that they deserved. Like Marius he remembered the adulation of the People when he had returned to the city in victory and realized that only when fighting a great war did he truly outshine the rest of the Senate. Pompey began to look for another major war to fight and in 67 BC found his opportunity.

Piracy was a feature of life in the Mediterranean for most of the classical period. When strong kingdoms with powerful navies existed, it was usually reduced to a minimum or even for short periods eradicated. However, Rome's defeat of Macedonia and the Seleucid Empire, combined with the inexorable decline of Ptolemaic Egypt, removed the fleets which had kept piracy in check in the eastern Mediterranean. Many of the coastal communities in Asia Minor, especially in Cilicia, Crete and the other smaller islands, took to raiding by sea, finding the rich profits of plunder and ransom a welcome addition to the meagre rewards of fishing and agriculture. The spread of piracy was further encouraged when Mithridates of Pontus gave the pirate chieftains money and warships to aid him in his war with Rome. In spite of coming from so many different communities and lacking any formal political hierarchy, the pirates appear to have rarely fought amongst themselves and often sent forces or money to aid those under threat. Travel became difficult – the young Julius Caesar was just one of the prominent Romans taken hostage and ransomed by pirates – and trade began to suffer.

The population of Italy and especially the city of Rome had long ago expanded beyond the level at which it could be fed solely by home-grown produce and now relied on massive grain imports from Sicily, Egypt and North Africa. The pirates' activities began to threaten this lifeline, causing grain supplies to diminish and prices to soar.

In 74 the Senate had sent the former praetor Marcus Antonius against the pirates. Antonius was given wide-ranging powers and considerable resources but, unlike his more famous son Mark Antony, had little ability and was defeated in a naval battle fought off Crete in 72. Antonius died soon after his defeat, and in 69 the consul Quintus Caecilius Metellus was sent against the strongholds on Crete. He proved a competent commander, but the campaign involved besieging one walled town after another and progress was slow. In spite of his successes, the pirate problem became even worse, and in one instance two praetors along with their lictors and entire entourage were kidnapped as they travelled through a coastal area of Italy, whilst Ostia itself was raided.[15]

By 67 the shortage of grain had become critical and the tribune Aulus Gabinius proposed the re-creation of the massive province and extraordinary powers which had been allocated to Antonius. At first Gabinius made no mention of Pompey as the most obvious recipient of this command, but it is clear that there was already a close association between the two men. Cicero claims that Gabinius was heavily in debt and it is most probable that Pompey secured his support by assisting him financially. The *Lex Gabinia* was passed by the Popular Assembly and Pompey granted proconsular *imperium* not only over the Mediterranean itself, but for a distance of 50 miles inland. It is not entirely clear whether his *imperium* was equal or superior to that of any other proconsul whose province overlapped with his, but probably the former was the case.

To assist him he was given twenty-four legates – all of whom were to have held a military command in the past or at least to have been praetor – each assisted by two quaestors. His forces would eventually consist of a fleet of 500 warships, supported by an army of 120,000 infantry and 5,000 cavalry, along with the money and resources of food and other essentials needed to maintain them. Many of these troops were probably not well-trained and disciplined legionaries, but hastily raised local levies. The figures may also have included existing garrisons in the provinces covered by Pompey's extended *imperium*, who fell under his control for the duration of the campaign. In spite of its vast scale, this was to be essentially a policing action. Pompey needed numbers, so that he could put pressure on the pirates from all directions simultaneously, and only a small fraction of his forces were likely to face heavy fighting.[16]

Although Antonius had been granted similar *imperium*, it was only Pompey's personal prestige which secured the enormous resources placed at his disposal, making this command utterly unprecedented in scale. Strikingly the command was secured for him by the tribunate, whose powers he had himself restored during his consulship. The manner in which this province was allocated to him conformed to the way that Marius had been appointed to fight Jugurtha, the Cimbri and Teutones, and Mithridates. Only a handful of generals possessed sufficient popular support to subvert the normal senatorial allocation of provinces and resources in this way. Such was the People's faith in Pompey that the price of corn in the Forum is supposed to have fallen as soon as he was appointed. Even many senators who were reluctant to grant so much power to one man – let alone a man whose prestige and wealth already outstripped all rivals – seem to have acknowledged that this was the best way to deal with the scourge of piracy. Pompey's legates were a highly distinguished group, consisting primarily of men from the old-established noble families.

Pompey's strategy was made possible by the huge forces under his command, but was also a tribute to his organizational genius. The Mediterranean was divided into thirteen zones – six in the west and seven in the east, each commanded by a legate with military and naval assets at his disposal. The western commands were allocated to Aulus Manlius Torquatus, Tiberius Claudius Nero, Marcus Pomponius, Publius Atilius, Lucius Gellius, and Aulus Plotius who was entrusted with the Italian coast. In the east were Cnaeus Lentulus Marcellinus, Cnaeus Cornelius Lentulus Clodianus, Marcus Terentius Varro (the same man who had written the manual on senatorial procedure), Quintus Caecilius Metellus Nepos, Lucius Sisenna, Lucius Lollius and Marcus Pupius Piso. These men were given strict orders not to pursue any enemy beyond the boundaries of the region allocated to them. Pompey himself was tied to no set area and kept a squadron of sixty warships at his immediate disposal. The role of the other legates is not specified in our ancient sources. Some may have been involved in supervising the enormous logistical exercise required to maintain this massive effort. It is also more than likely that others were given mobile squadrons like that commanded by Pompey himself to pursue pirate ships from one region to another.

In early spring of 67 the campaign opened in the western regions, which Pompey is said to have swept free of pirates in a mere forty days. The pirates, allowed to go about their business almost unmolested for many decades, were unprepared for his onslaught and gave way with little fighting. After a brief stop in Rome, where one of the consuls from 67 had been cheerfully attempting to undermine his authority and had ordered the demobilization of some of his troops, Pompey took his mobile command eastwards to deal with the pirates' heartland. Here the fighting was expected to be tougher, but the pirates still appear to have been utterly wrong-footed and for all their teamwork in easier days, now tended to respond as individuals. Some tried to flee, but a growing number began to surrender. The Roman attitude to brutality was pragmatic, and now was not the time for mass executions. The pirates and their families were not mistreated, and many began to act as informants, providing the Romans with information to plan operations against other chieftains.

As word spread of the reception given to these men, more and more of the enemy gave themselves up. Pompey had prepared siege equipment for taking the strongholds along the mountainous coast of Cilicia, but found that almost all capitulated as soon as he arrived. Occasionally the pirates fought and were defeated, but their resistance swiftly crumbled. Florus describes ships' crews throwing down oars and weapons and clapping their hands – the pirates' gesture of surrender – almost as soon as they saw Roman galleys approaching. This time the campaign lasted forty-nine days. Pompey's forces captured seventy-one ships in combat and had a further 306 handed over to them. About ninety of these were classed as warships and fitted with rams. An inscription set up to mark the triumph, and conforming to the tradition which required victory to be quantified as much as possible, claimed that 846 vessels were taken throughout the entire campaign, although this figure may well have included even the tiniest of craft.

Pompey's treatment of his 20,000 captives showed a shrewd understanding of the causes of piracy, for he knew that they would swiftly resume their profession if allowed to return to their coastal communities. The old pirate strongholds were slighted or destroyed and the prisoners settled in more fertile regions. Many went to the coastal city of Soli in Cilicia, which was renamed Pompeiopolis, and became a prosperous trading community. The wholesale transplanting of troublesome warriors and their families to better land had been employed by the Romans before in Liguria and Spain and proved just as effective with the pirates. Raiding and piracy were not permanently eradicated from the Mediterranean, but they never again occurred on a similar scale to the early decades of the first century BC. Under the emperors the Roman navy would be established on a more permanent basis and fill the vacuum left by the decline of the Hellenistic powers.[17]

In the war against the pirates the Roman Republic had mobilized huge resources and, under the skilful command of Pompey, won a swift and, on their side, almost bloodless victory over numerous if disunited enemies. This was a considerable achievement of planning and logistics as much as fighting, and it was unfortunate that it ended with an incident which reflected less well on Pompey. In 67 Metellus was still operating against the pirates of Crete in a campaign which would earn him the honorary title of Creticus. Hearing of Pompey's generous treatment of prisoners, representatives from a stronghold under siege by Metellus' legions were sent to him in Cilicia offering to surrender. Pompey readily accepted, seeing this as further proof of his great fame, but Metellus resented any interference in his own war and refused to acknowledge this. The former sent one of his legates, Lucius Octavius, who is said even to have fought for the pirates against Metellus' men, although this did not prevent their eventual defeat. The desire of both Pompey and Metellus to win sole credit for winning a war and to place this before the interests of the State was typical of the mentality of the senatorial élite. Yet in Pompey's case it suggests a petty jealousy and refusal to allow anyone else any credit whatsoever, given that the scale of his own achievements was already so much greater than those of Metellus or indeed anyone else.[18]

MITHRIDATES AND THE EASTERN WARS

Pompey spent the winter with his main army in Cilicia. At the beginning of 66 another extraordinary command was bestowed upon him by the Popular Assembly at the behest of a tribune, giving him control of the eastern Mediterranean and the ongoing war with Mithridates of Pontus, whom Sulla had defeated but not destroyed. Gabinius' year of office was over and he was soon to be employed as one of Pompey's legates, so this time the law was brought forward by one of the new tribunes, Caius Manilius. There was considerable support for the *Lex Manilia* both from senators and, especially, from the equestrian order. Marcus Tullius Cicero, who later published the speech he delivered in favour of the bill, declared that Pompey possessed in abundance the four chief attributes of a great general, namely 'military knowledge, courage, authority and good luck' (*scientam rei militaris, virtutem, auctoritatem, felicitatem*). When Pompey heard of his appointment he publicly complained that the State gave him no opportunity to rest and spend time with his family. Even his closest friends found this feigned reluctance embarrassing, for he had long desired to take the field against Mithridates and had certainly encouraged, even if he had not actually engineered, the political manoeuvrings which eventually gave this to him.[19]

In 74 Mithridates had overrun the Roman province of Bithynia and driven into neighbouring Asia. His opponent was Lucius Licinius Lucullus, the man who as quaestor in 88 had been the only senator to follow Sulla in his march on Rome. Lucullus was a strategist and tactician of truly exceptional talent, who, in spite of limited resources, consistently outmanoeuvred Mithridates and defeated his armies either in battle or through starvation. The invaders were expelled from the Roman provinces, and Pontus itself attacked. When the king formed an alliance with Tigranes of Armenia, the Roman army drove deep into the latter's territory. Both Armenia and Pontus produced armies which were exceptionally large in numbers, but contained only a few units of real fighting ability. Tigranes is supposed to have joked that Lucullus' men were 'too few for an army, but too many for an embassy', shortly before the legions cut his great host to pieces in a matter of hours.

By 68 the war seemed virtually over, but in spite of his skills as a general, Lucullus lacked the knack of winning his soldiers' affection and was deeply unpopular with the army. He was also disliked by many influential groups back in Rome, in particular the equestrian businessmen whose companies operated in provinces. Lucullus had severely restricted the illegal activities of many of their agents, a measure which did much to win back the loyalty of the provincials to Rome. In 69 Asia was taken from Lucullus' province, and a year later Cilicia was also removed and placed under the command of another. On the point of total victory, the Roman general was starved of troops and resources, whilst his own legionaries became mutinous. As Roman pressure relaxed, the enemy counter-attacked and in 67 the legate Triarius was defeated by Mithridates. Losses were heavy, with no fewer than twenty-four tribunes and 150 centurions falling. Such high casualties amongst officers may well indicate the need for junior leaders to take too many risks in an effort to inspire dispirited soldiers. In the aftermath of the battle Mithridates was almost killed by a centurion who mingled with the king's entourage and managed to wound him in the thigh before being hacked to pieces by the enraged royal bodyguard.

By the end of the year both Mithridates and Tigranes had recovered most of their kingdoms, and Lucullus was left with a pitiful remnant of the forces he had once controlled. Even these had no great affection for him and refused his pleas to disobey the order which summoned these legions to join the newly arrived Pompey. Plutarch describes the Roman commander wandering the camp with tears in his eyes as he begged his men to stay with him. It was a rather pathetic end to the military career of a very able soldier. A meeting at which Pompey formally took over the command seems to have degenerated into a shouting match. Rather meanly, his successor only permitted Lucullus to take 1,600 soldiers – men so mutinous that Pompey considered them to be utterly useless for active service – home with him to march in his triumph.[20]

Pompey's province included Bithynia, Pontus and Cilicia, and he was given all the resources which his predecessor had lacked, especially since he continued to hold the Mediterranean command granted by the *Lex Gabinia*. He also had the power to begin a new war or establish a peace at his own discretion. One of Sulla's laws had forbidden a governor to lead troops beyond the borders of his own province without the express permission of the Senate, and Lucullus' unauthorized invasion of Armenia had provoked some criticism at Rome, even though it made sound military sense. From the beginning Pompey was given far greater freedom of action. Whilst his fleet – apart from those squadrons still tied to specific regions – patrolled the Mediterranean coast and the Bosporus, Pompey mustered an army of 30,000 infantry and 2,000 cavalry. Mithridates had about the same number of infantry, but 1,000 more horsemen, with him on the western border of his kingdom.

This region had been fought over several times during Lucullus' campaigns and had been thoroughly devastated and plundered, and the Pontic army had difficulty finding food as they waited to meet the Roman invasion. Desertion was punished by crucifixion, blinding or burning alive, but in spite of such brutal punishments, the king lost a steady flow of men. Wondering whether Pompey's lenient treatment of the pirates might be extended to him, Mithridates sent ambassadors to the Roman camp, only to be faced with a demand for unconditional surrender. As the supply situation grew worse, the king retreated into the interior of his kingdom. The Romans were better prepared, and as Pompey followed the Pontic army his legions were supplied by convoys bringing food from his bases back in the province. Mithridates sent his cavalry to strike at the Roman lines of communication, but although this caused some shortages it was not enough to deter his pursuers.[21]

By this time the armies had reached a part of the Pontic kingdom known as Lesser Armenia. It was a fertile area, largely untouched by war, but Pompey's foraging parties had difficulty operating in the face of the confident enemy cavalry and his own supply dumps were now a great distance away.

Mithridates had pitched his camp on high ground, making it unlikely that a direct attack against such a good defensive position would succeed. Pompey shifted his own camp into a more wooded region where the Pontic cavalry could operate less freely. The move encouraged Mithridates, who judged that his opponent had overextended himself and was now admitting his weakness. He readily accepted the challenge when Pompey sent forward most of his own cavalry to demonstrate outside the Pontic camp on the next morning. Mithridates' horsemen attacked, and pursued when the Roman cavalry began to retreat. The Pontic troops were led on and on, until Pompey sprang his ambush. A force of 3,000 light infantry and 500 cavalry had been concealed during the night in a scrub-filled valley between the two camps. This force suddenly attacked Mithridates' cavalry in the rear. Some of the Pontic horsemen were caught at the halt by the Roman infantrymen and, denied cavalry's chief advantages of speed and momentum, were massacred. This brief action – in many ways reminiscent of tactics used by Sertorius against Pompey in Spain – shattered both the morale of Mithridates' proud cavalry and the king's faith in them.[22]

The precise chronology of the campaign is uncertain, but at some point Pompey was reinforced by the three legions which had formed the garrison of Cilicia, bringing his strength up to well over 40,000 men in spite of attrition suffered in the campaign. This gave him a marked numerical advantage over the king, but the latter showed no inclination to risk a battle other than from highly advantageous ground. Therefore, Pompey resolved to starve the enemy out of his strong position and, using his own increased manpower, constructed a ring of forts connected by a ditch and wall around the enemy army. The entire system measured almost 19 miles in length (150 *stades*) and compares to similar lines built by Crassus in Southern Italy and Caesar in Gaul.

The Roman army was now drawing its supplies from Acilisene on the Upper Euphrates, whilst the king's foraging parties operated only under great risk of attack and ambush. Soon the Pontic soldiers were reduced to slaughtering and cooking their pack animals. Whether the Roman line of fortifications was incomplete or was designed to have some gaps in it because of difficult terrain, Mithridates was able to escape under cover of darkness, concealing his move by leaving fires burning in his own camp. As a further deception he had arranged a number of meetings with potential allies in the immediate future. Having thus skilfully disengaged, the king marched towards the neighbouring kingdom of Armenia, hoping to join forces with his old ally Tiridates. He seems to have continued moving mainly at night, relying on local knowledge of the paths, and camped each day in a position too strong for Pompey willingly to attack. The terrain was mountainous and such easily defensible positions were common.

Keeping pace with the king, but unable to catch him as he moved, Pompey sent patrols a considerable distance in advance of his troops to scout the routes through the mountains. These men discovered a pass which eventually led by a roundabout route to rejoin the path being followed by Mithridates. Pompey force-marched his army along the new path, gambling on being able to move fast enough to get behind the king. As usual he marched by day, driving his men on over the rugged terrain under the hot sun. His legionaries must have been very weary by the time they began to take up ambush positions in a narrow defile through which the main road passed. Mithridates was unaware of the Roman move, and may even have dared to hope that the Romans had given up the chase altogether. At nightfall his army continued its retreat in its usual manner, the column a disorganized mixture of units, individuals and baggage, and encumbered with wives, servants and other camp followers so that it was in no way prepared to resist attack.

As soon as the enemy army was fully in the defile Pompey sprang his ambush, ordering his trumpeters to blare out their challenge whilst the legionaries yelled their war cry and drummed their weapons against their shields, and the army's servants clashed cooking pots with anything else metal that they could find. The deluge of noise was immediately followed by a barrage of missiles – *pila*, javelins, arrows and even stones rolled or hurled down the slope. Then the Romans charged into the panicking mass. The moon was behind them and its eerie light cast long shadows ahead of the legionaries, causing those few of the enemy who attempted to resist to misjudge the range and throw their own javelins too soon. In some places the crowd was so densely packed that men could neither escape nor fight and were cut down where they stood.

A few of the Pontic soldiers resisted bravely, but the issue was never in doubt and Mithridates' army was almost destroyed. Plutarch and Appian both say that 10,000 men were killed and others, along with the baggage train, captured. The king escaped with a small body of cavalry and later joined up with a few thousand foot soldiers. Plutarch claims that at one point he had only three companions, one of them his concubine Hypsicrates, whose masculine nickname had been won by the bravery with which she fought in battle on horseback. The king fled to his stronghold at Sinora, where he had stored many valuables, some of which he used to reward those followers who were still loyal. When Tigranes refused the fugitives admission to Armenia and placed a price on his head, Mithridates fled to the north-ernmost part of his realm in the Crimea, taking the land route round the eastern shore of the Black Sea to avoid the Roman fleet patrolling its waters.[23]

Pompey sent only a small force after the king, and even this soon lost contact. His priority now was to deal with Tigranes and Armenia. A Parthian invasion, encouraged by Roman diplomacy and supported by his rebellious son who was also called Tigranes, had prevented the king from aiding his ally and son-in-law Mithridates. In spite of his age – he was now well into his seventies – Tigranes had repelled the invaders when they attacked his main fortress of Artaxata. Yet as Pompey's army advanced against him, he seems quickly to have decided that it was better to seek peace, even if this meant giving up some land and power. After initial negotiations, the king came in person to the Roman camp to surrender. Obeying the instruction to walk on foot rather than ride up to the tribunal on which Pompey sat, Tigranes then threw down his royal diadem and sword. Such an open admis-sion of utter helplessness in the face of Roman power, and of willingness to trust to whatever mercy they chose to extend, was a highly proper con-clusion to one of Rome's wars, and Pompey readily seized the chance to display his clemency in victory. The king was ordered to pay Rome an indem-nity of 6,000 talents, but was allowed to retain all of the territory which he still controlled. The outcome delighted Tigranes, who paid on his own initiative a bounty to each of Pompey's soldiers, with considerably larger sums for the centurions and tribunes. His son had joined Pompey after the failure of the Parthian invasion, but was dismayed to be given only the rule of Sophene. Soon afterwards he became rebellious and was imprisoned by the Romans.[24]

Pompey had driven Mithridates from his kingdom and received Tigranes' surrender in his first year of operations. If the speed of his success owed much to the victories won by Lucullus in previous years, this should not entirely detract from the skill with which Pompey had fought the campaign. By the end of the campaigning season of 66 when his main army divided into three and constructed camps for the winter, the Roman general was beginning to consider how he might best use the great resources placed at his disposal to win further glory on the Republic's behalf. In December the army's winter quarters were suddenly attacked by King Oroeses of Albania. The assaults failed, and Pompey took a column in pursuit of the retreating enemy, inflicting heavy losses on them when he caught their rearguard crossing the River Cyrus. Deciding that this punishment was enough for the moment and reluctant to embark on further winter operations for which he had not had time to prepare, he then returned his men to camp.

In the following spring he discovered that Oroeses' neighbour, King Artoces of Iberia, was also preparing to attack him, and decided to launch an immediate pre-emptive strike. Pushing down the valley of the River Cyrus he reached the strong fortress of Harmozica before the bulk of Artoces' army had advanced to support the position. With only a small force at his immediate disposal, the king retreated, burning the bridge over the Cyrus behind him, a move which prompted the garrison of Harmozica to surrender after a brief resistance. Leaving a force of his own to control both the city and the pass, Pompey pushed on into the more fertile lands beyond. Artoces continued to retreat, in one case even after he had begun negotiations with the Romans. In a repeat of the previous summer's campaign against Mithridates, Pompey force-marched his legions to get behind the king and cut off his retreat. The result was a battle rather than an ambush, but the Roman victory was just as complete. The Iberian army included large numbers of archers, but Pompey ordered his legionaries to charge at speed, ignoring the loss of formation and order this entailed, swiftly closing the range and sweeping the enemy bowmen away. Artoces is said to have lost 9,000 dead and 10,000 captured and capitulated soon afterwards.[25]

From Iberia Pompey now turned west towards Colchis and the Black Sea coast. Nature, more than any human foe, was the chief obstacle in this stage of the campaign, as his army marched through the rugged Meschian mountains. Strabo tells us that his men constructed 120 bridges to cross the river winding through the valley. One of the most marked differences between the professional legions of the Late Republic and their predecessors produced by the old militia system was their much greater technical and engineering skill. Spectacular feats of building roads through apparently impassable terrain and bridging rivers were celebrated almost as much as victories won by the army in battle. On reaching the Black Sea Pompey discovered that Mithridates had reached the Crimea and, never one to be daunted by repeated failure, was once again seeking to build up his power for a renewal of war with Rome. Judging that the fleet was sufficient to contain and blockade the king, the main Roman army moved on once more. Pompey had decided that the Albanians deserved another and greater display of Roman might and invaded King Oroeses' realm. The legions forded the River Cyrus, a line of cavalry horses stationed upstream to provide some protection from the fast-flowing water for the men on foot and the baggage animals. The advance to the next obstacle, the River Cambyses, proved difficult, especially when the local guides led them astray – always a danger when operating in previously unknown terrain. Few maps existed in the ancient world, and scarcely any contained information detailed enough for an army to plan its movements – but eventually the river was reached and crossed without opposition.

Oroeses had mustered a sizeable army, numbering some 60,000 foot and 22,000 horse according to Strabo, although Plutarch gives the number of cavalry as 12,000. Roman numbers are not stated in our sources, but may well have been substantially less than the 40,000–50,000 Pompey had mustered against Mithridates in the previous year. Many troops were needed to act as garrisons or to mop up the last fragments of resistance in the recently conquered territory, whilst the problems of supplying men and animals in the often difficult terrain anyway discouraged the use of too large a force. Pompey may have had a force half the size of the one he had led in 66 and could well have been heavily outnumbered by the Albanians. The latter certainly had an advantage in cavalry, some of whom were heavily armoured cataphracts, and Pompey needed to find a way of dealing with these as the king, obviously intent on forcing a pitched battle, advanced to meet him.

Throwing out his own horsemen as a screen, he advanced down onto a level plain flanked by hills. Some of his legionaries were concealed in defiles on this high ground, the men covering their bronze helmets with cloth to prevent the sun from reflecting on the metal and giving away their position. Other cohorts of legionaries knelt down behind the cavalry, so that they could not be seen from the front. Oroeses advanced against what seemed to be no more than a line of horsemen. Pompey repeated another tactic he had used against Mithridates, ordering his cavalry to attack boldly and then, feigning panic, to withdraw. The Albanian cavalry pursued them eagerly, confident both in their own numbers and in their individual superiority, and as they did so lost much of their order. The Roman auxiliary horsemen retired through the gaps between the infantry cohorts, which then stood up. Suddenly the Albanians were faced with a fresh and well-formed line of infantry who came forward against them, yelling their battle cry. Behind the legionaries the Roman cavalry rallied and moved round behind the line to attack the enemy flanks, whilst more cohorts emerged from the concealing defiles to threaten the enemy rear. The position of the Albanian army was hopeless, but in spite of this the warriors appear to have fought very hard. One account claims that Pompey fought hand-to-hand with the king's brother and killed him in the best traditions of Alexander the Great or Marcellus.

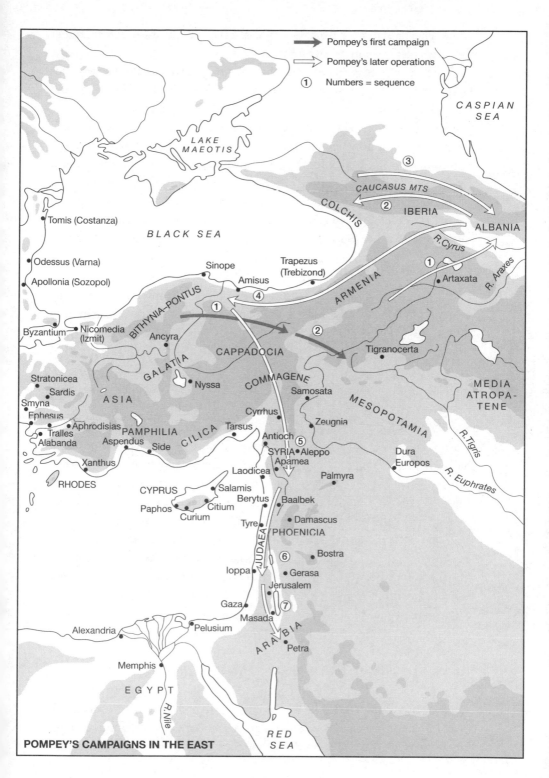

Pompey's first campaign

Pompey's later operations

① Numbers = sequence

CASPIAN SEA

LAKE MAEOTIS

③

CAUCASUS MTS ② IBERIA

COLCHIS

ALBANIA

R. Cyrus

BLACK SEA

Tomis (Costanza)

Odessus (Varna)

Apollonia (Sozopol)

Sinope

Trapezus (Trebizond)

Amisus ④

① ARMENIA

R. Araxes

Artaxata

Byzantium

Nicomedia (Izmit)

BITHYNIA-PONTUS

Ancyra

① ②

Tigranocerta

GALATIA

CAPPADOCIA

Nyssa

COMMAGENE

MEDIA ATROPA-TENE

Stratonicea

Sardis

Smyrna

Ephesus

Aphrodisias

Tralles

Alabanda

ASIA

PAMPHILIA

Aspendus

Side

Samosata

MESOPOTAMIA

Cyrrhus

Zeugnia

R. Tigris

Tarsus

CILICA

Antioch ⑤

SYRIA Aleppo

Apamea

Dura Europos

R. Euphrates

Xanthus

RHODES

Laodicea

CYPRUS

Salamis

Paphos

Curium

Citium

Berytus

Tyre

Baalbek

Palmyra

JUDAEA

PHOENICIA

Damascus

⑥

Bostra

Ioppa

Gerasa

Jerusalem

Gaza

Masada

⑦

ARABIA

Petra

Alexandria

Pelusium

Memphis

EGYPT

R. Nile

RED SEA

POMPEY'S CAMPAIGNS IN THE EAST

Although a hard fight, the battle proved decisive, for Oroeses soon accepted the peace terms imposed on him.[26]

After the victory in Albania, Pompey began to march towards the Caspian Sea, but is said to have turned back when only three days' journey from its shores, according to Plutarch deterred by lands infested with poisonous snakes. Instead he returned to Pontus where most of Mithridates' strongholds had now been reduced or persuaded to surrender, yielding enormous spoils. Along with the gold, silver and artwork, one stronghold yielded detailed accounts of the murders of family members and collections of passionate love letters written to concubines, as well as the Pontic king's collection of biological specimens and his scientific studies, which the general ordered one of his freedmen to translate into Latin. After this Pompey annexed Syria, dissolving the last remnants of the Seleucid monarchy which had briefly returned after Tigranes' withdrawal from the area. A civil war raging in the Hasmonean kingdom of Jerusalem prompted Roman intervention, and Pompey captured the city after a three-month siege, much of the fighting taking place in and around the great Temple. The first man over the wall in the final successful assault was Faustus Cornelius Sulla, the dictator's son. After the storming, Pompey and his senior officers entered the Holy of Holies inside the Temple, following the Roman urge to be the first to do anything, but out of respect removed nothing from it.

This was followed in 63 by a campaign against the Nabataean Arabs whose capital was at Petra, but on his way to besiege the city Pompey was halted by the arrival of a courier carrying a report of Mithridates' death. The army had not yet completed the construction of its marching camp and there was no tribunal from which the commander could address his men. Instead, the soldiers heaped up pack saddles into a mound and Pompey announced the news to the ecstatically cheering legionaries who hailed him as *imperator* for this completion of his victory. Mithridates, at last despairing of his ability to rebuild his strength and return to glory and power when most of his officers and his own son turned against him, had ordered a Galatian bodyguard to kill him, since years of dosing himself with antidotes to poison had rendered him immune to its effects.[27]

The war which Pompey had been sent to the east to fight was now over. For the last two years it had effectively provided a pretext for other operations against peoples of the same general area, but Pompey seems to have achieved just about all that he wanted to do. He had, for instance, declined opportunities for starting a war with Parthia, perhaps aware that this empire was more powerful and militarily strong than any of the opponents whom he had faced so far and could not be defeated in anything other than a long war. Pompey had won fame and glory enough in a region associated with Alexander, the greatest conqueror of all. Although the fighting was at an end, his task was not complete. More than a year was still to be spent on the reordering of the eastern Mediterranean. Provinces were organized, cities founded or re-founded – including Nicopolis, dedicated to Nike the Greek god of victory and intended to commemorate the defeat of Mithridates – and client kingdoms regulated. Many aspects of Pompey's settlement would endure until the end of Roman rule in the region. The scale of his activity was massive and once again a testament to his genius for organization. In a sense Pompey personified Roman imperialism, where destructive and fero-cious war-making was followed by the construction of stable empire and the rule of law. Later in the first century BC the poet Virgil would have Jupiter state that it was Rome's destiny 'to spare the conquered and overcome the proud in war' (*parcere subiectis et debellare superbos*), imposing law and order on the world. From the Roman perspective, that was essentially what Pompey had done.[28]

THE RETURN HOME AND THE 'FIRST TRIUMVIRATE'

In 62 Pompey landed in Brundisium. In the months before his arrival some senators are said to have been concerned that he might seize power by force just as Sulla had done after his war with Mithridates. Crassus conspicuously left Rome and took his family to a rural estate, although this seems likely to have been a gesture intended to add to the growing hysteria rather than motivated by genuine fear. Yet the circumstances were in no way like 83, for there were no armed opponents waiting for Pompey, and the returning general soon made it clear that he had no wish to become dictator. Instead he came back to Rome and, after celebrating a spectacular two-day triumph in late September which commemorated both the pirate campaign and all his eastern wars, disbanded his legions. In later years he would use some of the spoils from the war to construct Rome's first stone theatre – a complex of buildings greater in scale than any previous triumphal monument. His achievements as a general dwarfed those of any senator alive, and indeed of all but a handful of those in former generations. It was noted that his three triumphs commemorated victories on different continents – Africa, Europe and Asia.

Yet Pompey's homecoming was not entirely happy. Almost immediate-ly he divorced his wife, who had been scandalously unfaithful during his absence, but for a while he failed to find a suitably well-connected replacement. The fear which had preceded the victorious commander's return soon turned to hostility as senators began to resent any individual having so much prestige and looked for means of clipping his wings. He was criticized for attempting to bribe the electorate into voting for one of his former legates, Lucius Afranius, in the race for the following year's consulship. More importantly he failed to secure the formal ratification of his Eastern Settlement or to have grants of land made to those veterans from his army whom he had not already settled in Asia. Neither proposal was at all unreasonable or contrary to the Republic's best interests, but still many of the most influential senators chose to thwart them and, once again, Pompey's inexperience as a political operator made it difficult for him to get what he wanted at Rome.

In the end he was forced into more desperate measures and, sometime in 61–60, he formed a secret political alliance with his old rival Crassus and Caius Julius Caesar. To strengthen the bond Pompey married Caesar's daughter Julia, and in spite of the huge age difference the marriage proved to be an extremely happy one. At first the political association was equally successful. Supported by the money and influence of the other two, Caesar won the consulship in 59 and during his year of office confirmed the Eastern Settlement in law and distributed land to Pompey's veterans. He also set himself on the road to rivalling Pompey's wealth and military record. Just over a decade later the Roman Republic would once again be plunged into civil war when these two former allies fought for supremacy.

CHAPTER 8

CAESAR IN GAUL

Caius Julius Caesar (c. 100–44 BC)

He would sometimes fight a battle after careful planning, but also on occasion on the spur of the moment – often at the end of a march, or in very bad weather, when everyone least expected it … He never let a routed enemy rally, and always therefore immediately stormed their camp.[1]

'ALL GAUL IS DIVIDED INTO THREE PARTS' (*GALLIA EST OMNIS DIVISA IN PARTES TRES*) – the opening words of Caesar's *The Gallic War* still prompt fairly widespread recognition.[2] For many generations of schoolchildren Caesar's elegantly simple and grammatically correct prose provided their first acquaintance with Latin literature, so that recognition can often be tinged with bitter memories. Even now, when Classics rarely forms a part of the school syllabus, Julius Caesar is one of a handful of figures from antiquity whose names are generally remembered, thanks in part to his famous affair with Cleopatra and his spectacular murder, both of which have provided much inspiration for drama and cinema.

Whatever their main interests, military historians will probably know a little about Caesar's campaigns, for he continues to be included amongst the ranks of the most successful and gifted generals of all time. Napoleon named Caesar as chief amongst the Great Captains from whose campaigns much could be learnt, and at St Helena devoted some time to producing a detailed critique of the Roman's generalship as described in *The Gallic War* and *The Civil War*. The French emperor was not the first to suggest that Caesar was sometimes prone to exaggeration in his account, although, given that his own official pronouncements in the Imperial Bulletins inspired the proverb 'to lie like a bulletin', it is unclear just how serious an offence he considered this to be. More recently a number of historians have used Caesar's own narrative to assess his ability as a commander.

The sheer detail of Caesar's *Commentarii* (*Commentaries*) ensures that more is known about his campaigns than those of any other Roman general. There are seven books describing operations in Gaul from 58–52 BC and three dealing with Civil War in 49–48 BC. Additional books, not written by Caesar himself but produced after his death by officers who had served under him, cover the final operations in Gaul in 51 and the remainder of the Civil War. It is not clear whether each book was published at the end of the year's campaigning or whether the entire collection was released simultaneously. The former seems more probable, and it is likely that they were intended to advertise Caesar's achievements to the people of Rome whilst his operations were still continuing. Several sources attest to the great speed with which Caesar wrote and no less an authority than Cicero declared the *Commentarii* to be one of the highest expressions of the Latin literature. Few openly criticized their reliability, although one of Caesar's own subordinates claimed that he took little care to verify accounts of events which he had not himself witnessed. Very rarely, especially for the Gallic campaigns, does any hint of an alternative version survive in the other sources covering this period. Therefore Caesar's ability as a commander is assessed almost exclusively from his own narrative, a situation which it is probable many generals throughout history would envy.

The *Commentarii* certainly report events in a manner which is favourable to their author, although his use of the third person throughout the text makes this a little less obvious. It is, however, unlikely that Caesar had complete freedom to invent as he pleased, for it should be remembered that the many senatorial officers with the legions in Gaul wrote frequently to family and friends back in Rome. Cicero's brother Quintus served as one of Caesar's legates and the brothers corresponded regularly. A good deal was known about the army's activities, and it is highly probable that the basic narrative in the *Commentarii* is accurate.

It is after all from Caesar's own writings that many historians have felt able to criticize some of his actions on campaign. For many he appears as a flawed genius, a man prone to sudden rash acts, whose talent often shone out most clearly in extricating his army from desperate situations which his own mistakes had created. It is also often assumed that he was a maverick who commanded in a way very different from the mass of Roman generals, whom modern commentators are all too inclined to dismiss as plodding amateurs. The Romans certainly never developed any formal institution for training men for command and thus all their commanders, including Caesar, were in this sense amateurs. It is important now to discuss Caesar's campaigns in the context of the operations of other Roman generals, and in particular his contemporaries such as Pompey, and judge whether or not he differed fundamentally from them in his style of command.[3]

EARLY LIFE AND CAREER UP TO 58 BC

Caius Julius Caesar was born around 100 BC. His family, the Julii Caesares, were patricians who claimed descent from the goddess Venus, but had only managed to produce a single consul during the entire second century. Caesar first attracted widespread attention during Sulla's dictatorship when he publicly displayed images of Marius at the funeral of his aunt, and Marius' widow, Julia. In 80–78 he began his military service, fighting in Asia and winning the *corona civica*. Whilst returning to Italy his ship was attacked by pirates and he was taken hostage. Throughout his captivity he continually declared that he would return and see every one of the pirates crucified. After his ransom had been paid, on his own initiative he raised forces from the nearest allied communities and went back to fulfil his promise, although as an act of mercy he ordered that the pirates should have their throats cut before they were fixed to the crosses. Caesar may have been a military tribune in 72 and perhaps served against Spartacus. In 63 he won both the praetorship and the office of Pontifex Maximus, Rome's senior priesthood, the latter with the assistance of a tribune who passed a law changing the election procedure.[4]

In most respects Caesar's early career was conventional, but there was a flamboyance about his behaviour which seemed to court controversy and won him many enemies. He spent lavishly, far beyond his resources, to win the favour of the poor by giving them feasts and entertainment and by associating himself with the popular causes of the day. All young senators pursuing a public career attempted to stand out from their peers, but Caesar took everything to extremes so that he was widely disliked, especially since his talents and intelligence were so obviously exceptional. Many senators believed that he was associated with Catiline's rebels who attempted to stage a coup in 63, a suspicion which was strengthened when he argued in the Senate against imposing the death penalty on the conspirators. Most people also believed that Crassus was involved, but since so much of Rome's aristocracy owed him money, it was felt politic not to make an issue of this.

Caesar was seen as politically unstable, a rake whose natural gifts and overweening ambition made him potentially dangerous. His affairs – almost always with senators' or equestrians' wives – were legion and frequently the subject for gossip. Rumour persisted that during his service in the east he had had a homosexual affair with the ageing King Nicomedes of Bithynia, so that he was dubbed 'a husband to women, and a wife to men'. Such crude invective was the common coin of Roman politics, making it very difficult to know whether the story had a basis in truth, but Caesar's womanizing was certainly both frequent and blatant. He is said to have seduced both Crassus' wife Tertullia and Pompey's third wife Mucia, whom the latter divorced on his return from Asia. A century later it would become a matter of some pride amongst the Gallic aristocracy to claim that a great-grandmother had become Caesar's mistress during his campaigns.

At Rome Caesar seemed to attract scandals, though not all were of his own making. One of his duties as Pontifex Maximus was to employ his house for the celebration of the festival of the Bona Dea, a ceremony at which only women were allowed to be present. However, on this occasion a disreputable senator named Clodius was discovered to have dressed as a woman to gain access to the secret rites and was alleged to be conducting an affair with Caesar's wife. Caesar claimed publicly to believe that there was no truth in this story, but divorced his wife anyway, declaring that 'Caesar's wife should be above suspicion'. Once again he set himself apart from other men, and, whilst his personal charm won over many – not least the numerous women who became his lovers – it was this attitude of superiority which made those who did oppose him so bitter in their hatred. Cato the Younger was the most prominent of these, a man whose fame rested upon a strict manner of life reminiscent of his famous forebear. His loathing for Caesar was deep and had as much or more to do with their conflicting characters as with differing politics. During the debate over the Catilinarian conspiracy Cato noticed that Caesar had just been slipped a note and demanded that it be read aloud, obviously hoping that it contained something incriminating. Caesar demurred and, when pressed, finally passed the note to Cato who was dismayed to find that it was in fact a passionate love letter from his own half-sister Servilia (the mother of the Brutus who would lead the conspiracy against Caesar in 44 BC).[5]

After his praetorship Caesar had gone as governor to Further Spain, where he had conducted a policing action against rebellious tribes and been awarded a triumph. However, faced with deliberate obstruction by his political rivals on his return to Rome, he voluntarily gave up the right to celebrate this honour in order to stand for the consulship. The sacrifice of a triumph gives an indication of just how confident Caesar was of gaining the higher office and winning even greater glory. His impatience to succeed quickly was matched by Crassus and Pompey and their support, in the latter's case the physical support of gangs of his veterans who were active in the Forum, ensured that his election campaign and year of office were marred by disturbances and violence. Yet only gradually did most senators realize that these three men had joined in an alliance to dominate the Republic. The other consul for 59, Marcus Calpurnius Bibulus, was backed by more conservative elements in the Senate and at first attempted to block all of his colleague's actions. Caesar responded by becoming ever more radical in his methods to force through his measures, most of which were objected to not because of their content but simply because he was proposing them. In one incident Bibulus had a basket load of dung emptied over his head and after this he virtually retired from public life for the remainder of the year. One wit declared that there were two consuls for the year – Julius and Caesar.

Traditionally the Senate still allocated provincial commands and his opponents, along with a large majority who were dismayed at the consul's tactics, determined that Caesar should receive the non-job of caring for the roads and forests of Italy. Thus was the dangerous radical to be deprived of the chance for winning glory and enriching himself – his debts were widely known to be on a staggering scale. This move was thwarted when once again a tribune brought a bill before the Popular Assembly to confer a province on an individual. Caesar was given both Cisalpine Gaul and Illyricum, to which Transalpine Gaul was added when news arrived that its current governor had died. His command was to last for five years – later extended to ten. Although not quite on the same scale as Pompey's Mediterranean or eastern commands, this was still a huge responsibility for a single magistrate. It was all the more unusual because there was no war, or even known major threat, in this region to justify putting so many resources in the hands of one man. Caesar set out for his province desperately needing to win glory and plunder, but it is not at all clear that he had already decided where he would find these. It is more than likely that he planned a Balkan campaign against the strong and wealthy kingdom of Dacia (roughly in the area of modern-day Romania). Then an opportunity suddenly presented itself on the Transalpine frontier and the balance of his war effort moved in that direction instead.[6]

THE MIGRATION OF THE HELVETII, 58 BC

At the beginning of spring in 58 BC a people known as the Helvetii – a Gallic people occupying an area roughly equivalent to modern Switzerland – began to migrate, following a route which would take them across the River Rhône and through the Roman province of Transalpine Gaul. The move was motivated by a growing population which created a demand for more extensive and fertile land to cultivate, and Caesar states that they planned to move to the west coast of Gaul near the mouth of the Garonne. He also claims that, with much of their tribal territory surrounded by mountains, the Helvetii felt confined because they had only limited opportunity to raid their neighbours. Warfare was endemic amongst the Gallic and German tribes and most often took the form of plundering expeditions which allowed chieftains to win glory and loot and so maintain a band of warriors as their personal attendants. Many of the tribes, especially of Southern and Central Gaul, were evolving from primitive chiefdoms into organized states governed by elective magistrates. However, individual noblemen still controlled considerable power, based around the warriors in their train and supported by men tied to them by bonds of kinship or debt.

Caesar's account is filled with attempts by such men to seize supreme power within their tribe and sometimes beyond. Just such a man, one Orgetorix, who had skilfully married off his female relatives to powerful noblemen in neighbouring tribes to gain wider influence, originally inspired the Helvetii with a desire to migrate, in 61 BC. However, while the Helvetii prepared for the migration, Orgetorix's ambitions brought him into conflict with the tribe's magistrates. After a failed attempt to overawe them with a display of the force at his disposal, he was placed on trial and died in slightly mysterious circumstances. Even so, at least one of Orgetorix's connections, his son-in-law the Aeduan nobleman Dumnorix, was to assist the Helvetii during their migration. It may well be that factions in several Gallic tribes welcomed the arrival of the migrants, and hoped with their aid to win power amongst their own peoples or to dominate their neighbours. An army of Germanic tribesmen under King Ariovistus had several years earlier been invited into Gaul by a people called the Sequani and had subsequently come to dominate a wide area in the centre of the country. There was probably a good deal of political background to the Helvetii's migration which Caesar chose not to explain, and some perhaps of which he was unaware.[7]

Orgetorix's death certainly did nothing to deter the Helvetii from their enterprise and they continued to mass food supplies for the journey. As a mark of determination not to turn back, they burned their own villages and farms before setting out. Caesar claims that altogether some 368,000 people were on the move, stating that the figure was based on records kept by the Helvetii themselves and written in Greek characters which his legionaries captured at the end of the campaign. As usual we have no way of checking the reliability of this estimate and can say little more than that a substantial number of warriors and their families were migrating. Like the Cimbri and Teutones, they did not move in a single massed column but in many separate groups spread over a wide area. Caesar notes at one point that it took them twenty days to cross the River Arar (modern Saône), which reinforces the picture of many individual trains of settlers, much like the waves of wagon trains which swept across the American West in the nineteenth century AD. In his narrative Caesar made a concerted effort to raise the spectre of the Cimbri and Teutones, reminding his readers on several occasions and in some detail that some of the Helvetii, especially the Tigurini clan, had taken part in those earlier movements and defeated the army of the consul Silanus in 107.[8]

Caesar received a report of the migration whilst he was still in Rome, and immediately rushed to Cisalpine Gaul – the speed with which he could travel, either riding or in a light carriage, continually amazed his contemporaries. He was already determined to prevent any incursions into Roman territory and, more than this, scented an opportunity to fight the dramatic and successful war he so desperately craved. The garrison of his great province of the Two Gauls and Illyria consisted of four legions, numbered VII, VIII, IX and X, supported by an unspecified number of auxiliaries. The latter included Spanish cavalry, Numidian light infantry, and perhaps also horsemen, Cretan archers and Balearic slingers, along with numbers of locally raised Gallic troops. However, only one legion – Caesar does not say which one – and some auxiliaries were in Transalpine Gaul and immediately available to meet the threat. To delay the Helvetii, Caesar ordered the bridge across the Rhône near Geneva to be destroyed.[9]

A deputation from the Helvetii now came to Caesar asking for permission to move through part of the Roman province during their journey and promising to do no harm whilst they were there. The Roman commander had already decided to deny the request, but for the moment answered that he needed time to consider his response and asked them to return in several days' time. In the meantime he ordered his soldiers to construct a line of fortifications stretching for more than 17 miles (19 Roman miles) from Lake Geneva to the Jura Mountains. When the envoys returned they were starkly informed by the proconsul that he would not grant them permission to pass through Roman territory and would forcibly resist any attempt to do so.

During the next few days small groups of tribesmen, most often under cover of darkness, tried to ford or cross the Rhône by raft and break through the Roman line. The delay imposed as they struggled to get over the Roman ditch and wall gave time for reserves to be summoned to the spot and each attempt was driven back under a shower of missiles. Rebuffed, the Helvetii turned back and, with the co-operation of Dumnorix who had some influence amongst that tribe and arranged friendly passage, took an alternative route through the lands of the Sequani. Leaving his legate Titus Labienus in charge of the troops holding the fortified line, Caesar went back to Cisalpine Gaul to fetch his three legions camped at Aquileia and raise two new formations, *XI* and *XII*. It is more than probable that orders had already been dispatched to set all of this in motion before he arrived. At the head of these five legions, he then returned by the shortest route, forcing his way through the Alpine passes in spite of attacks by the local tribesmen – the Alps were not fully conquered by the Romans until the lands all around them had long been under their control. The difficulty of operations in the mountains and the meagre plunder to be won made a campaign in this area an unattractive prospect for a magistrate out to win fame and fortune. It was not till the end of the first century BC, under the command of Caesar's adopted son and Rome's first emperor Augustus, that Roman authority was finally imposed here.[10]

Caesar had already crossed the Rhône when he received reports from allied tribes, most notably the Aedui, complaining that the Helvetii had been plundering their lands. He immediately advanced against them, and caught up with the rearmost of their columns, consisting mainly of the Tigurini, at the Saône. At the head of three legions, he left camp during the night and launched a sudden attack. Surprise was complete and the Gauls were massacred or dispersed with little loss to the Romans. (Apart from the significance of the Republic gaining revenge for 107, Caesar mentions at this point his personal satisfaction in the defeat of Tigurini, since his father-in-law's grandfather had been killed with Silanus). The Roman army then bridged the Saône and followed the main body of the Helvetii. Caesar now had all six legions, a force of perhaps 30,000 men, and 4,000 auxiliary cavalry, including a contingent of Aedui led by Dumnorix. Envoys from the tribesmen now asked the Romans for land, saying that they would happily settle wherever they were sent, but immediately refused Caesar's demand for hostages to be handed over. On the next day the Helvetii withdrew, but their outnumbered cavalry inflicted an embarrassing defeat on the Roman auxiliary horsemen who pursued incautiously. It was rumoured that the rout was led by Dumnorix and his men. Encouraged, some of the Helvetii stopped to offer battle. Caesar declined, and for the next two weeks shadowed the enemy, his vanguard staying about 5 or 6 miles behind the nearest of the tribesmen.

Supplying his forces was and is always one of the prime concerns of any commander, and Caesar's army was beginning to run short. He had been feeding his men from provisions brought up the Saône by boat, but as he moved further and further from the river this became impractical. The Aedui were supposed to have brought considerable quantities of grain to the army, but had so far failed to fulfil this obligation. Caesar summoned the two senior magistrates, or Vergobrets, of the tribe – one of whom was Dumnorix's brother Diviciacus. Dumnorix was blamed for deliberately holding back the collection of wheat and placed under open arrest, but as a favour to Diviciacus he was not punished further.[11]

On the same day, Caesar's scouts reported that the Helvetii had stopped for the night on a plain dominated by high ground some 8 miles from the Roman camp. A patrol was sent out to examine the hills themselves and the routes approaching them. These were discovered to be easy to traverse and Caesar decided to launch another surprise attack under cover of darkness. Labienus and two legions, guided by men who had taken part in the earlier patrol, were sent on ahead to seize the heights. Labienus was given strict orders not to engage until he saw the rest of the army going into the attack. An hour later Caesar himself took the main force along the same route. At the head of the column was the cavalry, preceded by scouting patrols all under command of the experienced Publius Considius, who had served under Sulla and Crassus and was probably a tribune. By dawn Labienus had secured the summit of the high ground and Caesar was no more than a mile and a half away. The Helvetii, who in common with many tribal armies moved clumsily and took little precaution to guard against surprise, were still blissfully unaware of the presence of either Roman force. However, Considius now galloped back to report that the hills were held by the enemy, claiming that he had recognized the troops holding these from their arms and insignia – probably shield devices or standards. Too far away to see such detail himself, Caesar had to assume that his advance party had at best got lost and at worst met with disaster. Halting, he led his men back to the nearest hill and formed them up for battle. It was several hours before patrols were able to establish that Labienus was in fact where he was supposed to be and by this time the Helvetii, still oblivious to all this enemy activity, had marched on. Caesar followed and camped 3 miles away from the nearest tribesmen.[12]

The attempt to surprise the enemy encampment had failed, but the incident is nevertheless highly informative. The method employed – initial scouting report confirmed by patrols who reconnoitre the ground and then act as guides for the main columns – would in essence not be out of place in the routine of a modern army. The ability to move large numbers of troops with confidence at night is a sign of a high level of military efficiency. Hannibal's army had shown a marked superiority over his Roman opponents in their capacity to move at night, most notably before Trasimene and in their escape from the Falernian Plain. Only a few of the legions produced by the old militia system were sufficiently well trained and disciplined to attempt such manoeuvres, but by the time of Pompey's and Caesar's campaigns they seem commonplace. Like the speed with which Caesar bridged the Saône in a day, it reflected the greater professionalism and skill of the legions under their command. Yet night operations were always liable to confusion and in this case a false report resulted in the attack being aborted.

By this time Caesar's army was running very low on supplies and, since the Aedui had not yet brought the promised grain, he decided to take the army to the supplies by marching to their main town of Bibracte some 18 miles away. News of this change in direction was carried to the Helvetii when some of the Gallic auxiliary cavalrymen deserted to them. They interpreted the move as prompted by timidity and decided that now was the best time to rid themselves of their pursuer. When the Romans turned away, the Gauls also changed direction and followed them, harassing the rearguard. Caesar led his men to a hill and, sending his cavalry to delay the enemy, formed the legions into battle. The four veteran units adopted the usual *triplex acies* halfway up the slope. Behind them were the raw *XI* and *XII* legions along with the auxiliary infantry and the baggage train. These were given orders to construct a camp, although it is unclear how far work on this proceeded. Caesar did not trust the recently recruited legionaries to stand in the main line of battle, but hoped that the sight of a slope filled with men would impress the enemy.

It is probable that a commander over and above the unit's tribunes was appointed for each legion. (In another battle later the same year Caesar's quaestor and five legates would each be placed in charge of a legion so 'that every man might have a witness of his valour'.)[13] Very visibly Caesar ordered his own horse, followed by those of his officers, to be sent to the rear. He also made an encouraging speech – probably several times as it would not have been possible to address the entire line simultaneously. Interestingly enough, Caesar very rarely recounts any of his speeches in detail except when wishing to make a political point. As the Romans prepared for battle the

Helvetii drove back his cavalry and formed a dense line of bands at the bottom of the slope – they are actually described as a phalanx by Caesar. Behind the warriors were many of their families in carts to observe the fight and witness their men's behaviour.

The Helvetii were extremely confident and readily advanced up the hill to attack the waiting Roman line. The legionaries waited until they came within the effective range of their *pila* – some 15 yards, or perhaps a little more given the slope – and then hurled a volley of these heavy javelins. The tactic was the same as that employed by Marius' men at Aquae Sextiae, as was the result. The small pyramidal points of the heavy weapons punched through shields, occasionally pinning two overlapping shields together, and, as they were designed to, the long slim shanks slipped through the hole to strike the man behind. Some Gauls were killed or badly wounded, many more found their shields encumbered by a heavy *pilum*, which could not easily be pulled out, and dropped them to fight unprotected. The combination of the advance up the hill and the devastating Roman volley had broken the Helvetii's formation and taken much of the impetus from their advance. When the Romans drew their swords and charged downhill in good formation they had a marked advantage.

Even so, it was a while – Caesar says *tandem* or 'at length' but it is as always difficult to quantify such an expression – before the Helvetii began to give way. They fell back for about a mile, and presumably for most of this distance the two fighting lines were not in contact. As the legions advanced to renew the battle they were suddenly faced with a new threat. The Boii and Tulingi, two subgroups within the migrants, had formed the rearguard and as a result had been late arriving at the battle. Now they threatened the Romans' exposed flank. The legions detached the cohorts of their third lines to form a new fighting line facing towards this threat, whilst the first and second lines pressed on against the enemy's main body. Fighting continued on the two fronts for about five hours, the Romans gradually forcing the Helvetii further and further up the hill and the Boii and Tulingi back amongst the carts and baggage, where they managed to push together numbers of carts to form a barricade. Some warriors threw javelins from the top of this improvised rampart while others flung missiles between the wheels, but in the end the legionaries forced their way in. Roman casualties were heavy enough for Caesar's men to spend the next three days tending the wounded and burying the dead. Gallic casualties were, as usual for a defeated army, considerably higher and numbers of distinguished prisoners were taken, including one of Orgetorix's daughters.[14]

The Helvetii retreated into the territory of the Lingones, but Caesar had sent messengers to the latter instructing them to withhold any aid and food from the fugitives or face a Roman attack. Threatened with starvation, the Helvetii sent envoys to beg for peace and this time submitted to his demand for hostages. The power of leaders within tribal societies was rarely absolute, and it may have been this independence of spirit which prompted one group of some 6,000 people to flee during the night. Caesar sent messengers to tell the tribes whose lands the fugitives might pass through to arrest them. Virtually all were returned to him and sold as slaves. The remainder of the Helvetii were instructed to return to their homeland. The Allobroges, a neighbouring people who lived within the Roman province, were told to give the Helvetii a considerable quantity of grain to tide them over as they rebuilt their own communities and planted seeds for the next year. However, one subgroup within the migrants, namely the Boii, were on the express request of the Aedui allowed to settle amongst the latter. The settlement was intended to secure the Roman province and Rome's allies. Caesar claims that only 110,000 Helvetii were left to return home, but, given the Roman desire to measure military success in spectacularly large and seemingly precise numbers of killed and captured, we must treat the implication that some 258,000 people had perished or been enslaved in the campaign with extreme scepticism.[15]

CAESAR ON CAMPAIGN, 58–53 BC

Shortly after the defeat of the Helvetii, Caesar received appeals from a number of Gallic tribes including the Aedui for aid against Ariovistus, who was said to lead an army of some 120,000 German warriors. There was an element of irony in this, for the German leader had recently been granted the title of King and Friend of the Roman People by the Senate during Caesar's own consulship.[16] Explaining that the need to protect Rome's allies and the Roman province overrode such a consideration, the Roman commander readily advanced to confront this new enemy. For all their general's confidence, it seemed for a while that the spirit of his army would fail as rumours were spread by traders and Gallic auxiliaries of the size and ferocity of the Germanic warriors. The tribunes and other senior officers were infected first, but the panic swiftly spread amongst the ordinary soldiers and nearly produced a mutinous refusal to advance any further.

Caesar called together the centurions – there were sixty in each of his legions – and other officers and sought to reassure them. He concluded by

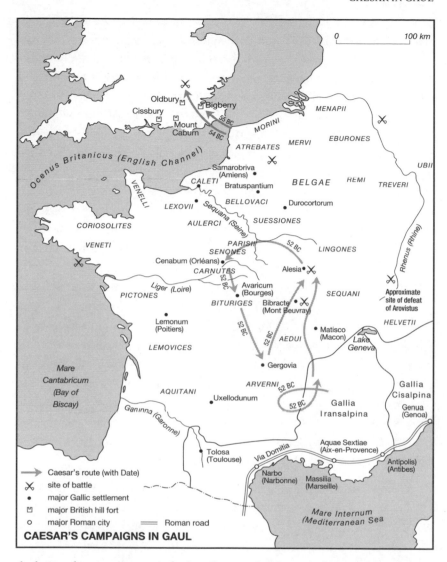

CAESAR'S CAMPAIGNS IN GAUL

declaring that, irrespective of what the rest did, he intended to advance alone with just *Legio X* on whom he was sure he could rely. This flattery immediately won over the soldiers of *Legio X*, who thanked their commander for his faith in them, and swiftly shamed the rest of the army who did not wish to be outshone by any other unit. This was one of the first instances where Caesar displayed his skill in manipulating the fierce unit pride of his legions. Ariovistus was soon brought to battle – Caesar had discovered from prisoners that the women who acted as soothsayers for the Germans had pronounced that the warriors could not win any battle fought before the new moon and so he deliberately provoked an immediate encounter – and defeated them after a hard fight. This time the newly raised legions were placed in the main battle line rather than in reserve, which suggests that participation in the previous campaign had increased their effectiveness. Throughout his campaigns Caesar attempted to prepare raw units for combat, promoting able centurions from veteran legions to senior positions within them, and gradually exposing them to the rigours of campaigning.[17]

The utter defeat of the Helvetii and Ariovistus in a single year represented massive achievements. Either victory would normally have satisfied a Roman governor as providing ample fame and plunder. Winning both together would guarantee a man a prominent place in the Senate. Yet for Caesar, secure in his special command, they were just the beginning. In the next year he responded to an attack on another allied tribe, the Remi, by moving against the Belgic peoples of north-eastern Gaul. An initial confrontation when both armies occupied a strong position and were reluctant to leave it and attack the enemy at a disadvantage ended when the Belgians ran out of food – a frequent problem for tribal armies without any organized commissariat. Disengaging when so close to the enemy was always a risky operation, and the warriors suffered badly as they straggled away under cover of darkness. Caesar then advanced and began systematically ravaging each tribe's territory as he came to it. It took some time for the Belgians to muster their main army again, but when it had re-formed they were able to launch a surprise attack on the Roman army as it was constructing its camp near the River Sambre. Caesar's description of this confused fight is one of the most famous passages in *The Gallic Wars*:

> Caesar had to do everything at the same time: to raise the standard, which was the signal to stand to arms, to sound the trumpet call which recalled the soldiers from work, to bring back the men who had gone further afield in search of material for the rampart, to form the line of battle, to address the soldiers, and to give the signal for battle.[18]

As he and his legates, who had been ordered to remain with their men until the camp's fortifications were complete, sought to create some semblance of a fighting line, Caesar rode along the battle line going from legion to legion.

> After addressing *Legio X*, Caesar hurried to the right wing, where he saw his men hard pressed, and the standards [*a shorthand term for the unit's formations*] of *Legio XII* clustered in one place and the soldiers so crowded together that it impeded their fighting. All the centurions in the fourth cohort had fallen, the standard-bearer [*signifer*] was dead and his standard captured; in the remaining

cohorts nearly every centurion was either dead or wounded, including the *primus pilus* Sextus Julius Baculus, an exceptionally brave man, who was exhausted by his many serious wounds and could no longer stand; the other soldiers were tired and some in the rear, giving up the fight, were withdrawing out of missile range; the enemy were edging closer up the slope in front and pressing hard on both flanks. He saw that the situation was critical and that there was no other reserve available, took a shield from a man in the rear ranks – he had come without his own – advanced into the front line and called on the centurions by name, encouraged the soldiers, and ordered the line to advance and the units to extend, so that they could employ their swords more easily. His arrival brought hope to the soldiers and refreshed their spirits, every man wanting to do his best in the sight of his general even in such a desperate situation. The enemy's advance was delayed for a while.[19]

In battle, Caesar was very mobile, riding – apart from the defeat of the Helvetii there is no mention of his commanding on foot in any other field action – along close behind the battle line to observe the combat and respond accordingly. In this case, as he says, 'there was no other reserve available' and so the commander went himself to join the fighting line. Once there he tried to inspire the flagging troops – calling out to the centurions as individuals, men whom he knew and recognized (and could therefore reward), and to the legionaries less specifically – and gave orders to reorganize and push forward the line. Although Caesar acknowledges the danger of the situation by his need to borrow a shield, he at no point says that he actually joined in the fighting. Instead he emphasizes his role in encouraging and directing the troops.

There are no stories told of Caesar equivalent to the tales of Pompey fighting sword or spear in hand and inflicting or receiving wounds. The heroic tradition embodied in Marcellus and to some extent Pompey had no place in Caesar's style of command. Throughout the *Commentaries* his physical courage is taken for granted, and his moral courage to cope with any crisis and never doubt that he would ultimately be victorious is more prominent. In Caesar's account his legionaries are disciplined, staunch, adaptable and brave; their centurions, both as individuals and collectively, utterly reliable and disdainful of danger. His treatment of more senior officers varies. Sometimes these take the wrong decision or become nervous and panic. Only very rarely do centurions or soldiers waver. The general himself never loses his calm certainty in his ultimate success. In battle he moves along just behind the fighting line, going from one crisis point to another.

All along the line his senior officers act in the same way, encouraging and directing the soldiers in a similar, if not quite so gifted, manner, but each of these men was tied to a particular sector and unable to rove at will. Only on a few occasions does Caesar admit that he had not anticipated a crisis, but usually another officer was able to respond. In the battle against Ariovistus, it was Publius Crassus – younger son of Caesar's political ally – 'who commanded the cavalry and was able to move more freely than those in the main line' who spotted a German threat to the Roman flank and ordered up the cohorts of the third line to meet it.[20]

The Sambre was one of the hardest fought of Caesar's battles. It was in many ways a soldiers' battle, won by the stubbornness of his legionaries who refused to give in, but the general and his commanders did what they could to direct the fighting. Caesar managed to stabilize his embattled right wing consisting of the *XII* and *VII*, but the position was only saved when Labienus, who had broken through on the left and taken the enemy camp, observed the situation and sent *Legio X* back to take the Belgians in the rear.

The rest of the summer was spent in suppressing the Belgic tribes. In 56 Caesar faced no strong confederation of tribes and divided his army to campaign in several regions of Gaul simultaneously. Perhaps the most notable achievement of the year was the defeat in a sea battle of the Veneti, who lived in what is now Brittany. Caesar was somewhat preoccupied by political worries in this year, for it seemed for a while as if the triumvirate was breaking down. Only a hastily arranged meeting with Pompey and Crassus, accompanied by over a hundred senators who wished to win their favour, at Luca in Cisalpine Gaul allowed him to resolve the argument between these two. Both men agreed to become consuls in the following year and arranged for Caesar's command to be extended to ten years.[21]

There is a strong similarity between Caesar's campaigns in Gaul and Pompey's operations in the Near East. In each case they enjoyed far greater resources and freedom of action than the vast majority of Roman governors. Both men also had the assurance that they would not find themselves replaced by a new proconsul until they were ready, and so could afford to plan ahead rather than simply scrabbling for immediate glory. The wars they fought were, at least by Roman standards, both justified and for the good of the Republic – Caesar was at pains to stress this throughout the *Commentaries*. They were waged to protect Rome's allies, interests or simply her power. An independent people who failed to show sufficient respect for Roman might were guilty of pride and thus a potential threat who deserved to be taught a lesson. The verb *pacare*, to pacify, was a common Roman euphemism for forcefully imposing their will on others and appears with some frequency in the *Commentaries*. In this way the legions marauded through Gaul until they had reached the Atlantic in the west, the Channel and North Sea in the north, and the Rhine in the east.

Caesar's and Pompey's activities differed from most Roman warfare because the key decisions of where they were to operate were made to a large extent by the commanders themselves with virtually no guidance from the Senate. The overwhelming majority of senators acknowledged that their operations were of benefit to Rome, however much they may have resented or envied two individuals winning so much personal glory, but as a body they had virtually no control over what these commanders were up to. Yet even political opponents could not help revelling in the legions' wonderful achievements. On one occasion Caesar was suspected of breaching faith by attacking a German tribe whilst engaged in negotiations with its leaders – a charge which even his own account suggests had some substance. Cato made a speech in the Senate suggesting that Caesar be handed over to the Germans, but may simply have wanted to confirm his reputation for pitiless virtue since he can have had no expectation that this might actually be done. Even he seems never to have questioned whether the campaigns being waged in Gaul were actually in Rome's interests. As with Pompey in the east, Caesar's opponents let him win wars for the good of the Republic, and waited to oppose him on his return to Rome when he would become a private citizen again.[22]

Caesar's operations in Gaul were consciously intended to be spectacular, for he had ever an eye on opinion back at Rome. In 55 he constructed a bridge across the Rhine, and he described the project in loving detail in *The Gallic War*, for such feats of engineering were almost as praiseworthy as successful battles or sieges. Crossing over the bridge he was the first Roman general to march against the German tribes on their own soil, though in fact they avoided battle and he achieved little other than to display his might and ability to reach them. In the next year the exercise was repeated, emphasizing to the tribes the legions' capacity to construct such wonders at will. In both 55 and 54 he also led expeditions across the sea to Britain, an island of mystery only barely part of the real world.

His own stated reason for mounting the invasion was that he believed that the Gauls had been aided by the Britons during recent campaigns. This is not impossible, but it is unlikely that such support had been on any great scale. Suetonius gives us another motive, claiming that his personal fondness for pearls led him to Britain which was believed to be rich in these. Yet more than anything else it was the Roman desire to achieve something never done before by another commander. Britain was a land of wonder, where the inhabitants fought from chariots in the manner of the heroes of the *Iliad*, a technique which the Gauls had abandoned centuries before. Caesar won the formal submission of the south-eastern tribes, imposing an annual tribute on them, although we do not know whether this was ever paid. More importantly the Senate declared a longer period of public thanksgiving for this achievement than had ever been declared before. It did not matter that both expeditions had come near to disaster when much of the invasion fleet was damaged or destroyed in storms and it seemed as if the expeditions would be stranded on the island. To many modern commentators the British expeditions seem ill prepared and rash to the point of dangerous recklessness. There is no indication that any of Caesar's contemporaries shared this view. Caesar was no more bold than the majority of senators placed at the head of an army, but he was certainly far more successful.[23]

In the winter of 54–53 BC he suffered his first serious reverse when a rebellion began amongst the Eburones and rapidly spread to other Belgic tribes. The recently recruited *Legio XIV* and another five cohorts were attacked in their winter quarters and, having negotiated with the chieftain Ambiorix, accepted a truce under which they would march away to join up with the rest of the Roman army. Whether by design or as a result of spontaneous action by individual warriors – the truth of such matters is usually very difficult to establish, as with the similar massacres during supposed truces at Fort William Henry in 1757, Kabul in 1842 and Cawnpore in 1857 – the Roman column was ambushed in wooded country and virtually annihilated. Caesar blamed the disaster on a divided command, for which he was obviously responsible though he does not mention this, and in particular to the craven and un-Roman behaviour of the legate Sabinus. Our other sources refer to this as one of his few serious defeats, blaming him even if he had not actually been present. Suetonius tells us that on receiving the news of the massacre he took a vow not to shave or cut his hair until his dead soldiers had been avenged.

After their success the main force of the Ambrones dispersed, each warrior content for the moment with their plunder and glory, but Ambiorix rode on with his bodyguard and persuaded the Nervii to attack the legion wintering in their territory. This was commanded by Quintus Cicero, the orator's brother, who led a much stauncher defence and refused to begin discussing a truce with the enemy. Caesar rapidly mustered the only immediately available forces – two understrength legions and some auxiliary cavalry which together numbered no more than 7,000 men – and marched to relieve Cicero's garrison. Although outnumbered and having sufficient supplies only for a very brief campaign, he managed to lure the Nervii into fighting in unfavourable circumstances and swiftly routed them. When the beleaguered legion was relieved, it was found that virtually all of its soldiers had been wounded.

It was still winter, making it very difficult to find food and forage, and so there was a lull in the fighting for several months, but it was still before the normal campaigning season that Caesar once again took the field, launching the first of a succession of fast-moving punitive expeditions against the rebellious tribes. In turn the tribes were surprised and unable to resist effectively as their lands were devastated. Most capitulated, but when the Eburones proved reluctant Caesar declared that anyone was free to plunder their land. He preferred that any casualties in the inevitable skirmishes occurring when the land was laid waste in this way should be suffered by the eager bands of freebooters who soon arrived from all over Gaul and Germany, rather than by his own legionaries.[24]

VERCINGETORIX AND THE GREAT REBELLION, 52 BC

Caesar's early interventions in Gaul had come at the invitation of the leaders of allied tribes, just as Ariovistus had been summoned to Gaul to assist the Senones in their struggle with the Aedui. Although the Gallic peoples shared a common language and culture, the individual tribes were fiercely independent and often hostile to each other. Neither tribe nor individual chieftain seeking to dominate his own people ever scrupled to seek external aid against an enemy or rival. Many tribes, most especially the Aedui, benefited from the arrival of the legions, but by the winter of 53–52 BC a widespread resentment of the Roman presence in Gaul had arisen. A group of noblemen from many tribes – both those who had suffered the attack of the legions and a few who had at first welcomed their arrival – met secretly and planned a co-ordinated rebellion. Their motives were neither nationalist nor entirely altruistic, since many hoped that the glory gained by defeating Rome would bring power or kingship amongst their own and other peoples.

The man who soon emerged as the principal leader of the rebellion, Vercingetorix of the Arverni, had first to overcome opposition from his own people when his followers proclaimed him king. Yet soon he was raising an army recruited not merely from his own tribesmen but from most of the peoples of western and central Gaul. Compared to the normal tribal armies, the force he created was both larger and a good deal more organized and disciplined, if still inferior to the Romans in the latter respects. More care was taken over supply than was usually the case in Gaul, giving Vercingetorix the capacity to remain longer in the field and not be forced into fighting a battle in unfavourable circumstances in the few weeks before his men would be forced to disperse for want of food. In 52 BC the Gauls were able to adopt a far more subtle strategy than had ever been the case in their earlier encounters with Caesar.[25]

The first outbreak of the rebellion came very early in the year at Cenabum in the land of the Carnutes, where two chieftains and their followers massacred all the Roman traders to be found in the town. The Roman army was currently dispersed in winter quarters throughout the conquered territory, whilst Caesar himself was in Cisalpine Gaul. It had been his habit throughout the campaigns to spend the winter months there, carrying out his judicial and administrative activities as governor as well as keeping a close eye on the politics of Rome. When Caesar heard of the rising he hurried to Transalpine Gaul. The only forces at his immediate disposal were some recently raised cohorts and local levies, and he was reluctant to send messengers summoning the legions to join him, in case they were attacked individually and overwhelmed. Such an apparent withdrawal could also have been interpreted as a sign of fear and weakness and encouraged other tribes to join the rebels. Therefore, the general himself would have to go to the legions, but before he could do this it was important to do as much as possible to protect the Roman province.

There had already been some raids against the provincial communities who were themselves Gauls and so might be persuaded to join the rebellion. Caesar sent some of his troops to the threatened sectors and concentrated a small striking force near the passes of the Cevennes which led into Arvernian territory. It was still winter and the main pass was considered to be impassable, but Caesar led his men through, clearing paths through 6-foot deep drifts to launch a raid on the enemy. Surprise was complete and for two days the Roman column plundered and ravaged at will, with the auxiliary cavalry galloping on ahead to spread panic through as wide an area as possible. Soon Vercingetorix was deluged with panicky messages from his countrymen demanding immediate aid. He shifted his main army in the direction of the incursions, but by this time Caesar had placed his force under the command of Decimus Brutus and himself ridden off, publicly announcing that he would return in three days with more levies. Instead he rode swiftly to Vienne where he joined a force of cavalry – probably including a unit of 400 Germans whom he had mounted on good horses and kept at his immediate disposal

– previously ordered to muster at this place. Not even resting for the night he took the horsemen on through the lands of the Aedui and into the territory of the Lingones and joined the two legions wintering in this spot. Messengers were dispatched instructing all the other legions to concentrate, and Caesar had united his army before the first intelligence reached Vercingetorix that his opponent was no longer with the raiding column.[26]

The Roman field army was together, but spring had not yet arrived and no great store of provisions had been mustered to allow them to operate together for any length of time. When Vercingetorix advanced to besiege Gorgobina, the main town of the Boii who had been permitted to settle in Aeduan territory in 58, Caesar was faced with a dilemma. His army was not provisioned for a long campaign and could not hope to draw significant quantities of food and fodder from the winter landscape, but any failure to protect allied communities would be interpreted as weakness and encourage defections to the enemy. Revolts were always weakest in their early phases as many potential rebels waited to see whether prospects of success were sufficiently good to make the risk of joining worthwhile. Roman defeats, however small, helped to encourage the waverers to commit themselves, and even inaction was usually interpreted as a sign of weakness. In the previous winter Caesar had moved immediately with a small and poorly supplied force to attack the Nervii and relieve Cicero's camp. In 52 he responded with similar boldness, deciding that it was better to assume the offensive immediately in spite of the risks than to remain inactive and appear impotent. This was the characteristic Roman response to rebellion, wrenching back the initiative from the rebels at the first opportunity and then trying to keep it by launching one attack after another with whatever troops were quickly available rather than waiting to muster a stronger force. The approach suggested supreme confidence in the inevitability of Roman victory and, even if this was no more than a façade and the attacking troops poor in numbers or quality or inadequately supplied, it was often enough to overawe and crush the rebellion.[27]

Caesar ordered the Aedui to gather grain and bring it to him as soon as possible and, leaving two legions to guard the army's baggage, immediately advanced to the aid of the Boii, reducing any hostile strongholds he passed en route and confiscating any supplies and pack animals he could find. One of these strongholds was Cenabum, which was thoroughly plundered and burnt as punishment for the killing of the Roman businessmen. The advance of the legions persuaded Vercingetorix to abandon his blockade of Gorgobina and close with the enemy. Caesar had just accepted the surrender of another walled town, Noviodunum, when the Gallic army appeared, reviving the townsfolks' enthusiasm for resistance. Fighting developed between the cavalry of the two armies, the advantage swaying one way then the other in the usual whirling manner of such combats. Finally, Caesar fed in his German horsemen and this reserve of fresh men, combined with the significant moral advantage Germanic warriors enjoyed over their Gallic counterparts, prompted the flight of the enemy. The town surrendered once more, and the legions pressed on to attack Avaricum, one of the most prosperous and important of the communities of the Bituriges. Caesar was confident that capture of this town, coming after his earlier successes, would be enough to persuade the tribe to capitulate.[28]

Vercingetorix decided that it was better for the moment to avoid direct confrontation with the enemy and instead to wear the legions down by depriving them of food. He camped some 16 miles from Avaricum and ordered his cavalry to harass Roman foraging parties. A cat and mouse game developed as the Romans became more cautious and tried to avoid using the same routes more than once and so falling into ambush. The Bituriges were persuaded to carry off or destroy their animals and food stores to prevent their falling into enemy hands, and even went so far as to burn many of their own towns and villages. Caesar sent back frequent messages calling for the Aedui and Boii to bring him fresh supplies of grain, but the latter were few in number and what they could supply was swiftly exhausted. The Aedui could have done more, but were beginning to waver in their loyalty and so sent virtually nothing.

Undeterred, Caesar set about the siege of Avaricum, ordering the construction of a huge siege ramp across the valley between his camp and the hilltop town. Eventually, after twenty-five days of toil, a ramp 80 feet high and 330 feet broad led up to the Gallic wall. It was another example of the legions' skill in engineering and willingness to undertake prolonged heavy labour, in this case while the weather was cold, the rain heavy and frequent, and their rations small. Caesar personally supervised the project and talked to the work party from each legion as it went about the task, telling the legionaries that he would abandon the siege if they felt the lack of food had become too serious. The soldiers' pride in themselves and their units kept them going, so that each group assured their commander that they would finish what they had begun.

As the siege progressed, the Gallic army also began to run short of provisions. Vercingetorix's authority over the army was by no means absolute and the other chieftains persuaded him against his better judgement to move closer to the town and attempt to relieve it. An attempt to ambush a Roman foraging party was detected and prompted Caesar to march out with the bulk of his forces. Vercingetorix offered battle from a very strong hilltop position, but refused to come down and fight in the open. Although the legions were eager and confident of their ability to beat the enemy on any ground, Caesar refused to attack, announcing to his soldiers that he valued their lives too highly to win a victory with heavy casualties when it could be achieved at lesser cost by other means. Vercingetorix managed to send 10,000 warriors in to reinforce the townsfolk, but was otherwise unable to assist them.

The defenders were very active throughout the siege, launching sallies to burn the Roman siegeworks. As these grew in size, and siege towers were raised so that men could shoot down on the defenders on the town's wall, the Gauls added wooden turrets protected by stretched hides to raise the height of their own positions. Many of the locals worked in nearby iron mines and put this experience to good use in tunnelling underneath the ramp. When the latter was virtually complete the Gauls filled the mine with incendiary material and tried to set fire to the ramp during the night. The attempt was backed by groups of men running out to fling torches onto the Roman works, whilst others hurled flaming missiles from the wall.

It was the practice during the siege for two legions always to be in a state of readiness and these quickly moved forward to meet the attacks. The fighting was vicious and Caesar himself paid particular tribute to a Gallic warrior who stood above one of the gateways hurling lumps of grease and pitch. The man was shot with a scorpion, one of the Roman army's light catapults, which fired a heavy-tipped bolt with great accuracy and terrible force, but another immediately took his place, only to be picked off in turn. Again and again a warrior came forward to continue the task and was killed. Only when the sallies were finally repulsed and the fire extinguished did the Gauls give up.

The Gauls now realized that the defence was hopeless, but an attempt by the warriors to break out was thwarted. On the next morning, during a heavy rainstorm when the enemy would least expect an attack, Caesar ordered his legionaries to assault. The walls were swiftly taken, but for a short while dense knots of warriors formed up in the lanes and marketplace of the town to meet the attack. The Romans ignored them, concentrating on securing the key points of the defences, and the Gauls swiftly gave way to panic. The sack of the town was brutal in the extreme, as the weary legionaries vented their frustration after their prolonged and difficult labour and extracted another revenge for Cenabum. Men, women and children, virtually all were slaughtered as the soldiers ran amok. The army remained in the town for several days to recuperate and Caesar was pleased to discover sizeable stores of grain there. It was now almost spring and certainly no time to slacken the pace of his offensive, so after this short break he took the main force of six legions against the Arvernian town of Gergovia and sent the other four under Labienus against the Parisii and Senones to the north. Rarely in the *Commentaries* does the author give precise figures for the number of troops under his command, but it seems probable that his veteran legions were by now somewhere between 50 and 75 per cent strength – some 2,500–4,000 men – although the more recently raised units may still have been larger.[29]

If anything the loss of Avaricum, against whose defence he had counselled, reinforced Vercingetorix's influence and he was able to persuade more tribes to join the alliance. For a while even the favoured Aedui rebelled, although swift action by Caesar was able to stamp out this rising quickly. The main Gallic army was camped on a ridge outside Gergovia. The Roman general rode out to reconnoitre the town in person and swiftly decided that a direct assault was unlikely to succeed. He was also reluctant to commit himself to a long blockade until he had made arrangements to secure his supply lines. He therefore pitched camp and waited. During the next few days there were frequent skirmishes between the cavalry and light troops of the rival armies. In a night march Caesar secured a hill nearer the town, taking the small enemy force there by surprise and setting two legions to occupy and fortify the position. The Roman camps were then connected with each other by a route defended by a ditch on either side to ensure uninterrupted communications. After some time, for part of which he was absent dealing with the Aedui, he resolved on mounting a major attack against an exposed part of the ridge on which the Gallic army was camped. As usual his planning was based on personal observation of the ground and interrogation of prisoners, which informed him that the enemy had reduced the number of men there in order to fortify another section which they felt to be vulnerable.

That night the Romans sent out cavalry patrols with orders to range in all directions, making as much noise as possible. At dawn Caesar sent out a great mass of camp followers and slaves wearing basic equipment and mounted on pack animals in a rather similar ploy to the one used by Pompey. These were ordered to rise in a wide circle around the enemy-held high ground and it was hoped that from a distance they would be mistaken for real cavalry. One legion very visibly marched in the same direction, but, once in dead ground, it concealed itself in a wood. The feint worked, and the great bulk of the Gallic army shifted over to meet this apparent threat, leaving their main camp virtually empty. Gradually, during the morning, small parties of legionaries went from the main camp to the smaller one, until the bulk of the army had in this way shifted its position. Then Caesar led them into the attack, each of the legions working its way up one of the series of re-entrants leading up to the ridge, with 10,000 auxiliary infantry provided by the once again loyal Aedui taking another route. The attack was swiftly successful, and there was virtually no resistance as they broke into three of the Gallic camps dotted around the ridge. In one of these King Teutomatus of the Nitiobriges was almost captured, awaking from his slumbers just in time to gallop off half-naked on a wounded horse.

The attack had been highly successful, and Caesar now tells us that he ordered the recall to be sounded by the trumpeters. The unit he was with, his favourite *Legio X*, immediately halted, but the signal did not carry well along the rolling ridgeline and was not heard by other units. He claims that he had specifically ordered the legates and tribunes not to let the soldiers get out of hand and press the attack too far. However, in spite of all their efforts, these men were unable to restrain the exhilarated legionaries who swarmed on up the slope to attack the walls of Gergovia itself. At first it seemed as if the impetuous and ill-organized attack would succeed through sheer enthusiasm as panic spread amongst the few defenders of the town:

> Married women hurled down clothing and silver from the wall and, baring their breasts, stretched out their hands to beg the Romans to spare them, and not massacre women and children as they had done at Avaricum. Some of the women even lowered themselves by hand from the wall and gave themselves to the soldiers. Lucius Fabius, a centurion of *Legio VIII*, who was known to have announced to his unit that he was inspired by the rewards at Avaricum, and would not permit anyone to climb the wall before him, got three of his legionaries to lift him up so that he could climb on top of the wall. He then pulled each of them up onto the rampart.[30]

However, the Gauls swiftly began to recover and large numbers of warriors moved to meet the incursion, forming up in dense blocks behind the wall. The women stopped begging for mercy and began to cheer their menfolk on. As yet only a small number of Romans had broken into the town and they were both tired and disorganized. For a long time the enthusiasm of Caesar's men did not permit them to give up, but they were fighting at a great disadvantage and casualties were heavy. The appearance of the Aeduan auxiliaries on the attackers' flank created a panic when they were mistaken for the enemy, in spite of the fact that they had their right shoulders bared to mark them out as allies and not enemy warriors.

> At the same time the centurion Lucius Fabius and those who had climbed the wall with him were surrounded, killed and flung from the rampart. Marcus Petronius, another centurion from the same legion, who had tried to hack through the gate, was being overwhelmed by numbers and was now in a desperate situation. Wounded many times, he called out to the men of his unit who had followed him: 'Since I cannot save both myself and you, whom I led into danger through my own lust for glory, I can at least manage to save your lives. When you get the opportunity look after yourselves.' Straight away he charged forward into the midst of the enemy, killed two of them and forced the rest back from the gate a short distance. His men tried to come to his aid, but he said, 'There is no hope of you saving my life, for my life's blood and strength are draining away. So escape whilst you have a chance and make your way back to the legion.' So, before long he fell fighting and saved his men.

Fabius and Petronius were two of the forty-six centurions and just under 700 men who were killed during the fighting. Caesar's only criticism of his troops in the *Commentaries* is to say that they were simply too confident and eager to win his praise, whilst the prominent place given to the heroism and self-sacrifice of a few individuals helped to conceal the scale of the defeat. During the fighting he summoned two cohorts of *Legio XIII*, who had been left to guard the smaller camp, to support *Legio X* as he tried to cover the flight of his men. On the following day the army was paraded and reprimanded for its disobedience of his orders, but he issued no punishments. He then marched them out of the camps and deployed into battle order in a very strong position. Vercingetorix not surprisingly refused to attack in such unfavourable circumstances, and the Roman commander was able to assure his men that, in spite of their recent reverse, the Gauls were still frightened of them. He then withdrew, deciding that there was little point remaining outside Gergovia and anyway there were renewed problems with the Aedui, some of whom had massacred the Roman garrison at Noviodunum. The town was then put to the torch, and great quantities of grain which had been massed there taken, burnt or spoiled in other ways.

Following up their success, the rebels sent out many small groups of cavalry to threaten the Roman supply lines from Transalpine Gaul. Caesar had lost the initiative at Gergovia, and his reverse was enough to encourage more tribes to join the rebels, but now he launched a counter-offensive in a different direction, hurrying back towards the Roman province by forced march. His army forded the swollen Loire, with cavalry forming a screen upriver and the infantrymen lifting arms and equipment above their heads as they waded through the chest-deep water, just as Pompey's men had crossed the Cyrus. Further north Labienus had campaigned with considerable success against the Parisii and Senones, but now felt that it was better to rejoin Caesar and confront the enemy with their full strength. Caesar fully approved his decision, and provides a detailed account of the skill with which his legate deceived the Gallic leaders about his intentions and was able to cross a river unopposed before engaging and smashing the enemy army. According to *The Gallic War*, as the battle opened Labienus encouraged his men by asking them to imagine that Caesar himself was present to observe their behaviour. However gifted a legate, the *Commentaries* make it clear that their author was always the true hero.[31]

For a short while both sides regrouped. Vercingetorix was able to increase the number of warriors in his main army and encourage other tribes to attack the Romans wherever they could. Caesar had been joined by Labienus and also mustered more levies from his provinces and hired more German horsemen and light infantry from across the Rhine, replacing the small ponies they rode with more expensive mounts, mostly provided by his officers. Then he advanced against the Sequani and Lingones of eastern Gaul. Vercingetorix mustered a large force of cavalry to attack the Roman army on the march, the warriors binding themselves with a solemn oath not to leave the field until they had each ridden twice through the enemy column. The Gallic leader divided his men into three groups and threatened both flanks and the head of the column simultaneously. To counter this Caesar also divided his auxiliary cavalry into three detachments and sent one against each of the opposing groups. Whenever the Gallic horsemen seemed to be gaining an advantage, cohorts of legionaries were ordered to form up in close support of their own horsemen. This helped to stabilize the combat, since it provided a solid refuge behind which the auxiliaries could rally and reform before returning to the fray, but it also slowed down the army's progress.

In the end the German cavalry, who were facing the enemy attacking the right of the Roman column, forced their way to the top of some high ground and, charging down the slope, routed their opponents. This defeat prompted the retreat of the rest of the Gallic cavalry. Discouraged by the failure of an attack launched by what was felt to be their strongest arm, Vercingetorix and the Gallic army retreated to the town of Alesia. Caesar pursued, forcing the pace with the main body while leaving his baggage train protected by two legions on a convenient hill. For the rest of the day the

Roman harassed the Gallic rearguard, inflicting heavy losses. The next morning the entire Roman force moved on Alesia, where they discovered the Gallic army camped on high ground outside the town.[32]

With his army now concentrated and carrying with it ample supplies, this time Caesar did not hesitate to begin the blockade of the town and Vercingetorix's camp. Whilst his cavalry screened the work and fought a number of skirmishes with their Gallic counterparts, the legionaries began construction on a line of fortifications some 11 miles in length with twenty-three forts connected by a ditch and rampart. Before the circuit was closed, the Gallic commander ordered his cavalry to escape, telling each contingent to return to their own tribes and raise troops for a massive relief army which would return and defeat the enemy. Caesar claims that some 80,000 Gauls remained encamped outside the town, and that they had sufficient food for at least thirty days. However, it seems highly unlikely that the Gallic army was as large as this, especially since it let itself be besieged by a Roman force of perhaps 40,000 men – Caesar does not state his own strength, and the size of each legion in 52 BC as well as the number of auxiliaries is not precisely known.

The Roman commander learned of the flight of the enemy cavalry and Vercingetorix's determination to withstand a siege. The legions were set to strengthening the Roman siege lines which at first had consisted of a ditch and wall no more than 6 feet high. Now a trench 20 feet wide with steep sides surrounded the enemy position. This was intended to slow down any enemy trying to cross and provide sufficient warning of an attack for troops to be rushed to the spot. The main earth and timber rampart was set back about 400 paces from the ditch, and this was protected by two more ditches, each 15 feet in width and the inner one flooded wherever this was possible. The wall itself was 12 feet high, topped with a parapet and walkway and with a high turret every 80 feet. Sharpened stakes were set in tight rows in front of the rampart, and in advance of these were rows of smaller stakes concealed in pits – traps which the soldiers nicknamed 'lilies' from their circular appearance – and, even further forward, rows of iron spikes fitted to pieces of wood and buried so that the sharp point just projected above the ground. These obstacles might in some cases wound or even kill enemies who charged across them too quickly and carelessly, but this was not their main purpose. Men moving carefully and slowly would probably be able to thread their way between them without suffering injury, but this would inevitably rob any massed attack of momentum.[33]

The construction of the fortifications at Alesia was an enormous task, effectively doubled in scale when Caesar ordered that another, almost identical line of contravallation (i.e. wall facing outwards) should be built to prevent any relieving army from attacking the lines of circumvallation (i.e. wall facing inwards). Archaeological excavation, begun on a large scale under the aegis of Napoleon III and backed up by more modern expeditions, has substantially confirmed the accuracy of Caesar's description. Once the fortification was completed Caesar's army, which had carefully massed food and forage sufficient for a month, was protected from attack from any direction. Although Vercingetorix had attempted to launch attacks intended to hinder the work, he had not been able to prevent its eventual completion. In the meantime the tribes were putting together a relief force and, if we are probably wise to take Caesar's figure of 8,000 cavalry and 250,000 foot soldiers with more than a pinch of salt, this was certainly substantial and may well have enjoyed a marked numerical advantage over the Roman army. Such a force mustered slowly and took a considerable time to provide itself with food and other supplies. As the siege lengthened, the entire population of Alesia which could not fight – women, children and the elderly – was expelled from the town in order to preserve the dwindling store of food.

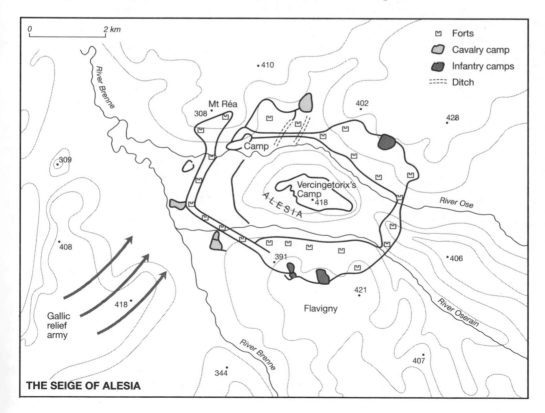

THE SEIGE OF ALESIA

Caesar was not willing to let the refugees through his lines, and these unfortunates were left to starve to death in the no-man's-land between the rival armies. Whether he feared that in the confusion the enemy might launch an attack or simply wished the Gauls to be depressed by this terrible sight, Caesar does not say.[34]

Soon afterwards the relief force arrived and camped on high ground a mile from the Roman lines. On the following day they paraded their great strength in a plain clearly visible to the besieged, the cavalry spread over some 3 miles and the infantry behind. Vercingetorix led his men out of the camp and town and began to fill in sections of the wide ditch 400 paces ahead of the Roman lines. Caesar divided his own troops to defend against attack from either direction, and then sent out his own cavalry to engage the Gallic horsemen. Interspersed amongst the latter, and not at first visible, were small knots of archers and javelinmen, whose unexpected missiles caused some loss to the auxiliaries. When a few of the Roman cavalry were driven back the relieving army and besieged warriors sent up a great shout of triumph. Yet cavalry combats often involved withdrawals by men who would swiftly rally and go forward again, and this combat was no exception, continuing sporadically for most of the afternoon. Once again Caesar's German cavalry proved their superiority over Gallic horsemen and launched a final charge which routed the enemy. The Gallic light infantry, abandoned by their own horsemen, were almost all cut down.[35]

There was no fighting on the following day, as the Gauls prepared ladders to scale the ramparts and fascines to fill in the ditches. Their main attack came at midnight and was begun by the relieving force. The noise of battle announced their arrival to Vercingetorix, who ordered a trumpet sounded which sent his own men in to battle. The Gauls flooded in to the attack, weaving their way between the obstacles and filling in the ditches as a barrage of slingstones, arrows and javelins was sent at the rampart in an effort to drive the defenders back. The Romans replied with javelins and stones which had been collected and placed in readiness on the walkway and with the fire of the scorpions from the towers. The fighting was fierce and confused, for the darkness made control difficult, but two of Caesar's legates – one of whom was Mark Antony – took troops from forts in an area which was not threatened to reinforce the legionaries under attack. Both of the main assaults were eventually beaten back.

On the next morning the Gauls launched their main effort against the most vulnerable section of the line, a fort held by two legions on a gentle reverse slope which gave little advantage to the defender. A picked force –

60,000 strong according to Caesar – moved before dawn and concealed themselves behind high ground in a position previously discovered by scouts from
which they could launch an attack on this fort. At midday this assault went in,
while other groups of warriors made demonstrations and feint attacks on
other parts of the line. Vercingetorix was not in communication with the
relieving army and once again only ordered his own men to advance when
he saw their attacks going in.

Caesar rode to a vantage point – his lines of fortification followed the
contours of the rolling landscape – and began directing the battle. Whenever
he saw a section of his line hard pressed he sent orders for reserve troops to
reinforce the men there. The greatest threat was against the camp on the
hill, and as the Gauls managed to fill its protective ditches and even cover
most of the stakes and pits, a breakthrough seemed imminent. This time
the general sent Labienus at the head of five cohorts to strengthen the two
legions in the fort. This trusted legate was given considerable freedom in
his orders, Caesar expressly permitting him to concentrate the cohorts and
fight their way out if he felt that the position could not be held. The general
himself now also began to move around the lines, encouraging the
hard-pressed legionaries.

Vercingetorix's men, aware of their desperate need to make contact
with the relieving army, managed to drive most of the defenders from one
section of the wall with concentrated missiles. The warriors charged, and
some started to tear down the earth wall with tools. Caesar ordered Decimus
Brutus with several cohorts to drive them back. Soon afterwards another
legate, Caius Fabius, was given more reserves and told to reinforce this sector.
Finally, he placed himself at the head of another group of cohorts, some of
whom he pulled out from one of the forts which was not under heavy attack.
He ordered some of his cavalry to leave the line by one of the gates away
from the fighting and told them to move round to the camp on the hill by
a wide circuit. Caesar himself led the rest of his men to the camp's relief.
There the hard-pressed Labienus had been forced back from the rampart,
but had put together a solid fighting line inside the fort from his own troops
and any others that he had been able to gather. The battle had reached its
crisis. Perhaps it is best to allow Caesar himself to describe the conclusion: his

> arrival was known through the colour of his cloak, which he always wore in
> battle as a distinguishing mark; and the troops [*turmae*] of cavalry and the
> cohorts which he had ordered to follow him were also visible, because from
> the higher parts of the hill these downward slopes and dips could be seen. Then

> the enemy joined battle: both sides cheered, and the cry was taken up by a shout from the men within the fortifications and rampart. Our troops threw their *pila* and got to work with their swords. Suddenly [the Gauls] spotted the cavalry behind them; other cohorts approached. The enemy turned around and were caught as they fled by the cavalry; and a great slaughter ensued ... seventy-four captured war standards were carried to Caesar; very few of this vast host escaped unscathed to their camp.[36]

The Roman victory was completed the next day when Gallic envoys came to his camp and accepted his demand for their unconditional surrender. Caesar sat in state on the tribunal in front of the rampart as the leaders each arrived to give themselves up. According to Plutarch Vercingetorix dressed in his finest armour and rode in on his best charger. After walking the horse around the tribunal he dismounted, laid down his weapons and sat on the grass waiting mutely to be led away. The number of captives was vast – every soldier in the army being given a prisoner to sell as a slave – adding to the vast total taken by Caesar's men during the Gallic campaigns. Pliny believed that more than a million people were sold into slavery as a result of his conquests, and as many again killed. Caesar had gone to his province massively in debt, but the profits of his campaigns not only allowed him to pay off his creditors, but made him one of the wealthiest men in the Republic. Twenty days' public thanksgiving was decreed by the Senate to celebrate the defeat of Vercingetorix.[37]

The operations in Gaul were not quite over. Another smaller rebellion occurred in 51 BC and Caesar met this in his accustomed manner, immediately sending columns out to attack any signs of resistance. The town of Uxellodunum was taken by siege, and the warriors who had defended it had their hands cut off as a permanent and highly visible warning of what happened to those foolish enough to oppose Rome. It was not the first time that Caesar had imposed such a harsh punishment – he had once ordered the execution of the entire ruling council of a tribe – nor was it unusual for a Roman commander to act in this way. Again like other Roman generals Caesar also acted generously when this seemed likely to bring practical advantage. Both the Arverni and the Aedui were treated leniently after the 52 BC rebellion, their captured warriors being returned to them rather than sold. Caesar's attitude did much to win these tribes back to their traditionally friendly attitude to Rome. For Vercingetorix, as for Jugurtha and so many other leaders who had opposed Rome, there was no leniency. He was held captive for years until he could be led in procession and ritually strangled at the end of Caesar's triumph.

CHAPTER 9

CAESAR AGAINST POMPEY

The Civil War (49–45 BC)

All this has made Caesar so strong that now hope of resistance depends on one citizen. I wish that citizen [Pompey] had not given him so much power rather than that he now resisted him in the hour of his strength.[1]

THE DIE IS CAST

CAESAR'S GALLIC VICTORIES GAVE HIM THE MILITARY GLORY AND WEALTH HE had craved in 59 BC, but there was now a question as to whether he would be permitted to assume a position of importance in public life at Rome. He knew that he had made many bitter opponents during his turbulent career and expected to face prosecution, not least from Cato who had wanted to hand him over to the Germans. Innocence or guilt played only a minor part in determining the outcome of Roman political trials and by the autumn of 50 BC he was not sure just how many friends he could count on in the Senate. Crassus had been killed by the Parthians in 53 BC, having invaded their country in an unnecessary war inspired largely by his desire to rival the military achievements of the other two triumvirs. Julia had died in child-birth the year before, severing the closest of all links between Caesar and Pompey. Although a marriage dictated by political convenience, the union appears to have been a genuinely happy one for both parties. Pompey seems always to have craved and responded well to devotion, whether from a wife or an army.

Although he had not desired a province after his second consulship held with Crassus in 55, Pompey had gained massive power when repeated outbreaks of politically motivated rioting caused chaos in Rome and led to his appointment as sole consul for 52. He was given all of the Spanish provinces and their garrisons to command for five years, but was permitted to remain in Rome and govern through legates. In many ways this was a greater subversion of the traditional Republican system than any of his earlier activities. In the same year he took another bride young enough to be his daughter, when he married Cornelia, daughter of Publius Metellus Scipio, a prominent critic of Caesar. The two allies seemed to be drifting apart.

Caesar announced that he wished to go straight from his Gallic command into a second consulship, standing for election *in absentia* and remaining in Gaul until he could enter Rome to celebrate his triumph and become consul on the same day, just as Pompey had done. As a magistrate he would be immune to prosecution and he could then take another province and military command to win further glory. There was much talk of the need to avenge Crassus' defeat at Carrhae and the subsequent Parthian raids on Syria, and it was felt that either Caesar or Pompey should be given control of this war. However, Caesar's bitterest opponents were determined to prevent his escaping prosecution in this way and set in hand measures to ensure that he had to return as a private citizen. Pompey's attitude remained ambiguous, but he seems to have expected that his former ally, who in 59 had been very much the junior of the three, should simply trust to his protection.

Caesar was unwilling to do this, in part because Pompey's record in defending his friends against political enemies was somewhat patchy. He had done nothing to prevent Cicero's exile in 58, although he had assisted his recall in the following year. Caesar was also reluctant to admit that he required the assistance and protection of any other senator. As far as he was concerned, his Gallic victories had earned him a place of influence as high as or higher than that held by Pompey. The latter had been Rome's greatest military figure for thirty years and was unwilling to accept a man whose fame was so recent as his peer. It may also be that he feared being overshadowed if Caesar were allowed to return to public life at Rome, for even he probably realized that the younger man was a far more gifted political schemer. Caesar's frequent pronouncements that he would rather be the first man in the tiniest village than the second man in Rome, or that it would be far easier to push him down from second to last place in the Republic than from first to second, may even have made Pompey uneasy.[2]

The politics in the months leading to the Civil War were extremely complex, with a range of proposals being presented but nothing actually being done. Some asked for Caesar to lay down his command and his army, others for Pompey to do the same, and then it was suggested that both men give their troops up, which only led to bickering over which one should go first. Pompey's failure to support Caesar's requests encouraged Cato and his other opponents in the Senate in the belief that they could use one man against the other. Pompey was certainly the lesser of two evils, since he was a less capable politician and might more easily be disposed of in the future. In return he doubtless considered it useful to appear as the champion of the 'best men' (*optimates*) in the Senate against a man intent on flouting the laws of the Republic. It is difficult to know whether the numerous offers of conciliation made by the partisans of either Caesar or Pompey were anything more than attempts to gain the moral high ground in the struggle which both now viewed as inevitable. Caesar believed that he was faced with a choice between laying down his command and facing trial and political extinction or fighting a civil war. His opponents wished to destroy him, one way or the other, and so a war began to protect one man's status, or *dignitas* – no English word quite embraces the full power of this concept for a Roman aristocrat. The rival sides did not have significantly different ideologies, or even policies. Instead it was personal pride, and in the case of Cato and some other senators deep personal emnity, which plunged the Roman Republic into another civil war, spread devastation all around the Mediterranean and costs many tens of thousands of lives.

In the early hours of 11 January 49 BC, a two-horse carriage approached the little River Rubicon which marked the boundary between the province of Cisalpine Gaul and Italy proper. Some distance behind were 300 cavalrymen and, further back again, *Legio XIII*. On one side Caesar still legally held *imperium* and had the right to command troops, but as soon as he crossed over at the head of soldiers he would be violating the law. The *Commentaries* pay no attention to the moment, but other sources, which may draw upon the accounts of some of the officers with him, claim that Caesar got down from the carriage and hesitated for a long time. Finally, he appeared to make up his mind and, employing the gamblers' expression 'the die is cast' (usually quoted as the Latin *alea iacta est*, though he may in fact have spoken in Greek), continued his journey across the Rubicon. In this way the Civil War openly began, although since a party of centurions and legionaries wearing civilian clothes had already crossed into Italy and seized the nearest town of Ariminum (Rimini), in some ways it had already started.[3]

THE MACEDONIAN CAMPAIGN, 48 BC

The pretence on both sides of hoping for a negotiated settlement had prevented either leader from overtly massing troops. In previous months Pompey had blithely declared that all he had to do was stamp his foot and legions would spring up from the soil of Italy. There were only two trained and experienced legions at his immediate disposal, but both had recently served under Caesar in Gaul and their loyalty was somewhat questionable. Pompey left Rome in mid January, announcing that it could not be defended, and he and his allies set about raising levies. While this decision made military sense, it helped to create a mood of panic amongst senators such as Cicero who were sympathetic rather than devoted to his cause. Caesar had only a single legion and a few auxiliaries, with no other units nearer than Transalpine Gaul, but decided to launch an immediate offensive. Over the next weeks small forces of Caesarean troops drove deep into Italy, taking towns and defeating or forcing the surrender of any Pompeian cohorts which opposed them. At this stage training and experience, allied with aggression and boundless confidence, proved more than a match for sheer numbers.

From the beginning Pompey was hindered by the refusal of many of his allies to follow orders. A number of senators whose pride greatly outweighed their ability, and whose political influence demanded that they be given responsible roles, all too boldly rushed to meet Caesar with inadequately trained or prepared forces. Victory followed victory as Caesar's reinforced, but still outnumbered, troops overran the entire peninsula in just two months. With the situation growing ever more hopeless, at least one senator tartly suggested that perhaps it was time for Pompey to start stamping his foot. Yet Pompey was not especially concerned by his former ally's successes, for he had already resolved to transfer the war to another theatre. He concentrated all of his newly raised legions at Brundisium and, after fighting a skilful rearguard action, embarked them on ships and took the army across the Adriatic to Macedonia. Caesar had won control of Italy for the moment, but his victory was far from complete and the war would go on.[4]

It is difficult to say when Pompey decided that Italy could not be defended and that it was better to shift his forces to Macedonia, but he may even have been toying with the idea before Caesar crossed the Rubicon. He knew that it took time to train men and fit an army for battle, especially when they would be facing legions hardened by years of successful campaigning in Gaul. Caesar's support was limited to a few of the younger and more disreputable senators, whereas the bulk of the Senate and the provinces actively favoured, or were at least well disposed towards, Pompey and his allies. An immediate encounter was likely to favour Caesar, but a longer war would give more scope for his own talents as an organizer and planner to come into play. Moving to Macedonia gave him ready access to the massive resources of eastern provinces of the Empire. It was an area where virtually every community and ruler was personally bound to him as a result of his settlement of the region in the 60s and soon troops, money and supplies were flooding into his camp. A great fleet of warships was also assembled. The 57-year-old Pompey showed all the energy of his youth as he threw himself into marshalling these forces and training his soldiers, showing off his own skill at arms and as a horseman as he joined in the men's exercises. The rest of the year was spent in creating a large and effective army, strong enough to face Caesar should he choose to attack, but the long-term aim was always a return to Italy. As Pompey himself frequently remarked, 'Sulla did it; why shouldn't I?'[5]

In March 49 Caesar was in no position to follow his enemy. Many of his legions had still not reached Italy and anyway he had no fleet to transport them across the Adriatic. To have done nothing would simply have played into Pompey's hands as he built up his strength, so Caesar chose to turn west and attack the Pompeian armies in the Spanish provinces. These consisted of seven legions, all of them properly equipped and trained, and at least as many Spanish auxiliaries. The rival commanders seem almost to have spent the Civil War dreaming up dramatic pronouncements, and Caesar declared that he was going to fight 'an army without a general', before returning to beat 'a general without an army'. The campaign lasted from April to August and culminated in the surrender of the Pompeian legions. Caesar had deliberately chosen to avoid a pitched battle to prevent unnecessary loss of Roman lives. Instead he had outmanoeuvred his opponents, eventually cutting them off from a water supply and compelling them to give up. Caesar then followed his practice from the beginning of the war of releasing his aristocratic prisoners and allowing them to go wherever they wished, while demobilizing or recruiting their soldiers. It was a considerable success, and an operation which had demonstrated the determination of his troops and his own tactical skill. However, although Pompey had lost some of his best legions – his defeated legates soon rejoined him, but this was a somewhat questionable reinforcement – the campaign had bought him much precious time. The utter defeat of an initially successful expedition to Africa led by one of Caesar's subordinates helped in part to balance the loss.

By the end of 49 Caesar's position was still extremely precarious and news that four of his legions had mutinied at Placentia in Northern Italy was especially discouraging. These units, chief amongst them the veteran *Legio IX* which had served throughout the Gallic campaigns, complained that many soldiers were overdue for discharge and that none of them had received the donative of 500 denarii (more than two years' salary) per man which Caesar had promised to them in the spring. The general's reaction was stern as he told the men that they would receive everything when the war was won and that he had never reneged on any promise to them in the past. He then declared that he would decimate *Legio IX*, but allowed himself to be 'persuaded' by the pleas of officers and men only to execute twelve of the 120 soldiers seen as ringleaders. The mutiny – like so many others throughout history – had been partly the product of a period of idleness which had allowed minor discontent to fester, but was another reason why Caesar could not afford to go onto the defensive and wait for Pompey to return.[6]

On 4 January 48 BC, Caesar embarked seven of the twelve legions he had concentrated in Brundisium in the small fleet of merchant ships he had managed to gather. It is unlikely that any of these units were much above half strength – by the end of the year *Legio VI* would muster fewer than 1,000 effectives – so that his force probably numbered significantly under 20,000 men with 500 auxiliary cavalry. With them went the barest minimum of servants and baggage to pack in the maximum number of fighting troops. The small number of cavalry reflected the much greater space required for transporting horses more than the Roman emphasis on heavy infantry. Only a handful of warships were available to protect the transports from the vast Pompeian fleet commanded by Bibulus, Caesar's old consular colleague from 59 and a man with a personal score to settle. However, the decision to set sail outside the normal campaigning season surprised the enemy, and Caesar's luck held as usual so that he was able to land unopposed at Paeleste on the coast of Epirus.

Bibulus managed to catch some of the empty ships on their return journey, and soon imposed a blockade which effectively cut Caesar's army off from both reinforcements and supplies. Food was the most critical problem, for the season – at this time January in the Roman calendar fell in late autumn – meant that it would be several months before significant quantities of food and fodder could be foraged from the land itself. Caesar's army was also significantly outnumbered. In a short time Pompey was able to concentrate nine legions – each at something like full strength – supported by 5,000 light infantry and 7,000 cavalry. Two more legions were on the way to join him from Syria under the command of his father-in-law, Scipio.[7]

On the night after he had landed, Caesar force-marched to Oricum, a town where Pompey had massed some of his great store of supplies, and forced its surrender. Although a Pompeian convoy of grain ships managed to escape with or destroy their cargo, this was still an important prize. Even more valuable was the larger city of Apollonia which surrendered soon afterwards. These successes prompted Caesar to launch an immediate attack on the biggest of all Pompey's supply dumps at the great trading port of Dyrrachium (in modern-day Albania). Pompey's scouts reported the enemy's march and a race developed, which he narrowly won. Caesar was not strong enough to risk a battle and withdrew to guard Apollonia and Oricum.

As the weeks passed he became ever more desperate for reinforcement from Mark Antony who had remained with the rest of his troops at Brundisium. Several attempts to cross the Adriatic were thwarted and most of our sources maintain that Caesar grew so desperate that he became convinced only his own presence would hurry up the shipment. Setting out in a small boat in bad weather, blithely telling the nervous captain not to be afraid because he carried 'Caesar and Caesar's good fortune', he ordered them to hold their course in spite of the storm. Yet in the end, even such determination had to give way to the elements and he was forced to return to the shore. These months were a desperate time, with expeditions seeking food having to go ever further away. Pompey was content to let starvation do his work for him, especially since even his well-prepared army could only operate with difficulty in this season. It was not until 10 April that Antony was able to bring the rest of the army – four legions and 800 cavalry – over to Greece, and even then the operation was extremely fortunate to succeed with only minor losses to the enemy fleet. Pompey responded too slowly to prevent the two parts of the Caesarean army from uniting.[8]

Caesar now had eleven legions, each probably smaller in size than the enemy but more experienced. However, he was still heavily outnumbered in cavalry and light troops. It was certainly no easier to feed this increased force off his meagre resources, for no substantial quantities of food were likely to make it across the sea from Italy and spring was still some weeks away. Once again, staying on the defensive was likely to prove of more benefit to the enemy, and Caesar decided to attack Dyrrachium. He managed to outmarch Pompey and get between his army and the city, but failed in his attempt on Dyrrachium itself. The Pompeian army fortified a camp on a hill named Petra, which dominated a bay forming a natural harbour. He was thus able to bring in sufficient food for his men, while Caesar's army, camped on high ground inland and to the north, continued to go short.

In order to make it easier for his patrols and foraging parties to go about their business unmolested by the enemy cavalry, Caesar ordered the construction of a line of fortifications running along the line of hills facing Pompey's position. He swiftly decided to extend the line with the object of completely enclosing the enemy, effectively besieging the larger army. To prevent this, Pompey set his own legionaries to constructing a line of fortifications facing Caesar's, and a number of skirmishes were fought as the sides struggled to control key positions. Caesar's men hurried to extend their wall and ditch to meet the sea, while Pompey's soldiers tried to construct their own line so that it would stop this from happening. Pompey had the advantage of greater manpower and a shorter distance – some 15 miles as opposed to 17 – to cover as he was hemmed in nearer the coast.

The use of lines of fortification to wholly or partially surround an enemy and restrict his movements and access to supplies had been used by Roman armies in the past and most notably by Crassus against Spartacus, Pompey against Mithridates, and Caesar against Vercingetorix. It was another reflection of the engineering skill and tenacity when undertaking massive projects which were the hallmark of the professional legions. In many respects it was also an extension of the traditional days or weeks of tentative manoeuvring between armies before fighting a battle. The defensive advantages offered by field works should not distract from their use on these occasions in a highly aggressive manner to restrict the enemy's activities and force the opposing commander to fight when he did not wish to, to withdraw, or, in the most extreme cases, to watch the slow destruction of his army by hunger.[9]

Both armies had supply problems as they toiled to extend the lines of fortification to the south and eventually to the sea. At times Caesar's men were living almost exclusively on meat, instead of the balanced grain, vegetables and meat ration which was normally issued – the claim that the legions were vegetarian and ate little or no meat is a myth based on a misreading of this and another passage in Caesar. Some of them foraged for the roots of a plant called charax and managed to turn this into an unpleasant, but edible substitute for bread. On seeing one of these Pompey is supposed to have declared that he was fighting animals rather than men. Morale does not seem to have suffered, and many of the veterans will have recalled similar privations at Avaricum. Pompey's army suffered more from a shortage of water than of food itself, for the main streams leading into their positions had been dammed by Caesar's men. Wells were dug, but could not offer a complete solution to the problem. Apart from his soldiers, his army had a very large number of cavalry mounts and baggage animals. The former were given priority after the men, and the train mules and horses soon began to die or had to be slaughtered in considerable numbers. Disease – possibly typhus – also began to spread amongst the soldiers.

The pitch of fighting increased as Caesar's men made a last, unavailing effort to complete the enemy's encirclement. Antony led *Legio IX* to secure a vital hill, but was driven from this by a Pompeian counter-attack, although he managed to withdraw with only minimal losses. Pompey then launched a series of attacks against the forts in one sector of Caesar's lines. Some initial headway was made, but the extremely stubborn resistance of the garrisons gave time for reserves to arrive and beat the enemy back. Pompey's attacking troops were supported by very large numbers of archers and slingers who laid down a barrage of missiles on the ramparts. In one fort the majority of men in the three-cohort garrison was wounded and four out of six centurions in one cohort lost an eye. The shield of a centurion called Scaeva was later found to have been hit by 120 missiles and he too was wounded in the eye. Feigning surrender, he waited until two Pompeian legionaries came towards him, before suddenly lopping the arm off one and killing the other. Somehow the position held and by the end of the day the attackers were fleeing in disorder. Many of Caesar's officers are supposed to have believed that had they might have won the war if they had followed up this advantage with an all-out attack, but Caesar's legate Sulla decided against this, feeling that it was not a subordinate's duty to take such a critical decision. Caesar, who was at a different sector of the line, fully concurred with this attitude in his account.[10]

The heroic defenders of the fort were lavishly rewarded with extra pay, a number of promotions, and, which at the time may have been most satisfying, extra rations for all. The desertion to Pompey of two Gallic noblemen along with their personal warriors and retainers provided him with information which inspired a fresh attack on what they assured him was a weak spot in the enemy lines. This time the main column of legionaries advancing from the Pompeian lines was supported by a force of light infantry which had been taken by sea and landed behind Caesar's positions. Their target was the unfinished section of fortifications and once again the assault made some headway before bogging down. As Caesar and Antony both led reserves up to the threatened sector, the enemy began to collapse into rout.

This time the commander was present to order his own counter-attack, which focused on a camp originally built by his own *Legio IX*, but subsequently abandoned and now occupied by the enemy. Concealed in woodland and dead ground, the Caesarean legionaries were able to approach unobserved and storm the position in a sudden onslaught. Yet, as the Pompeians themselves had found, such success often led rapidly to disorder and confusion. One column of Caesar's men got lost, mistaking a wall leading off in another direction for part of the camp's rampart and following it. Now it was Pompey's turn to hurry all available reserves to the area and overwhelm the attackers. Beginning with the most advanced units, panic spread through the bulk of the thirty-three cohorts Caesar had committed to the attack. Caesar himself was on the spot and tried to stop the rout by grabbing at standard-bearers as they fled. Seizing a standard or its bearer and trying to persuade the routers to rally around this symbol of their unit pride and identity was a common gesture for a Roman commander faced with such a situation. Sulla once did this successfully when fighting Mithridates' army in Greece. Two years later during the African campaign Caesar would take hold of one of his own signifers and physically turn the man round, telling him, 'Look! That's where the enemy are!' This time his presence had no such steadying influence. At least one man left the standard in his commander's hands and ran on. Other accounts, though not the *Commentaries*, even maintain that one of the fleeing men tried to stab Caesar with the heavy iron butt of his *signum* (standard), and was only stopped when the general's bodyguard sliced his arm off.

The losses in this action were very heavy, amounting to 960 men and thirty-two tribunes or centurions killed and others captured. Pompey did not follow up his advantage, prompting Caesar to declare that the enemy 'would have won today, if only they were commanded by a winner'. However, the speed with which initial success had degenerated into heavy defeat for both sides suggests that Pompey was right. Lines of fortifications staunchly defended and closely supported by strong reserves were exceedingly difficult for even another Roman army to capture. The already uneven and broken ground, divided further by walls and ditches, made it difficult for a commander to control any attack and so introduced an exceptionally high level of chance into the outcome of any combat. Pompey had won a victory and, as from the beginning of the campaign, time was on his side and there was no real advantage in seeking a rapid decision. The captured Caesarean soldiers were executed, although even Caesar says that this was not ordered by Pompey himself, even if he did not overrule the decision. Instead it was his old legate Labienus who harangued the captives and then had them killed. Labienus had switched sides at the beginning of the Italian campaign – whether through dissatisfaction with the rewards and praise he received from his commander, an older loyalty to Pompey, or sheer political conviction is unclear. Caesar had ordered his personal baggage sent after him, but however lightly he treated the defection in public, it was a major blow which had deprived him of the ablest of his commanders. Labienus appears as a far more brutal figure in *The Civil War* than in *The Gallic War*, and was especially loathed by the officers who added books to Caesar's account.[11]

On the following day, just as he had done at Gergovia, Caesar assembled his soldiers and tried to restore their morale. Several standard-bearers were very publicly demoted for cowardice. Caesar made no effort to offer battle to the enemy as he had done in Gaul, probably judging that this was too risky in case the enemy accepted. It was now clear that he had no prospect of blockading Pompey into submission, and he resolved to march away into central Greece and rebuild his army's confidence and health. Sending the wounded and sick ahead, he sent the baggage train out of camp at night and then followed with the main army. A few Pompeian cavalry noticed the retreat quickly enough to harass the rearguard, but these were soon driven off. The numerically inferior Caesarean cavalry were closely supported by a cohort of 400 picked legionaries marching ready for battle rather than weighed down with packs. Caesar had skilfully disengaged from close contact with the enemy, which was never an easy operation, but this and his own confident tone in the *Commentaries* should not hide the fact that he had suffered a serious defeat.[12]

Crops were by this time beginning to ripen and as Caesar's army marched through land which had not been subject to the rampages of campaigning armies the men were able to harvest sufficient grain to meet their needs. To some Greek communities Caesar's legions looked like a beaten force and they were reluctant to offer them any aid lest it earn them the antipathy of the victors. After Gomphi had shut its gates to his officers and refused to hand over any food, Caesar stormed the city and put it to the sack. According to some of our sources the army's progress on the next day was more a drunken revel than a disciplined march. After this brutal object lesson, most towns and cities did not dare to refuse him anything.[13]

Pompey followed, but kept at a distance, and seems to have wanted to continue his strategy of wearing his enemy down by depriving him of supplies. Many of the eminent senators in his camp were loud in their criticism, demanding that he get the war over with quickly by defeating Caesar in battle. Caesar, who obviously was not an unbiased source, claimed that they were already squabbling over who would receive the offices and honours currently in the possession of his own supporters. The pressure on Pompey was considerable, but it is by no means clear whether it was this which finally persuaded him to seek battle. It was now August, and both the season and freedom to move meant that Caesar's supply situation had greatly eased. The Pompeians had a marked superiority in infantry and an even greater one in cavalry, which made a battle, especially a battle in open country, an attractive prospect. At the beginning of the month the rival armies were near Pharsalus and spent several days in the familiar offers of battle and tentative manoeuvring. On the morning of 9 August 48 BC Caesar was about to march to a new campsite, for his men had largely exhausted the forage immediately available to them in their current position, when he noticed that the Pompeian army was once again offering battle. For the first time they had advanced beyond the high ground in front of Pompey's camp and were deploying in the level plain bordered by the River Enipeus. It was a sign of determination to risk an action which Caesar welcomed. Issuing an order for the men to down packs and prepare for battle, he led his troops out to face the enemy.

Caesar had 22,000 legionaries divided into some eighty cohorts – a further seven cohorts were left to guard the camp – and 1,000 cavalry. Resting his left flank on the river, he deployed the legions in the usual *triplex acies*. His best unit, the veteran *Legio X*, took up the place of honour on the right of the line, flanked by all the cavalry supported by some light infantry. On the left he placed a composite unit formed from *Legio VIII* and *Legio IX*, both heavily under strength, for the latter in particular had suffered heavily at Dyrrachium. Dividing the line into three sectors, Caesar placed Mark Antony in charge of the left, Cnaeus Domitius Calvinus in the centre and Publius Sulla on the right. The commander himself was free to move to any section of the front, but was in fact to control the battle from the right wing, spending much of his time with his favourite *Legio X*.

Across the plain Pompey's eleven legions were also deployed in three lines. Altogether they mustered some 45,000 men, and each of his cohorts was formed ten ranks deep – Caesar's units, barely half their size, were probably in only four or five ranks. The best legions were stationed on the flanks and in the centre, and the entire line was divided into three commands, with Lucius Domitius Ahenobarbus on the left, Pompey's father-in-law Scipio in the centre and Lucius Afranius on the right. Pompey himself joined Ahenobarbus and the troops immediately opposite Caesar. According to

Frontinus, 600 cavalrymen were placed on the right flank next to the river. The remaining 6,400 horsemen – or in all other sources the entire mounted arm – were concentrated on the left with large numbers of slingers, archers and other infantry skirmishers in support. Placed under the command of Labienus, it was this force which was to deliver the main, and Pompey hoped decisive, attack, sweeping aside Caesar's outnumbered cavalry and then turning to take his legions in the flank and rear. The plan was not especially subtle, as the concentration of so many thousand cavalry in one section of the plain could not be concealed, but that did not mean that it would be easy for Caesar to devise a countermeasure. His response was to take one cohort from the third line of each legion and station them as a fourth line behind his own cavalry and probably echeloned back to the right. The Caesarean horsemen will have prevented the enemy from observing this move.

Both armies were confident. Passwords were issued on each side to reduce the confusion inevitable when fighting against opponents wearing the same uniforms and speaking the same language. Caesar's men had 'Venus, the Bringer of Victory' in a reference to his divine ancestor, whilst Pompey's soldiers took 'Hercules the Unconquered'. In an exchange similar to those which were to shape the Napoleonic legend, a former chief centurion of *Legio X* now serving as commander of an ad hoc unit of 120 veterans called out to Caesar that 'Today, I will earn your gratitude whether I live or die.' This man, Caius Crastinus, was in the front line, which now opened the battle by beginning to advance towards the Pompeians. The latter did not move. This was an unusual tactic, for Roman infantry normally advanced to meet enemy foot soldiers. Even Marius' men at Aquae Sextiae and Caesar's when he faced the Helvetii, although they had waited as the enemy wore themselves out attacking uphill, had at the last minute hurled their *pila* and then immediately charged some 10 or 15 yards into contact. Caesar says the order to remain stationary originated with Caius Triarius, who had persuaded Pompey that it would prevent the cohorts from falling into disorder and would permit them to gain the best possible protection from their shields against enemy missiles. The belief that their formations would break up if they moved may have been a reflection of the perceived inferior quality of the Pompeian legionaries compared to Caesar's men. On the other hand Pompey may simply have wanted to bring Caesar's infantry as far forward as possible so that it would be easier for his cavalry on the left wing to envelop them. In the *Commentaries* Caesar is highly critical of the decision, arguing that an advance helped to encourage the soldiers and that a passive defence was detrimental to morale.

Before the lines of legionaries clashed, Labienus' cavalry charged against their Caesarean counterparts, driving them back after a brief struggle. In the process the Pompeian horsemen fell into disorder. It was rare to concentrate so many cavalrymen on such a narrow frontage and most of the units were very inexperienced. Neither Labienus nor his subordinate officers had much experience of leading and controlling so many mounted troops, and their task can only have been made harder by the thick clouds of dust stirred up by so many hoofs. These factors, combined with the natural tendency for a large number of horses packed so closely together to grow excited, seems to have turned the Pompeian left wing from ordered lines of individual squadrons into a single unwieldy mass. Before they could rally and re-form, Caesar ordered his fourth line to counter-attack. These cohorts suddenly appeared from the dust and confusion and advanced towards the stationary crowd of milling cavalry. The legionaries were ordered to use their *pila* as spears. On other occasions when Roman infantry tried to panic enemy cavalry they yelled and clashed weapons against shields. In one of the very rare instances where infantry have successfully charged cavalry in the open, Labienus' men began to give way, confusion turning to rout as the entire mass of horsemen stampeded to the rear. We do not know whether Caesar's own horsemen had rallied and were able to pursue the enemy, but it is clear that the enemy cavalry played no further part in the battle.

Pompey's main attack had failed and exposed the left flank of his heavy infantry, providing yet another reason why it might be unwise for these to advance. Caesar's cohorts had advanced and, in the usual fashion, accelerated into a running charge preparatory to throwing their *pila* when they were at most some 30 or 40 yards from the enemy line. When the Pompeians failed to conform to normal legionary tactics and finally advance to meet them, Caesar's soldiers checked and did not waste their own missiles when still out of effective range. For a while the entire line halted, the centurions and their subordinates re-forming the ranks which had become ragged during their abortive charge. The coolness of this manoeuvre when the enemy was so close testified to the quality, training and experience of Caesar's legionaries and their officers. Then, after this pause, the line moved forward again. It closed to within 15 to 10 yards, threw a volley of *pila*, and charged home, the men raising their battle cry and drawing their swords. To their credit, and to some extent in confirmation of Pompey's tactics, the Pompeians met them steadily enough and delivered a volley of their own *pila*. The fighting was fierce, the extra depth and tight formations of the Pompeian cohorts keeping them in the fight against their more experienced opponents.

Crastinus was killed by a sword thrust to the mouth which was so powerful that the tip of his opponent's *gladius* emerged from the back of his neck. The cohorts of Caesar's second line, which always operated in very close support of the first, were soon fed into the fighting.

For a while neither side gained any marked advantage in this combat, until Caesar's fourth line turned to attack the left flank of Pompey's line. The Pompeian fighting line started to edge backwards and Caesar gave the signal which ordered his third line – fewer in numbers than was usual owing to the creation of the fourth line, but composed of fresh troops – to advance and join the combat. The pressure was too much and Pompey's legions collapsed into flight. Caesar claims that 15,000 enemy soldiers were killed and 24,000 captured along with nine legionary eagles and 180 *signa* (standards). He is supposed to have given orders for his men to spare fellow citizens whenever possible, but to slaughter the foreign auxiliaries. His own losses amounted to 200 soldiers and thirty centurions – a proportion which reflects the aggressive and therefore risky style of leadership encouraged in the legions.[14]

Pompey seems to have played little role in the battle after the failure of his cavalry attack. Caesar even maintains that he left the field before the fighting was over, despairing of his eventual victory in a manner unworthy of a Roman, and returned to his camp. When he saw that his own army was about to collapse, he took off his general's insignia and galloped away. Even in accounts favourable to him there is no trace of the vigour he had shown in earlier campaigns. As far as the *Commentaries* are concerned it was clear that the better man – certainly the better Roman – had won.

Joining his wife, Pompey fled to Egypt, where he was murdered by the courtiers of King Ptolemy XII, who hoped to gain favour with the victor. The first blow was actually struck by a centurion who had served under Pompey during his eastern campaigns, but was now with one of the two legions left in Egypt for some years who were generally believed to have 'gone native'. When Caesar arrived on 2 October 48 BC he was presented with Pompey's head, but refused to look upon it and granted his former ally honourable burial. Publicly he claimed that he regretted not being able to extend his famous clemency to his most distinguished opponent. This may simply have been for public consumption, but it is also possible that he still retained considerable affection and respect for his old friend.[15]

DICTATORSHIP AND THE IDES OF MARCH

Caesar spent the next six months in Egypt, thus giving time for the surviving Pompeians to form a new army in North Africa. The long delay before he returned to Rome baffled many of those such as Cicero who hoped that the Civil War was now over. Perhaps Caesar believed that without Pompey opposition to him would collapse, or maybe for the moment he found less satisfaction in his victory than he may have hoped. He became involved in the dynastic struggle between the teenage Ptolemy and his 21-year-old sister Cleopatra. The latter – lively, intelligent, charismatic and attractive if not strictly beautiful by the standards of the day, and well educated in both Hellenistic and the older Egyptian culture – is famously supposed to have had herself delivered to Caesar's headquarters hidden in a carpet or blanket, which was then unrolled to reveal its remarkable passenger. The pair, who matched each other in great wit, learning and massive ambition, were soon lovers, and the Egyptian queen made a far greater impression upon the promiscuous middle-aged Roman than perhaps any of his other paramours with the possible exception of Servilia, the mother of Brutus and great love of Caesar's youth.

Caesar defeated Ptolemy, who died in the confusion, and installed Cleopatra on the Egyptian throne. Even then he did not want to leave Egypt and the lovers are said to have gone for a long and luxurious cruise along the Nile. It was only the arrival of bad news from around the Mediterranean that finally forced Caesar to disturb his reverie. Pharnaces, the son of Mithridates who had turned against his father and been permitted by Rome to keep a much reduced kingdom, had invaded the Roman province of Pontus and defeated a Roman army. At the end of May 47 Caesar mustered a small force from the legions immediately available and marched against him. The Pontic army was utterly defeated at Zela on 2 August and the swiftness of his victory prompted the famous comment 'I came: I saw: I conquered' (*veni, vidi, vici*). Yet for a moment the issue had seemed in doubt when Pharnaces broke all the rules of generalship in this period and attacked Caesar's army whilst it was constructing a camp on high ground. Attacking an enemy in a strong position gave the Pontic army the initial advantage of surprise, but the legions recovered quickly and swiftly destroyed the enemy. In a jibe at Pompey, Caesar commented on how fortunate a general was who won his reputation fighting such fragile opponents.[16]

Returning to the west and his Roman enemies, Caesar's conduct of the remainder of the Civil War was energetic, impatient and increasingly ruthless.

In December 47 he led an ill-prepared invasion of Africa, which was in some ways even bolder than the landing in Macedonia two years before. Once again his talent for improvisation and his refusal to question his ultimate success, combined with the high quality of the officers and men under his command, allowed the Caesarean army to survive its initial weakness until reinforcements arrived and the supply situation improved. In April 46 he faced the Pompeian army outside the town of Thapsus. The author of *The African War* for once suggests that Caesar was not in full control of his army:

> Caesar was doubtful, resisting their eagerness and enthusiasm, yelling out that he did not approve of fighting by a reckless onslaught, and holding back the line again and again, when suddenly on the right wing a *tubicen* [trumpeter], without orders from Caesar but encouraged by the soldiers, began to sound his instrument. This was repeated by all the cohorts; the line began to advance against the enemy, although the centurions placed themselves in front and vainly tried to restrain the soldiers by force and stop them attacking without orders from the general.
>
> When Caesar perceived that it was impossible to restrain the soldiers' roused spirits, he gave the watchword 'Good Luck' [*Felicitas*], and spurred his horse at the enemy front ranks.[17]

In another, even less favourable tradition Caesar had to leave the field altogether because of an epileptic fit. Whatever the truth of these accounts, Caesar's legions won a rapid and decisive victory. It was not quite the end of the war, however, for Pompey's son Cnaeus Pompeius took control of Spain and had to be defeated at Munda in 45 BC.[18]

Caesar had won the Civil War, spreading devastation throughout Italy and the provinces to defend his personal honour, but it remained to be seen whether or not he could win the peace. As dictator for life he held power equalled in the past only by Sulla, whom he declared a political illiterate for retiring from public life. The honours voted to him were greater than those ever granted to any one individual and the scale of his planned projects truly staggering. Throughout the Civil War Caesar had paraded his *clementia*, pardoning captured opponents, in some cases more than once. Many had feared that this was simply a cynical ploy, remembering how Sulla had at first acted in a conciliatory manner until victory allowed him full rein to his brutal vengeance. Fears that Caesar would do the same proved unfounded, for there were no proscriptions and the Senate came to include a large number of his former opponents, some of whom were even given high office. Yet if the dictatorship was not repressive, it was also clear that elections were closely controlled and the Senate had no real power or independence. Rumours were rife claiming that Caesar wished to be made a king – a title which was still an anathema to the Romans centuries after the expulsion of the monarchy – and to be deified. Sometimes it was said that he wished to rule with Cleopatra, whom he had brought to Rome, as his queen and establish a new dynasty. The motives of the conspirators led by Brutus and Cassius were many and varied, but had more to do with fears about Caesar's future plans than anything he had so far done.

The dictator's intentions cannot now be established, for the sources for the period were thoroughly muddied by the propaganda put about by both his supporters and his enemies after his death. It is, for instance, impossible to know whether the boy Caesarion was in fact the illegitimate offspring of Caesar and Cleopatra. Caesar himself may not have been clear about his ultimate objectives, for his immediate plan was to revert to what he did best, leading an army in war. When he was stabbed to death at a meeting of the Senate on 15 March 44 BC, having publicly dismissed his bodyguard some time before, he was just about to depart for a campaign against the Dacians and then a further war with Parthia. The latter in particular was a task which would inevitably take several years to complete, and we cannot know what he expected to happen at Rome during his absence. With Caesar's assassination Rome was once again plunged into civil war. By a final irony the dictator's corpse fell at the foot of a statue of Pompey, for the Senate was on that day meeting in a temple attached to Pompey's theatre complex.[19]

SOLDIER AND GENERAL: CAESAR THE LEADER

In the last chapters we have dealt with generals – Marius, Sertorius, Pompey and Caesar – all of whom at some point led their legions against other Roman armies. From the earliest days of the Republic, Roman politics had been fiercely competitive, but it was not until the first century BC that squabbles between rival senators erupted into civil war. It seems extremely doubtful that Scipio Africanus ever dreamed of fighting against the regime which forced him into premature retirement from public life. Had he done so, it is hard to imagine that any of his former soldiers – now retired and dispersed to their homes – would have been willing to use force in defence of their old commander. The legions were recruited from a cross section of the propertied classes, all of whom were able to contribute to the political life of the Republic through voting in the Assemblies.

Yet within a century the relationship between the army, its commanders and the Republic had altered, so that in 88 BC and on many subsequent occasions generals both could and did lead their legions against other Roman armies. The change was profound and connected to the rise of the professional army, where the majority of legionaries were recruited from the poorest elements in society. For such men military service was not a duty owed to the State which interrupted their normal life, but a source of employment and a steady, if low, income. When they were discharged from the army the *proletarii* had nothing to go back to in the way of property or work in civilian life. Successive commanders such as Marius, Sulla, Pompey and Caesar all at times pressed for the establishment of colonies and the grant of farmland to their veteran soldiers. In each case the plan was bitterly unpopular, largely because no senator wanted another to place so many citizens in his debt. The Senate as a whole was also reluctant to acknowledge that the legions were now recruited from the poor and refused to take responsibility for their welfare after discharge. This encouraged a closer bond between commander and troops so that the legionaries' loyalty focused far more in the person of their commander than in the Republic which offered them so little. The legions in effect became 'client' or private armies of popular and powerful commanders.

This traditional view of the changes brought about as a result of the Marian Reform is a little simplistic, and has been widely criticized, especially by those scholars who believe that the evolution of the army was gradual and that there was no sudden change under Marius. They note, for instance, that it is certainly untrue that every Roman general in the first century BC was capable of turning his legions against rivals in the State. Lucullus led his army in years of highly successful campaigning in the east and yet never succeeded in winning his soldiers' affection, so that they refused all his pleas to resist his replacement by Pompey. On numerous occasions during the civil wars unpopular generals were deserted or even lynched by their own men. Yet if many, perhaps even most, Late Republican generals could not hope to persuade their legions to fight against other Romans, the essential point is that some of them both could and did. Such an action had been impossible in the heyday of the militia/conscript army which had won Rome dominance in the Mediterranean and, though perhaps the intensity and high stakes of political competition had increased, civil war only became a possibility with the new nature of the legion. This is something which the advocates of a gradual change rather than sudden military reform have failed adequately to explain, although really there is no reason why the former should have any less powerful an impact than the latter.[20]

Since some Roman commanders were able to build up such a close bond with their legionaries that the latter were willing to fight other Romans on their behalf, it is important to consider how they did this. Pompey was able to raise an army at his own expense and largely from his own family's estates in spite of his youth and lack of any legal authority. Few other men had the wealth to attempt such a venture, but a good deal of his success rested on personal charisma and traditional attachment of the local population to his family. In 88 Sulla was able to persuade his men to march on Rome because they were afraid that Marius would take other legions to the lucrative war in the east. However, although occasionally a man was able to rally the support of soldiers before they had campaigned with him, a shared period of successful active service did most to tie legionaries and general together. Pompey's and Sulla's men were confirmed in their loyalty in this way, while ten years of shared hardship and victory in Gaul ensured that there was never any question that Caesar's army would refuse to follow him across the Rubicon. Usually long and successful campaigning created a strong bond between general and soldiers, although Lucullus' experience shows that occasionally this did not prove to be the case. One of the chief reasons for his unpopularity was the belief that he was miserly in his distribution of plunder captured from the enemy. Marius, Sulla, Pompey and Caesar all rewarded their men, and especially their officers, lavishly. At some point, possibly during the Civil War, Caesar doubled the pay of his legionaries to 225 denarii a year.

In the *Commentaries* Caesar repeatedly justifies his cause, often in passages claiming to recount addresses he made to his troops. This was a way of reinforcing his message for his literary audience, but similar appeals feature in most historians' accounts of the civil wars. To a greater or lesser extent, all the soldiers in an army during a civil war probably had some knowledge of the nature of its causes. Centurions and more senior officers such as tribunes certainly do appear to have taken an active interest in politics and needed to be persuaded of the justification and legitimacy of their commander's actions. Army officers, and especially the ordinary soldiers, doubtless had a different perspective on political disputes to the senatorial class, but that does not mean that their concerns or ideas of legitimacy were any less deeply held. It seems often to have been an army's officers who initiated widespread defections to the opposing side or the assassination of a general. Early on in the Civil War each of Caesar's centurions formally offered to pay for and equip a cavalryman at their own expense, identifying themselves strongly with his cause.[21]

Marius was noted for introducing a less rigid form of discipline, except when actually on campaign; and on occasions, as at Gomphi, Caesar allowed his men licence to celebrate in the most disorderly manner. He is supposed to have boasted that his men fought just as well 'if they were stinking of perfume'.[22] Neither man overlooked serious offences and both were perceived to be very fair in their treatment of offenders regardless of their rank. A number of officers were publicly humiliated and dismissed when they failed to meet Caesar's standards. Marius, Pompey and Caesar were all also noted for the rigorous training programmes which they imposed upon their troops. Suetonius tells us that Caesar

> never gave advance warning of a march or battle, but always kept them [his troops] ready and prepared for a sudden move whenever he chose. He often turned them out even when there was no emergency, particularly in wet weather or during festivals. And he would warn them to keep a close eye on him, and would then suddenly slip out of camp at any hour of the day and night, and make an especially long and hard march, to wear out those who followed too slowly.[23]

Like Sertorius he equipped his men with impressive armour and weapons, the latter or their scabbards often inlaid with gold and silver, wanting them to take a pride in themselves and their appearance. The legionaries were encouraged to feel that their general, or senior officers who would report to him, always watched their behaviour and would as rapidly reward the brave as he would punish the cowardly. When Caesar addressed his men he always called them *commilitones* or 'comrades'. In Gaul he is said to have had flagstones carried with the baggage train so that his tent could be provided with a paved floor, but in spite of such luxuries, which may in part have been intended to impress local chieftains, he tried to share the hardships of his men. Suetonius mentions how he

> showed remarkable powers of endurance. On the march he led his army, usually on foot but sometimes on horseback, bareheaded in the sun or rain, and could travel very fast over great distances in a light carriage, taking minimal baggage; he would swim unfordable rivers or float across on inflated animal skins, frequently arriving at his destination before the couriers he had sent to announce his coming.[24]

Although the *Commentaries* describe the heroic actions of many individual soldiers, it is very rare for ordinary legionaries to be named. Most often their courage is praised collectively and specific legions often singled out for praise.

We have already noted Caesar's talent for manipulating unit pride, as when he announced that he would advance against Ariovistus with only *Legio X* if the rest of the army was too timid. Following an incident in which part of this legion was temporarily given horses to ride so that they could act as Caesar's bodyguard, the unit adopted the informal title of *equestris* or 'knights', and soldiers joked that they would be elevated to the equestrian order by their generous commander. Soldiers identified strongly with their legions, especially in the best units, and the rivalry to prove that they were superior to the rest of the army was intense and actively encouraged.[25]

Caesar's narrative pays particular attention to the deeds of his centurions. Successes are often attributed in no small part to their courage and inspirational example and defeats mitigated by their heroism. The praise they received in his formal accounts of the campaigns was matched by tangible rewards and promotions bestowed on them immediately. During the Gallic campaigns Caesar's army more than doubled in size, creating many opportunities for promotion to higher grades of the centurionate. Little is known about the origins of centurions in this period and it is uncertain whether most were directly commissioned or promoted from the ranks, although the latter course is never explicitly mentioned in the *Commentaries*. It is possible that they were mainly drawn from what might loosely be called the 'middle classes' in Roman society – families which owned some property and possessed some education and may even have been quite prominent in smaller Italian communities. Certainly, once they became centurions they enjoyed pay and service conditions massively greater than those of the ordinary legionaries. The potential for advancement and reward was also on a greater scale. Scaeva, the centurion who distinguished himself defending one of the forts at Dyrrachium, was promoted to the rank of *primus pilus* and given a bounty of 50,000 denarii (100 years' pay for an ordinary legionary). An inscription which probably dates to the 30s BC refers to a Gallic auxiliary cavalry unit known as the *ala Scaevae* (Scaeva's regiment) and it seems very likely that this is the same man. A handful of Caesar's centurions were even enrolled in the Senate during his dictatorship. Centurions were rewarded lavishly but suffered disproportionately high casualties in their desire to win distinction. Appian claims that Caesar ordered his men to search carefully for the body of Crastinus amongst the carnage of Pharsalus and had him buried in a tomb away from the mass grave. He is also supposed to have laid a number of decorations for valour on the corpse, which, if true, would be an extremely powerful gesture since the Romans did not normally issue posthumous medals.[26]

Caesar praised and rewarded his men, shared their dangers on campaign, and trained them hard. Successive victories, broken only by a handful of defeats all of which were swiftly avenged, confirmed his legionaries' faith in his skill as a commander. Caesar himself continually reminded the world that he was not simply a gifted general, but also a lucky one. Only a few commanders in history have been able to win comparable devotion from their troops. Occasionally the relationship wavered from the absolute obedience depicted in the *Commentaries*, and the Civil War witnessed two major mutinies. In late 49 *Legio IX* protested that many men were overdue for both pay and discharge, but quickly gave way when their general arrived and berated them for ingratitude and lack of faith. Caesar put on an act of such fury, announcing that he would decimate the legion, that the soldiers were almost relieved when he ultimately ordered the execution of only twelve ringleaders.

His performance when much of the army, including his beloved *Legio X*, mutinied before the African campaign was even more overpowering. Once again it was probably inactivity and an absence of purpose whilst Caesar had been away in Egypt as much as anything else which had caused old discontents to come to a head. Sallust, the future historian and then one of Caesar's officers, narrowly escaped lynching as the mutineers angrily demanded back-pay and bounties. Then their commander arrived suddenly and appeared on the tribunal. An invitation to state their grievances shocked the assembled troops into silence, until voices yelled out that they wished to be discharged from service. Caesar, who was about to embark on a major campaign and so was obviously in great need of troops, replied without any visible emotion that they were demobilized, that he would win the war with other troops, but still give them everything he had promised after his victory. There does not seem to have been any real desire for discharge and the legionaries' mood swung from hostility to a sense of sorrow and shame that their old general did not appear to value their services.

Caesar said nothing more, until some of his senior officers – quite possibly instructed in their role before the confrontation began – loudly begged him to forgive the men who had endured so much under his command and excuse a few rash words. Hopes that he might relent were dashed when he spoke again and began by addressing them as 'Civilians' (*Quirites*) instead of his habitual 'comrades'. The mutineers started to shout out their repentance and begged to be allowed back into his service. When Caesar turned to leave the platform the shouts grew even louder, and the legionaries pleaded with him to punish the ringleaders in the disturbance and take the rest with him to Africa. The general made a show of indecision, letting the men grow ever more desperate, until he finally announced that he would take all of them on campaign apart from *Legio X*, whose ingratitude after his repeated favours could not be excused. Men from this unit now went so far as to beg him to decimate them if only he would take the legion to war. In the end, he decided that the flood of emotion was so strong that it was unnecessary to take any further steps. *Legio X* fought with distinction at Thapsus and made the critical breakthrough at Munda. After Caesar's assassination the remnants of this veteran unit remained loyal to his memory and fought for years and with great effectiveness on behalf of his adopted son Octavian.[27]

Caesar knew how to play on his soldiers' emotions, most of all on their pride in their units and their own status as good and brave soldiers. Success in public life required all Roman senators to develop some skill in dealing with and winning over people, whether as individuals or in crowds in the Forum or military camp. Caesar through instinct and experience developed the knack of winning over and inspiring soldiers to a degree unrivalled by any of Rome's other great commanders, with the possible exception of Pompey.

CHAPTER 10

AN IMPERIAL 'PRINCE':
GERMANICUS BEYOND THE RHINE

Claudius Germanicus Caesar (15 BC–AD 19)

How well had Germanicus been tutored by his [Tiberius'] instructions, having so thoroughly absorbed the essentials of military knowledge under his command that he was later to welcome him home after the conquest of Germany! What awards did he pile upon him, in spite of his youth, so that the splendour of his triumph matched his great deeds![1]

THE CONSPIRATORS WHO MURDERED JULIUS CAESAR DO NOT SEEM TO HAVE had a very clear idea of what to do next, and may have hoped that, once the dictator was dead, public life would simply return to its traditional pattern. Within months a new civil war erupted, as Mark Antony rallied many of the Caesarean legions to avenge his death. For a while the Senate, which was broadly in sympathy with the conspirators, tried to use Caesar's adopted son Caius Julius Caesar Octavianus – conventionally known to historians as Octavian – as a figurehead to weaken Antony's control over the veteran legions. Octavian was only 19, and seemed of little account apart from his famous name. Cicero is supposed to have said that the Senate should 'praise the young man, reward him, and then discard him' as soon as he had served his purpose. In the meantime they gave him proconsular *imperium*, making official his command of the large number of Caesar's veterans, including *Legio X*, who had rallied to his cause. Realizing the Senate's attitude to him and anyway eager to fight against the conspirators, in 43 Octavian defected to join Antony and Marcus Lepidus. Together they formed the Second Triumvirate, which, unlike the alliance between

Crassus, Pompey and Caesar, was given official status in law, each man taking the title *triumvir rei publicae constituendae*. The wording echoed Sulla's rank as dictator, as did the triumvirs' behaviour when they captured Rome, instituting new proscriptions ordering the deaths of a huge number of senators and equestrians.

Cicero paid the price for his Philippics, a series of vitriolic speeches attacking Antony which he had delivered and published: Antony ordered his head and his hand to be nailed to the Speaker's Platform in the Forum. Within a year Brutus and Cassius had died by their own hands following the defeats of their armies in the two battles of Philippi. The triumvirs divided control of the provinces, but gradually their alliance broke down. Lepidus was sidelined peacefully, but the struggle between Antony and Octavian was decided by armed force at the naval battle of Actium in 31 BC. Antony fled to Egypt, where both he and Cleopatra – who had been his lover for over a decade and openly his wife for a year – committed suicide.[2]

After Actium Octavian commanded greater military forces than had ever been controlled by any Roman general in the past, with no fewer than sixty legions bound by their oath to obey him – a total which he would soon reduce to twenty-eight permanent units. With Antony gone there was no longer any serious rival to his supremacy and indeed battle, proscriptions and suicide had done much to thin the ranks of the senior members of the Senate. Caesar had been murdered because his power was blatant. His adopted son survived through creating a regime in which his control of State affairs was veiled. Octavian – he would later be voted the name Augustus by the Senate, which helped him gradually to disassociate himself with his brutal past as a triumvir – was neither dictator nor king, but *princeps senatus*, a traditional honorific given to the most distinguished senator. From this title the regime he created is known today as the Principate, or sometimes the Empire, as opposed to the Republic. In reality emperors with absolute power, Augustus and his successors pretended to be no more than the most senior magistrate in the State.

Many of Rome's traditional institutions persisted, but real power was now firmly and irrevocably in the hands of the *princeps*. The Senate survived and openly flourished, gaining new responsibilities and marks of distinction at the price of losing its independence. Young aristocrats continued to pursue a career in public life which brought them more military and civil responsibilities, but all important posts were now appointments of Augustus rather than won through open elections. Public life was carefully controlled to prevent a regression back into civil war. The Augustan regime was not an instant creation, but the product of a gradual development, of trial and at least some error. Its success owed a good deal to Augustus' politic skill, to the deep desire for stability after decades of upheaval, and also to the *princeps'* own longevity. When Augustus died in AD 14 virtually no one was left alive who could remember a time when the Republic had functioned in its traditional way.

Augustus was not himself a great commander and it was rumoured that he had fled the field when his wing of the army was routed at the first battle of Philippi. Strong enough to admit his own limitations, he relied heavily on a few trusted subordinates to control his forces for him. His attitude to the soldiers under his command was a lot stricter and more formal than Caesar's. After Actium he never addressed troops as 'comrades' but always as 'soldiers' (*milites*), and enforced very strict discipline. On several occasions he decimated cohorts which had panicked and fled. His officers risked public humiliation if they failed in their duties, and Suetonius tells us that he used to order centurions to stand to attention outside his tent all day, perhaps holding up a lump of turf. Usually they were instructed to remove their weapons belt, so that without this restraint the hem of the long military tunic fell almost to ankle height, resembling a woman's dress more than a military uniform. Yet alongside the punishment came decorations and promotion for distinguished service, even if these were no longer issued with quite the freedom typical amongst the commanders of the civil war era. Even more importantly, Augustus ensured that the soldiers were paid regularly and provided on discharge with either land or a sizeable bounty. In AD 6 a special treasury, the *Aerarium Militare*, was established and kept under the emperor's direct control to undertake these tasks. Augustus had no intention of repeating the Senate's mistake by neglecting the needs of the legionaries and so encouraging them to give their loyalty to charismatic generals.[3]

Augustus brought internal peace to Rome, an achievement which was conspicuously celebrated throughout his principate. His regime relied heavily on the glory derived from continuous and spectacular warfare against foreign opponents. Under its first emperor Rome continued to expand as intensively as it had done in the last decades of the Republic and by AD 14 had brought under its control almost all of the territory which would compose the Empire for over four centuries. The *Res Gestae*, a long inscription set up outside Augustus' mausoleum recounting his achievements, lists a vast array of peoples and kings defeated by the emperor. In style the text is identical to the monuments set up by triumphing generals for many generations, but in sheer numbers of vanquished enemies it dwarfs the victories even of Pompey and Caesar.

In a very Roman way these spectacular military successes justified the prominence of the emperor as *princeps*, the greatest servant of the State. Most of these victories were actually won by his *legati*, but the main credit went in the normal way to the supreme commander. Augustus had no intention of being rivalled by the dead, and still less by the living. When in 29 BC Marcus Licinius Crassus, the grandson of Caesar's ally, completed his defeat of the Bastarnae by killing their king in single combat, he was denied the right to dedicate the *spolia opima* on a legal technicality. Augustus himself subsequently celebrated this rite, even though he had never actually performed such a feat. No one was permitted to win sufficient personal glory to detract in any way from the deeds of the *princeps*. After 19 BC no senator unrelated to Augustus and his family was granted the right to celebrate a triumph, although success was still sometimes rewarded with triumphal honours (*triumphalia*), permitting a man to display the symbols of victory without actually riding in procession through the city. Apart from Africa, all provinces which contained a legionary garrison were directly controlled by Augustus and governed by his *legati* who held delegated *imperium*. Not only were all but one of the legions in service under the direct command of his representatives, but over time the command in all important wars was given only to members of the emperor's extended family.[4]

From the beginning of his career, Octavian had relied heavily on his close friend Marcus Vipsanius Agrippa to lead his troops. It was Agrippa who controlled the fleets which defeated Sextus Pompeius – last surviving son of Pompey the Great – at Naulochus in 36 BC and Antony at Actium in 31 BC. From an obscure family, he never threatened to overshadow Caesar's adopted son, and was able to rise with him, eventually marrying Augustus' daughter Julia. Until his death in 12 BC Agrippa was frequently dispatched to fight the Empire's most important wars, campaigning in Spain, Gaul and Germany, the Balkans and the east with great success. He was evidently a very capable commander, but very few sources survive for his campaigns and none that would allow us to reconstruct these in any detail. This may not be entirely coincidental, for his greatest successes were always publicly attributed to the emperor.

As the younger members of the Augustus' extended family reached maturity, most were given important responsibilities at an early age. The most successful militarily were his stepsons Tiberius and Drusus, both of whom were placed at the head of large armies in their early twenties.

Offspring of an earlier marriage of the emperor's wife Livia, they were very much members of the old senatorial élite, being members of the Claudian patrician clan on both their mother's and their father's side. Few families were believed to have a character as distinct as the Claudians, all of whom were extremely proud, self-confident and conscious of their own worth. As a result they produced some of the State's greatest heroes as well as some of its most hated villains. Drusus was very much a hero in the traditional mould, charismatic and popular both with the troops and the citizens of Rome. Desperate to win the *spolia opima*, he is said to have chased Germanic chieftains round the battlefield in the hope of defeating them in single combat. There was widespread dismay when Drusus died in 9 BC as a result of injuries received when falling from his horse on his way back from a campaign in Germany.[5]

Tiberius lacked his younger brother's charm and seems never to have possessed the knack of making others, especially other senators, like him. Even when young he never appears to have adopted the rather flamboyant leadership style of Drusus or Pompey. He was considered a very strict disciplinarian, even by the standards set by Augustus, reintroducing archaic methods of punishment. On one occasion he cashiered a legate commanding a legion for employing some of his soldiers to escort a slave on a hunting expedition in hostile territory. Suetonius describes how in expeditions across the Rhine he ordered that no unnecessary items be included in the baggage train, personally inspecting each wagon's load before the army advanced. Having denied luxuries to his officers, he conspicuously did without them himself, sleeping on the bare earth and often without even a tent. He was careful about his routine, ensuring that all his orders were written down and making himself always available to his officers to explain what he required of them. Velleius Paterculus, who served under him as a prefect in command of auxiliary cavalry and later as a legate, recounts how he always rode on the march rather than travelling in a carriage, and ate his evening meal (to which officers were usually invited) sitting, rather than reclining on a couch in the normal relaxed Roman manner.

For all his strictness both to himself and others, Tiberius was solicitous for his officers' welfare, placing his own surgeon and servants at the disposal of any who were sick or wounded and providing them with transport. As a leader he was tough but fair; as a general careful, successful and trusted by his soldiers. Velleius wrote after Tiberius had succeeded Augustus as emperor and so was much inclined to flatter his old commander, but may well present an accurate picture of the respect and even affection in which he was held by the army.[6] His description of the almost ecstatic welcome from the army of Germany when Tiberius arrived to take command in AD 4 rivals accounts of some of Napoleon's reviews:

> Truly words cannot describe the reaction of the soldiers at their meeting, their tears of joy and exultation at saluting him, their desperate longing to touch his hand, and inability to restrain such cries as 'Do we really see you, general?' 'Have you truly come back safely to us?', and then 'I served with you, general, in Armenia!' 'And I in Raetia!' 'I was decorated by you in Vindelicia!' 'I also in Pannonia!' and 'I in Germany!'[7]

THE SITUATION ON THE RHINE FRONTIER IN AD 14

Augustus trusted Tiberius, just as in the past he had trusted Agrippa, with nearly all of the most important commands during the second half of his principate, but for a long time did not favour him as successor. A number of other, often younger, male family members linked to him by blood and not simply marriage were preferred, but each in turn died prematurely. Rumour blamed Augustus' wife Livia – whom the emperor Caligula later dubbed *Ulixem stolatum* or 'Odysseus in a frock' after the scheming hero of Homer's poem – for arranging these deaths in order to ensure that her son became the next emperor. It is impossible now to know the truth of the matter, but the imperial family seems to have suffered an exceptionally high rate of mortality, even by the standard of the day. What is clear is that in the end Augustus turned to Tiberius, adopting him as his son and sharing power with him during the last years of his life. Tiberius had a son of his own, known as Drusus the Younger, but was also instructed to adopt his late brother's son, Germanicus. The name was an honorific granted to Drusus for his victories over the Germanic tribes, and was extended to his children following his accidental death. Germanicus was 6 years old in 9 BC, but the name proved singularly appropriate for as an adult he would win his greatest fame campaigning in Germany. His mother was Antonia, daughter of Mark Antony and Augustus' sister Octavia, the Octavia whose rejection in favour of Cleopatra had added a personal element to the civil war.[8]

When Julius Caesar overran Gaul, he made it clear that he intended no permanent occupation of territory east of the Rhine, but had brought under his control all lands to the west of the river. The *Commentaries* emphasized that the Rhine was the boundary between the Gallic and Germanic peoples, showing that his 'pacification' of Gaul was complete. Newly conquered

Gaul, the old Roman province of Transalpine Gaul and Italy itself would only be secure if the Germans, more primitive and savage than the Gauls, were kept at bay beyond the Rhine and prevented from emulating the Cimbri and Teutones. In truth Caesar admits that the situation was a little more complicated, and that a number of Germanic peoples had already settled west of the river. Archaeologically it has proved very difficult to confirm the clear distinction Caesar and other ancient authors maintain between German and Gallic tribes on the basis of their material culture – settlement pattern and style, metalwork and most of all pottery. This does not necessarily mean that there was no difference between these peoples, simply that this type of evidence can in this case neither confirm nor deny it. Linguistic analysis of surviving names of places and persons tends broadly to back the picture presented in our ancient sources. The literary sources make clear that apart from sharing a common language and culture, there was little sense of unity or common cause amongst the Gauls and especially the Germans. A warrior identified with his own tribe or clan, such as the Chatti, Marsi or Cherusci, or sometimes to a degree with a broader group of kindred peoples such as the Suebi. In no important sense did he think of himself as a German.[9]

Caesar presented a picture of the Gallic tribes as inherently unstable, the tribes riven by power struggles between ambitious chieftains seeking supremacy and almost annually at war with their neighbours. The Germans became deeply involved in the area either when their aid was sought by Gallic leaders, or when a people migrated across the Rhine in search of more fertile and secure land on which to settle. Caesar may have exaggerated the situation in order to justify his intervention in defence of Rome's and her allies' interests – which in itself was no different from his support for the Sequani, as Ariovistus had pointed out – but it is probable that his version is substantially accurate and fits into a pattern which prevailed in much of Europe throughout the Bronze and Iron Ages. Warfare and especially raiding was endemic. At times a tribe grew in power, often under the rule of a charismatic war-leader, and sometimes bringing neighbouring peoples under control. Usually this proved temporary, rarely outliving the powerful leader. Frequently civil wars and aggressive expansion prompted factions or nearby tribes to migrate, which resulted in pressure on the peoples whose lands they moved into. Migrations could have a knock-on effect over a very wide area. Caesar also exaggerated when he depicted the Germanic tribes as semi-nomadic pastoralists, drawing on a centuries-old stereotype which saw such societies as inherently more primitive and savage than communities which farmed the land and ultimately built themselves cities. Thus in Homer's *Odyssey* the Cyclops planted no crops because they were too lazy, ate meat and drank milk, and had no political assembly – all indications of their barbarity. Archaeology has shown that many farms and villages in Germany were occupied for centuries, but such stability need not conflict with a potential for tribes, or parts of tribes, suddenly to seek land elsewhere.[10]

Caesar left Gaul conquered – there is no evidence for any serious rebellions whilst he was away fighting the civil war – but not yet fully settled as a province. The process involved the imposition of a new administrative structure, including the holding of a census to assist with taxation on at least three occasions from 27 BC, and at times prompted widespread resistance. Agrippa operated in Gaul on several occasions between 38 and 19 BC and there were several other campaigns fought on a smaller scale under other commanders. Just as in Caesar's day, the Gallic tribes nearest the Rhine often sought help in the form of warrior bands from among the Germans. The latter even more frequently raided the rich lands of Gaul, and at times these attacks were on a very large scale. In 16 BC an army drawn from three tribes, the Sugambri, Tencteri and Usipetes, ambushed a detachment of Roman cavalry and, following up their success, surprised the main army of the provincial governor Marcus Lollius, inflicting a sharp defeat on him. During this battle one Roman legion, *Legio V Alaudae*, suffered the humiliation of losing its eagle standard. This campaign had opened when the Germans seized and crucified the Roman traders operating in their lands. As elsewhere Roman and Italian merchants operated well ahead of the army. Their activities and practices may sometimes have been resented and they were certainly often the first target when the tribes became hostile to Rome. Both to secure the stability and peace of Gaul and in response to raiding and violence against citizens, Augustus' legions were drawn ever more often into punitive action against the Germans.

Germanicus' father Drusus was the first Roman commander to reach the Elbe, where the official version of events claimed that he was warned from going any further by the appearance of a goddess. After his death Tiberius spent several years operating in the same area. Over time a Roman province between the Rhine and Elbe began to take shape. In AD 6 an attack was planned and prepared against Maroboduus, king of a great confederation of the Suebic tribes and a number of their neighbours in the lands between the Rhine and Danube. However, a widespread rebellion in Pannonia and Dalmatia unexpectedly broke out and required the attentions of Tiberius and a large part of the Roman army to suppress. The Pannonians were extremely warlike, their armies based on the Roman model from the experience of many of their men as auxiliaries in Roman service. At one point during this campaign Tiberius found himself at the head of a force of ten legions, supported by seventy cohorts of auxiliary infantry, fourteen cohort-sized units or *alae* of auxiliary cavalry, and large numbers of allied troops. Interestingly, he considered this too large an army for one general to control effectively and so divided it into two independent groups, and subsequently into much smaller columns. It took the greater part of three years of hard and costly fighting to defeat the rebellion.[11]

Almost immediately news reached Augustus of an appalling disaster in Germany. As in Gaul, the process of turning conquered territory into a formal province provoked renewed resistance. The most important rebel leader was a prince of the Cherusci named Arminius who was serving as commander of a contingent of his tribesmen with the Roman army. At some point in the past he had been granted not only Roman citizenship but equestrian status, and was an intimate of the provincial legate, Publius Quinctilius Varus. Varus' family had a somewhat questionable military reputation, since both his father and grandfather had backed the wrong side in civil wars and ended up taking their own lives, but he was very experienced, having previously served as governor of Syria where he had suppressed a rebellion in Judaea in 4 BC. His appointment to the German command conformed with Augustus' tendency to rely primarily on his extended family, for he was married to a daughter of Agrippa.

Late in the summer of AD 9 Varus received reports of a revolt and, just as he had done in 4 BC, responded in the traditional Roman way by gathering his army and marching immediately against the enemy. The need to react as quickly as possible to a rising was considered reasonable justification for a Roman general taking the field with a small or poorly supplied force consisting of the only troops available at short notice. In contrast Varus weakened his strength by sending off many small detachments of troops and marched with an army encumbered by a great baggage train and accompanied by a horde of camp followers and the soldiers' families. Abandoned by Arminius and its German scouts, the lumbering column walked into an ambush in a difficult area of marsh and thick woodland, the Teutoberg Wald. By sudden attacks over a period of days Arminius' warriors weakened the Roman column until they were able to overrun the last pitiful remnant. Three legions – *Legiones XVII, XVIII* and *XIX* – along with six cohorts of auxiliary infantry and three *alae* of cavalry were massacred. Varus did what no Roman general should have done and despaired, committing suicide before the end.

Excavations at Kalkriese (near modern-day Osnabrück) have in recent years discovered grim evidence of probably the last main action fought by this army. Most of the small detachments of troops scattered throughout the province suffered a similar fate in the following days. A few survivors managed to reach the Rhine where the two surviving legions in the region expected at any moment to come under attack.[12]

The disaster in the Teutoberg Wald was a terrible blow to the ageing Augustus, who let his hair and beard grow unchecked for a month as a mark of mourning and is supposed to have wandered through his palace banging his head against the walls and yelling out, 'Quinctilius Varus, give me back my legions!' For a while the army was reduced to a strength of twenty-five legions, and the numbers XVII, XVIII and XIX were never reused. Tiberius was immediately sent to the Rhine frontier and all available troops transferred from other provinces to reinforce his army. Soon there would be eight legions and at least as many auxiliary troops in the two provinces of Lower and Upper Germany which ran along the west bank of the river. The expected German invasion did not materialize, Arminius' warriors having apparently followed the practice of most tribal armies throughout history and dispersed to their homes to show off their plunder and revel in their glory. When strong enough Tiberius began to send punitive expeditions against the German tribes. The Roman reputation for invincibility had been shattered by Varus' defeat, and it would take several years of hard campaigning to begin to restore it. In AD 11 Tiberius was joined by Germanicus, who had first gained experience under his command during the Pannonian rebellion at the age of 22. Augustus was now very elderly and in AD 13 Tiberius returned to Rome, both to assist the *princeps* and to ensure that the succession proceeded smoothly on his death. Germanicus replaced him as supreme commander on the Rhine frontier.[13]

MUTINY

Like his father, Germanicus was extremely popular both with soldiers and people of Rome, affection which would remain deeply felt long after his death. We know that at least one Roman auxiliary unit, and perhaps the entire army, was still annually celebrating his birthday in the early third century AD. Urbane, handsome, fair-haired, athletic – he had worked especially hard to develop his legs which had originally been rather thin – his manner was easy and courteous. Again like his father, Germanicus took his wife and children with him to his province. She was Agrippina, child of

Agrippa and Augustus' daughter Julia and so his cousin, for the imperial family were much inclined to arrange marriages between different branches of the extended family in order to prevent giving too many outsiders some blood link to the emperor. In many respects she personified the ideal Roman matron, a group much celebrated in Augustan propaganda as virtuous, hard-working both in running the home and supporting her husband in his career, and producing the next generation of Roman citizens. The couple had nine children, well above the average in an age when birth rates amongst sena-torial and equestrian families were in decline, but only six of these – three boys and three girls – survived childhood. The youngest son, Gaius, was born in AD 12 and as an infant was often dressed by his parents in a minia-ture version of legionary uniform. The soldiers nicknamed him Caligula, or 'Little Boots', after the hobnailed military boots or *caligae*.[14]

Augustus' death in AD 14 sent shock waves throughout the Empire, for most of its population could scarcely remember a time without the *princeps*. Uncertainty combined with virtually no active campaigning during that summer to produce mutinies amongst the legions, first in Pannonia and then on the Rhine. Soldiers complained of the heavy deductions made from their pay, both official for uniforms, equipment and tents and unofficial in the form of bribes to centurions to avoid unnecessary fatigues. Under Augustus the process of turning the Roman army into a professional force had almost been completed. At the beginning of his principate legionaries were expected to serve for sixteen years, followed by four more as veterans, who were supposed to be exempt from normal duties but still required to fight. The near constant warfare of these decades led to these terms being extended to twenty and five years respectively. The change was resented, especially since even longer service was required from large numbers of men after the great crises in AD 6 and 9. So desperate had been Augustus' need for men that in both those years he had reintroduced conscription, something that was now deeply unpopular especially in Italy. Suetonius tells us that Augustus actually sold into slavery an equestrian who had cut off his sons' thumbs to make them unable to hold a weapon and so ineligible for call-up. The legions' strength was boosted by men reluctant to serve or of a calibre not normally accepted by recruiting parties. Most drastic of all, the State purchased large numbers of slaves and freed them to become soldiers in a repeat of the desperate days of the Second Punic War. Although such men received citizenship with their freedom, Augustus insisted that they serve in distinct units, the *cohortes voluntariorum civium Romanorum*, rather than in the legions.[15]

The worst outbreak began in the army of Lower Germany commanded by Aulus Caecina, a very experienced officer of the type who seem often to have been appointed as senior subordinates to the younger members of the imperial family. On this occasion he remained strangely inactive, until all four of his legions – *I*, *V*, *XX* and *XXI* – threw off all discipline. The first targets of the soldiers' resentment were the centurions, many of whom were seized and flogged. Germanicus was away in Gaul supervising the collection of taxation, but soon hastened to the army's camp. He was greeted by a parody of the normal parade of welcome for a commander, and was only with some difficulty able to impose any order on the occasion, as men bombarded him with complaints about overdue discharge and the poor conditions which rewarded their loyal service. Some of the troops even shouted out that they were willing to make him emperor instead of Tiberius. Shocked, Germanicus tried to leave the meeting and, when men blocked his way, even went so far as draw his sword and threaten to kill himself if they did not instantly return to their proper loyalty. It was the sort of theatrical gesture commonly used by a Roman senator in the Forum or with the army, but in this case the impact was mixed, for while some men held his arm to restrain him, at least one is said to have offered the general his own sword, saying that it had a sharper edge.

Concessions for a while prevented more violence, but some senators sent by Tiberius to investigate the legionaries' grievances were roughly handled and one ex-consul narrowly escaped death. Acting on the suggestion of his *consilium*, Germanicus resolved to send Agrippina and the 2-year-old Caligula to safety in one of the nearer Gallic towns. Roman legionaries were hard men, capable at times of extreme cruelty, but they were also often deeply sentimental, and the sight of the tearful party of refugees fleeing from the camp prompted a radical change of mood. Seizing on this change, Germanicus again addressed them, and this time was able to demand that the ringleaders be brought before him, summarily condemned and executed. However, to prevent a recurrence of the problem he also dismissed a number of centurions who were found guilty of taking bribes from their men.

A number of concessions, including immediate discharge for those overdue for it and return to the earlier pattern of sixteen years' ordinary service and four as a veteran, were announced around the same time. The reduction in length of service does not appear to have lasted long and soon reverted once more to a total of twenty-five years, but in other respects the main grievances of the mutinies do appear to have been answered. After further summary executions and some actual fighting in another camp, the mutiny of the army of Lower Germany was at an end. On seeing the aftermath of this last incident, Germanicus is supposed to have said that 'This was not a cure, but a disaster!' With his entire army – the non-citizen auxiliaries appear to have remained loyal throughout – once again restored to discipline, Germanicus was able to turn his attention to foreign enemies.[16]

It was now late in the campaigning season, but even so Germanicus put together a punitive column consisting of elements of all four of the recently mutinous legions, altogether some 12,000 men, along with twenty-six cohorts of auxiliary infantry and eight *alae* of cavalry. Crossing the Rhine this force moved rapidly against the Marsi. Rather than following the normal, easiest trail into this tribe's territory, Germanicus took a longer, less well-known route. In the lead were the auxiliary infantry, marching quickly and carrying only their equipment, tasked with finding and clearing the path of obstructions, and behind came the main body of the legions with a small baggage train. The Romans moved by night, clear skies and bright starlight allowing them to find their way without difficulty. Surprise was increased because the night was a festival which the Germans were celebrating with feasting. Before dawn a number of Marsian villages were surrounded by Roman troops. There was virtually no resistance when the attack went in and slaughtered the occupants. Germanicus then divided his army, creating smaller battle groups each based around one of the four legions present, and sent these off individually to devastate the land for some 50 miles around. Roman punitive expeditions were normally brutal affairs – on one occasion in 51 BC Caesar had achieved great surprise simply by ordering his men not to torch every building they passed – but this one was even more ferocious than usual. Prisoners were not taken and any Germans encountered were massacred irrespective of their age or sex. Usually the Romans had a degree of respect for local religious sites, but an important shrine was deliberately burnt to the ground by the troops.[17]

The Romans did not face any serious opposition until the columns had reunited and begun the march back to the Rhine, for it took time for tribal armies to muster. The Marsi had been too stunned by the onslaught to react at all, but the neighbouring Bructeri, Turbantes and Usipetes gathered an army and took up position along the route which they rightly guessed the Romans would take on their return journey. Germanicus had learned of their intentions and moved with his army in a hollow square, the baggage train now swollen by plunder in the centre, and the individual cohorts ready to deploy quickly into battle order. When the Romans reached a narrower spot the Germans sprang their ambush, launching their main attack against the rear. According to Tacitus, Germanicus galloped up to the troops from *Legio XXI Rapax* (or 'greedy', in the sense of greedy for glory) who were on the left wing, 'crying out in a great voice that now was the time to eradicate the disgrace of mutiny. They were to charge and turn shame into glory.' Enthusiastically, the cohorts of this legion drove the Germans back, inflicting heavy losses. Chastened, the tribesmen allowed the Roman column to complete its march unmolested. Germanicus returned his men to winter quarters in Lower Germany.[18]

ROME'S VENGEANCE, AD 15–16

In many respects the operations of the next two years were similar to the punitive expedition against the Marsi, but on a much larger scale. The war was being fought to avenge the disaster of AD 9 and, even more importantly, to re-establish a deep fear of Roman might amongst the Germanic tribes. Arminius was the main enemy, but the success of the Cherusci had encouraged many other peoples to become openly hostile. The power of chieftains amongst the tribes was by no means absolute and relied on their prestige. Most warriors would choose to follow a successful war-leader, but he could not compel them to do so. Arminius was not the only prominent figure amongst the Cherusci, and some of the other princes resented his current dominance. Therefore the tribes' war effort was usually uncoordinated and some groups did not recognize the dominance of the Cherusci at all. Rome's war was therefore waged against many different enemies simultaneously and each had to be persuaded that the alternative to alliance and peace with the Empire was too terrible to endure. At this stage the Romans do not appear to have planned the physical reoccupation of the lost province west of the Elbe. In the campaigning season Roman armies drove into Germany, laying waste the land (the Romans had a verb, *vastare*, for this action) and defeating anyone who dared to oppose them, but by the autumn they always returned to secure bases on the Rhine. At no point were significant garrisons left behind in the way that Caesar had always wintered his troops in the most recently overrun sectors of Gaul during his campaigns.

Germany also differed from Gaul in other important respects. Sizeable settlements equivalent to the Gallic *oppida* were extremely rare, most of the population living in scattered villages. Caesar had often drawn considerable quantities of grain and other supplies, sufficient to support his army for weeks at a time, from the Gallic towns, either by demanding these from allied communities or seizing them by force from the enemy. Germanicus could not hope to do this in Gaul and, since foraging would slow the march of his columns and leave small detachments engaged in the task vulnerable to attack, was forced to carry most of his requirements with the column. There is some rhetorical exaggeration in Tacitus' picture of Germany as mainly forest and swamp, but it was certainly true that much of the terrain was difficult to traverse for a large army. Even in spring and summer there were few routes suitable for taking the wagons required by the baggage train. Many of these were trails which had been established, and often improved by the construction of bridges or causeways, by earlier Roman armies who had operated in the area under Drusus and Tiberius. Roman armies made little use of maps in the modern sense, and had a tendency to think in terms of routes to a place, but in Germany they had far fewer options open to them for alternative paths. Both sides understood this, and the Germans were frequently able to anticipate the direction the enemy would take in time to muster an army in a suitable ambush position somewhere along it.

Tribal armies took time to muster as warriors came in from scattered settlements, and then, lacking formal discipline and somewhat casual in obedience to leaders, moved slowly. For this reason such large-scale ambushes usually took place, as in AD 14, when the Roman expedition was on its way home. It may also be that the Roman withdrawal after an attack was interpreted as an encouraging sign of timidity. Germanicus, like all other Roman commanders who had led or would subsequently lead armies in this theatre, had to be very careful in balancing the forces he committed to punitive expeditions. If too few troops were sent then there was the risk that they would be overwhelmed, especially if they penetrated deep into hostile territory. Larger columns required a substantial baggage train of pack animals and wagons to transport even the barest minimum of supplies and so inevitably moved more slowly. It was for this reason that Tiberius had paid such careful attention to the loading of baggage carts during his expeditions across the Rhine. A large supply train was also inclined to force a Roman column to spread over a wider area, especially if it had to traverse a narrow pass or causeway, making it much harder to defend against ambush.

The Romans' aim was to strike as fast and as hard as they could, spreading devastation and terror over as wide an area as possible, and then to withdraw without suffering any significant losses. Their intention was to convince each of the tribes that it was vulnerable and could not hope to stop an attack if the Romans chose to target it. The defeat of a tribal army in a battle, whether fought on the way in or the way out, could add to the impression of Roman military might, but was not essential. What was vital was that the Romans should never suffer a reverse, however small, which would encourage the tribes in future.[19]

In the new campaign, Germanicus planned to use the armies of both Upper and Lower Germany, giving him a force of eight legions supported by auxiliaries. He launched his attack at the very beginning of spring AD 15, striking with his main force of four legions and the bulk of the auxiliaries at the Chatti, while Caecina with the rest of the army demonstrated towards the Cherusci. The winter had proved unusually dry and the main column was able to ford with ease streams that were normally much deeper. A detachment was left behind to construct a proper road and bridges where necessary to carry it over water. Surprise was complete and many of the Chatti were captured or killed, although the bulk of the warriors swam across the River Eder. Under cover of light artillery and auxiliary archers, the legionaries rapidly threw a bridge across the river and attacked, dispersing this force. In subsequent days the tribal centre at Mattium was burnt and the lands around laid waste. Germanicus then withdrew, his army marching away completely unmolested, for the Chatti were in no state to muster an army and Caecina's actions prevented either the Cherusci or the Marsi from intervening.

Germanicus, like any good Roman commander, was always ready to employ diplomacy in conjunction with force where it seemed likely to bring an advantage. Envoys had arrived from Segestes, an older leader of the Cherusci whose influence had been eroded by the rise of Arminius, asking for protection from his rival. The German leader's message emphasized his past loyalty to Rome, in particular his unsuccessful attempt to warn Varus of the planned revolt and Arminius' treachery. Acting on these earlier negotiations, Germanicus' army collected Segestes and his party during their march. A number of the latter's warriors, including his own son, had fought against Rome in AD 9 and even brought with them trophies taken from Varus' men. Past misdemeanours were overlooked given the political advantage to be gained from the defection of such a famous chieftain. Tiberius granted a pardon for all misdemeanours and gave the exiles a place to live within the Empire and a pension for life. A less willing member of the party was Segestes' daughter who had been previously abducted and married by Arminius, and then as forcibly taken back by her father. She was now pregnant with Arminius' son, who would be born and grow up in exile.[20]

Arminius was enraged, both by the defection and by the loss of his wife, and swiftly began gathering a large army, being joined by his uncle,

Inguiomerus, another powerful figure amongst the tribe who in the past had been considered pro-Roman. Such was their combined prestige that many bands of warriors from neighbouring tribes joined the Cherusci. As reports of this reached Germanicus, he and Caecina attacked tribes considered to be sympathetic to the enemy, and in particular devasted the territory of the Bructeri. During these operations the eagle standard of *Legio XIX* was recovered. Since he was not far from the site of Varus' disaster, Germanicus decided to march into the Teutoberg Wald and bury the dead. Caecina went in advance to reconnoitre the ground and where necessary construct bridges and causeways across the most marshy areas. For a while they followed the same route as the earlier army. Tacitus gave a dramatic description of what they saw:

> Varus' first camp with its size and proper layout showed the efforts of three legions; then a half-collapsed rampart and shallow ditch marked the spot where the last shattered remnants had camped. In the plain between were whitening bones, scattered where the men had fled and heaped in piles where they had stood at bay. Lying nearby were broken weapons and bits of horses, while the skulls of men were nailed to tree trunks. Not far away were groves containing barbarian altars, where they had sacrificed the tribunes and senior centurions. Witnesses of the massacre, who had survived the fighting or escaped the chains of captivity, described where the legates fell, where the eagles were taken, where Varus was first wounded and where at last he had met death by his own hand; and they told of the tribunal from which Arminius had given his victory speech, of the gibbets and pits for burying prisoners, and the arrogance with which he insulted the eagles and other standards.
>
> Now, six years after the disaster, a Roman army had come to the spot and buried the bones of three legions, no man knowing whether he laid to rest the remains of a stranger or a kinsman ... but with anger rising against the enemy, all simultaneously mourned and hated.[21]

A mound was raised as a memorial over the mass grave. Germanicus himself laid the first section of turf to show his respect for the fallen, although such an act was not really appropriate since he was a member of the priestly college of augurs and the Romans had strong taboos about such priests having physical contact with the dead. Having completed its grim task, the army advanced against Arminius. At first the Germans withdrew ahead of them, but when the auxiliary cavalry were sent a little further in advance of the main column than was usual they were ambushed and routed. Auxiliary infantry sent up in support became infected with panic and were in turn driven back.

The Germans' pursuit was only halted when Germanicus arrived with the legions and deployed them into battle order. Arminius was not ready to risk a full-scale battle and withdrew, content with the success already achieved. It was now late in the season and the Roman commander was reluctant to risk delaying his return to winter quarters for the uncertain chance of provoking and winning a decisive battle. He decided to withdraw, taking half of the army himself by the northern route where some could at times be transported by river or sea, and sending Caecina with the remaining four legions along a trail frequently used by the army in the past and known as the 'long bridges'. Originally built by an army under the command of Lucius Domitius Ahenobarbus more than a decade before, these causeways across the marshes were in a state of disrepair and required some attention before it was safe to send the baggage train over them. However, the Romans' choice of such a well-known route was quickly noticed by Arminius, who rushed his warriors by other, shorter paths to reach the bridges before Caecina and take up position in the woods and high ground to their flank.[22]

The Roman commander divided his men between building a fortified camp and repairing the causeways, keeping some units in formation to cover each working party. Throughout a long day they were harassed by the Germans, who mainly skirmished from a distance, but occasionally charged home when they detected a vulnerable spot in the rough Roman lines. It was not a landscape well suited to the operations of a drilled and disciplined army, for there were few patches of open, solid ground where units could operate in formation. The situation was made even worse when some of Arminius' warriors dammed a stream, directing the flow of water down into the already half-flooded plain. The lightly equipped Germans were more used to such marshy terrain and coped far better than the encumbered legionaries. Tacitus claims that the legions were close to breaking under the pressure when night fell and brought an end to the fighting. Drawing on a literary set-piece which has often been employed by authors throughout the centuries – most famously in Shakespeare's *Henry V* – he then contrasted the nervous silence of the sleepless Romans with the drunken carousing and boasting audible from the German encampments.

On the next morning Caecina formed his army into the hollow square often employed in these campaigns, with *Legio I* in front, *Legio V Alaudae* on the right, *Legio XXI Rapax* on the left and *Legio XX* in the rear. His hope was that these could set up a strong enough fighting line somewhere amidst the marshland to cover the movement of the baggage train and wounded across the 'long bridges'. However, whether through confusion over their orders or, as Tacitus hints, a measure of panic, *V Alaudae* and *XXI Rapax* hurried on too quickly, not forming up in battle order until they were past the marsh-land and had reached a more open plain beyond. The movement left the train exposed when Arminius led his warriors in a massed attack. Fighting was confused as the Germans swarmed down on the wagons and the marching column. Caecina's horse was wounded as he tried to bring some order to the chaos, throwing the ageing commander – he was now around 60 – to the ground. Only the quick actions of some soldiers from *Legio I* prevented his being killed or taken by the enemy.

Eventually the bulk of the Roman army managed to reach the open ground already occupied by the two legions who ought to have covered the flanks. Once there the weary men were forced to labour on for several hours to construct a basic ditch and rampart around their camp. Much of the baggage had been taken by the enemy, whose preoccupation with plunder-ing had done much to permit the escape of the main force. That night few of the wounded had dressings or proper medicine and scarcely any of the men tents in which to sleep. When a horse broke from its tether and galloped through the camp spreading confusion, a mob of frightened men led a panicked rush to the gateways, believing that the position was overrun by the enemy. Caecina only stopped them by throwing himself down in the open gateway and daring them to trample on him. Afterwards the tribunes and centurions carefully explained what had happened and calmed the men.

Arminius and Inguiomerus appeared to have the Roman army at their mercy, trapped in difficult country and worn down after days of ambushes just as Varus' men had been in AD 9. However, while Arminius planned to permit Caecina to leave his camp and march once again into close country before launching an attack, his uncle was convinced that they had already won. His suggestion that their bands of warriors should encircle the Roman camp and launch a direct assault was warmly received by the other chief-tains. This was what Caecina had expected them to do and he had prepared accordingly. His men were formed ready to sally out from each of the camp's four gateways, the attack led by a picked body of the bravest soldiers mounted on horses publicly taken from the commander and his senior officers. In such a desperate situation Caecina wanted it known that he would not gallop away and abandon his men, but share whatever was their fate.

The legionaries were kept under tight control as daylight revealed a dense ring of German warriors advancing to the attack. Caecina let them come close, hoping that the apparent reluctance of the Romans to come out and fight would reinforce the barbarians' contempt for them. Only at the last minute did he order the legions to charge out of the gateways, trumpets blaring and the men raising a cheer. Almost immediately the enemy's soaring confidence was shattered, panic rapidly spreading through their ranks. Where they did not instantly flee, the open plain allowed the Romans to take best advantage of their superior training and equipment. German casualties were heavy, including Inguiomerus who was badly wounded, as the Romans pursued them for the rest of the day. For the remainder of its march back to the Rhine the Roman column was free from attack. However, rumours of disaster had preceded Caecina's men, and caused a panic amongst the garrison commanders on the frontier. Only the intervention of Germanicus' wife Agrippina is said to have prevented the destruction of the bridge across the river at Vetera (modern Xanten). She was also there to greet the returning column, personally thanking the men, distributing clothes to those who had lost them and caring for the wounded.[23]

The return journey of Germanicus' own half of the army had been less eventful, although one section of this force endured considerable hardship and some loss when the coastal plain along which they marched – roughly along today's northern Dutch coast – was flooded by an unusually high tide.

THE TRIBES OF GERMANY

This incident, along with the troubled withdrawal of Caecina's column, reduced the impact of the successes of this campaigning season for they suggested that the Romans were not invincible. Arminius may not have won any great successes, but he had avoided being decisively beaten and his prestige was high. Germanicus decided that in the next year he would aim to seek a direct confrontation with the German war-leader. This time all eight legions would fight in a single force. To this end he spent the winter months in preparation, rebuilding the army. The western provinces of the Empire, notably Spain and Gaul, vied with each other to send grain and replacement mounts and baggage animals to the army, although Germanicus was aware that the drain of the long wars in Germany had pushed these regions to the limit of their resources. This made a major, and hopefully final, success in the next campaigning season all the more imperative.

It was decided to insert as much of the army as possible by water, sailing along the North Sea coast past the Frisian Islands to land deep in enemy territory. Therefore much of the army was set to the task of building almost 1,000 boats to add to the fleets already stationed on the Rhine. The diplomatic campaign to win over German chieftains continued, with Segestes' brother, Segimerus, and his son defecting to the Empire. The son had not only fought against Rome in AD 9 but was believed to have dishonoured the corpse of Varus, but once again the immediate advantage to be gained from welcoming enemy deserters outweighed Roman anger. Apart from the practical preparations, Germanicus paid particular attention to the health and morale of his men, personally touring the hospitals in the winter quarters, talking to the men as individuals and praising their feats of courage.[24]

In the spring of AD 16 the army met up with the fleet in the territory of the Batavi, a tribe which occupied the 'island' between the Rhine and the Waal, and who provided many auxiliaries for the Roman army. The Batavi were an offshoot of the Chatti, and had crossed the Rhine and settled there after an internal dispute. Before the main campaign began Germanicus sent a small flying column to attack their kindred the Chatti. At the same time news arrived that a Roman fort built near the site of Varus' disaster was under attack, so he led six legions to its relief. Neither operation resulted in any serious fighting, but Germanicus discovered that the tribesmen had destroyed both the mound erected over the mass grave of Varus' men and a nearby altar and monument set up decades before by his father. Such symbols of Roman power erected in their territory appear to have been seen as deeply humiliating to the local warriors. Germanicus re-erected the altar, but decided against repairing the burial mound.[25]

Marching back to rendezvous with the fleet, the Roman army embarked and sailed along the coast to the estuary of the River Ems. They landed on the western bank, although this then imposed a delay as the legions constructed a bridge across the river and allowed Arminius' army to muster. News of a rebellion amongst the Angrivarii prompted the dispatch of a column to ravage their land in immediate punishment. Then Germanicus advanced to the Weser and found the German army massed on the eastern bank. Tacitus tells the story that Arminius called out to summon his brother Flavus, who had remained loyal to Rome and was still serving as an auxiliary commander. The two are supposed to have had an argument, yelling at each other from opposite banks and contrasting their fortunes, but it is more than possible that this is a rhetorical invention, or at least an exaggeration of a real incident. Reluctant to attempt a direct assault across the river until he had secured a foothold and given the legions time to construct a number of bridges, Germanicus sent a force of auxiliary cavalry across by a ford. With them went Chariovalda, the war-leader (or *dux*) of the Batavi, and his warriors. At first things went well, but the Batavi were lured into an ambush by the Cherusci and swiftly surrounded, their warriors forming a circle of shields facing outwards in an episode which conformed with the most heroic traditions of intertribal warfare. After some time Chariovalda led a breakout, but was killed in the act. The remnants of his men were saved when the Roman cavalry came to their aid.[26]

In subsequent days the rest of the Roman army was able to cross the Weser. Scouts reported that Arminius had withdrawn to a position from which he planned to give battle, near a sacred forest, dedicated to a god whom the Romans equated with Hercules. A deserter claimed that the German leader planned to mount a night attack on the Roman camp, but this was not pressed home when the legions were discovered to be on the alert. Earlier the same night Germanicus is supposed to have disguised himself in an animal-skin hood, probably of the type worn by standard-bearers, and wandered through the tent lines, hoping to gauge the soldiers' spirits. (Directly or indirectly, the incident was most likely the inspiration for the very similar episode in Shakespeare's *Henry V.*) Eavesdropping on campfire conversations, the 31-year-old Roman commander is supposed to have been overwhelmed by his men's affection for and trust in him. Even more encouragement came when a German warrior who was able to speak Latin – perhaps the legacy of service as an auxiliary – rode close to the rampart and called out an invitation for anyone to desert, promising them land and a wife each, along with 25 denarii a day till the end of the war. Since the legionary's annual salary was at this time only 225 denarii, this was an extremely lavish offer. However, the men were insulted at the thought that they might betray their own side, and cheerfully declared this a good omen, claiming that it meant that the Germans' lands and women were theirs for the taking.[27]

On the next morning the commander addressed his army, although since eight legions and auxiliaries were present it is probable that either he or his officers repeated the speech to several smaller groups. According to Tacitus he told them that:

> The open plain is not the only good battleground for a Roman soldier, for if he thought carefully, then woods and forest pastures were just as suitable. For amidst the trunks of trees and undergrowth the barbarians' great shields and enormous spears were not as handy as the *pilum*, *gladius* and well-fitting cuirass. What they [the legionaries] needed to do was strike hard and fast, aiming for the face. The Germans wore no armour or helmets, and their shields were not strengthened with metal or hide, but simply wickerwork or thin painted boards. Only the front ranks carried proper spears, the rest had only short clubs hardened with fire. While their stature was impressive and powerful in a quick attack, they could not stand being hurt.[28]

Encouraged by this denigration of the enemy, and the promise that victory would bring an end to their labours, the soldiers cheered enthusiastically, before the parade was dismissed and the army marched out to deploy for battle. Arminius, Inguiomerus and the German army waited for them on a wooded plain backed by high ground near the Weser. The place was known as Idisiaviso, but has never been precisely identified. Arminius and most of the Cherusci were in reserve – an unusually subtle refinement for a tribal army – on the high ground. The Roman army marched to the battlefield in a formation which could readily convert into battle order. Tacitus says that the Romans advanced with Gallic and German auxiliaries supported by foot archers in front, followed by four legions along with Germanicus himself and two cohorts of the Praetorian Guard (the élite imperial bodyguard) and the pick of the cavalry. Behind them came the other four legions with light infantry and horse archers as rearguard. It is uncertain what formation each section was in; whether for instance each group of four legions was deployed in the hollow square so often used in these campaigns. At the start of the battle Germanicus claimed to have seen eight eagles flying in the direction of the Roman advance, and announced to his men that this was an omen of victory.

Tacitus' account of the battle does not allow a clear reconstruction of the sequence of events. Some of the Cherusci appear to have surged forward to the attack against Arminius' orders and were soon taken in the flank and rear by units of auxiliary cavalry. The Roman infantry also pushed steadily onwards, driving the tribesmen back. Arminius himself led a charge against the archers in the vanguard of the Roman army, and was only stopped by the auxiliary heavy infantry. Almost cut off, he smeared his face with his own blood to avoid recognition and escaped, thanks to the quality of his horse. Rumour suggested that German auxiliaries from the Chauci let him go deliberately. In heavy fighting the German army was routed and suffered heavy losses. Some warriors drowned or were shot as they tried to swim the Weser, others were picked off by the archers as they tried to hide in the branches of trees. Roman casualties were extremely light, although Tacitus gives no figure for these. After the battle the army paraded and hailed Tiberius as *imperator*, for any victory, even one won by his adopted son, was always credited to the *princeps*. A trophy was made from captured weapons and inscribed with the names of the defeated tribes.[29]

Enraged by this visual symbol of their defeat, tribesmen began to harass the Roman column as it withdrew. An army was once again mustered and took up position at a spot along the trail the Romans were following, near a rampart marking the boundary of the lands of the Angrivarii. Next to this were forests and marshes flanking a narrow waterlogged plain. The German infantry concealed themselves near the rampart, while the cavalry were in woodland further back, ready to attack the rear of the Roman column. The Romans were aware of the presence of the enemy and Germanicus decided that another massed engagement would be to his advantage. Leaving the cavalry to cover the open ground, the infantry were divided into two forces, one to attack the rampart and the other the woodland near the main path. The commander himself led the assault on the fortification, for he judged this to be the best-defended area.

The first attack made little headway, the soldiers suffering casualties as they tried to scramble up the turf wall. Germanicus ordered the recall and then brought up slingers and skirmishers to bombard the defenders. Light artillery (scorpions), picked off the most conspicuous warriors, shooting their bolts over distances greater than any hand-held weapon and with such force that neither shield nor defensive armour could stop them. Suppressed in this way, the defenders were unable to reply effectively – archers appear to have been rare in German armies – and a second attack carried the rampart. Germanicus led the way with the two praetorian cohorts as the Romans advanced into the woodland to exploit this breakthrough. He had removed his helmet so that his men would more easily recognize him. Fighting was bitter, but the Romans seem to have coped better with the restricted visibility of the woods than their opponents, who had trouble in gaining much advantage from their considerable numbers. Arminius' leadership was for once rather lethargic, and Tacitus speculates that this may have been the result of the wound he had taken in the last battle. Near the end of the day Germanicus drew off one legion to begin construction of a camp. Once again very heavy losses had been inflicted on the enemy and another trophy was erected to commemorate the victory.[30]

It was now near the end of summer and time to return to the frontier provinces. The bulk of the Roman army retired the same way it had come, taking ship and sailing along the North Sea coast. A great storm scattered the fleet, blowing some of it over to the coast of Britain, and sank a number of ships. On his return – at one point he had found himself with just a single ship and landed in the territory of the allied Chauci – Germanicus quickly organized some punitive expeditions to show that the Roman army was still formidable. The Chatti and Marsi were again attacked, the raid on the latter resulting in the recapture of another of the eagles lost with Varus.[31]

RECALL AND MYSTERIOUS DEATH

At the end of AD 16 Tiberius summoned Germanicus back to Rome where he celebrated a triumph over the Germans. Two cohorts of the Praetorian Guard were ordered to meet him in full parade uniform, but such was his popularity that in the event all nine cohorts of the Guard insisted on taking part as a mark of their respect. Tacitus claims that Germanicus had begged for one year's extension of his command to complete the victory. It may be that this was an officially approved rumour which was supposed to show that Rome could have easily achieved full victory if only she had chosen to do so. Germanicus was soon sent to Syria to oversee the eastern provinces where it seemed likely that there might be problems with the Parthians over Armenia.

Tiberius' attitude to his adopted son cannot be established with certainty. Rumour maintained that he envied him as a potential rival, remembering the mutineers' offer in AD 14 to make the popular young commander emperor. Agrippina's very public role in caring for the soldiers and the parents' dressing of their son in a miniature uniform seemed to indicate a desire to subvert the troops in their loyalty. It was said that the imperial legate sent to govern Syria, Cnaeus Calpurnius Piso, had been ordered by Tiberius to watch and hinder Germanicus. There was certainly considerable friction between the two men, which ended in Piso's dismissal. Shortly afterwards Germanicus fell ill and died amidst rumours of poison and claims that Piso or Tiberius was to blame. Piso tried to re-enter his province and resume command, rallying some troops to his cause before he was defeated. He later stood trial in the Senate and committed suicide shortly before a guilty verdict was delivered. The popular reaction to news of Germanicus' death was massive and testament to the great affection for him. His corpse was carried back to Rome with great ceremony.[32]

Whether or not Tiberius was jealous of Germanicus, and whether the latter was in fact murdered, is now impossible to say. In the next few years he would certainly send into exile or execute both Agrippina and her two oldest sons. The Augustan regime presented itself as a modification of the traditional Republic, but in spite of this façade it was from the very beginning a monarchy – and few monarchs have not been suspicious of rivals, real or imagined. In Rome the emperor's reputation rested heavily on the continued success of his armies, but it was vital that no else, not even a relative, should gain too much military glory of his own. The changed conditions of the Principate gave some members of the imperial family great opportunities for military command at a very early age, but did not entirely relieve them from suspicion of plotting against the emperor.

By a strange coincidence AD 19 also saw the death of Germanicus' great opponent, Arminius, who was murdered by his chieftains when they felt that his power had grown too great. Earlier in the same year Tiberius had refused an offer by a Cheruscan nobleman to assassinate the war leader, declaring that Rome did not need to employ such dishonourable methods. Clearly the victories of Germanicus were considered sufficient vengeance for the Teutoberg Wald and the German leader was no longer felt to be a threat, since other Roman wars – most notably that against Jugurtha – had been concluded by similar acts of treachery. Power was always precarious amongst the tribal peoples and perhaps Tiberius simply trusted to this fact to remove Arminius in due course, as in fact occurred. Arminius had succeeded where others such as Vercingetorix had failed, rebelling against Rome and not being overcome. The tribute paid to him by the historian Tacitus in the early second century AD was certainly well deserved:

> Without doubt he was the liberator of Germany, a man who fought against the Roman People not in their earliest days, like other kings and war leaders, but at the height of their power; in indecisive battles and wars without being defeated he lived for thirty-seven years, and held power for twelve, and to this day is celebrated in tribal songs.[33]

CHAPTER 11

IMPERIAL LEGATE: CORBULO AND ARMENIA

Cnaeus Domitius Corbulo (died AD 67)

Domitius Corbulo used to say that the enemy was conquered with the pickaxe.[1]

ULTIMATELY, THE POWER OF AUGUSTUS AND HIS SUCCESSORS RESTED UPON their control of the army. An emperor needed political skill to placate the Senate and prevent popular unrest from becoming a threat, but none of this mattered if his generals were able to emulate Sulla or Caesar and use their legions to fight their way to supreme power. Augustus was able to rely on his extended family to fight the most important wars of his principate, but few of his successors were able to do the same. At first Tiberius employed Germanicus and the Younger Drusus in a similar role, but after their deaths in 19 and 23 respectively there was no one to replace them for the remaining fourteen years of his reign. Caligula, Claudius and Nero had no adult male relatives to fight wars on their behalf (and would probably not have trusted such persons even if they had existed). Unlike Augustus and Tiberius, who had campaigned with great success, their three successors had no military experience, making them all the more reluctant to permit any of their generals to win too distinguished a reputation or gain the affection of their troops.

An emperor could not afford to be outshone by a senator, most especially in the field of military endeavour which remained of central importance to the Roman aristocracy. Yet it was from the ranks of the Senate that the *princeps* had to draw the overwhelming majority of the men who would govern the provinces and command the legions stationed within them. Senators were considered – not least by themselves – the most suitable men for this task, but it was also important to provide them with opportunities to win fame and distinction in the traditional way. A good emperor ensured that there were enough important tasks given to members of the Senate, encouraging this body to acquiesce in his rule and so reducing the risk of conspiracies against him. The ideal was a relationship of mutual benefit to emperor and senators, but this always contained an element of risk that one of the latter would gain too much power and become a rival for the throne. Tiberius is said to have compared the emperor's job to 'holding a wolf by the ears', to a great extent because of this uneasy bond.[2]

Roman armies under the Principate were virtually all commanded by senators, just as they had been under the Republic, but these generals now operated in a profoundly different environment. This was reflected most obviously in their title, for they were no longer proconsuls or propraetors, but legates or representatives of the emperor. All save one of the legions maintained by Augustus were stationed in provinces controlled by the emperor, in an arrangement reminiscent of Pompey's indirect rule of the Spanish provinces after his second consulship. (The exception was the legion garrisoning Africa which was controlled by a proconsul. This arrangement lapsed during Tiberius' reign.) The emperor possessed *imperium* superior to other proconsuls (*maius imperium proconsulare*), although this bedrock of the Augustan regime was rarely mentioned publicly and never paraded in the manner of his other titles, most notably his possession of the powers of the tribune of the plebs (*tribunicia potestas*). The emperor's representative placed in charge of a province was entitled the *legatus Augusti pro praetore*, and his *imperium* was delegated, not his own by right. Soldiers took and regularly renewed an oath of loyalty to the emperor, and not as in the old days to obey their general as well as the Senate and People of Rome, and it was in the emperor's name that they received their pay and any additional rewards or decorations. In addition to its other standards, each unit in the army now carried an *imago*, bearing the bust of the *princeps* as an additional reminder of whose men they were.

A senatorial career under the principate continued in the traditional way to include a range of civil and military posts. In his late teens a man would usually serve as the senior tribune (*tribunus laticlavius*) of a legion for anything from one to three years. The other five tribunes (*tribuni angusticlavii*) in each legion were equestrians following a different career plan which involved commanding auxiliary units. In his early thirties a senator could hope to become the legate in command of a legion. (The ad hoc appointment of commanding officers for these units which had been usual in Caesar's day was turned into a formal position – *legatus legionis* – under Augustus.) On average a legionary legate served in this capacity for about three years. Finally, in his forties he might hope to become a *legatus Augusti pro praetore* in command of a province, which included the control of up to three, or in a few cases four, legions. Tenure in this post varied considerably, though the average was again three years, and a handful of men might be granted a second command in another province.

In terms of the broad range of different posts likely to be held in a career, and also in the relatively limited scope for gaining military experience, there was little difference between the Republic and the Principate. However, whereas under the former success had depended upon winning elections and gaining influence in the Senate, it was now reliant on the favour of the emperor. Not only that, but in all their military posts, most especially commanding a legion or an entire province, they were the emperor's men and not free agents. Caesar seems to have reflected a widely held belief when he stated that the freedom of action of a legate was considerably less than that enjoyed by the army commander. Under the Principate this was taken a stage further and the activities of provincial legates were far more closely monitored and regulated than those of any governor under the Republic. This affected not simply the occasions on which they were permitted to wage war, but also how they should do so. According to Suetonius, Augustus 'believed nothing less appropriate in a general than haste and recklessness and so, he often used these adages: "More haste, less speed"; "Better a safe commander than a bold"; and "That is done quickly enough which is done well enough."'[3] A legate was not expected to take risks in order to win a quick victory before a replacement arrived, but instead to act in the emperor's best interests. Each man received instructions (*mandata*) from the *princeps* and, although the scope and frequency of these is fiercely debated by scholars, it is clear that no major operations – especially offensive operations – were allowed without specific permission.[4]

The emperor allocated men to provincial commands and decided how long they would remain in a post. He also controlled their activities as governors far more closely than the Senate had ever been able to do. Yet sheer distance ensured that it would have been impossible for the emperor to direct his legates' behaviour in every detail, and their powers and opportunities for demonstrating their ability remained numerous. A governor was expected to lead his troops to war in response to internal rebellion or the invasion of his province without first seeking approval from Rome. An inscription recording the achievements of Tiberius Plautius Silvanus Aelianus as *legatus Augusti*

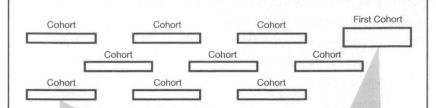

Cohort	Cohort	Cohort	First Cohort

Cohort	Cohort	Cohort

Cohort	Cohort	Cohort

Cohorts II–X

Century	Century	Century	Century	Century	Century
hastatus posterior	hastatus prior	princeps posterior	princeps prior	pilus posterior	pilus prior

Each century consisted of 80 legionaries and was commanded by centurion whose title is given inside box.

The First Cohort

Century	Century	Century	Century	Century
hastatus posterior	hastatus	princeps posterior	princeps	primus pilus

Each century consisted of 160 legionaries commanded by a centurion whose title is given inside the box. The centurions of the First Cohort were known as the primi ordines and possessed immense prestige

A Century from Cohorts II to X

● Centurion

○ ○
○ ○
○ ○
○ ○

● Optio

AN IMPERIAL (COHORT) LEGION

pro praetore of one of the Danubian provinces in the second half of the first century AD gives an idea of the range of military and especially diplomatic tasks which a governor might undertake:

> In this post he brought over more than 100,000 of the people who live across the Danube to pay tribute to Rome, along with their wives and children, leaders and kings. He suppressed an uprising among the Sarmatians, although he had sent a large part of his army to an expedition in Armenia; he compelled kings who had previously been unknown or hostile to the Roman people to worship the Roman military standards on the river bank which he was protecting. He sent back to the kings of the Bastarnae and the Rhoxolani ... their sons who had been captured or taken from the enemy. From some of them he took hostages and in this way strengthened and extended the peaceful security of the province. And the king of the Scythians was driven by siege from Chersonesus, which is beyond the Borysthenes. He was the first to help the corn supply in Rome by sending from his province a large amount of wheat.[5]

On the invitation of the emperor Vespasian – this courtesy was maintained by all good emperors – the Senate granted Silvanus triumphal honours (*triumphalia*) to mark his highly successful term as governor. The language of this monument differs in no significant way from traditional aristocratic celebrations of their achievements. Many of the actions themselves, such as resettlement of tribes, diplomacy aimed at instilling respect for Roman power in local peoples, putting down rebellion and defending allies from attack, were those performed by governors since the first permanent provinces were created. An imperial legate was expected to carry out these duties well, but not on his own initiative to extend them, still less to seek glory by new, unauthorized conquest.

CORBULO IN GERMANY

Cnaeus Domitius Corbulo was a large, virile man who looked every inch a soldier and had an instinctive knack of winning the respect of men, and especially soldiers. Relatively little is known about his early life, but the family was wealthy and well established. His father was consul (actually suffect consul) in AD 39 and he had a half-sister – his mother was married no fewer than six times – who was Caligula's last wife, Milonia Caesonia. In AD 47 Corbulo was appointed by Claudius to be legate of Lower Germany. Before his arrival in the province it was subjected to heavy raiding by the Chauci. From their lands on the North Sea coast the German warriors came in small ships, sailing along to attack parts of Northern Gaul wherever sea or river gave them access. It was a style of activity well established amongst the peoples of this area which in later centuries would become most famous with the Vikings. The Chauci were led by Gannascus, although he came originally from another tribe, the Canninefates (a people related to the Batavi). He was a deserter from a Roman auxiliary unit and thus another in the succession of enemies who were considered to be all the more dangerous because the Romans had taught them how to fight.

On reaching Lower Germany Corbulo responded quickly, employing both the army and the naval squadrons of the fleet which patrolled the Rhine and North Sea, the *classis Germanica*. Small bodies of troops were sent out to intercept any raiders who had landed, while Roman galleys chased down the German ships. Plundering bands were able to attack quickly and were difficult to stop, but tended to be vulnerable as they withdrew, carrying their spoils. After a brief period of operations the Chauci were expelled from the Roman provinces and Corbulo concentrated his army, subjecting the troops to a short, but very rigorous training programme. He is said to have executed two legionaries found labouring in the constructing of fortifications on a marching camp having laid aside their swords. Tacitus, who tells the story, thought that it might be an exaggeration, but felt that even so it hinted at the tough discipline actually imposed on the army. As we have seen, the general whose first task was to retrain and harden an undisciplined and soft army was a familiar figure in Roman literature, so there must always be some suspicion that a description of such activity was merely one of the clichés inevitably attached to famous commanders. However, since the Rhine army appears to have undertaken little serious campaigning for more than a decade before Corbulo's arrival, it is probable that many soldiers and units had no recent experience of active service. Also, in AD 43 a large part of the army from the two German provinces, including three legions and many auxiliaries, had been drawn off to form the invasion force for Claudius' exped-ition to Britain. It is likely that the most battle-ready units were selected for this, leaving the less well-trained soldiers and probably also the least ambitious and aggressive officers behind. It was anyway impossible to maintain the legionaries and auxiliaries in a permanent state of complete preparedness for war, especially since there were so many other tasks soldiers were called upon to perform.[6]

When he felt that the army was ready, Corbulo crossed the Rhine and advanced through the lands along the North Sea coast. The first tribe he encountered were the Frisii, who had openly attacked Roman troops in AD 28 and not yet been subjected to major reprisals. Impressed by the size and confidence of Corbulo's army, the leaders of the Frisii immediately surrendered and allowed the Romans to establish a garrison in their territory. The Roman commander then pushed on eastwards towards the lands of the Chauci. Ahead of the army went envoys demanding the tribe's submission. These men were also able to arrange the murder of Gannascus, who had escaped the defeat of his forces.

As with the betrayal of Jugurtha and murder of Viriathus, this incident again demonstrated the Romans' willingness to employ dubious and dishonourable methods to dispose of enemy leaders whose existence was prolonging a conflict. However, in this case the assassination provoked the Chauci to resist the Romans all the more fiercely, so Corbulo's army advanced against them to begin what he expected to be a major campaign. At this point he received instructions from Claudius instructing him to cease operations and return with the army to his province. It is not made clear in Tacitus' account how the emperor knew where his legate was and what he was doing, but the most probable source of this information would be Corbulo's own dispatches. Claudius did not desire a renewal of major operations east of the Rhine, especially while the conquest of Britain was still ongoing. Tacitus also claims that such an unmilitary emperor, crippled from birth and long considered even by his own family to be mentally incapable, had no wish to allow Corbulo to win great fame through conquest. Claudius had already faced one attempted rebellion by a provincial governor in AD 42 and had no wish to create an even more dangerous rival.

Corbulo immediately obeyed his orders – anything else risked a swift execution – but his wistful comment of 'How lucky Roman generals were in the old days' harked back to the Republic when there had been far fewer restraints on a magistrate's pursuit of glory. In spite of his recall, he was still rewarded triumphal honours. When all of the troops, including the garrison established amongst the Chauci, had been pulled back west of the Rhine, their commander set them to constructing a canal between that river and the Meuse. Such projects helped to keep the soldiers busy and fit, if not at the peak of their military training, and had the added advantage of benefiting the provinces. The legate responsible was often honoured by the emperor. Tacitus follows his account of Corbulo's German campaign with an incident involving Curtius Rufus, the legate of the neighbouring province of Upper Germany, who had employed his legionaries to establish a new silver mine. Many men were injured or killed during this project and the yield was poor, yet Rufus too was granted triumphal honours (*triumphalia*). Tacitus acidly claims that after this the legionaries wrote a letter to Claudius asking him to grant this honour automatically to each legate as he took up his appointment, rather than wait for them to order such arduous and pointless tasks.[7]

ROME, PARTHIA AND THE ARMENIAN QUESTION

Corbulo's conduct in Germany won him widespread success, but it was his later campaigns in the east which established his reputation as one of the greatest Roman generals of the first century AD. Before examining these operations in some detail, it is worth reviewing the history of relations between Rome and Parthia.

Parthia was the most powerful kingdom to emerge from the break-up of the Seleucid Empire in the late second century BC. Its Arsacid dynasty of kings came eventually to control a wide swathe of territory including much of modern-day Iran and Iraq. Within this area was a highly mixed population, varying from Hellenistic cities such as Seleucia and Ctesiphon to pastoral and semi-nomadic tribes. Parthian society was essentially feudal, with much of the power that was theoretically in the hands of the king being held in practice by the leaders of the seven great noble families. The army was formed from a combination of the king's own troops and the retainers of the leading noblemen, who at other times might easily become rivals for the throne. It was therefore not entirely in the king's interest to allow any aristocrat to create a force that was too large or too efficient lest this be used against him. The internal weakness of Parthia prevented her from becoming a serious rival to the Roman Empire, even for control of the eastern provinces, but she was certainly the strongest independent power encountered by Rome during the Late Republic and Principate.

Parthian armies were essentially cavalry forces, which presented a very different problem to the legions compared with the tribal peoples of the west. Most Parthian horsemen were horse archers wielding very effective composite bows and trained through long practice to fire on the move, presenting a difficult target for the enemy and never closing to close quarters unless they possessed an overwhelming advantage. More prestigious were the cataphracts, where both horse and man were heavily armoured. These men, who were mainly from the aristocracy and their closest followers, for the cost of such equipment was great, were at times willing to charge home, each man thrusting a long lance (*kontos*) two-handed. In combination, the archers wearing down an enemy before the cataphracts attacked, these horsemen could be devastatingly effective, but Parthian armies were not always well balanced between the two types, or skilfully led. Nevertheless, in spite of the appearance of similar troops in the armies of other nations, no other people at this period were able to match the best Parthian armies in this style of fighting.[8]

Pompey encountered the Parthians near the end of his eastern campaigns and wisely chose diplomacy instead of the hope of further glory offered by military confrontation. However, in 54 BC Crassus, eager to rival the achievements of his allies Pompey and Caesar, launched an invasion of Parthia. There was scant justification for the war even by Roman standards, although this opinion became more widespread when the expedition ended in disaster. Crassus was over 60 and his last experience of active service had been against Spartacus. At first his running of the campaign was lethargic, as he permitted most of the first year to slip by without pressing the enemy. Both the Romans and the Parthians were overconfident, for their armies were accustomed to defeating the forces fielded by the other kingdoms of the region with great ease.

In 53 BC Crassus encountered a force detached from the main Parthian army under the command of Surenas (which may have been a title rather than a personal name) at Carrhae. It was good cavalry country and the Roman legionaries found it impossible to catch their mobile opponents, who showered them with arrows. The Roman horse, many of whom were Gallic auxiliaries, were under the command of the general's son Publius, who recklessly led them away from the main force to be surrounded and annihilated. For the remainder of the day the horse archers continued to shoot at the square of legionaries, and the Romans' hope that the enemy would run out of arrows proved vain, for Surenas had a well-organized supply train of camels carrying spare ammunition.

Many of Crassus' men were wounded, mostly in the face, legs or right arm which were not covered by the shield, although the legions were not reduced to a state where they could be swept aside by a cataphract charge. Yet Crassus, who after Publius' death had shaken off his lethargy and tried to supervise and encourage his men in the best Roman manner, despaired and ordered a withdrawal. Retreating from close contact with the enemy was always dangerous, but when the enemy had plentiful cavalry and the terrain was open it was courting disaster. Most of the Roman army was quickly killed or captured. (There is an intriguing theory that some of the prisoners were subsequently sold on as slaves and eventually came into Chinese service, but the evidence for this is inconclusive.) Crassus was killed while trying to negotiate a truce and his head taken to the Parthian king. Only a few survivors led by the quaestor Cassius Longinus – one of the men who later murdered Caesar – escaped to Syria and managed to repulse some feeble enemy raids into the province. For a while the Parthians were too busy with internal problems to take great advantage of their victory. In the following months Surenas was executed by the king as a potentially dangerous rival. Obviously this did little to encourage the emergence of any equally talented commanders.[9]

As Rome was soon plunged into civil war, there was no opportunity to avenge Crassus. Caesar was killed before he could launch his planned invasion. Then in 40 BC King Orodes of Parthia sent an army to conquer Asia and Syria. With them was Quintus Labienus, the son of Caesar's old legate and later enemy, and some die-hard Pompeians. This was an almost unique case of a Roman aristocrat defecting to an enemy of the Republic, but even here the issue was blurred somewhat and this could be seen as a continuation of the Civil War. Carrhae had confirmed many Parthians in their conviction that their warriors were superior to any enemy, including the Romans. Overconfidence combined with poor leadership resulted in heavy defeats in 39 and 38 BC when Parthian armies rashly attacked well led and prepared Roman forces occupying strong positions. In the second of these defeats the king's son Pacorus was killed and the attempt to overrun Syria abandoned. Mark Antony had not been present during this campaign, command having rested in the capable hands of his legate Publius Ventidius Bassus. Another of his subordinates expelled a Parthian-backed regime from Judaea in the following year.

In 36 BC Antony himself launched a major attack on Parthia. Learning from Crassus' misfortune, he supported his legionaries with far more cavalry and light infantrymen armed with bows and slings, and kept where possible to regions which were unsuited to cavalry operations. Antony's main army pushed through Armenia into Media Atropatene (modern Azerbaijan) where he began to besiege the city of Phraapsa. A Parthian attempt to relieve the city was defeated – the legionaries clashing their weapons against their shields and shouting to panic the horses – but the mounted enemy managed to flee without suffering heavy losses. Antony had driven his army to advance so quickly during the invasion that his heavy siege train had lagged some distance behind. As the Parthians turned their attention to the Roman supply lines a force of their horsemen overwhelmed the train and its escort. Without artillery and other heavy equipment, there was no prospect of taking Phraapsa, and Antony was reluctantly forced to withdraw. As usual the Parthians harried the marching columns, inflicting heavy losses on the encumbered legionaries. Antony's expedition was not a disaster on the scale of Carrhae, but it was still a major defeat. The growing tension between Antony and Octavian prevented any attempt to renew the war.[10]

Augustus ignored the Parthians for almost a decade after Actium, but in 20 BC he sent the young Tiberius to the east to install a new ruler on the Armenian throne to replace the current Parthian puppet. Through a combination of diplomacy and the threat of force the Romans managed to secure all of their objectives, including the return of all the standards, most especially the precious legionary eagles, and prisoners lost by Crassus and Antony. The eagles were taken to Rome and installed amid great ceremony in the temple of Mars Ultor (Mars the Avenger), the centrepiece of the new Forum of Augustus. This diplomatic success avoided the risk of a full-scale war with Parthia when Augustus' army was already fully committed elsewhere. Both Romans and Parthians by this time had a healthy respect for the other's military might. The chief source of friction between them was Armenia, which both considered to be within their sphere of influence. For the Romans it was one of a number of client kingdoms and they expected its king to acknowledge openly that his power rested on Roman approval. One of the main reasons for sending Germanicus to the east in AD 18 had been formally to confer power on the new Armenian king at Artaxata. Yet culturally Armenia had much more in common with Parthia, and it was considered an appropriate, as well as advantageous, kingdom with which to reward loyal relatives of the Arsacid king.

In AD 35 a Parthian king established one of his sons on the Armenian throne, although he was swiftly defeated by a Roman-backed rival. In AD 52 Vologaeses I of Parthia took advantage of a period of confusion in Armenia following the murder of the king by his unpopular nephew to replace him with his own brother Tiridates. The ageing Claudius at first made no response to this move, but following his death in 54, his successor and adopted son Nero resolved to take action. In the following year Corbulo was sent to the region. The choice was extremely popular, for it appeared to suggest that the new regime would select men on merit – and of course from the senatorial point of view also on the basis of high birth and wealth.[11]

CORBULO IN ARMENIA

Corbulo was given an extraordinary province combining Cappadocia and Galatia. These were normally senatorial provinces, but the Augustan system was extremely flexible and the assignment of an imperial legate to control the area caused no difficulty. In fact, since legates were able to second officers and men from the army to form their large staffs, they usually had substantially more administrative personnel at their disposal than a senatorial proconsul. At some stage Corbulo was granted proconsular rather than propraetorian *imperium* and had a junior legate serving under him to carry out much of the day-to-day administration in his enlarged province. Cappadocia gave best access to Armenia, while Galatia had a large population, many descendants of three Gallic or Galatian tribes which had overrun the area in the third century BC, and was considered to be a fertile recruiting ground. Cappadocia was garrisoned by some auxiliary units, but neither of the areas contained a legion and the bulk of the forces placed at the new legate's disposal were drawn from the army in Syria. Corbulo received two of the four Syrian legions supported by about half of the auxiliary units in the province. Additional troops were to be provided by the client kingdoms of the region. From the beginning there was some friction between Corbulo and the legate of Syria, Ummidius Quadratus, who was forced to give up such a large part of his army and knew that he was bound to be overshadowed

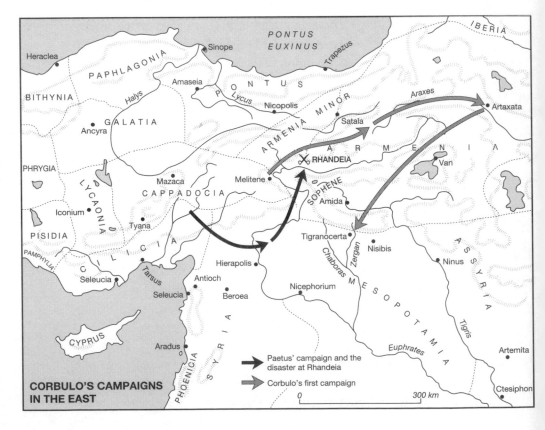

Corbulo's campaigns in the east. Paetus' campaign and the disaster at Rhandeia. Corbulo's first campaign.

by his more famous colleague. However, since Corbulo had superior *imperium* the dispute rarely produced anything more than minor bickering.

From the beginning it was hoped that a diplomatic solution, by which Tiridates would agree to travel to Rome and have the kingship formally conferred on him by Nero, would be possible. Accordingly Corbulo dispatched ambassadors – most often centurions – to Vologaeses, but at the same time he began to prepare his army for war in case these overtures were rejected. Nero had already ordered that the Syrian legions be brought up to strength by a levy (*dilectus*), although it is not clear just what this meant in the context of the Principate. In theory every Roman citizen remained liable for military service, but Augustus' experiences in AD 6 and 9 had shown just how unpopular conscription was, especially in Italy. The levy in the eastern provinces may have taken the form of organized conscription, widespread use of something like a press gang, or simply the dispatch of a larger than normal number of recruiting parties to find volunteers. By the middle of the first century the number of Italian-born men in the legions was declining, with most recruits being citizens from the provinces. From quite early on there does seem to have been a willingness to enlist non-citizens from some of the more settled regions in the east, the franchise being granted to them when they joined the legions. Augustus had formed an entire legion, *XXII Deiotariana*, from Galatian soldiers and the province was considered to provide high-quality recruits. Interestingly enough, the levy to bring the legions up to strength occurred at about the time of the Apostle Paul's missionary journey through Galatia, although there is some debate over his route through the province. His later letter to the Galatian churches contains a striking amount of martial vocabulary and imagery.[12]

Corbulo found the troops under his command to be in a poor state. Tacitus says that the Syrian legions were unfit and ill-disciplined because the army there had been idle for many years. He claims that there were old soldiers who had never seen or built a marching camp, and others who did not possess a cuirass or helmet. Having reviewed his troops, the general ordered the discharge of all those whose age or health made them unfit for service. Once again we encounter the cliché of the great commander who arrives to find a demoralized army and who swiftly imposes proper discipline and turns it into an effective army. It was also a common literary theme that long service in the east, especially in the major cities, corrupted the morals and destroyed the military efficiency of soldiers. Scholars have rightly pointed out that even the sources that appear to make the claim demonstrate that legions stationed in the east were not invariably of poor quality, and that their recruits were not in any way worse military material than those enlisted in the western provinces. However, this does not mean that in AD 55 Corbulo's troops were not in need of intensive training. The Syrian army spent the bulk of its time in policing the provinces, the soldiers often distributed in many small detachments. This gave units very little opportunity for regular training, especially at legion level or above. Corbulo's experience in Germany had already demonstrated how swiftly the combat readiness of troops in a peaceful province declined, so that there was nothing unique about the Syrian army. In addition the legions under him had just discharged many of their older men and received drafts of new recruits. There was a great need to train the latter and to integrate them fully into their new units. Hence, the rigorous training programme which Corbulo imposed on his men was a sensible and normal preparation for what could prove to be a tough campaign.[13]

The general took his men up into the mountains to train in cold conditions similar to those they might encounter in the highlands of Armenia. Tacitus tells stories of numerous cases of frostbite, of one man whose hands fell off when they became frozen to a bundle of firewood, and of sentries found dead of exposure at their posts. Throughout the winter the army remained under canvas rather than constructing more substantial winter quarters or returning to billets in the cities. Corbulo shared the hardships with his men and, 'lightly clothed and bareheaded, moved continually amongst the troops in the march column or as they laboured, praising the hardy, encouraging the weary, acting as an example to everyone'.[14] As well as trying to inspire his men, the general also punished any crime more harshly than was usual. Desertion was always a problem in the professional army, where men had to serve for twenty-five years and were subject to brutal punishment, and in such tough conditions many more men decided to flee from the army. Corbulo ordered all deserters to be executed, ignoring the normal practice of inflicting lesser punishment on first- and second-time offenders. Some men still ran, but the harshness of this directive ensured that his army lost fewer men in this way than most Roman forces. The two legions from the Syrian garrison, III Gallica and VI Ferrata, were joined by a third, which was most probably IV Scythica from Moesia, although Tacitus claims that the unit was posted to the east from Germany. We do not know when this reinforcement arrived, but it seems more than likely that this unit also underwent a period of training to prepare it for war. Even so, it does not appear to have played a major role in operations until near the end of the war.[15]

At first it seemed as if diplomacy alone would secure Roman aims, for Vologaeses responded to the envoys by giving hostages. Apart from a petty dispute between the ambassador sent by Quadratus and Corbulo's envoy over who should gain the credit for escorting these Parthian aristocrats back into the Empire, it seemed that the crisis was over and honours were voted by the Senate to Nero. However, Tiridates was supported by his brother in his refusal to go to Rome and tension once again mounted over the next year or so.

Much of the army was stationed near the border with Armenia and Corbulo established a series of forts manned largely by auxiliaries and placed under the command of a certain Paccius Orfitus, who was a former senior centurion or *primus pilus*. Under the Principate a *primus pilus* was automatically elevated to the equestrian order after holding this post, and Orfitus was probably now either an auxiliary prefect or a legionary tribune. He was also a self-confident, aggressive officer who reported to Corbulo that the nearest Armenian garrisons were in a poor condition and asked permission to begin raiding. In spite of a clear order to refrain from any such action, Orfitus was encouraged by the enthusiasm of some recently arrived troops (*turmae*) of auxiliary cavalry to launch an attack. The Armenians proved to be readier than he had anticipated, and routed the advance guard of the raiding party. Things grew worse when their panic infected the other troops who promptly fled back to their forts. A defeat, even in such a minor skirmish, was the worst possible start to a campaign, especially for an inexperienced army. Usually a general hoped to follow a period of training with some easy victories to boost the men's confidence. Corbulo was outraged and gave Orfitus and the other prefects a severe dressing down. When they and the units under their command rejoined the main army they were ordered to pitch their tents outside the camp's rampart, a symbolic humiliation which was often inflicted on the survivors of a decimated unit.

Corbulo may have hoped that isolating the defeated troops in this way and holding them up to the contempt of the rest of the army would prevent the bulk of the soldiers from being infected with a dangerously high opinion of the enemy's prowess. Later the general allowed himself to be 'persuaded' by a petition from the entire army – or more probably from its officers – to allow the units back into the camp. He may well have felt that the object lesson in the importance of obeying his orders had been properly made. It was possibly around the same time that a story reported by Frontinus occurred. According to this, Corbulo discovered that a prefect commanding an auxiliary cavalry unit which had been routed by the enemy had not kept his men properly armed and equipped. As a punishment he ordered this man, one Aemilius Rufus, to report to his tent and had his lictors strip him naked. Rufus was then left to stand to attention in this undignified condition until the general decided to dismiss him.[16]

With the enemy massing on his border, Tiridates began an active campaign to repress those communities within his kingdom who appeared sympathetic to Rome. Apart from his own retainers, he had been sent additional horsemen by his brother. Corbulo advanced against him and at first tried to intercept the attacks launched against friendly towns. At the beginning he hoped to draw the enemy into a pitched battle, but Tiridates had no intention of risking such a meeting and chose instead to make full use of his mobility. Corbulo broke his army up into a number of smaller columns, hoping to put pressure on the enemy at several points simultaneously. He also instructed the king of Commagene to raid the regions of Armenia nearest to his land. Diplomatic activity managed to win over the Moschi, a tribe on the eastern borders of Armenia some distance from the Empire, and persuaded them to attack Tiridates from yet another direction. At around the same time, Vologaeses was faced with internal rebellion and was no longer able to send significant military aid. Tiridates sent envoys asking why he was under attack in spite of the hostages handed over during the earlier round of negotiations. Corbulo simply responded with the same demand that the king go to Rome to receive his power from Nero.

A meeting was arranged, but the Roman commander ignored Tiridates' suggestion that he bring only an escort of unarmoured legionaries to face his 1,000 horse archers. Instead Corbulo took all the troops with him, including *VI Ferrata* reinforced with 3,000 men from *III Gallica* who paraded under a single eagle to make it look as if only one legion was present. He also ensured that the meeting took place at a location offering him a very good position in case a battle developed. In the event Tiridates, perhaps mistrustful of such a strong force, declined to come close. After several hours, both sides retired to camp for the night, but under cover of darkness the king withdrew and then sent the bulk of his forces in a raid against the Roman supply lines running down from the Black Sea port of Trapezus. Such a move was typical of the Parthian way of waging war and in the past had proved successful against Antony. Corbulo was better prepared, having established a series of forts guarding the road through the mountain passes leading to the sea and arranging for troops to escort each supply convoy.[17]

The chronology of Corbulo's campaigns is impossible to reconstruct with certainty, for Tacitus, who provides the only detailed account of these operations, is vague in this respect. For him the description of a war, even one in which a truly senatorial hero performed so creditably, represented little more than a useful digression to break up his account of Roman political life and the vices of the emperor and his court. It is unclear whether the operations described so far took place in AD 56 or 57, or even just possibly in 58. However, following his failure to force Tiridates into a decisive encounter in these initial operations, Corbulo decided to target instead the most important cities and strongholds loyal to the king. The threat to these was intended to draw the enemy forces away from his own supply lines and perhaps even force the king to risk a battle in their defence. Fortified places controlled the land around and were important sources of revenue and military resources, making them valuable in their own right. Even more importantly, a king who could not defend communities loyal to him and who watched impotently as these were taken by siege lost much prestige.

The Roman army moved across the high plateau Erzerum into the valley of the River Araxes. Corbulo himself led a force against the stronghold of Volandum (possibly modern Igdir), while simultaneously two of his subordinates moved against smaller or less heavily defended towns. After a personal reconnaissance of the position and time spent ensuring that his men were adequately supplied and had all the equipment needed for their task, he issued orders for the assault, encouraging the soldiers with his confidence in their courage and the hope of glory and plunder. Under cover of supporting fire from artillery, archers and slingers, some legionaries were formed into a *testudo* – holding their shields above their heads so that they overlapped to form a roof strong enough to deflect all but the heaviest missiles – and began to undermine the wall with picks and crowbars. Another group set ladders against the rampart and fought their way to the top. Volandum fell within a matter of hours without the Romans suffering a single fatal casualty. The defenders were massacred and the women, children and other non-combatants auctioned off as slaves. All the other plunder was given as a reward to the soldiers. Both the other strongholds had fallen to a similar onslaught on the same day. Terrified by the ease with which the Romans had taken these positions and fearful of sharing the same fate as their occupants, most of the nearby towns and villages surrendered to Corbulo without a fight.[18]

The Roman army concentrated once more and advanced on Artaxata. Before the siege could begin they needed to cross the Araxes, but since the bridge was within range of the city's walls, Corbulo led his men by a more roundabout route, crossing over by a ford. The threat to the regional capital prompted Tiridates to bring his army to its relief. He deployed for battle in an open plain in the path of the Roman army, hoping either to fight on this ground favourable to his numerically superior cavalry or to feign retreat and lure the Romans into an incautious pursuit. Corbulo's army was advancing in hollow square, each of the marching cohorts ready to change swiftly into battle order. He had been reinforced at some point by a vexillation – a detachment named after the square *vexillum* flag which they carried as their standard – from one of the legions left in Syria, *X Fretensis*, and these formed the front of the square. *III Gallica* formed the right and *VI Ferrata* the left, surrounding the baggage in the centre. The rear was brought up by 1,000 cavalry who had strict orders not to be lured out of position for any reason. More horsemen supported by bowmen on foot were deployed on the wings. Seeing that the Roman army was well prepared to meet a direct attack, Tiridates instead sent forward small groups of horse archers to probe the enemy. These light horsemen galloped forward, shooting arrows at the Romans, and then retired, often pretending to panic in the hope of provoking a careless pursuit. Corbulo kept most of his men tightly under his control – the earlier punishment of Orfitus a reminder of the price of disobedience. However, one decurion eager to make a name for himself charged out ahead of his men only to fall beneath a hail of arrows. It was a further warning that a Parthian apparently in flight remained an extremely dangerous enemy. At nightfall Tiridates withdrew his army.

Corbulo set up camp where he was and for a while considered force-marching the legions against Artaxata that same night, suspecting that the king had gone to the city and hoping to surprise him before he had a chance to organize its defence. He abandoned this idea when his scouts (*exploratores*) reported that Tiridates had in fact headed off in another direction and appeared to be fleeing to a distant region. Instead he sent out his light infantry at dawn the next day to encircle the city and prevent anyone from escaping, before following with the main force. Abandoned by their king, the inhabitants of Artaxata opened their gates and surrendered to the approaching Romans. They were allowed to go free; but the city was put to the torch and its walls slighted, for Corbulo had too few troops to detach a suitable garrison and the sheer distance from other Roman bases would anyway have made its position precarious. The victorious Roman army formally hailed Nero as *imperator* for the success won by his legate. It was a title the emperor was pleased to accept, as were the other honours which a sycophantic Senate showered upon him.[19]

Following on from this success, Corbulo marched on Tigranocerta, probably following much the same route taken by Lucullus' army over a century before. Communities and individuals who welcomed him were pardoned, those who resisted or fled were punished. In one case where he found that the locals had retreated to mountain caves with their moveable possessions the soldiers were ordered to pile brushwood into the entrances and set this on fire, burning or suffocating the occupants. The Iberians, who were currently allied to Rome, were instructed to plunder the territory of the Mardi, a hill tribe who refused to submit. Corbulo, like all other Roman commanders, employed force or diplomacy on a purely pragmatic assessment of which was most likely to bring advantage. Good treatment of those who submitted to Rome encouraged further surrenders and so helped to weaken the enemy.

It was a hard march through difficult terrain, and as Corbulo kept forcing the pace, provisions ran short; he had probably taken with him the smallest possible baggage train. For a while the soldiers' ration consisted almost entirely of meat, rather than the usual well-balanced issue, until arrival in the fertile plains around Tigranocerta gave more opportunity for foraging. Here resistance was a little more organized and while one fortified town was stormed quickly, the attack on another was repulsed and it had to be reduced by a formal siege. Around this time some Armenian noblemen who had deserted to join the Romans were arrested and executed on suspicion of plotting to assassinate the Roman commander. When the Romans finally reached Tigranocerta, the leaders of the city were uncertain whether or not to resist. A prominent local aristocrat, one Vadandus, had been captured in the recent fighting – or was perhaps one of the suspected conspirators. Corbulo ordered him to be beheaded and then had the head shot over the walls of the city by a *ballista*. Frontinus claims that 'by chance it fell in the midst of the council being held by the most important barbarians: the sight of this object, which seemed almost an omen, so stunned them that they rushed out to surrender'.[20] Corbulo was presented with a gold crown and, hoping that leniency would win over the population of such an important city, addressed the citizens announcing that they were not to be punished in any way.

Further fighting continued, as the Romans reduced the garrison of a place called Legerda only after a siege and carefully prepared assault. Tiridates was unable to do much to defend his kingdom, for Vologaeses was preoccupied with a serious rebellion by the Hyrcanians who lived near the Caspian Sea. The latter had sent envoys to Corbulo and formed an alliance with Rome. Tiridates did make one attempt to move back into Media, but was stopped when faced by a force of auxiliaries under the command of the legionary legate Verulanus Severus. Learning that Corbulo and the main army was hastening to the spot, he swiftly retreated. The Romans sent punitive expeditions to any part of Armenia which appeared to show loyalty to the Arsacid king, but no longer faced any concentrated opposition within the country. Nero dispatched a prince of the Cappadocian royal house – he was also related to the Herods – to become Armenia's new king. This man, Tiridates, had spent much of his life as a hostage in Rome and was considered to be reliable by the emperor. Corbulo and the main army withdrew from the kingdom and went to Syria which currently lacked a governor since Quadratus had died a few months before. Corbulo left behind him a force of 1,000 legionaries, three cohorts of auxiliary infantry and two cavalry *alae* to support the newly installed Tiridates.[21]

The Cappadocian proved somewhat over-bold, for in AD 61 one of his earliest actions was to launch a heavy raid across the border into Adiabene, a region controlled by Parthia. Complaints from the Monobazus, the ruler of Adiabene, that his Parthian overlord was not providing proper protection to his subjects forced Vologaeses into action to prevent a huge loss of face which would almost certainly be followed by a loss of land. Making a public restatement of Tiridates' loyalty and claim to the Armenian throne, he loaned him a detachment of his household cavalry under the command of Monaeses and a force raised from Adiabene. He also made peace with the Hyrcanians to allow Tiridates a freer hand in Armenia. With these and the remainder of his own troops, Tiridates set out to regain his throne. Corbulo responded by sending two legions, *IV Scythica* and *XII Fulminata*, into Armenia. Although there were three other legions currently under his command, he seems only to have had one immediately available to defend the Euphrates in case the Parthian king should decide to attack Syria. This unit was immediately put to the task of preparing defences, including the construction of a line of forts controlling all the main springs supplying fresh water. He also wrote to Nero requesting the appointment of a new legate to control the war in Armenia, since it was difficult for one man to supervise the conflict there and protect Syria.[22]

Monaeses led his army against Tigranocerta, but found that Tiridates was well prepared to defend the city, having stored large quantities of provisions and mustered a strong garrison including the Roman troops left by Corbulo. Parthian cavalrymen disliked siege work and were unsuited to performing the necessary tasks, while the need to feed their horses placed a great burden on locally available forage. The situation was made worse because much of the local vegetation had recently been consumed by a swarm of locusts. Therefore it was the contingent from Adiabene which both played a leading role in the subsequent assault on the city and paid a heavy price in casualties when this was repulsed and turned into a rout by a Roman sally. Corbulo sent a centurion as envoy to Vologaeses who had brought his court and army to Nisibis, some 37 Roman miles from Tigranocerta. The failure of the siege and the shortage of provisions persuaded the king to order Monaeses to pull back into Parthia. After negotiations it was agreed that Parthian ambassadors should be sent to Nero in Rome and in the meantime the Romans also withdrew from Armenia. Tiridates seems to have gone with them, for the Romans were still prepared to acknowledge Tiridates as long as he clearly acknowledged that he ruled with the emperor's permission. However, the details of this condition proved unacceptable to the Parthians and the war was renewed in AD 62.[23]

A new legate had arrived to take command of Cappadocia (and probably also Galatia) with responsibility for the war in Armenia. This was Caesennius Paetus, and it was rumoured that the news of his appointment had discouraged Corbulo from fighting rather than negotiating in the previous year, for he did not want to begin a campaign only to be replaced and let another man finish it. Tacitus does not neglect to mention that some people said that Corbulo was also afraid to risk suffering any reverse which might dent his record of unbroken success. On arrival Paetus took command of two of the Syrian legions, *IV Scythica* and *XII Fretensis*, reinforced by *V Macedonica* recently transferred from the Danubian frontier, while Corbulo retained *III Gallica*, *VI Ferrata* and *X Fretensis*. Both forces were supported by auxiliaries, but it is notable that Corbulo kept the legions which had campaigned with him in recent years. Paetus was given troops which may well have been poorly trained and certainly had far less experience. He failed to order – and may not anyway have had the time – a training programme comparable to that with which Corbulo had prepared his men for war. As with the earlier relations between Corbulo and Quadratus, there was little love lost between Nero's two legates. Paetus was keen to show that he was his own man, not a mere subordinate, and to equal or surpass the achievements of his more famous colleague, while Corbulo showed little enthusiasm for aiding him in this task.[24]

Little is known about Paetus, but his handling of the subsequent campaign was inept. It began well enough, as he led his army into Armenia in response to a Parthian invasion led by Tiridates. He took only two legions, leaving *V Macedonica* behind (perhaps because there had been insufficient time since its arrival to integrate it into the army). The Roman force marched through the Taurus Mountains and headed for Tigranocerta, but preparations had been hasty and they were inadequately supplied. Several strongholds were taken, but lack of food forced the army to withdraw back into the region bordering Cappadocia rather than winter in central Armenia itself. At first the Parthians seem to have planned to deliver their main attack against Syria, but Corbulo had thrown a bridge of boats across the Euphrates, covering the work parties with artillery mounted on ships, and deployed his troops in a strong position on the far bank. Deterred by his confidence and evident strength, the enemy instead sent the bulk of their forces into Armenia. Paetus was not prepared to meet them, having dispersed his legions and made lavish grants of leave, probably most of all to his officers. When Vologaeses and the main army arrived, Paetus' mood rapidly swung from overconfidence to panic. At first he advanced boldly across the River Arsanias to a position near Rhandeia, but the loss of some minor skirmishes persuaded him to abandon his intention of seeking battle. Much of the army became infected with their commander's nervousness and the result was the ignominious defeat of a number of outlying detachments. An additional shock came when a force of Pannonian auxiliary cavalry, who were considered to be élite troops, were routed by the Parthians. In country that should have offered good defensive positions for an infantry army, Paetus found himself outmanoeuvred and surrounded in some hastily constructed and poorly defended camps.

Increasingly desperate messages were sent to Corbulo asking for aid, but before any assistance arrived the Roman general began negotiations with the Parthian king which led to a humiliating surrender. According to Tacitus it was rumoured that Paetus' soldiers were sent under the yoke, and it is certain that he agreed to the evacuation of all Roman forces from Armenia, with supplies and fortified positions to be given to the Parthians. The legionaries even laboured to construct a bridge across the Arsanias so that Vologaeses could ride across on an elephant to celebrate his triumph. In the event a rumour spread that the soldiers had designed the bridge to collapse under the weight, so the king instead had the animal wade through the water. The retreat of the Roman army resembled a rout as the column was enthusiastically plundered by the local Armenians. They covered some 40 Roman miles in a day, abandoning the wounded and sick who could not keep up. Corbulo, who had taken a vexillation of 1,000 men from each of his three legions and reinforced them with auxiliary troops, was by this time very close and began to meet with stragglers as he crossed the Euphrates.

The column was accompanied by a large number of pack camels carrying grain, so that it could move quickly and avoid the need to forage.

Later, in his *Commentaries*, now sadly lost but available to Tacitus, Corbulo maintained that Paetus' men had burnt ample store of food when he left his camps and that the Parthians had been on the brink of giving up the siege because their own supplies were virtually exhausted. At the time some suggested that the veteran commander had been deliberately tardy in his relief expedition, hoping to heighten the drama of his arrival. Yet even if this were the case, the disastrous situation had been created by Paetus. Rejecting the latter's pleas to launch a joint invasion, since he was now legate of Syria and had no orders to invade Armenia, and lamenting the undoing of his earlier work, Corbulo marched back to his province. Paetus returned to winter in Cappadocia. In the following months Vologaeses demanded that Corbulo abandon the bridgehead he had established across the Euphrates and retire to the Syrian bank. The Roman countered by saying that all Parthian troops must leave Armenia first and only gave up their position once this had occurred. Another Parthian embassy was dispatched to Rome. Their demands, coupled with interrogation of the accompanying centurion, made it clear that Paetus' official dispatch had concealed the extent of his defeat. The legate was soon recalled to Rome, but Nero announced that he was to receive no more than a reprimand, acidly commenting that if such a nervous man were kept in suspense over his fate it would probably make him ill.[25]

Tacitus had little good to say of Nero, even at the beginning of his reign when his rule was not tyrannical. However, even he approved the emperor's decision to risk 'a hazardous war' rather than submit to a 'shameful peace'. A new governor, Caius Cestius Gallus, was sent out as legate of Syria, so that Corbulo was once again placed in charge of the Armenian situation with authority to make war if this were necessary to achieve Rome's aims. His *imperium* was made superior to all other governors in the region so that Tacitus compared his position to that of Pompey during the war against the pirates. He was also reinforced by an additional legion, *XV Apollinaris*, sent from Germany. This gave him seven legions, but *IV Scythica* and *XII Fulminata* were considered unfit for service and sent back to garrison Syria. A field army was assembled consisting of *III Gallica*, *V Macedonica*, *VI Ferrata*, and *XV Apollinaris*, along with vexillations from the legions in Egypt and the Danubian frontier, and a great force of auxiliary infantry and cavalry. Before the invasion of Armenia began, he carried out the proper religious ceremonies to purify the army and addressed the men, recounting his earlier successes and laying all the blame for Rhandeia on Paetus.

The arrival of such a large and well-led Roman force immediately made Vologaeses and Tiridates willing to negotiate and the two armies met near Rhandeia. Corbulo delegated Paetus' son, then serving as a tribune in one of the legions, to take a small party and bury the remains of the men killed in 62. After a period of negotiations, the Roman general and the Armenian king meeting each with an escort of twenty men between the lines and dismounting to greet each other as a mark of respect, a treaty was agreed. Tiridates laid his royal diadem in front of a statue of Nero and agreed to travel to Rome to receive it again from the emperor's hand. Both sides put on a display of force, parading their armies and sending them through a series of manoeuvres. In the midst of the Roman force was a commander's tribunal, on which a statue of Nero sitting in a magistrate's chair was set. When Tiridates and his followers were invited to a feast, Corbulo took great care to explain to them in detail the routine of the Roman camp, always emphasizing the organization and discipline of the army. Such displays of Roman might had been, and would remain, a staple of Roman diplomacy for many centuries. As far as the Romans themselves were concerned, such encounters were never the meeting of equals, but visible celebrations of Roman supremacy.[26]

In the end, the Romans had achieved their aim of making Tiridates formally acknowledge that his right to the throne relied upon the Roman emperor's approval. With this made clear, the conflict was considered properly ended. Corbulo was not permitted to occupy Armenia and create a new province, still less to launch a full-scale invasion of Parthia. Throughout these campaigns his freedom of action was constrained by the emperor's instructions. Yet the supervision of Nero and his advisers had also made it possible to transfer reinforcements from other provinces to bolster the forces in the east. Corbulo was also permitted a longer spell of command than any Republican general, with the exception of a Pompey or a Caesar, had ever been able to secure in normal circumstances. Although he had far less freedom at the highest levels of strategic decision making, in other respects Corbulo controlled and inspired his army in much the same way as Republican commanders. Though they now operated in a different political environment, Roman aristocrats continued to pursue glory for themselves and their families. The bickering between Corbulo and his colleagues governing neighbouring provinces as each man tried to outshine the other is highly reminiscent of the rivalry between Republican governors.

AN IMPERIAL LEGATE WAS EXPECTED TO PERFORM HIS TASKS COMPETENTLY, and most emperors sought out men of genuine talent to command in the most important campaigns since defeats reflected badly on the emperor himself. Yet unlike Republican commanders, who rarely faced any restraint on their actions until they had laid down their office and returned to Rome, legates were as closely supervised as distance and speed of communications permitted.

In AD 60 much of the province of Britain had erupted into rebellion under the leadership of Queen Boudicca of the Iceni. When the revolt began the legate Caius Seutonius Paulinus, with two out of the four legions stationed in the province, had just captured the Isle of Mona (modern Anglesey), the main centre of the Druidic cult. This was one of the few religions actively suppressed by the Romans, who were disgusted by the important role played in the druids' rituals by human sacrifice, and also aware that the religion helped to unite anti-Roman elements in Britain and Gaul.

While Paulinus was occupied in storming Mona and massacring the druids and their followers, the rebellion in the eastern part of the province had time to gather momentum. The colony at Camulodunum (Colchester) was the rebels' first target, for the locals resented the confiscation of their lands to give to the Roman veterans settled there at the end of their military service. Some of the veterans managed to hold out in the massive Temple of Claudius for two days, but the colony had no proper fortifications and the issue was never in doubt. The fury of the Britons resulted in widespread torture and mutilation as they massacred the entire population of the town. In the following weeks Verulamium (St Albans) and Londinium (London) suffered the same fate. Archaeologists have discovered a thick layer of burnt material on each of these sites dating to the Boudiccan revolt.

The first significant response by the Roman army came when a substantial vexillation of *Legio IX Hispana* marched straight into the heartland of the rebellion, hoping to break the Britons' spirit with a display of force. Instead the Romans encountered a much stronger army than anticipated. Perhaps in an ambush, or possibly in a night attack on their camp, almost all of the legionaries were killed and only the legionary legate and some cavalry escaped the disaster. Paulinus managed to reach Londinium before it fell, but had only a small body of cavalry with him as he had left the bulk of his army to march on behind. Some refugees left under the protection of the governor and his cavalry, but the bulk of the population remained to be slaughtered. Once he had withdrawn to meet the main army, Paulinus had something like 10,000 men at his disposal. *Legio IX* was too badly mauled to play any further part in the campaign, but the governor had sent messengers summoning the other legion in Britain, *II Augusta*, from its station in the south-west to join him. Its acting commander, the prefect Poenius Postumus, for an unknown reason refused to answer Paulinus' summons. Therefore it was with only his own troops – most of *Legio XIV Gemina* and part of *Legio XX* plus some auxiliary units – that the latter was forced to confront Boudicca, whose army was many times larger.

Paulinus chose a spot – which cannot be certainly identified – where a wooded defile offered protection to his flanks and rear. His deployment, with the legions in the centre, auxiliary infantry on their flanks and the cavalry on the wings, was entirely conventional. Like Marius at Aquae Sextiae and Caesar against the Helvetii, he kept his men stationary and silent as the mass of Britons advanced towards them. Only at the last minute did he order them to throw their *pila* and charge. The volley of heavy missiles robbed the British advance of momentum, but the tribesmen had become so tightly packed together as they had crowded into the defile to reach their enemies that they could not retreat. Like the Roman army at Cannae, they had degenerated into a great mass, incapable of manoeuvre or fighting effectively. Slowly and steadily they were cut down by the Romans, but the latter paid a heavy price for their success. A little less than 10 per cent of Paulinus' men were killed or wounded in the fighting – a very high casualty rate for a victorious army in the ancient world. In a single day's fighting the back of the rebellion was broken. Boudicca escaped, but soon afterwards took poison. Paulinus and his men waged a vicious campaign into the winter to stamp out all embers of resistance, their anger deep as a result of the atrocities the Britons had committed.

The defeat of Boudicca was one of the great triumphs of Nero's reign, the units involved being rewarded with the grant of new battle honours. *Legio XIV* was granted the title *Martia Victrix* (Mars the war god's own, Victorious) and *Legio XX* may also have earned the name *Victrix* for its service in this campaign. At the time the popular imagination pitted Paulinus against Corbulo as rivals for glory. Yet in spite of his achievement, in AD 61 Paulinus was recalled after a report from an imperial representative claimed that he was too brutal in the measures he was taking to stamp out all resistance. The concern was less for the welfare of the provincials and more a pragmatic assessment that leniency was more likely to lead to long-term peace and stability in Britain. Corbulo kept within the boundaries of action and behaviour required by the emperor and served as a legate for far longer than the average term. Another man who similarly managed to maintain imperial trust was Cnaeus Julius Agricola, the father-in-law of the historian Tacitus, who was legate of Britain for seven years between AD 78 and 84. During this time he was allowed to expand the province in the north, constructing forts in the newly conquered territory. Tacitus' biography dwells mainly on these years, seeking to show how a senator could still win fame and respect in a properly aristocratic way even under a repressive regime. The last years of Agricola's command were spent under the rule of Domitian, who would later order the execution of another governor of Britain, Sallustius Lucullus, simply for permitting a newly designed lance to be named after him.[27]

Corbulo and Agricola managed to demonstrate conspicuous ability without convincing their respective rulers to suspect them of imperial ambitions and so not grant them important commands. Both proved loyal and won wars on their emperor's behalf. In the process they also won themselves glory and the respect of other senators. Corbulo is the only general of the Principate from outside the imperial family to figure in Frontinus' *Stratagems*, a collection of clever ploys on the part of commanders written by Agricola's predecessor as legate of Britain. Yet once such men had won their victories and joined the ranks of the foremost senators they could seem to represent a major threat to an emperor who lacked personal military achievements. Prominence under the Principate, and particularly under certain emperors, was accompanied by high risk. In AD 67 – or just possibly earlier in 66 – Nero embarked on a tour of Greece. It was primarily an opportunity to display his artistic talents, although he also took part in the Olympic Games and became the only competitor in history to win all the events, including those which he did not in fact complete. Before Nero and his entourage left Italy a spate of executions had marked the discovery of a senatorial conspiracy – whether real or imagined is impossible to say. One of the alleged ringleaders was Corbulo's son-in-law Lucius Annius Vinicianus, who had also been legate of *Legio V Macedonica* in Armenia and had escorted Tiridates to Rome. Corbulo was summoned to join Nero in Greece where he was permitted to forestall execution by committing suicide, a gesture which usually permitted the condemned man's family to inherit his property. Shortly afterwards the legates of both the German provinces were similarly sent for and instructed to kill themselves. The position of imperial legate was in many ways even more precarious than that of commanding a Roman army during the civil wars which marked the fall of the Republic.[28]

CHAPTER 12

A YOUNG CAESAR:
TITUS AND THE SIEGE OF JERUSALEM, AD 70

Titus Flavius Sabinus Vespasianus (AD 41–81)

Perceiving that his safety depended solely on his personal prowess, he turned his horse's head and shouting to his companions to follow dashed into the enemy's midst, struggling to cut his way through to his own party ... Of all that hail of arrows discharged at Titus, who wore neither helmet nor cuirass – for he had gone forward ... not to fight, but to reconnoitre – not one touched his person.[1]

NERO, ABANDONED BY THE SENATE AND HIS OWN PRAETORIAN GUARD, ORDERED one of his last faithful slaves to kill him in AD 68. Thus died the last of the Julio-Claudians. He left no heir, and power was seized by Galba, the legate of Spain. He was backed by the legion which garrisoned his province and – following the promise of a sizeable bounty to any who joined him – the Praetorian Guard. However, the new emperor failed to deliver on this promise and was lynched by a mob of praetorians within seven months of seizing power. His successor, Otho, bribed his way to power, but lasted just ninety-five days before committing suicide on receiving news of the defeat of his army by a rival, Vitellius the legate of Germania Inferior. Vitellius had managed to rally the bulk of the Rhine armies to his cause and had invaded Italy. Soon he in turn faced a challenge from the legions of the eastern provinces, led by Vespasian, the legate of Judaea. His army defeated in the Po valley and Rome itself stormed by the enemy, Vitellius was brutally murdered eight months after he had come to power.

Vespasian was the fourth man to become *princeps* within twelve months, and recent events had demonstrated quite openly the power of the legions to make or break emperors. After almost a century of internal peace, the Empire had been plunged into a civil war as savage as any of those which had scarred the final decades of the Republic's life. Unlike the conflicts of the first century BC, the Civil War of AD 68–9 did not grow from long-held political rivalries. The leaders were in general fairly ordinary legates who found themselves in command of powerful armies at a time when there was a power vacuum at the centre of the Empire. With the exception of Vespasian, they were not men who had recently led legions on campaign and so had a chance to create a bond based on common experience and trust. Instead they relied upon winning over the army, and most of all the officers, within their own and the neighbouring provinces. Yet once again Roman soldiers had shown themselves willing to fight other Romans on behalf of individual generals who promised them rewards. Vitellius had dismissed Otho's praetorians and recruited new guard cohorts from his own legions. The Syrian legions' support for Vespasian was made all the more enthusiastic by a rumour claiming that Vitellius planned to post them to the Rhine and send the garrisons of those provinces to take over the more comfortable billets in the east.[2]

Vespasian proved a capable and decent ruler, one of the few men whose character did not steadily degenerate under the temptations of wielding supreme power. His family was not part of the old aristocracy and he and his brother Sabinus were the first to enter the Senate. The wealth that permitted them to do this came from a number of less than entirely respectable sources, including tax collecting and mule breeding, and Vespasian's own career had been chequered. In AD 43 he was a legionary legate, commanding *Legio II Augusta* which took part in Claudius' great expedition to Britain. Vespasian played a prominent role in the main battle – probably at the River Medway – against the strong tribal confederation led by the brothers Caractacus and Togodumnus, and subsequently operated independently with his own legion and supporting auxiliaries against the peoples of the south-west. Claudius was extravagant in his award of honours and decorations to the participants in this, his only major war, and Vespasian was one of those granted *triumphalia*, which was an unusual honour for someone of his rank. Even so, he never really became one of the most important men in the Senate and for a while virtually retired from public life. Later, he enjoyed Nero's favour for some time, until his habit of leaving abruptly before or dozing off during the emperor's musical recitals led to his exclusion from court.

Too obscure and poorly connected to be seen as a potential rival,

Vespasian's incurring of imperial displeasure did not lead to execution and in AD 67 he was sent as legate to Judaea where rebellion had broken out in the previous year. He had held all the posts normally held before the command of an imperial province and had won something of a reputation in Britain, but his appointment owed much to the same feeling that he would never pose a threat to the emperor. As added insurance, Nero kept Vespasian's younger son Domitian with him in Rome, effectively as a hostage. It is doubtful that anyone, including himself, seriously considered Vespasian as a possible candidate for the throne until the Civil War was well under way. Even after Nero's death, he openly acknowledged the authority of first Galba and then Otho, only declaring himself emperor after the latter's suicide.[3]

Victories won by his subordinates made Vespasian emperor, but only his own political skill prevented his principate from proving as brief as those of his immediate predecessors. Most important of all, he had to deny provincial governors the opportunity of turning their armies against him. Like Augustus, he was to make extensive use of relatives and partisans – all men whose own best interests were served by the continuance of the new regime – to fight the major wars of his reign. The new emperor needed military successes to celebrate, for glory of this sort was still one of the most important attributes of a *princeps*. Active service also kept the armies busy and less likely to mutiny or revolt, especially if their leaders were reliable men. One war was especially important to Vespasian, for in spite of the steady progress he had made in its suppression, the Civil War had prevented his completion of the campaign in Judaea. Although most of the province was once again under Roman control, the great city of Jerusalem, along with a handful of small fortresses, remained in rebel hands. A new and still insecure emperor could not afford a personal association with a war which had not yet resulted in outright Roman victory. Jerusalem needed to be taken, as soon as possible and in a manner which did not detract from Vespasian's earlier achievements in the conflict. Therefore, in the spring of 70 the task of besieging the city and crushing the centre of rebellion fell to the emperor's older son, Titus, then 29 years old.

The siege of Jerusalem is described in greater detail than any other major operation undertaken by the Roman army. The city occupied a strong natural position and was heavily fortified with three main lines of walls, so that during the five-month siege the Romans were forced to take it section by section, one difficult assault being followed by another and another. The cost of this was high, both in casualties and in the enthusiasm of the survivors, and at times the legionaries' morale slipped to a low ebb. Titus was faced with an extremely difficult task, but one that had to be performed as soon as possible for political reasons. The capture of Jerusalem provides a very good illustration of the nature of siege warfare and the peculiar problems it presented to a commander. Our understanding of the campaign is greatly enhanced by the archaeological work which permits fairly accurate reconstruction of the layout of Jerusalem in the Second Temple Period. The principal literary account is provided by the Jewish historian Josephus who wrote his history of the Jewish Rebellion at Rome under the patronage of Vespasian and Titus. His flattery of both, and especially the latter who is often called simply Caesar, is both frequent and obvious, for instance in the following passage:

> Thus, if, without a syllable added in flattery or withheld in envy, the truth must be told, Caesar personally twice rescued the entire legion when in jeopardy, and enabled them to entrench themselves in their camp unmolested.[4]

For all his sycophancy, Josephus was present with Titus' headquarters during the operation and describes events in great detail, giving by far the best portrait of the army of the Principate on campaign. He was also peculiarly well suited to describe the conflict, for he had begun the war as a general appointed by the rebel government and had fought against the Romans, before surrendering and becoming a collaborator. His attitude towards the rebel leaders was extremely hostile, but he was content to describe the heroism of many of the Jewish fighters and the defeats they inflicted upon the Romans. More than any other conflict outside of the civil wars, we are able to see the Jewish Rebellion from the perspective of both sides, and not simply from the Roman point of view.[5]

THE JEWISH REBELLION

Judaea became a directly ruled province following the death of Herod the Great in 4 BC. This prompted a rebellion which was then brutally suppressed by Varus, the legate of Syria. Herod had been a consummate politician, backing Antony in the Civil War and yet still winning favour with Octavian after Actium, thus managing to retain his throne. Yet he was never popular amongst his subjects, who saw him as a foreigner – he was an Idumaean and so not considered properly Jewish – imposed on them by a Gentile power. The Roman governors who succeeded him had even less success at winning the hearts and minds of the population. These men were not senators, for Judaea was a minor province with a small auxiliary garrison, but equestrians with the title of prefect, although around AD 40 this was changed to procurator.

It was not an easy province to control, for the culture and religion of its monotheistic population set them apart from the rest of the polytheistic Roman world. By pagans the Jews (and later Christians) were seen as perverse, almost indeed as atheists, for they denied the very existence of other gods.[6] Even if they were granted Roman citizenship, religious taboos prevented Judaean aristocrats from following a career in imperial service. Therefore it proved impossible to absorb them into the élite of the Empire in the same way that over time the noble families of other provinces enjoyed increasingly senior posts in the army and administration, eventually becoming equestrians and even entering the Senate. The high-priestly families of Jerusalem were given a dominant role in administration and especially the running of the Great Temple by the procurators, but their capacity to control the wider population was limited. Many Jews were willing to recognize religious leaders from outside the aristocracy, and these were often men of humble origins, such as John the Baptist or the Bannus whom the teenage Josephus followed for a time. As a whole the Jews had a much stronger sense of their own identity as a nation than most other peoples who came under Roman rule. Every year the festival of the Passover reminded them of their escape from bondage in Egypt and, more recently, they had the memory of the Maccabees' successful rebellion against the rule of the Seleucid Empire in the second century BC.[7]

Religion and the rituals associated with the Great Temple in Jerusalem acted as continual reminders of Jewish identity, but society was also fiercely divided into sects and doctrines over the interpretation of the law. Judaeans did not quite consider Galileans to be proper Jews, while both loathed the Samaritans who occupied central Palestine and had their own cult and temple. The three major Jewish religious sects, Pharisees, Saducees and Essenes, disagreed on most issues and were frequently split by internal dissent. The proper attitude towards Roman rule was often a vexed issue and many of the popular religious leaders who appeared periodically were perceived as revolutionaries inciting rebellion. In the 30s Jesus was publicly questioned over his attitude to taxation – 'Render under Caesar that which is Caesar's, and to God that which is God's' – and finally executed as a rebel – 'We have no king but Caesar'. Economic problems further divided society, with lawlessness and banditry being a recurrent challenge to peace and stability. Violence appears just beneath the surface in the Gospels, with stories of travellers being attacked and beaten or of absentee landlords, and disciples with revolutionary names such as Simon the Zealot or Judas Iscariot. Barabbas who was released by Pontius Pilate in place of Christ was, according to Mark, in prison for having led an insurrection in Jerusalem. At least some of the bandits probably had religious or political motives, but the impact of their actions was (as has so often been the case throughout history) felt most heavily by the poor.

Judaea was a troubled region, struggling to fit into the Roman system and frequently subject to procurators who failed to understand its peculiarities and who were all too often corrupt and repressive. Sporadic outbreaks of rebellion occurred from 4 BC onwards and finally erupted in the summer of AD 66 into a major rebellion. The procurator marched on Jerusalem to quell the rising with a show of force, but suffered defeat. Within a few days the garrison of Jerusalem was massacred. The legate of Syria, Caius Cestius Gallus, hastily assembled a field army to move against the rebels, arriving outside the city in October. His force was based around *Legio XII Fulminata*, which had been humiliatingly defeated with Paetus at Rhandeia four years earlier, reinforced by vexillations from *III Gallica*, *VI Ferrata* and X *Fretensis*. These were supported by some regular auxiliaries, and a large number of recently raised and ill-disciplined levies. It was not an army carefully prepared, trained or adequately supplied for war, but Gallus was following the normal Roman practice of responding as quickly as possible to insurrection in the hope that an immediate, confident counter-attack would stop the rebellion before it gathered momentum.

Surprised at the strength of resistance, Gallus suffered some minor defeats and, deciding that he could not hope to take the city, abandoned the siege and withdrew. His retreat rapidly turned into disaster, the Roman column being remorselessly harried as it descended through the narrow Beth-Horon pass. By the end of the campaign 5,780 Roman soldiers had been killed and *XII Fulminata* had lost its eagle. (Josephus makes no mention of the rebels' capturing this trophy, so it may be that it was genuinely lost in the confusion. This would not have altered the disgrace of the loss of the precious standard and symbol of the legion's pride.) Gallus died soon afterwards, probably from disease.[8]

Late in 66, or early in 67, Vespasian was sent to take command of the war in Judaea, while Caius Licinius Mucianus became legate of Syria to deal with the normal administration of the province. The arrangement was similar in many ways to the command structure when Corbulo was sent east to deal with the Armenian problem. By the time that Vespasian was appointed to Judaea, Corbulo was probably already dead, but it is unlikely that he would have been given another command even if he had not fallen from favour. The ideal of the senatorial class – if not always of the individual senator – was that opportunities to win military glory should be shared out as widely as possible. The 57-year-old Vespasian had not yet served as a provincial legate, but had a competent military record and the qualified trust of an emperor, who had recently become very nervous about the ambitions of more prominent senators. Tacitus described him as the ideal Roman commander, 'active in war and accustomed to march at the head of the column, to select the place to camp, and to harry the enemy day and night by his generalship and, if occasion required, by his own hand; his ration was what fortune provided, in dress and lifestyle he was much the same as a private soldier'.[9] In 67 Vespasian launched a full-scale and properly prepared invasion of Galilee, storming those walled towns and villages who did not surrender.

Throughout the rebellion the Jews never managed to form an effective field army and the conflict was dominated by sieges. At Jotapata Vespasian received the surrender of the rebel commander Josephus, who had been hiding in a cave with a group of devoted followers, all of whom had determined to commit suicide rather than give themselves up. The future historian, who admits that he felt no enthusiasm for such a gesture, persuaded his companions to draw lots, determining who should kill the others. Miraculously – though the reader is inclined to suspect a more disreputable cause – Josephus and one other were selected to be last to die and, having watched the rest dispatch each other, they decided that surrender was in fact the only reasonable course of action. The rebel general was brought before Vespasian, whom he grovellingly declared would one day become emperor – an action that would later lead to Josephus' release and favourable treatment when the 'prophecy' was fulfilled.[10]

In 68 the Roman army divided to suppress Idumaea, Peraea and virtually all of Judaea itself, but the following year witnessed little fighting as Vespasian concentrated his efforts on his bid for the throne. The unbroken succession of defeats which the Jews had suffered since their initial victory in 66 had by this time discredited the essentially aristocratic government formed at the start of the rising. Instead a number of far more radical leaders had seized power. At the beginning of 70 Jerusalem was split between three factions, two based on the Zealot movement and the other led by Simon bar Giora. Left alone by the Romans, these leaders had taken to fighting amongst themselves as each struggled for power. After considerable bloodshed, the rift in the Zealot movement was repaired and John of Gischala – a man who had been Josephus' bitter rival for control of Galilee – was acknowledged as its leader. Hostility between the Zealots and Simon's men continued unabated, involving heavy loss of life to the general population and much destruction of food stores whose want would be greatly felt in later months. Only the arrival of the Romans outside the city finally brought a grudging and mistrustful union against the common enemy.

TITUS AND HIS ARMY

Until his father's sudden elevation to supreme power, Titus' career had been fairly conventional. He served as the senatorial tribune in a legion in Germany and Britain, perhaps at the time of Boudicca's rebellion in AD 60–61. When Vespasian was given the Judaean command, he was appointed as legate of *Legio XV Apollinaris*, a unit which had seen a little service at the end of Corbulo's campaign but lacked the experience of much of the rest of the army. At 27 Titus was younger than most legionary legates, and his selection reflected the long-established tradition of senators relying on family members to serve as their senior subordinates. In Armenia one of Corbulo's legions had been commanded by his son-in-law Vinicianus, whilst Caesenius Paetus' son was a tribune under his command. It was another example of a practice which was not altered by the creation of the principate, although it may only have been especially favoured commanders who were permitted to choose their own legates. The young Titus was a dashing figure, athletic and handsome – his face as round as his father's but softer – and, in the familiar cliché, as skilled at riding and handling his personal weapons as he was at directing the troops under his command. He played a distinguished role in the Galilean and Judaean campaigns, leading successful assaults at Japha, Tarichaeae – where he led his cavalry through the waves of the Sea of Galilee to enter the town from its un-defended side – and Gamala, and persuading Gischala to surrender or face a similar attack.[11]

Jerusalem was a far bigger and tougher proposition than any of these smaller communities, and for the task Titus took control of a field force larger than any that his father had ever concentrated in one place. It was based around four legions, *V Macedonica* commanded by Sextus Vettulenus Cerealis, *X Fretensis* led by Aulus Larcius Lepidus Sulpicianus, *XII Fulminata*, and *XV Apollinaris* under the command of Marcus Tittius Frugi. Also present and given a prominent place in the general's *consilia* was Tiberius Julius Alexander, an Alexandrian Jew who had abandoned the formal practice of his religion for a career in the imperial service. The identity of the commander of *XII Fulminata* is unknown. This was the first time that the legion was to see active service after the disastrous 66 campaign and its reputation remained poor, although Josephus claims that the soldiers were especially eager for revenge. A pair of inscriptions suggest that one of the unit's senior centurions transferred into *X Fretensis* at a lower grade of the centurionate following the disaster. Such a demotion – whether forced or voluntary to disassociate himself from the stigma of defeat – has no parallel amongst our evidence for centurions' careers.

All of the legions, most of all *V*, *X*, and *XV*, were under strength as a result of campaign casualties and attrition, and also from sending detachments with the army which had gone to Italy to defeat Vitellius. To compensate for this the army had been reinforced by a vexillation of 2,000 men from *III Cyrenaica* and *XXII Deiotariana* stationed in Egypt and further drafts from the Syrian army.[12] The Egyptian contingent included few if any men with combat experience, but was to perform with conspicuous gallantry on at least one occasion. It was commanded by the prefect Fronto Haterius. Supporting the legions were eight *alae* of auxiliary cavalry and twenty cohorts of infantry, along with the forces sent by the local client kings, many of whose troops were trained and equipped on the model of the regular auxiliaries. Altogether, Titus may have had anything between 30,000 and 40,000 fighting troops under his command, along with great numbers of army slaves and camp followers.[13]

It was a formidable force, including a good proportion of seasoned soldiers, but the task it faced was an extremely difficult one, for Jerusalem was strongly protected by both natural and man-made fortifications. It lay upon two hills, the one to the east markedly lower than the other. In the Old Testament period the city had been confined to the lower hill, which was still enclosed with its own wall and included the Great Temple – known as the Second Temple (as opposed to the First, originally constructed by Solomon). The Second Temple had been rebuilt on a lavish scale by Herod the Great who left his mark on much of the city. He had added a large tower, topped by a turret at each corner, to the north-east corner of the Temple, naming it the Fortress of Antonia after his patron Mark Antony. Even without this reinforcement the Temple was itself virtually a fort, although work on some of its internal features was still in progress just before the outbreak of the rebellion against Nero. Later, under the Hasmoneans, the city expanded to cover the second, larger hill, a region which was subsequently surrounded to the north by another wall, usually known as the second wall (the first being around the Old Town). Herod's palace and a number of other monuments, notably the three massive towers named after his family (an area today known as 'the citadel') were built in the New Town. In the first century AD Jerusalem continued to expand, with many dwellings being built outside the second wall, but it was not until 66 that a third, outer wall was constructed to defend this suburb. This was the weakest of the fortifications, for the older structures were works of exceptional scale and quality of materials and workmanship. To the east the lower hill was further defended by the Kidron valley, on the opposite side of which rose the Mount of Olives. An assault from this direction would have proved extremely difficult and was not, in fact, attempted.[14]

Our ancient sources do not provide any reliable figures for the size of the city's population in AD 70 and the number of active defenders. Jerusalem was certainly an exceptionally large community by the standards of the Roman world, but a total of over 1,000,000 occupants according to Josephus or even some 600,000 according to Tacitus seems much too high. Josephus claims that Simon led a force of 10,000 of his own partisans and 5,000 Idumaean allies, whereas John had 8,400 Zealots under him. These well-armed and highly motivated men would bear the brunt of the fighting during the siege, but at various times their numbers would be swelled by many of the ordinary citizens. The Zealots controlled the Temple and much of the surrounding area, while Simon's men held most of the New Town.[15]

THE PRELIMINARIES AND TAKING THE FIRST WALL,
LATE APRIL–MAY 70

The Roman army approached in several columns, mostly from the west, apart from X *Fretensis* which had been garrisoning Jericho for much of the last year and advanced from that direction. Although it was unlikely that the Romans would encounter a major enemy force in the open field, the army did not advance in battle order, but still moved carefully and under the close control of Titus and his officers. The order of march of the main column was very similar to that adopted by Vespasian in AD 67. The vanguard consisted of auxiliaries and allied troops, most in close formation, but probably screened by cavalry pickets and parties of archers and light infantry tasked with exploring any potential ambush sights. Following close behind were the officers and men tasked with laying out and beginning construction of the night's marching camp. Then came the officers' baggage train, followed by Titus and his staff, guarded by his *singulares* – an élite bodyguard of infantry

1. The Romans attack the Third Wall, making a breach after fifteen days. The Jewish rebels abandon this part of the City.

2. The Romans breach the Second Wall, but their attacking columns are defeated after an initial success. The Wall falls permanently four days later.

3. Siege ramps are built against the Fortress of Antonia. The defenders' countermining undermines their fortifications, which collapse.

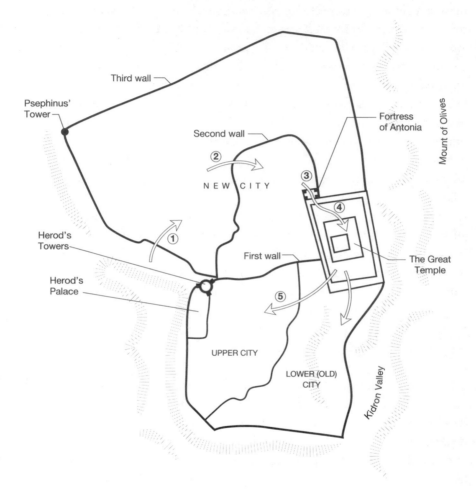

4. After weeks of heavy fighting the Romans break in to the Great Temple and burn it down.

5. The Romans launch attacks from the Temple into the Old City. After eighteen days of preparation they storm the area around the former palace of Herod the Great.

THE SIEGE OF JERUSALEM

and cavalry picked out from the auxiliary units – and the 120 cavalrymen which each legion maintained. Next there was the artillery train required for the siege, and then the commanders of the auxiliary units each with a small escort. Presumably they were collected together rather than staying with their units so that it was easier for Titus to issue an order to them. Behind came the legions, each preceded by its eagle and other standards massed together and escorted by trumpeters, and followed by their baggage trains and slaves. Finally the rearguard was formed by the remainder of the auxiliary and allied troops.[16]

As his forces closed in on the city, Titus rode ahead to reconnoitre, escorted by 600 cavalry, most probably his *singulares*. He was wearing neither helmet nor armour, for he did not plan to fight, simply to observe and to judge the mood and enthusiasm of the defenders. At first the appearance of the Roman patrol provoked no response from the city until, as they incautiously rode along parallel to the walls, a group of rebels launched a sudden sally. For a moment the Roman general was cut off with a small group of followers – the rest had fled believing that no one had been left behind – and was forced to lead a headlong charge to break out. Titus escaped unscathed, although two of his bodyguard were cut down as they tried to get away. Personal reconnaissance provided a commander with useful information, but was seldom without risks, as Marcellus' death had shown centuries before.[17]

On the following day the three legions, approaching along essentially the same route followed four years earlier by Cestius Gallus, reached Mount Scopus, a height about a mile to the north of Jerusalem and overlooking the city. *XII Fulminata* and *XV Apollinaris* pitched camp together on this high ground, with *V Macedonica* a few hundred yards away and slightly to the rear. Presumably the auxiliaries and allied troops were distributed amongst these camps. As arranged *X Fretensis* also arrived on the far side of the city and began to construct a camp on the Mount of Olives, the soldiers dispersing into work parties. Deciding to unite against the common enemy, the Jews launched a combined attack out of the eastern wall of the city, swarming across the Kidron valley and attacking the isolated legion. The suddenness and enthusiasm of the attack surprised the legionaries, who seem complacently to have assumed that the rebels were not capable of serious aggression. Many panicked and fled, and their officers struggled to form any sort of coherent fighting line as the rebels drove uphill and captured the Roman campsite. The ease with which they had taken such a naturally strong position testifies to the Romans' lack of precautions. Titus and his *singulares* rode to the spot, but it would take time before more reinforcements could march to join the fighting.

Rallying some of the fleeing soldiers and getting them to form up and re-engage the enemy, Titus then supported their advance by charging against the rebels' flank with his cavalry. Throughout the rebellion the Jewish partisans, who never mustered cavalry in any significant numbers, proved especially vulnerable to the fast-moving and disciplined Roman horsemen. As the Roman counter-attack gathered momentum the Jews were driven back down the way they had come. Having crossed over the Kidron stream they managed to halt on the far bank and bring their pursuers to a halt. For a while the fighting seems to have petered out into sporadic exchanges of missiles and half-hearted charges. By noon Titus decided that the threat was over and ordered much of the legion to return to the task of building the camp, establishing a covering force of auxiliary cohorts and other men brought up as reinforcements. The rebels had a man on the walls watching the Romans who signalled this partial withdrawal by waving a cloak. This prompted a new attack by a fresh band of rebels who poured out of one of the gates and

> sprang forth with such impetuosity that their rush was comparable to that of the most savage of beasts. In fact not one of the opposing line awaited their charge, but, as if struck [by the missile] from an engine, they broke their ranks and turned and fled up the mountain side, leaving Titus, with a few followers, half way up the slope.[18]

Galloping around the hillside, the Roman commander led whatever men he could find in a series of desperate charges, fighting hand-to-hand at their head. After a while, parts of the legion broke off work to join the fight and these were joined by some of the rallying troops. After a while Titus was able to halt the enemy attack and put together his screening force once more, permitting the legionaries to return and complete the camp.[19]

In the following days a party of soldiers were lured forward to within missile range of the walls by a group of rebels pretending to surrender, and suffered heavily before they escaped. Titus made an angry speech to the survivors, condemning their indiscipline in running forward without orders. The young commander announced that he intended to execute them in accordance with the strictest traditions of military discipline. Hearing this a great crowd of the condemned soldiers' comrades clustered around him begging him to forgive the men and declaring that they would make sure that there was no repeat of this misadventure. It was a piece of theatre similar to some of Julius Caesar's confrontations with his troops and typical of the way that Roman senators often interacted with a mass of soldiers much as they handled a crowd in the Forum. Titus yielded to their entreaties, realizing anyway that it was not practical to execute so many men at once and also guessing that the importance of his point concerning the need for strict obedience had been well made.

At around this time he ordered the three legions to move from Mount Scopus and camp nearer the city on its western side. Since the rebels had shown their willingness to attack any detachment which appeared vulnerable, the Romans deployed facing the city to cover the movement of the baggage and camp followers. Titus formed his infantry in three ranks, backed by a fourth rank of foot archers and closely supported by three ranks of cavalry. Once again the three legions were divided between two camps, Titus himself with *XII Fulminata* and *XV Apollinaris* taking position within a quarter of a mile of the walls, while *V Macedonica* was a little further to the south, facing the tower of Hippicus, one of the trio of massive turrets built originally by Herod.[20]

Before launching the assault on the third, or outer, wall, Titus again rode out with his cavalry bodyguard to examine the fortifications and select the most suitable spot for breaching the wall. The easiest approach proved to be near the tomb of a high priest, the location of which is not precisely known, although it appears to have been not far from the modern-day Jaffa Gate. Orders were issued for the legionaries to clear all the ground outside the walls in preparation for the siegeworks and to begin collecting the timber which would be needed in their construction. The defenders attempted to harass the workers with missiles fired from scorpions and larger *ballistae* which they had captured in the fortresses of the city or during the defeat of Cestius Gallus in AD 66. Instructed by Roman deserters, their shooting was at first wildly inaccurate, but would steadily improve as the siege went on. The legions used their own artillery – one late source claims that each unit had sixty scorpions and ten larger stone-throwing *ballistae*, but it is probable that the numbers varied considerably depending on the nature of the operation – in an effort to suppress the defenders on the wall. This was the main role of artillery during a siege, the attacker trying to make it impossible for defenders to remain in positions from which they could impede the siegeworks and the defender trying to do just that. Fortifications on the scale of the walls and towers at Jerusalem could not be breached by the missiles of ancient artillery.

Although the Romans suffered casualties during this exchange of bolts and stones shot from the engines, in the end this was insufficient to slow the progress of the work parties significantly. The greater numbers and size of their machines – those of X *Fretensis* were especially renowned – and the quality of their crews allowed them to win the artillery duel, although this encounter was by no means one-sided. Josephus tells us that at the beginning the lightly coloured catapult stones – which may well have been quarried and carved on the spot – were easy for the defenders to see in flight. Sentries on the wall would yell out 'Baby on the way!' in time for most of the defenders to duck or take cover. Learning this, the Romans began to paint their ammunition a much darker shade, making it far less visible and greatly increasing the casualties caused. The force of such projectiles was truly appalling. Josephus recalled seeing a man's head flung a quarter of a mile away from his body by the impact of a catapult stone during the siege of Jotapata. Even more gruesomely, he describes a missile which hit a pregnant women, instantly killing her and flinging out her unborn child.[21]

Since the walls could not be broken by artillery, the principal method of creating a breach was to employ a massive battering ram, the iron head usually shaped like that of the animal after which it was named. The bulk of the Romans' efforts had been to construct three ramps allowing these engines to approach the wall. Calculating the distance to the wall by throwing a plumb line – the only method which allowed the engineers to avoid exposing themselves to enemy missiles – to confirm that the ramps were ready, the legions brought up these massive machines. Titus had ordered the construction of artillery positions to cover the ramps and prevent the defenders from hindering the work of the rams. At Jotapata one giant of a Galilean had hurled a boulder down to snap the iron head off a ram. On another occasion the defenders lowered straw-filled sacks to cushion the blows and reduce the force of the battering. Roman convention dictated that until the first blow of the ram struck the wall of a city its occupants could still surrender and hope for reasonable terms. Josephus tells us that a great moan went up from the people of Jerusalem when the noise of the first strike echoed across through the streets. Another uneasy truce developed between Simon and John, the former permitting the Zealots to pass through the sectors held by his men in order to reach the threatened section of wall. From the rampart they began hurling down incendiary missiles or shooting at any Roman who was visible. A few groups sallied out from the walls to set torches to the rams and siegeworks. In spite of the boldness of the attacks, each one was beaten off by a combination of archers and artillery backed by cavalry charges sent in by Titus who directed the battle.[22]

Although the Romans had successfully defended their works, the rams initially made little impression on the wall, apart from the one operated by *XV Apollinaris* which managed to weaken the corner of a tower. As the day wore on many of the Roman units were allowed to return to camp, for it seemed that the main threat had been repulsed. Yet once again they had underestimated the determination of their opponents, who launched a second attack, this time from a concealed doorway near the Hippicus tower. It was on this occasion that the stubborn resistance of the vexillations from the Egyptian legions won fame by stopping an advance which seemed on the very brink of success. This time Titus himself led his cavalry in a charge against the rebels, allegedly killing twelve of them himself. A single prisoner was taken in the fighting and the Roman commander ordered him to be crucified within sight of the walls as a warning of the fate awaiting those who fought against Rome. Yet the very fervour of the rebel sallies had surprised the besiegers and created an air of nervousness. When one of the siege towers fell down during the night there was widespread panic until officers were sent around to explain the cause of the confusion. There were three of these towers, one for each of the ramps, and their purpose was to provide a platform from which archers and scorpions could shoot down onto any defenders on the wall's parapet. Gradually the defenders were losing the ability to fight from their own fortifications just as the battering began to take effect, as one of the rams at last opened a breach. Most of the rebels decided that the position was hopeless and pulled back to the second wall. When the Roman storming party climbed the breach, the few remaining men fled. The outer wall of the city had fallen after fifteen days of the siege. Titus ordered most of the wall to be demolished, along with many of the buildings, gardens and other structures in this section of the city. The legions – with the exception of *X Fretensis* which remained on the Mount of Olives – advanced to camp in the area levelled in this way.[23]

THE SECOND WALL

Although the defenders had abandoned the third wall, their defence of the second line was as determined and aggressive as any of the earlier fighting. Continual raids were made against the Roman soldiers labouring to prepare for the assault, resulting in many fierce skirmishes. Josephus tells us that the rebels were still confident of their ability to defend the city and eager to win favour from their leaders. By contrast, for the Romans the incentives to valour were the habit of victory and inexperience of defeat, their continuous campaigns and perpetual training, the magnitude of their empire, and above all Titus, ever and everywhere present beside them all. For cowardice when Caesar was with them and sharing the contest seemed monstrous, while the man who fought bravely had as a witness of his valour one who would also reward it.[24]

During this period a horseman from one of the auxiliary *alae* made a lone charge into a dense block of the enemy formed up outside the walls, killing three before galloping unscathed back to his own comrades. There was a long tradition in the Roman army, stretching back at least to Polybius' day, of rewarding such acts of bravado. In this case Titus praised the man, a certain Longinus – the name was a common one, especially amongst auxiliaries – but also warned his men not to be too reckless in their bids for honour.

The Romans found the approach to the second wall easier than the first, and within five days a battering ram had created a breach in one of the towers. Titus took his *singulares* and 1,000 legionaries into the city, and at first encountered little opposition. However, he neglected to order work parties to widen the breach – Josephus claims that this was because he hoped that Jerusalem would still surrender and wished to avoid unnecessary destruction, but this seems unlikely – and the storming party soon had difficulty making its way through the maze of narrow streets. The rebels launched a counter-attack, their numbers and local knowledge giving them a marked advantage. The Romans suffered heavily and were soon forced to retreat, but the narrowness of the breach made it difficult for them to exit quickly, or for reinforcements to come to their aid. A desperate rearguard action developed as Titus and a force of auxiliary archers kept the rebels back to cover the retreat of the rest. On this occasion the Roman commander is supposed to have demonstrated as much skill with the bow as he had earlier shown with spear and sword, shooting down twelve men with as many arrows.[25]

Encouraged by the repulse of the enemy, the defenders held the wall with renewed determination for three more days, until a second Roman assault proved successful on the fourth day. This time the legions were ordered to demolish most of the walls and buildings in that quarter to allow themselves more room for movement. The reverse had proved temporary, but it is notable that several days had to pass before the Romans felt ready for a second attack. Assaulting an enemy-held fortification placed very heavy demands on the courage of the soldiers taking part, probably heavier than those during a battle. In an effort to give his soldiers more time to recover and to cheer them up, Titus ordered a suspension of the main work of the siege while the army held a formal parade to receive its pay. The army was normally paid three times a year, on the first day of January, May and September. Since the parade at Jerusalem took place early in June, this would mean that the pay was overdue by at least a month.

It was an affair of great ceremony, the units parading in turn over four days to receive the money they were due. A great deal of time and effort was devoted to polishing armour and weapons as individuals and units vied to produce the best possible turnout. The result was a scene of great splendour as the serried ranks, their brightly painted shields for the first time unveiled from the protective leather covers, paraded within full view of the city. For the Romans themselves it was a reminder of their pride in themselves and their units, and also of the tangible rewards of military service. To the rebels it was a display of the might and overwhelming power of the Roman army. Although it did not prompt sudden surrender, this return to the formal routine and ritual of peacetime soldiering helped to prepare the troops for the even greater tasks ahead of them.[26]

ANTONIA AND THE TEMPLE

The next phase of the siege involved the construction of assault ramps against the Fortress of Antonia and a stretch of the first wall. *V Macedonica* worked to construct the first ramp against Antonia, while *XII Fulminata* built another some 30 feet away. *X Fretensis* and *XV Apollinaris* constructed two more ramps about 45 feet apart against the wall, probably not too far from the modern Jaffa Gate. (It is possible that each pair of legions was in fact labouring on either side of a single ramp, but this theory cannot be proved and it does not affect the basic narrative of the siege if there were in fact two ramps instead of four.)[27] The height of the walls, and especially of Antonia, combined with the growing accuracy of the rebels' artillery, made the labour on these projects extremely difficult. In addition the defenders mounted frequent sallies so that large numbers of troops were required to remain under arms to protect the siegeworks. In spite of this the Romans persevered and completed the ramps after seventeen days of heavy labour. The need for timber in the construction work had already meant that the hills for several miles around were stripped bare of trees.

The great sense of achievement at the completion of these works was rudely shattered when the ramps were destroyed before the rams had been moved into position. As the Romans had toiled in their construction, John of

Gischala's men had been tunnelling out from Antonia beneath the ramps nearest to it. The roof of the mine was supported by timber props which were coated in bitumen and piled around with combustible material. Finally these were set on fire, the blaze consuming the timbers and causing the mine to collapse, bringing the Roman works down with them. What was not immediately shattered was burnt in the fire which spread rapidly amongst the dry timbers of the ramps. Two days' later Simon equalled his rival's success when his men sallied out and set fire to the ramps facing their section of the first wall. The Romans were thrown into such confusion by this attack that the rebels came close to storming part of the camp and were only repulsed by the picket stationed in front of the rampart, its members oath-bound not to abandon their position. Titus, who had been at Antonia inspecting the damage there, then arrived at the head of his *singulares* and charged the enemy in the flank. Once again the Jewish infantry proved vulnerable to well-handled cavalry and they suffered heavy losses as they were driven back into the city. This did little to diminish the scale of their victory in destroying the product of so much labour by the enemy.[28]

Morale amongst the besiegers dropped alarmingly following these setbacks. Dio tells us that some soldiers so despaired of ever taking the city that they deserted to join the rebels inside. Titus summoned his senior officers to a *consilium* in order to discuss the problem. Some argued for an immediate all-out attack using the entire army in the hope of overwhelming the defenders and storming the city, but this risked a costly failure which would quite probably irrevocably shatter the men's spirit. Others suggested that it was better to surround Jerusalem with a wall and simply starve it into submission, although this would inevitably take a long time and was scarcely the sort of dramatic victory Titus' father needed to cement his hold on power. Titus sided with the more moderate opinion, deciding that they should continue the assault and begin new ramps even though this would require quantities of timber which might prove difficult to find and could certainly not be quickly replaced if destroyed by the enemy.

Before the army resumed this work, however, he ordered the construction of a line of circumvallation all round the city. Each legion and sub-unit in the army was given a stretch of rampart to construct, probably from dry stone much like the smaller circuit still visible at Masada. This was a normal Roman method of undertaking any major project, employed for instance in the building of Hadrian's Wall where many inscriptions have been found recording the completion of a set distance of wall by a specific century of a legion. Division of labour in this way made practical administrative sense, but it was also intended to exploit the soldiers' pride in their own units as they competed to finish their allotment before everyone else. Titus continually visited the work parties, encouraging the troops to believe that their commander noticed everything that they did and would reward ability as swiftly as he punished sloth. In three days a line some 5 miles long and including fifteen forts was built completely enclosing the city. Each night Titus himself went on a tour of inspection, visiting the sentries and outposts all the way around the wall. In the second watch Tiberius Alexander undertook this task, and in the third one of the legionary legates was selected by lot for the same duty.[29]

Titus had given his men a task which, although involving considerable effort, could be and was completed swiftly. The satisfaction felt at its completion helped to renew their spirits. To the defenders the Romans' wall sent a clear message that there could be no escape and made it much more dangerous for small groups to leave the city in the hope of finding food. Food supplies were by now running very short in Jerusalem, especially for the ordinary population who were unable to prevent the partisans from seizing anything they could find. Yet any attempt to leave the city and surrender to the Romans risked immediate execution. Nor was it always safe to enter the Roman camp. At one stage during the siege some civilians who had given themselves up were observed picking gold coins out of their own faeces, having swallowed these to prevent their confiscation by soldiers on either side. The rumour spread that deserters were full of gold, leading to a gruesome massacre as camp followers, auxiliaries and some legionaries pounced on any prisoners they could find and slit their stomachs open in search of wealth. Horrified, not least because such atrocities would only deter others from defecting to the Roman camp in the future, Titus harangued his troops and promised to execute anyone found responsible for this crime, although in fact the culprits were not discovered. Even so the dream of concealed gold led to more instances of such dreadful murders whenever no senior officer was in sight.[30]

After completing the line of circumvallation the Romans began to construct new ramps facing Antonia. Materials were in short supply, and men had to be sent as much as 11 miles away to find trees to fell. In twenty-one days the new assault ramps were ready, the work having been once again made difficult by the continued activity of the defenders. Yet when John led his men out to burn the completed works he found the Roman troops guarding the positions very determined and well supported by archers and scorpions. The raid was poorly organized and not pressed home. The rams were now brought up to batter the walls of Antonia, a barrage of artillery missiles being laid down on the ramparts in an effort to pin down the defenders. Some legionaries formed *testudo* with their shields making an overlapping roof above their heads and set to work trying to prise the stones out of the wall with crowbars. Little impression had been made after a day's concerted effort, but overnight everything changed when Antonia, undermined by the earlier tunnels dug by John's men, suddenly collapsed. A massive breach opened in the tower-fortress to the amazement of the Romans. The Zealots had suspected the danger and hastily built a new wall running behind it, to cut off the route which otherwise led straight into the Temple Court. Rubble from the collapse of the great tower had piled up against this, however, making it relatively easy to scale.[31]

The Roman troops displayed a surprising reluctance to assault this makeshift fortification, in spite of an encouraging speech from Titus promising rewards to the first men over the parapet. Only a dozen auxiliaries responded, led by a Syrian called Sabinus, whose thin frame and swarthy skin in no way conformed to the ideal image of the brave soldier. Calling out to the watching general, Sabinus led the charge up the slope, only to be killed along with three of his comrades. The remainder were all wounded, but brought back into the Roman lines. The rest of the troops had made no effort to follow the lead of these brave men. However, two nights later a group of twenty legionaries on outpost duty, joined by a standard-bearer (*signifer*), a trumpeter and a couple of auxiliary cavalrymen, on their own initiative climbed up to the enemy rampart. Killing or driving off the Jewish sentries, they had the musician sound his trumpet.

As far as we can tell this exploit had not been ordered by higher commanders, but was simply a bid by these soldiers to win fame and reward. Even so, Titus quickly discovered what had happened and formed up a body of troops to secure the foothold. Exploiting this success, he sent his men into the Temple Court where a furious combat developed as the rebels struggled to defend this most sacred of sites. In the darkness there was little that leaders could do to organize the fighting, but the combat raged for over half of the next day before the Romans were finally driven back. In the course of the fighting a Bithynian centurion named Julianus made a one-man charge across the Temple Court, driving back the enemy, but failing to persuade the Roman soldiers to follow him. In the end his hobnailed sandals – the *caligae* after which Caligula was nicknamed – slipped on the smooth flagstones and he was surrounded by a group of rebels and hacked to pieces. It seems more than likely that such tales of heroic death, so similar to stories

Caesar told to soften the impact of his own reverses, were included in Titus' own *Commentaries* which Josephus claims to have consulted.[32]

The next assault into the Temple was to be better prepared than the first, and the Roman general ordered the remains of Antonia to be levelled, creating a wide ramp up into the Court. Only a single turret was left as an observation post. The Roman general also sent Josephus to carry a message to John of Gischala, formally challenging him to come out and fight a battle. The gesture was in part intended to emphasize to the wider population of the city that they only suffered because of the actions of the radical leaders, but it may also have been intended to encourage his own troops by suggesting that the enemy were afraid to fight them fairly. Desertions, especially from amongst the aristocracy, were now occurring frequently, whenever these men could evade the guard set by the partisans.

A few days later Titus formed a special assault force which he placed under the command of the legate Cerialis. It consisted of temporary units of 1,000 men, commanded by a tribune and drawn from the bravest thirty legionaries in each century. In this way these men were marked out as special in the hope that their pride would make them fight all the harder to justify their selection. The attack was to go in at night, observed by Titus from the remaining turret of Antonia. Josephus claims that the young commander had had to be restrained by his officers from personally leading the storming party as he had done in earlier sieges. Certainly, every commander faced a difficult choice between remaining in the rear, where it would be difficult to see what was going on and still harder to do much to influence the fighting, or going forward and risking death or capture. At the first, ultimately unsuccessful assault on Gamala in AD 67, Vespasian had grown frustrated with not being able to direct the attack and had entered the town with his *singulares*. When the Romans were routed by a rebel counter attack, Vespasian was cut off and suffered a wound to the foot before he and his guards fought their way out. At Jerusalem Titus again emphasized to the soldiers that his main reason for staying behind was so that he could better observe their individual conduct.

The attack achieved initial surprise, but the defenders swiftly rallied and came in ever growing numbers to contest the wide Temple Court. Once again the night battle continued well into the following day without either side gaining any marked advantage. Most of the Court apart from a narrow corner was left in Jewish hands. Within seven days the road over the ruins of Antonia was complete, allowing the Romans to commit troops more easily in support of their attacks. With this task finished, work began on ramps to permit rams to be brought against the first wall, although the wood required for the task was now having to be brought from over twelve and half miles away. For a while there was a lull between major attacks, but still each day there were skirmishes and raids. Titus ordered the execution of a cavalryman from a group which had let their horses roam freely while they were out on a foraging expedition only to have them stolen by the enemy. Shortages within the city were now extreme as a result of the blockade, and John and Simon joined forces to launch an all-out attack on the camp of *X Fretensis* on the Mount of Olives, hoping to break the Romans' line at this point. They were repulsed after a very hard fight and pursued back across the valley by the Roman cavalry. One auxiliary horseman, a member of the less well paid and prestigious cavalry troops forming part of certain predominantly infantry cohorts, galloped into the midst of the fleeing enemy and picked one up by the ankle. The four-horned saddle used by the Romans gave a rider a very secure seat, but even so this was a remarkable feat of strength as well as a display of contempt for the enemy. The man carried his prize to lay before Titus. The soldier was praised, his captive crucified within sight of the walls. At various times during the siege the Roman legionaries amused themselves by nailing victims to their crosses in a variety of grotesque postures.[33]

Bitter fighting continued in the Temple Court, both sides setting light to sections of the porticoes to make their own positions stronger against attacks. As before the defenders did their best to harass the men labouring on the siege ramps. During this period Josephus tells of a small man named Jonathan who challenged any Roman to meet him in single combat. A cavalryman – obviously on foot and an indication that horsemen were expected to play their part in a dismounted role in the dangerous operations of a siege – came forward and was killed after he slipped. Jonathan's triumph proved short-lived, for he was promptly killed by an arrow shot by a Roman centurion named Priscus. The defenders had more success when they abandoned a section of portico which they had already prepared to set on fire, luring forward some impetuous legionaries into a trap where they must either perish in the flames or be killed or captured by the enemy. Some days later an attempt was made to capture the rest of the Temple by escalade. Ladders were set against one of the porticoes and the stormers climbed up onto the top, but were unable to make any headway. Near the front were several standard-bearers, who could do little to defend themselves while carrying these heavy burdens. After a vicious fight around these symbols of unit pride, all the Romans who had reached the top were killed and the standards captured. In subsequent days more of the outer porticoes were put to the torch by the Romans, but the sheer size and quality of the stonework prevented the rams from having much effect.[34]

According to Josephus, Titus then held a *consilium* in which he made it clear that he still hoped to avoid the destruction of the Temple. For the Jewish historian it was important that blame for this dreadful catastrophe should fall not on his hero, but on the shoulders of the radical rebel leaders. Fighting continued in what was left of the Temple Court, on one occasion Titus sending in his bodyguard cavalry to reinforce the infantry line when it looked about to break. On this occasion he was once again observing the combat from the vantage point of the ruins of Antonia. Gradually the Romans were taking more and more of the Temple until the rebels were forced back into the inner court. In further confused fighting they were driven from this and the most sacred heart of the Temple put to the torch. Whoever started the blaze, it soon raged out of control and many of the Roman soldiers were reluctant to do anything to quell it. Titus tried to organize fire-fighting parties, telling a centurion and some of his men to use force against any men who disobeyed, but failed to bring any semblance of order. The soldiers were keen to plunder the fabulous wealth rumoured to be found in this place, and as eager to destroy the most sacred site of an enemy who had fought them with such bitter determination. In the confusion of the final capture of the Temple most of the buildings were burnt to the ground and most of the civilians sheltering nearby massacred. It was now late August.[35]

Later, when some order had returned, the Roman army celebrated more formally, by parading their standards in the Temple Court and offering a sacrifice. The Old Town was soon taken and given over to the sack. Josephus mentions that so much plunder was taken by the troops at Jerusalem that the value of gold fell by half throughout Syria when the men returned to their garrisons. Sometimes the looters encountered rebels engaged on the same task. One legionary cavalryman – each legion in this period included a small force of 120 horsemen – was captured, but escaped before he could be executed. In another rather theatrical performance Titus gave in to his soldiers' entreaties not to have the man killed for being captured in the first place, but still made him suffer the humiliation of being dismissed from his legion. There were still minor setbacks, but the heart had gone out of the defenders with the fall of the Temple. John of Gischala and Simon bar Giora had attempted to begin negotiations, but their approach was rejected so late in the siege. Eighteen days were spent in constructing ramps against the walls of the upper city, but the rebels were now demoralized and suffering badly from lack of food so that resistance was feeble. Before the Roman storming party had even reached the top of the breach created by the rams, the defenders fled and dispersed. The siege of Jerusalem was at an end. John of Gischala surrendered and was sentenced to life imprisonment. Simon was kept to be the most important captive in Titus' triumph. It was nearing the end of September.[36]

After the siege Titus held a formal parade to thank and reward his men.

> A spacious tribunal having accordingly been constructed for him in the centre of his former camp, he here took his stand with his principal officers so as to be heard by the whole army. He expressed his deep gratitude to them for the loyalty which they had continuously shown him...
>
> He accordingly forthwith gave orders to the appointed officers to read out the names of all who had performed any brilliant feat during the war. Calling up each by name he applauded them as they came forward, no less exultant over their exploits than if they were his own. He then placed crowns of gold upon their heads, presented them with golden neck-chains, little golden spears and standards made of silver, and promoted each man to a higher rank; he further assigned to them out of the spoils silver and gold and raiments and other booty in abundance. When all had been rewarded as he judged each to have deserved, after invoking blessings on the whole army he descended amidst many acclamations and proceeded to offer sacrifices of thanksgiving for his victory. A vast number of oxen being brought up beside the altars, he sacrificed them all and distributed them to the troops for a banquet.[37]

It was a ritual confirming the commander's role as judge of his men's behaviour, ending in three days of feasting. Afterwards *Legio X Fretensis* was to become the garrison of the captured city. *XII Fulminata* had evidently not fully atoned for its earlier defeats, for it was not permitted to return to its old base at Rhaphanaeae in Syria but was transferred to a far less comfortable position on the frontier between Cappadocia and Armenia. After various celebrations and ceremonies, Titus returned to Italy, dispelling fears of a return to civil war by immediately greeting his father most warmly on arrival. The emperor and his eldest son then celebrated a joint triumph over Judaea which culminated in the ritual strangulation of Simon bar Giora. Vespasian himself found the slow crawl of the procession extremely tiresome and was heard to mutter something about serving himself right for wanting to have such an honour at his age. Yet the new dynasty had gained the spectacular victory needed to justify its rule and took care to parade this achievement thoroughly. In the following years the Arch of Titus was built, which still bears reliefs depicting his triumph. This was part of a building programme including the Colosseum with which Vespasian provided employment for the Urban poor and helped to rebuild the centre of a Rome devastated by fire and Nero's grandiose projects.[38]

Vespasian managed to restore stability to the Empire. His only serious fault was considered to be his avarice, but this may well have been due mainly to the need to restore a treasury drained by Nero's excesses. He died in AD 79, his final words a joking reference to the convention by which emperors were almost always deified after their deaths – 'I think I am becoming a god'. In his funeral procession the actor wearing his mask and symbols of office called out to the officials organizing the ceremony and asked how much it all cost. When they replied with an enormous figure, the actor offered them 1 per cent of the total and suggested that they just tip the body into the River Tiber instead.

During his father's life Titus commanded the Praetorian Guard and undertook much of the emperor's dirty work. It came as something of a surprise and relief when his rule proved to be benevolent and just. For the sake of propriety he gave up his long-time mistress, Queen Berenice, a descendant of Herod the Great, as well as the band of eunuchs and homo-sexuals who had normally attended his entertainments. Like his father, Titus became far more popular after he had become emperor than he had ever been before. Yet his reign proved short, and in AD 81 he too died in his fortieth year, to be succeeded by his far less popular and gifted younger brother Domitian.[39]

CHAPTER 13

THE LAST GREAT CONQUEROR:
TRAJAN AND THE DACIAN WARS

Marcus Ulpius Traianus (AD 56–117)

He always marched on foot with the rank and file of his army, and he attended to the ordering and disposition of the troops throughout the entire campaign, leading them sometimes in one order and sometimes in another; and he forded all rivers that they did. Sometimes he even caused his scouts to circulate false reports, in order that the soldiers might at one and the same time practise military manoeuvres and become fearless and ready for any dangers.[1]

AFTER THE DEATH OF AUGUSTUS, THE ROMAN EMPIRE GAINED LITTLE NEW territory. Throughout the remainder of the first century AD a number of allied kingdoms were annexed to become directly ruled provinces, but the only major new conquest came when Claudius sent an army to invade Britain in AD 43. The great conquerors of the last decades of the Republic had also been the principal leaders in the civil wars which had torn the State apart, and it was simply too great a risk for an emperor to permit any of his commanders to win fame and glory in a similar way. It was absolutely vital that the military achievements of the *princeps* never be overshadowed by those of any other senator. Even Augustus had sacked a Prefect of Egypt who had celebrated his victories too boldly, and forced him to commit suicide, though the man in question had only been an equestrian and not a member of the Senate. Tiberius, Vespasian and Titus already had distinguished military records before they came to the throne, but Caligula, Claudius, Nero and Domitian had not this advantage and were thus even more reluctant to permit potential rivals to gain too much prestige. We have already seen how Claudius recalled Corbulo from beyond the Rhine rather than permit him to expand the war and reoccupy part of the German province lost in AD 9. The same emperor made sure that he was in at the kill for the culmination of the first campaign of his British expedition in AD 43.

Claudius spent less than a fortnight in Britain, but was present at a major defeat of the Britons north of the Thames and the capture and occupation of the tribal capital at Camulodunum (Colchester). How active a role he actually played in the running of any of these operations is questionable, but it is significant that he felt it was worth considerable travel and six months away from Rome to preside over the army's success. Brief though the visit was, it helped to associate the emperor very personally with the subjugation of a mysterious island visited, but not conquered, by Julius Caesar. Claudius was then able to return to Rome and ride in triumph along the Sacra Via, something emperors did not normally do as a result of the victories won vicariously through their legates. In the flood of propaganda, which included games, the construction of a number of monuments, and both Claudius and his son adopting the name Britannicus, it was always made clear that this was the emperor's victory. For a man whose reign had begun when he was discovered hiding behind a curtain in the chaos following Caligula's murder and raised to power by the praetorian guard in spite of the wishes of the Senate, it was a great proof of his right and capacity to be Rome's first citizen.[2]

In the long run, the political system created by Augustus discouraged further expansion of the Empire. Most emperors were reluctant to spend the long periods of time on campaign carrying out fresh conquests and did not trust anyone else to do this for them. Some authors in Augustus' day were in any case already proclaiming that Rome controlled all the best and most prosperous parts of the earth and that further expansion would prove more costly than any profits it might yield. There was some truth in this, although the suggestion put forward by some modern scholars that the Romans stopped expanding because they now bordered on peoples whom their military system could not readily defeat is not supported by the evidence. Yet it is certainly true that the professional army as constituted under the Julio-Claudians could not quickly or easily be expanded in size to provide troops for new military adventures. Conscription was deeply unpopular, as Augustus had found in AD 6 and 9, and avoided if at all possible by all subsequent emperors. The imperial army was on average a far more efficient fighting force than the pre-Marian militia, but it lacked the seemingly limitless pool of reserve manpower which had proved such a strength in the Punic Wars.

Under the Principate the army's main roles were controlling the provinces – a task which involved them in everything from minor policing to putting down rebellions; and securing the frontiers – usually achieved by a combination of diplomacy and the aggressive domination of neighbouring peoples through real or threatened punitive expeditions against them. Wars of conquest were rare, although the ideology of the Empire and its rulers remained for centuries essentially one of expansion. It was still considered a fundamentally good thing for the *imperium* of Rome to increase, but as had always been the case, this did not necessarily require the acquisition of more territory. Roman power could be respected in a region even when it was not physically occupied by the army or governed by a Roman official, and many areas which were never controlled in this way were still felt by the Romans to be part of their empire. The determination to protect and increase Rome's *imperium* provided the motivation for most of the wars fought under the Principate.

Domitian spent several years supervising his armies fighting on the Rhine and Danubian frontiers, although it seems unlikely that he ever exercised direct battlefield command. A line of frontier forts was established in Germany further forward than had been the case in the past, but only a relatively small area was annexed in this way. In the main these conflicts were especially large-scale versions of the frequent campaigns to maintain Roman dominance over the tribes bordering on her frontier provinces. Dacia was invaded in response to heavy raids on the province of Lower Moesia, but it is unlikely that permanent occupation was anticipated, and in the event the operations there met with little success. One army – commanded by the Praetorian Prefect Cornelius Fuscus, much to the annoyance of the Senate who felt that any army ought to be led by a member of their class and not a mere equestrian – was defeated, and perhaps annihilated, by the Dacians in AD 86.[3] Domitian's relationship with the senatorial class steadily worsened throughout his principate, denying him the popularity – and favourable treatment in our sources which were mainly written by senators for senators – of his father and brother. In the end he was murdered in AD 96 through a palace conspiracy and replaced by the Senate with one of their own members, the elderly Nerva.

Nerva was the first of what Edward Gibbon termed the 'five good emperors' who presided over the Roman Empire at the height of its power and prosperity in the second century AD. He was succeeded by Trajan, who

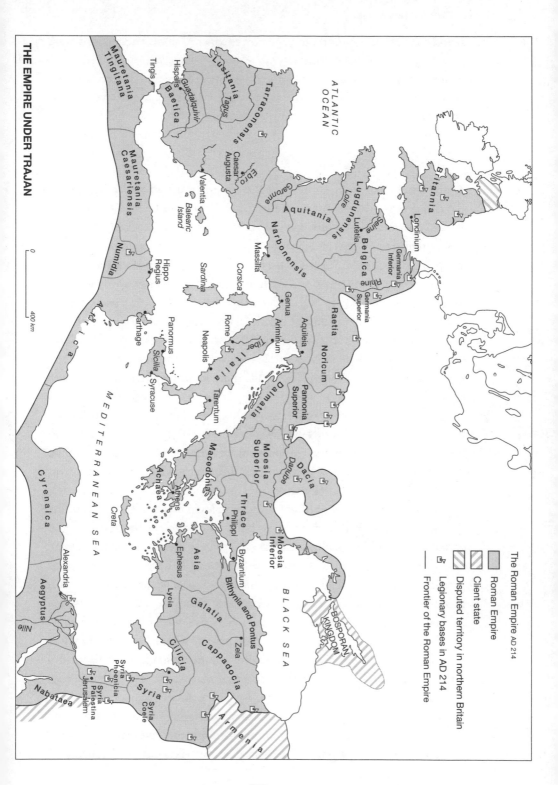

THE EMPIRE UNDER TRAJAN

The Roman Empire AD 214

Roman Empire
Client state
Disputed territory in northern Britain
Legionary bases in AD 214
Frontier of the Roman Empire

0 400 km

Mauretania Tingitana · Tingis · Hispalis · **Baetica** · *Guadalquivir* · **Lusitania** · *Tagus* · Caesar Augusta · *Ebro* · **Tarraconensis**

ATLANTIC OCEAN

Valentia · Balearic Island · *Garonne* · **Aquitania** · **Narbonensis** · Massilia · **Lugdunensis** · *Loire* · *Seine* · Lutetia · **Belgica** · Germania Interior · Londinium · **Britannia**

Mauretania Caesariensis · **Numidia** · Hippo Regius · Carthage · Sardinia · Corsica · Rome · Genua · Ariminum · Aquileia · *Tiber* · **Italia** · **Raetia** · **Noricum** · Germania Superior · *Rhine*

Africa · Panormus · **Sicilia** · Syracuse · Neapolis · Tarentum · **Dalmatia** · **Pannonia Superior** · **Pannonia Inferior**

MEDITERRANEAN SEA · **Cyrenaica** · Creta · **Achaea** · Athens · **Macedonia** · **Moesia Superior** · *Danube* · **Dacia** · **Moesia Inferior** · Philippi · **Thrace** · Byzantium

BLACK SEA · **BOSPORAN KINGDOM**

Alexandria · **Aegyptus** · *Nile* · **Lycia** · Ephesus · **Asia** · **Galatia** · **Bithynia and Pontus** · Zela · **Cappadocia** · **Cilicia** · **Syria** · Syria Phoenicia · Jerusalem · Syria Palestina · Syria Coele · **Nabataea** · **Armenia**

319

devoted much of his efforts to renewed expansion. His conquest of Dacia grew from Domitian's unsatisfactory campaigns in the area and had its root in frontier problems. In contrast the invasion of Parthia and the march to the Persian Gulf had little motive beyond the traditional desire of a Roman aristocrat to win glory by defeating powerful enemies.

TRAJAN'S BACKGROUND AND RISE TO POWER

Trajan was born and brought up at the city of Italica in Spain. His family claimed descent from some of the original Roman and Italian troops who formed this colony established by Scipio Africanus after his victory at Ilipa in 206 BC. Italica prospered and grew to be one of the largest and most important cities in Spain. Its citizens seem to have had Latin status, although the local aristocracy could gain full Roman citizenship through the holding of local magistracies. If they had sufficient wealth – and political success even at a local level always required money – then these families were able to become equestrians and send some of their sons into imperial service. Over time some gained the riches and favour to enter the Senate. In the first century BC, especially under Augustus, many Italian noblemen were made senators. Under his successors a growing number of men from the provinces joined the House. Some of these men were descendants of Roman colonists, but an increasing number were drawn from the indigenous aristocracy who had been granted citizenship. Claudius introduced a number of Gauls into the Senate. By the end of the first century there were also men from Spain, North Africa and the Greek east.

All of these men were Romans, both in law and in culture, regardless of their ethnic background, and their behaviour in public life differed in no significant way from that of senators of Italian or strictly Roman ancestry. Under the Principate Rome's ruling élite gradually absorbed the rich and powerful of most of the provinces without losing its traditional ethos. This process did a great deal to make widespread rebellion extremely rare throughout most of the provinces, save for those where the local aristocracy remained outside the system. Trajan was the first emperor whose link with Italy was extremely distant. He was succeeded by his cousin Hadrian, another Spaniard whose provincial accent earned the scorn of many other senators when he first came to Rome. Near the end of the century the throne would be seized by Septimius Severus, a senator from Lepcis Magna in North Africa. Later there would be Syrian, Greek, Pannonian and Illyrian emperors.[4]

Trajan's father and namesake, Marcus Ulpius Traianus, had had a fairly distinguished senatorial career, although it is not clear whether he was the first of the family to enter the Senate. In AD 67 he was the legionary legate commanding X *Fretensis* under Vespasian during the campaign in Galilee, and supported him during the Civil War. This brought him a consulship, perhaps in AD 70, and appointment as *legatus Augusti* first of Cappadocia and then of Syria. During this time there appears to have been some friction with the Parthians and Traianus' skilful handling of this affair led to his being awarded triumphal ornaments. It is uncertain whether the operations involved actual fighting or just vigorous diplomacy. During these years the family was granted patrician status. Scarcely any genuine patricians still survived by this time, for such prominent men had inevitably suffered much in the purges of successive emperors, and Vespasian had decided to create new patricians to add dignity to his Senate. Most of the beneficiaries were men who had shown themselves to be reliable during the Civil War, includ-ing the family of Tacitus' future father-in-law, Julius Agricola.[5]

Trajan's own upbringing appears to have been fairly conventional by the standards of the senatorial class, although it was claimed that he proved no more than adequate at rhetoric and other academic pursuits. At an early age he developed a passion for hunting which persisted throughout his life, and excelled at physical and especially military exercises. At the end of his teens, probably around AD 75, he became a senatorial tribune (*tribunus laticlavius*) in one of the legions in Syria, serving under his father's command in the manner of many young aristocrats. Later he transferred to a legion on the Rhine frontier and saw further service against the local tribes. Some tribunes were notorious for wasting their military tribunate, but Trajan embraced the military life with great enthusiasm and served for far longer than was usual. The Younger Pliny in his *Panegyric* – a written version of a speech praising the emperor and originally delivered in the Senate – claimed that he served for ten years, the traditional term required to make a man eligible for political office in the Republic. This may be an exaggeration, but his account of Trajan's time as tribune may well give an accurate picture of the enthusiastic young officer:

> As a tribune ... you served and proved your manhood at the far-flung bound-
> aries of the empire, for fortune set you to study closely, without haste, the
> lessons which you would later teach. It was not enough for you to take a distant
> look at the camp, stroll through a short period of duty: while a tribune you
> desired the qualifications for command, so that nothing was left to learn when
> the moment came for passing on your knowledge to others. Through ten years'

service you learnt the customs of peoples, the localities of countries, the opportunities of topography, and you accustomed yourself to cross all kinds of river
and endure all kinds of weather … So many times you changed your steed, so
many times your weapons, worn out in service![6]

A number of civil posts followed this spell in the army, until in the late 80s AD
Trajan became the legate of *Legio VII Gemina* at the town of Legio (the root
of its modern name, Léon) in the peaceful province of Hispania
Tarraconensis. In AD 89 Lucius Antoninus Saturninus, the legate of Germania
Superior, rebelled against Domitian. Trajan was ordered to march from
Spain to confront the rebel army. In the event he did not arrive before
Saturninus had been defeated, but his loyalty and prompt action won him
the emperor's trust. It seems that his legion remained on the Rhine and
mounted a successful punitive expedition against a German tribe – perhaps
the Chatti who had made an alliance with Saturninus. In the 90s he gained a
further reputation as a commander, and served as a provincial legate, perhaps
in both Germania Superior and Pannonia on the Danube. During his tenure
in the latter he fought and defeated some of the Suebic tribes. When
Domitian was murdered and Nerva elevated to the throne, Trajan was widely
respected as one of the gifted generals of an age for active service – he was
then in his fortieth year. Facing pressure from the praetorians who demanded
the punishment of Domitian's murderers, and probably nervous of rivals
emerging from amongst the provincial legates, in AD 97 Nerva adopted
Trajan, marking him out as his heir. The choice was a popular one, especially with the army, and did much to secure the new regime. A year later
Nerva died and Trajan became emperor. Within a year he was touring the
Danubian frontier, and in 101 he began a major campaign in this area, aimed
at the defeat of King Decebalus of Dacia.[7]

THE DACIAN WARS, AD 101–2 AND 105–6

In 58 BC Julius Caesar had considered attacking Dacia (an area roughly equivalent to modern-day Transylvania) until the Helvetii gave him an even more
attractive alternative opportunity for winning military glory. Only his murder
in 44 BC prevented a revival of his original plan for such a war from being
fulfilled. The Dacians were at that time united under the rule of Burebista,
a charismatic war leader who controlled a far larger force of warriors than
most tribal leaders. Not long after Caesar's death the Dacian king was himself
assassinated, and no comparably strong ruler emerged amongst his people for

over a century. This changed when Decebalus rose to power in the last decades of the first century AD, once again massing a strong force of warriors – he was especially keen to recruit deserters from the Roman army – and subjecting many neighbouring peoples, such as the Sarmatians and Bastarnae, to his rule. Dio described him in conventional terms as the ideal commander, who was:

> shrewd in his understanding of warfare and shrewd also in the waging of war; he judged well when to attack and chose the right moment to retreat; he was an expert in ambuscades and a master in pitched battles; he knew not only how to follow up a victory well, but also how to manage a defeat.[8]

Under Decebalus' aggressive leadership the Dacians had raided across the Danube, and inflicted serious defeats on the Romans. Domitian's campaign against them ended in a deeply unsatisfactory way with a treaty by which the Romans paid Decebalus an annual indemnity and provided him with engineers and artillery to strengthen the fortifications of his realm. Such terms indicated that Rome had not won the war and even hinted that she had lost, and added to Domitian's unpopularity with the Senate. When Trajan launched an invasion of Dacia in AD 101, its main aim was to achieve a far more satisfactory peace, based on a Roman victory which would allow the imposition of an appropriate treaty, making Rome's superiority over Dacia obvious to all. At first he does not appear to have planned to annex the kingdom.

Trajan subsequently wrote *Commentaries* describing his Dacian Wars, but only a few tiny fragments of these have survived. Cassius Dio, a senator of Greek extraction who wrote in the early third century AD, provides our best narrative of these operations, but even this remains only in the form of epitomes produced centuries later and lacking detail. A few other sources provide a little information, but it is impossible to produce a narrative of this conflict in anything like the detail of the other campaigns examined so far. The spoils from the conquest of Dacia funded the great Forum complex later constructed by Trajan in Rome. Little of this has survived beyond its massive centrepiece, a column 100 Roman feet high (97 feet 9 inches), decorated with a sculpted spiral frieze telling the story of the wars. Several hundred scenes depicting thousands of individual figures of Roman soldiers and their enemies were laid out to form a clear narrative. Originally it was highly colourful, the figures painted and equipped with miniature bronze weapons, the sculpture incorporating levels of detail which cannot possibly have been visible to the observer at ground level.

Trajan's Column tells a story, but it is a narrative which we can read only with difficulty. The task would be similar to looking at the Bayeux Tapestry, but without the captions and with only the haziest idea of the events and personalities of the Norman Conquest. Although many attempts have been made to relate the reliefs to the topography of Romania and to reconstruct the course of the wars in detail, none of these have ever carried much conviction and can never move beyond conjecture. Yet in another sense Trajan's Column provides us with a fascinating glimpse of how Roman commanders liked to be depicted in art. A range of artistic conventions influenced its style, but much of it drew on a centuries-old tradition of Roman triumphal art, for generals riding in triumph through the city almost invariably included in their processions paintings showing their own and their armies' deeds. Such pictures were often used to decorate temples or other monuments constructed with the spoils of war. The Trajan of the Column represents the ideal commander of Roman art, and it is interesting to compare this to the literary figure of the great general. Scenes from another monument at Adamklissi in Romania probably also show episodes from the war, but the story they tell is even harder to reconstruct. Trajan may be one of the officers depicted in the Adamklissi metopes, but these are too badly weathered to allow definite recognition.[9]

Preparations for the campaign were extensive and probably occupied at least a year. Ultimately nine legions – at full strength or at least in the form of a substantial vexillation – were concentrated on the Danube to take part in or support the operations. Other legions sent smaller vexillations and the already substantial auxiliary forces of the region were augmented by whole units and detachments from other provinces. Perhaps a third of the Roman army as then constituted was to take part in the war, although these troops were never massed in a single field army but operated in a number of separate forces and in supporting roles. It was a formidable force, but the task ahead of them would not prove easy. Dacia was defended by the natural strength of the Carpathians. The kingdom was rich in gold deposits and Decebalus had used this wealth to create a large army and to establish well-fortified strongholds controlling the main passes through the mountains. Excavation at a number of these sites has confirmed their formidable nature, with walls and towers which combined native, Hellenistic and Roman methods of construction.

Dacian warriors were brave, though perhaps no more disciplined than those of other tribal peoples. Their religion, based around the worship of the god Zalmoxis, often prompted men to commit suicide rather than surrender. In battle few appear to have worn armour, apart from the allied Sarmatian cavalry who fought as cataphracts, with both horse and man covered in metal or horn armour. Weapons consisted of bows, javelins, Celtic style swords, and also the scythe-like *falx*, a two-handed curved sword with the blade on the inner side and ending in a heavy point. This last weapon was capable of reaching past a shield to inflict terrible wounds, and appears to have encouraged some Roman legionaries to be equipped with greaves and an articulated guard to protect their exposed right arm.

Trajan's Column begins with scenes showing the Roman frontier posts along the Danube and a force of legionaries marching behind their massed standards over a bridge laid across river barges – the Roman equivalent of a pontoon bridge. Then the emperor appears, holding a *consilium* of senior officers to discuss the forthcoming operations. Trajan usually appears to be slightly larger than the men around him, but he never dominates by sheer size in the manner of the monumental art of other ancient rulers, such as the pharaohs of Egypt. High-level planning and the issuing of orders to the army's high command is followed by other preparations from the campaign. His head veiled in accordance with his office as *pontifex maximus*, Rome's senior priest, the emperor puts a circular ritual cake, or *popanum*, onto the flames of an altar, as around him the rite of the *suovetaurilia* is performed with the sacrifice of a bull, a ram and a boar to Mars. This important ceremony was held outside the ramparts of the army's camp near the start of any major campaign to purify the troops and ensure the support of Rome's deities. Just as they did in political life in Rome itself, magistrates played a central part in the regular religious ceremonies of the army. There is then a curious scene which shows Trajan watching a peasant clutching a large circular object fall off a mule, and which may be connected with an anecdote in Dio in which allied tribes sent a message to the emperor written in Latin on an enormous mushroom. Then the commander mounts a tribunal and makes a speech to a parade of his legionaries, an address known as an *adlocutio*. Afterwards the soldiers fortify several positions – presumably on the enemy bank of the Danube – the emperor moving amongst them as they labour and supervising the work.

Its crossing place secure, the main army advances into the hills, probably moving towards the pass in the Carpathians known as the Iron Gates. Trajan and one of his officers are shown inspecting an enemy hill fort, which appears to have been abandoned, before he returns to oversee a group of legionaries clearing a path through the thick woodland. A prominent theme on the Column, as indeed in much literature, is the engineering skill and dogged perseverance of the citizen soldiers of the army, and very often Trajan and his officers are shown overseeing the labour. He is also shown interrogating a Dacian prisoner, just as Caesar and other commanders had done, before the action moves rapidly on to the first major battle. In this the legionaries are shown formed up in reserve, while the auxiliaries, who include amongst their number bare-chested barbarians – probably Germans or perhaps even Britons from the irregular units known as *numeri* – wielding wooden clubs, do the actual fighting.

The savagery of these non-citizen soldiers is emphasized in this and other scenes. One regular auxiliary infantryman grips in his clenched teeth the hair of an enemy's severed head so that his hands are free to keep fighting. To the rear two more auxiliaries present severed heads to the emperor. In this scene Trajan appears to look away, but in a later, similar scene, he is shown reaching out to accept two such ghastly trophies. The Romans had outlawed headhunting in the provinces of the Empire, but it was evidently acceptable for soldiers to practise this when fighting against foreign enemies. Yet with one possible exception, only auxiliaries are shown on the Column taking heads and it seems likely that such behaviour was acceptable amongst these less civilized troops, but not amongst legionaries.

The bringing of trophies to the commander echoes incidents in the literature, such as the cavalryman at Jerusalem who picked up a rebel and brought him to Titus. The general, and even more the emperor, could reward such heroic feats and his role as witness to his men's behaviour was vital. Such a task meant keeping relatively close to the fighting, so that the men believed that they could be seen as individuals. One of Domitian's generals is supposed to have ordered his men to paint their names on their shields to make themselves feel more visible. Later on the Column Trajan is shown distributing rewards to auxiliary troops, although other evidence suggests that these men no longer received medals (*dona*) like the legionaries so that the awards must have taken another form. Auxiliary units gained battle honours, and sometimes an early grant of the citizenship which was normally given on discharge, so perhaps promotion and sums of money or plunder were the most common form of reward to an individual auxiliary soldier.[10]

This first battle probably took place near Tapae, where in AD 88 one of Domitian's generals had won a victory which did something to remove the shame of Cornelius Fuscus' defeat. A god hurling thunderbolts at the Dacians is shown in the top of the frieze, but it is unclear whether this is simply intended to show Rome's deities fighting on her behalf or indicates an action fought during, or perhaps terminated by, a storm. Some commentators have suggested that the reliance on auxiliaries to do the fighting while the legionaries remain in reserve reflected a Roman desire to win victories without the loss of citizen blood. Tacitus praised Agricola for winning the battle of Mons Graupius in this way, but in fact such a sentiment is rarely expressed.

It does seem to have been fairly common by the late first century AD to form the first line of infantry from auxiliary troops, while the legions formed the second and subsequent lines. This was certainly logical, for the higher organization of the legions, with ten cohorts coming under the command of a legate and being used to operating together (unlike auxiliary cohorts which were all independent units), made them easier for the army commander to control. For this reason legionaries were more effective as reserve troops to be committed as and when the fighting line needed reinforcement. In some cases, the battle may have been won by the auxiliaries without the need for any reserves. It is impossible to tell whether this was the case at Tapae in AD 101. It is equally possible that the sculptors chose simply to represent the opening phase of the battle begun when auxiliary infantry and cavalry launched an attack on the enemy. Dio tells us that the fighting was extremely fierce and that victory cost the Romans heavy casualties. When the Roman medical aid stations – medics are shown treating soldiers in one of the later scenes on the Column – ran out of bandages, Trajan sent them much of his own store of clothes to cut into strips and make up the shortage. To commemorate the fallen, he also established an altar on the site of the battle.[11]

Following up on their success, the Romans are shown continuing the advance and putting captured settlements to the torch. The parapet of one Dacian fort is shown decorated with a row of heads mounted on poles, while in front of the rampart are stakes concealed in pits, resembling the 'lilies' made by Caesar's men at Alesia. Dio tells us that in one such captured fort the Romans found standards and equipment captured from Fuscus' army.[12] The Romans then cross a river, this time without the benefit of a bridge. One legionary is shown wading through the water with his armour and equipment carried in the rectangular shield raised over his head. After this Trajan addresses another parade, before meeting with a group of Dacian ambassadors, and subsequently a group of native women. Then the action moves to another area as the Column shows Dacian warriors and Sarmatian cataphracts swimming – and in some cases drowning in the attempt – across the Danube to attack some Roman garrisons held by auxiliary troops. One group of enemies employ a battering ram with an iron tip shaped like the animal's head in an effort to breach a fort's wall, and this may perhaps be an indication of the knowledge of siege techniques which Decebalus had acquired from deserters and the treaty with Domitian.

In response to this new threat, we see Trajan and a mixture of praetorian guardsmen and auxiliaries embarking on a warship and a barge. They are bareheaded, wearing travelling cloaks (*paenulae*) and burdened with bundles – perhaps folded tents or simply supplies. The force moves along the Danube, then disembarks. Trajan is always at their head, and rides with a group of auxiliary infantry, cavalry and barbarian irregulars to hunt for the enemy raiding force. Two auxiliary cavalrymen seem to report to the emperor – presumably scouts who have found the Dacians – and this is followed by a massed Roman cavalry attack. Surprise appears complete – the goddess of Night is shown at the top of the scene suggesting an attack under cover of darkness – and the Sarmatians and Dacians are routed and cut down around their four-wheeled wagons. Caesar noted that Gallic armies were always accompanied by carts carrying their families, and it is possible that the Dacians followed a similar practice. However, it may be that these scenes represent not a raiding force, but a migration by some of the local peoples, perhaps tribes allied to Decebalus.

The Adamklissi metopes also show fighting around barbarian wagons and a dramatic Roman cavalry charge led by a senior officer, perhaps Trajan himself. Although cruder in style, these reliefs are less stylized than those on the Column and appear to show three distinct types of barbarian, probably Sarmatians, Bastarnae and Dacians. It is possible that the Adamklissi metopes correspond with these scenes on the Column, but they might equally depict entirely different events.

After this Roman victory Trajan is seen receiving another Dacian embassy, this time consisting of aristocratic 'cap-wearers' (*pileati*) rather than the socially inferior warriors who were sent by Decebalus at the start of the war. Dio mentions several attempts at negotiation, which failed due to Decebalus' mistrustful nature and, most likely, the uncompromising nature of Roman demands.[13] This is followed by a major battle, in which legionaries are shown fighting alongside auxiliaries. The Roman troops are supported by a scorpion mounted in a cart drawn by a team of two mules and known as a *carroballista*. Trajan supervizes from behind the fighting line, an auxiliary presenting him with a captive – perhaps one he had captured personally. Behind him is the famous field dressing station scene, which may mean that Dio's story about the bandages should be associated with this battle rather than the earlier encounter. As always with the Column, we simply cannot know.

After the defeat of the Dacians – many of whom are shown held captive in a compound – Trajan mounts a tribunal to address his paraded soldiers, and then sits on a folding camp chair to dole out rewards to brave auxiliaries. Yet in the midst of these scenes of Roman celebration is a bleaker scene off to the side, where several bound, naked men are brutally tortured by women. The men are most probably captured Roman soldiers and the women Dacians – in many warrior societies the task of humiliating and killing with torture enemy captives has often been performed by the women of the tribe. The scene may well be intended to show that the war was still not finished, for such a savage enemy needed to be defeated utterly.

At this point the narrative of the Column contains a clear break, perhaps indicating the end of the first year's campaigning, so that subsequent scenes should be assigned to AD 102. Another river journey is shown, then a column of legionaries marches across a bridge of boats and two Roman armies join together. In these and the following sections we see Trajan formally greeting arriving troops, making speeches to parades, taking part in another *suove-taurilia* sacrifice to Mars, receiving Dacian embassies, and accepting a prisoner or other trophies brought to him by soldiers. As the army advances through the mountains, making roads, building forts, fighting battles and besieging forts, the emperor is always with them, watching, directing and inspiring. He does not wield a tool or a weapon to join the soldiers in their tasks, for his role is to direct their efforts rather than share in them. Eventually the Romans overcome the difficult terrain and their stubborn and ferocious enemies. The First Dacian War ends with the formal surrender of Decebalus and the Dacians, kneeling or standing as suppliants before the emperor, who sits on a tribunal surrounded by the massed standards of his praetorian guard. Then Trajan stands on this or another tribunal to address his parading soldiers. Trophies and the goddess Victory mark the end of the conflict.

The peace was to prove temporary. Decebalus agreed to the loss of some territory, gave up his siege engines and engineers, handed over Roman deserters and promised not to recruit any more of these. In most respects the war had ended in an entirely satisfactory way for the Romans, with their enemy reduced to the status of a subordinate ally, and Trajan was justified in taking the honorary title Dacicus. Yet in the following years Decebalus broke most of the terms, beginning to rebuild his army and strengthen his power, occupying some of the lands of the Iazyges, a Sarmatian people, without seeking Roman approval for this expansion. The king was clearly not behaving in an appropriate manner for a Roman ally and war, which was threatened in 104, was openly renewed in 105 when the Dacians began to attack some

Roman garrisons. The commander of the most important garrison, Cnaeus Pompeius Longinus – a former *legatus Augusti* who may still have been holding this rank – was treacherously imprisoned during negotiation. However, Decebalus' attempts to use him as a hostage came to nothing when the Roman managed to obtain poison and committed suicide. At some point the Dacian also enlisted a group of deserters to assassinate the emperor, but this plan also failed.[14]

Trajan was in Italy when the Second Dacian War erupted, and the Column's narrative begins with his voyage across the Adriatic to be greeted by local dignitaries and the wider population. Two scenes of sacrifice follow. Even greater forces seem to have been mustered for the Second War. Trajan raised two new legions which were named after him, *II Traiana Fortis* and *XXX Ulpia Victrix*, both of which probably served in the Second War, although it is unclear whether they took part in the First. In the conventional Roman way the emperor combined force with vigorous diplomatic activity in AD 105, accepting the surrender of individual Dacian chieftains who abandoned their king, and negotiating with ambassadors from all neighbouring peoples. Decebalus appears to have had far fewer allies as a result. Even so the Column shows a heavy attack against some auxiliary outposts, which held out until relieved by a force led by Trajan himself.

The main Roman offensive may not have been launched until 106, and most probably followed a different route to the earlier campaign. It began with another sacrifice on the bank of the Danube, before the army crossed the river at Dobreta. This time they did so not on a temporary bridge of boats, but on a monumental arched bridge, built in stone and timber and supported by twenty piers each 150 feet high, 160 feet in width and 170 feet apart. It was designed by Apollodorus of Damascus – who would later plan Trajan's Forum complex and presumably had much to do with the construction of the Column – and built by the soldiers. A roadway was cut into the cliffs of the Danube to permit easier approach to the bridge. Dio's account describes this feat of engineering in loving detail strongly reminiscent of Caesar's account of his bridge across the Rhine. It was a great and magnificent victory for Roman engineering, in its way as admirable to the Romans as any feat of arms. The Column provides a detailed, if stylized depiction of the bridge as the background to the scene of sacrifice.[15]

After this Trajan joins the army – the soldiers are shown cheering him enthusiastically, much as Velleius described the legionaries welcoming Tiberius – takes part in another *suovetaurilia* purification ceremony, with the ritual processions walking round the camp, and then addresses legionaries and praetorians at a parade. At a *consilium*, Trajan briefs and discusses the campaign with his senior officers. The usual preliminaries over, the army advances, harvesting grain from the fields to supplement their supplies. The Column suggests some fighting, though not perhaps as much as in the First War, and Dio tells the story of an auxiliary cavalryman who, discovering that his wounds were mortal, left the camp to rejoin the battle and died after performing spectacular feats of heroism. The culmination of the campaign was the siege of Sarmizegethusa Regia, the religious and political centre of the Dacian kingdom set high in the Carpathians. After a stiff resistance, and it seems an unsuccessful Roman assault, the defenders despaired and set fire to the town before taking poison. The war was not quite over, but its issue was no longer in doubt as the Romans pursued the remaining Dacians. Decebalus was eventually cornered by a group of Roman cavalry scouts, but slit his own throat rather than be taken alive.

The leader of the Roman patrol was a certain Tiberius Claudius Maximus, who had joined the army as a legionary before becoming a junior officer in the *auxilia*. On the Column he is depicted reaching out to Decebalus, and by chance his tombstone has survived, carrying an inscription describing his career and giving another version of the scene. Decebalus was beheaded and the head taken back to Trajan, who ordered it to be paraded before the army. The war was over, and victory was completed by the discovery of the king's treasure, buried in a river bed, after much labour by Roman prisoners.[16]

A new province was created, guarded by two legions supported by auxiliaries and with its main centre at the newly founded colony of Sarmizegethusa Ulpia – a grand city built on fertile land at the foot of the Carpathians, unlike Decebalus' mountain fastness. Settlers came from many parts of the Empire, but especially the eastern provinces, and Roman Dacia soon prospered. The fate of the Dacians, whether they were completely expelled or simply absorbed in the more normal way, has been the subject of fierce debate in recent centuries, most especially amongst the Romanians – contemporary politics has had a major influence on whether they believe their ancestors to be Romans or Dacians.

EMPERORS ON CAMPAIGN

A massive programme of propaganda, of which the Forum complex was only a part, celebrated the victory in Dacia. Had Trajan simply wanted military glory to confirm his position as emperor, it is unlikely that he would have sought other opportunities for aggressive warfare. His rule was as popular as that of any emperor, and subsequent generations preserved his memory as the *Optimus Princeps*, the best of emperors, only rivalled in prestige by Augustus himself. His relations with the Senate – always the most critical factor in determining a ruler's treatment in our literary sources – were generally very good, his rule considered both just and successful. Even Trajan's vices – he was prone to infatuations with boys and youths – were pardoned, since his behaviour never reached a stage which Romans considered excessive or made him vicious. His decision to launch an invasion of Parthia in AD 114 was, according to Dio, motivated by a desire to win renown.

Trajan had spent more of his life with the army than most Roman aristocrats, and certainly appears to have enjoyed the military life. The pretext for war was, once again, a dispute over the relationship of the Armenian king to Rome, for a new monarch had been presented with his diadem of authority by the Parthian ruler and not by a Roman representative. The peace with Parthia had always been uneasy, since for the Romans their eastern neighbour represented a deeply unsatisfactory thing – the former enemy who had not been reduced to subordinate status and remained fully independent and strong. Trajan appears to have planned to win a permanent victory, for his campaign was from the beginning far more than simply a struggle to show dominance over Armenia. Massive Roman and allied forces – some seventeen of the thirty legions went in their entirety or as a substantial vexillation to the war – were backed by huge quantities of supplies which had been massed in the east for several years in preparation for the conflict. At the back of his mind the emperor was eager to emulate the great conquests of Alexander in the very region through which the Macedonian king had passed centuries before. The culture of the Roman Empire was firmly Greco-Roman and the heroes of the Hellenic world every bit as worthy of emulation as earlier generations of Romans.[17]

Trajan's eastern war began well, as in successive years he overran Armenia, Mesopotamia and most of Parthia itself. The Parthian capital of Ctesiphon and the major city of Seleucia were both captured, after which Trajan sailed down the Tigris to reach the Persian Gulf. If Trajan had any plans to follow further in the footsteps of Alexander – and it seems unlikely that he did – these were then dashed when major rebellions erupted throughout his newly acquired territories in AD 116. Roman columns had to operate throughout the new provinces, putting down insurrection. Matters were made worse by a major rebellion by the Jewish communities in Egypt and other provinces – though not Judaea itself – which required substantial numbers of troops to defeat. Trajan himself began a siege of the desert city of Hatra in Arabia. During the siege, when his own guard cavalry took part in at least one of the assaults, Trajan himself was almost struck by a missile as he rode past the walls. Dio notes that the emperor was not wearing any symbols of rank, hoping not to stand out amongst the other officers, but his age – he was now 60 – and grey hair made his seniority clear. He was missed, but a cavalryman riding beside him was killed. Hatra withstood the Roman onslaught until Trajan's men, desperately short of water and other provisions, withdrew. The emperor was planning fresh operations when he suffered a stroke and died soon afterwards.[18]

Trajan was succeeded by his relation Hadrian, but there was considerable doubt over whether in fact he had formally nominated him before he died. Thus, at the beginning of his reign, Hadrian's position was somewhat insecure, making him reluctant to spend several years away from Rome fulfilling his predecessor's eastern ambitions. This, combined perhaps with a feeling that Rome's military resources were overstretched, led to the abandonment of the territories taken from the Parthians. Another casualty was Trajan's great bridge across the Danube, which was partially demolished to prevent its ever being taken and used by an enemy. There were to be no wars of conquest during Hadrian's reign from AD 117 to 138, and in most cases the wars which developed in response to rebellion or attack were fought by the emperor's legates without his on-the-spot supervision. Lacking Trajan's aggressive ambitions, Hadrian nevertheless spent much of his reign touring the provinces and in particular visiting and inspecting the army. Dio noted that he 'subjected the legions to the strictest discipline, so that, though strong, they were neither insubordinate or intolerant'.[19] A cult of *Disciplina* – one of a number of Roman deities personifying virtues – flourished in the army at this time, especially with the troops in Britain and Africa, and may well have been encouraged by Hadrian himself. Even when the army was not at war, the emperor could still conform to the ideal of the good general by ensuring that the troops were well trained and ready to fight if necessary. According to Dio:

> He personally viewed and investigated absolutely everything, not merely the usual appurtenances of camps, such as weapons, engines, trenches, ramparts and palisades, but also the private affairs of the men serving in the ranks and of the officers themselves – their lives, their quarters and their habits – and he reformed and corrected in many cases practices and arrangements for living

that had become too luxurious. He drilled the men for every kind of battle, honouring some and reproving others, and he taught them all what should be done. And in order that they should be benefited by observing him, he everywhere led a vigorous life and either walked or rode on horseback on all occasions ... He covered his head neither in hot weather nor in cold, but alike amid German snows and under scorching Egyptian suns he went about with his head bare. In fine, both by his example and his precepts he so trained and disciplined the whole military force throughout the entire empire that even to-day [i.e. a century later] the methods introduced by him are the soldiers' law of campaigning.[20]

Hadrian watched the troops on exercise, just as a commander did in battle, praising and rewarding skill and criticizing and punishing poor performance. An inscription set up by an auxiliary soldier named Soranus survives, recording – albeit in rather poor Latin verse – an incident when the emperor commended his skill as an archer.[21] Much fuller inscriptions found at Lambaesis in North Africa include selections from a number of speeches delivered at a parade of the provincial army as a culmination to a series of rigorous exercises. Hadrian's style is very direct, referring to *Legio III Augusta* as 'his' legion and its commander as 'his' legate. He shows a detailed knowledge of the legion's recent history, noting that it was seriously under strength through having detached a cohort for service in a neighbouring province. He also mentions that it had subsequently sent a cohort, strengthened by men drawn from the rest of the unit, to reinforce another legion. Stating that under such conditions it would have been understandable if *III Augusta* had failed to meet his high standards, he reinforces his praise by declaring that they had no need of any excuse. The centurions, especially the senior grades, are singled out for specific praise. Both in this section of the speech and in those parts delivered to individual auxiliary units, the emperor repeatedly pays tribute to the diligence of the legate Quintus Fabius Catullinus. His address to the cavalry element of a mixed cohort (*cohors equitata*) gives a good indication of the style of these speeches:

It is difficult for the cavalry of a cohort to put on a pleasing display anyway, and especially difficult not to displease after an exercise performed by an *ala*; the latter fills a greater expanse of plain, has more riders to throw javelins, makes frequent wheels to the right and performs the Cantabrian ride in close formation, and, in keeping with their higher pay, has superior horses and finer equipment. However, you have overcome these disadvantages by doing everything you have done energetically, in spite of the hot temperature; added to this, you have shot stones from slings and fought with javelins and everywhere mounted quickly. The special care taken by my legate Catullinus is very obvious…

Some criticism is contained in the speeches, for instance when a cavalry unit is reprimanded for pursuing too quickly and falling into disorder which would have made them vulnerable to a counter-attack. Yet overall Hadrian sought to encourage his soldiers and make them feel that they and their units were valued and respected. Apart from the specific details there is little that would seem out of place in a similar address by a modern general or manager.[22]

Hadrian's successor Antoninus Pius was not a military man, and spent no time on campaign. It was a mark of the security of the time that he was content to trust his legates to fight the major conflicts of the time. These were all in response to problems on the frontiers. From the late first century AD the military bases on the fringes of the Roman Empire had taken on more and more of an air of permanence, with old timber fortifications and internal buildings being replaced by stone. Hadrian had taken the process further in his visits to the provinces, ordering the construction of new installations and frontier boundaries. In Northern Britain the army laboured to construct the Wall which bears his name and stretched for 80 Roman miles from coast to coast. Such barriers were only ever intended to restrict outsiders, and never to hinder the movements of the Roman army, instead providing them with secure bases from which to launch aggressive operations. Rome sought to dominate its neighbours, not merely to repel any invasion or raid on the provinces, but attempts at permanent occupation of new territory were rare.

CHAPTER 14

A CAESAR ON CAMPAIGN: JULIAN IN GAUL, AD 356-60

Julian the Apostate (AD 332–363)

And if it becomes necessary to engage the enemy, take your post staunchly amongst the standard-bearers, wait carefully for the right time to inspire your men with an act of boldness, inspire the fighters by example without being rash, support them with reinforcements when they are under pressure, modestly rebuke the lazy, and be present as a true witness to the deeds of both brave men and cowards. Therefore, urged on by the gravity of the situation, go as a brave man to lead other brave men.

Constantius' advice to Julian following his appointment as Caesar in AD 355.[1]

EXPANSION UNDER TRAJAN WAS FOLLOWED BY RETRENCHMENT AND THE reorganization of the frontiers under Hadrian and Antoninus Pius. When Pius died in AD 161 his successor Marcus Aurelius inherited a war with Parthia. Problems on the Danubian frontier also meant that Marcus spent much of the last decade of his reign on campaign, and he may even have been planning to create new provinces east of the Danube just before his death in 180. Although the second century AD witnessed a number of major conflicts, it was in general a time of great prosperity, when the Roman Empire in many respects reached its zenith. In the eighteenth century Edward Gibbon would see the years between AD 96 and 180 as the 'period in the history of the world during which the condition of the human race was most happy and prosperous'. For him Rome's decline began with the reign of Marcus' son, the brutal Commodus, which broke the recent precedent of an emperor choosing an able senator to adopt as his heir rather than looking to blood relations.

Certainly, Commodus' murder produced an outbreak of civil war surpassing in scale even the 'Year of Four Emperors' which followed Nero's suicide. The eventual winner, Septimius Severus, spent much of his reign fighting rivals or waging war against the Parthians and subsequently against the Caledonian tribes of northern Britain. Severus died in York, advising his two sons who succeeded him to 'look after the soldiers and despise everyone else'.[2] Within a few months the elder son, Caracalla, had murdered his brother and assumed sole power.

Caracalla enjoyed the military life and liked to be seen dressed in an ordinary soldier's uniform and using a hand-mill to grind his grain ration into flour just as the legionaries did.[3] Yet such gestures did not prevent his being stabbed to death by a cavalryman from his own guard as he crouched behind a bush to relieve himself on his way to fight another war with Parthia. After Caracalla emperors came and went with alarming frequency, most being murdered or executed by rivals, and a few dying in battle with foreign enemies. Civil wars were common, and as the Roman army wasted its strength fighting against itself, defeats on the frontiers became more and more frequent. Occasionally a strong emperor was able to maintain a measure of stability for a few years, perhaps even an entire decade, before upheaval and chaos returned.

While it is extremely difficult to describe in detail any of the wars of the second century AD, the sources for the campaigns of the third century make this task altogether impossible. Certainly they do not allow us to scrutinize the generalship of any of the army's commanders with any certainty, although the few anecdotes which are preserved suggest that their behaviour had much in common with that in earlier centuries. Against this measure of continuity, the relationship between the general and the state changed profoundly during this period, as the old tradition of relying on senators to provide the army's commanders ended. The relationship between the *princeps* and his senatorial legates had always been uneasy, for such men were always potential rivals. Marcus Aurelius promoted a number of equestrian officers to high command, though usually only after admitting them into the Senate. Such men were often virtually professional soldiers, spending many years in successive commands rather than interspersing military with civil posts in the traditional way. Whether this made them markedly more competent than the mass of senatorial officers is impossible to know, but they were clearly seen as more loyal, since their elevation depended entirely on imperial favour. Severus encouraged the trend when he placed equestrian prefects rather than senatorial legates in command of the three new legions – *I, II* and *III Parthica* – which he formed during his reign. In the third century equestrians replaced senators in all senior military posts and only a handful of senators saw any military service at all.

Although the growing reliance on equestrian officers was mainly motivated by successive emperors' fear of their own troops being turned against them by ambitious subordinates, in the long term the result was in fact to make such usurpation much easier. Marcus Aurelius spent almost half his reign with the army, as did Septimius Severus. Those seeking the emperor's patronage were forced to go to him, so that over time a good deal of the imperial court's activity came to take place in the headquarters of whichever army the emperor was with. Rome steadily diminished in importance as rulers spent less and less time there. The importance of the Senate also declined, both because the emperor rarely visited it and because its members were losing their prestigious military role. By the close of the third century, the Senate was politically irrelevant, and the city of Rome itself retained little more than symbolic significance. The focus of political activity was now with the army, which openly provided emperors with their only security. A man only remained in power for as long as he retained the loyalty of sufficient troops to defeat the forces of any rival. Whereas in the past a man seeking to make himself emperor had needed to win the support – however grudging – of the majority of the Senate, now he required the acquiescence of the army's senior officers, virtually all of whom were equestrians. Increasingly these men found leaders from amongst their own number and raised them to the purple. Failure to bestow sufficient rewards and favours on the faction of officers who had made them emperor led only to a ruler's swift murder and replacement by another. Becoming emperor was a lot easier than it had been under the early Principate, but remaining in power was considerably more difficult. Since newly created emperors were expected to shower honours and promotions on the leaders of the army which had backed their claim, men serving in other provinces gained little benefit from their elevation. As a result they often proved eager to seek from their own number a suitable candidate for the throne and back his claim in battle, eager to share the benefits of his victory.

It was extremely difficult for one man to retain the loyalty of the army throughout the empire, and the situation was made worse by the disappearance from the army's command structure of a rank equivalent in authority to the old provincial legates. Under the Principate there was a gradual reduction in the number of legions stationed in a single province. Under Augustus a number of provinces permanently contained four legions, but by the late first century it was rare to have even three legions under the same command. In the second century the same trend continued, so that for instance the three-legion province of Britain was divided into two. As emperors became less and less secure, they proved increasingly reluctant to entrust command of an army numbering some 20,000 or more men to any potential rival. By the fourth century most of the old provinces had been divided into five or six regions with only comparatively small garrisons. Even then, civil and military power was split between different officials, which often made the organization of supply for a field force difficult.

Such a system coped well enough with border skirmishing, but was utterly inadequate when faced with a major raid or invasion. If something on such a comparatively large scale occurred, then the emperor had either to go in person to deal with the problem or to send a senior subordinate with suffi-cient troops, running the risk that the latter would use his command to make a bid for power. Distrustful of their own senior officers, most third- and fourth-century emperors spent a great deal of their reigns on campaign, performing duties which in the past had fallen to provincial governors. Since a man could only deal with one problem at a time, it became increasingly common for emperors to share power with a colleague. This had first occurred when Marcus Aurelius appointed Lucius Verus, his brother by adoption, as his co-ruler or Caesar. It was Verus who presided over the war with Parthia, although, in spite of some extremely sycophantic histories painting him in heroic mode, it is unlikely that he played a very active role in the campaign.[4]

In the late third century Diocletian created a system known as the Tetrarchy, where the Empire was divided into an eastern and western section, each controlled by a senior emperor, known as the *Augustus*, aided by a junior partner or *Caesar*. A statue showing the four men, standing in a group and each resting one arm on the shoulder of a fellow emperor, symbolized the ideal of co-operative rule. In its purest form the Tetrarchic system barely outlived Diocletian himself, but the principle of multiple emperors remained the norm, save for occasional periods when one man, most notably Constantine the Great, was able to take all power back into his own hands and rule alone. Regions felt neglected if an emperor failed to pay sufficient atten-tion to their problems. Such discontent often prompted the troops stationed there to appoint a new emperor who would better meet their needs.[5]

JULIAN'S APPOINTMENT AS *CAESAR* IN GAUL, AD 355

When Constantine died in 337, having ruled for thirteen years as sole emperor, imperial power was divided between his three sons, Constantine II, Constantius and Constans, but it was not long before these began to fight amongst themselves. By 350 only Constantius survived, and much of the western empire had been seized by the usurper Magnentius. The latter was not finally defeated for another three years. The Empire had once again been united under a single *Augustus*, but Constantius had swiftly discovered the need for at least one assistant to aid him in his task. Most of Constantine's extended family had been killed in the power struggles after his death, leaving only the two sons of his half-brother Julius Constantius. In 351 the older of this pair, Gallus, was appointed *Caesar* and given the task of supervising the eastern provinces while Constantius dealt with Magnentius.

Within a year of the suppression of the usurper, Gallus himself was executed by an *Augustus* who had grown to mistrust both the judgement and the ambitions of his *Caesar*. Yet Constantius could still only be in one place at a time, and the disruption caused by civil war had encouraged a number of problems to break out on the frontier. The *Augustus* sent Silvanus, the Master of Infantry (*Magister Peditum*, a term which did not imply any particular association with foot soldiers more than horsemen and simply denoted a senior general) to restore the situation in Gaul, which had suffered badly with barbarian raids and some settlement. However, the risk inherent in trusting anyone with an independent command was soon demonstrated when this man was proclaimed as *Augustus* by his army. The danger of a new civil war was averted when one of Constantius' officers bribed some disaffected soldiers to murder Silvanus. The problems in Gaul remained, and the *Augustus* decided to send Gallus' brother Julian to deal with them, deciding that a relative might be marginally more trustworthy than anyone else. To enhance the bond further, Julian married Constantius' sister Helena.

Julian was proclaimed *Caesar* in Gaul on 6 November AD 355 at a formal parade of the army, the soldiers showing their approval by banging their shields against their knees. Such a ceremony openly demonstrated the trans-ferral of political power to the military. The new *Caesar* was 23 and had never held any public position or spent time with the army. Like Gallus until his elevation to power, Julian had spent his early years in comfortable imprisonment, engaging enthusiastically in academic study at Nicomedia and subsequently Athens, where he was heavily influenced by mystical Neoplatonism. Constantine the Great had made Christianity the official religion of the Empire, although he had not actively suppressed the majority of pagan cults, and his family were also Christians. Encouraged by his deep dislike for Constantius – a feeling only reinforced by the execution of Gallus – the student's rebellion took a religious path. Publicly Julian followed the new faith, but he secretly embraced paganism, a decision described by Christians as his apostasy. Later he claimed that the Sun God appeared to him in a dream instructing him in the formation of a new cult which he would seek unsuccessfully to introduce. Both in his own writings and in other accounts Julian comes across as a clever man, but one lacking much understanding of the views and feelings of others, especially of those with a less academic outlook. As a general he was to prove competent, if uninspired, and his inclusion here owes more to the relative wealth of material concerning his campaigns in comparison to any other fourth-century general than to any great genius.[6]

Constantius had deliberately hidden the scale of the problem in Gaul from his junior colleague until the latter was on his way to the region. Most serious of all was the news that Colonia Agrippinensis (Cologne) had been overrun by the Franks, but there had also been widespread raiding by another group of tribes, the Alamanni. Neither of these peoples were known in the early Principate and it has often been suggested that the smaller Germanic tribes faced by Caesar and Germanicus coalesced in the second and third centuries AD to form more united and coherent tribal confederations which presented a far more dangerous threat to the Roman frontier than their predecessors. Yet a more detailed examination of the military and political organization of the Germanic peoples in the fourth century suggests that little or nothing had actually changed. Divided into tribes and clans each with their own chieftains, they had very little political unity or sense of common purpose, and the power of kings and leaders proved as transitory as ever. Whether the tribes long known to the Romans had simply changed their names or been supplanted by other peoples is unclear, but the problem presented to the Roman army by these warlike tribes remained the same, as in general were the methods used in any effort to solve it.

Whenever the Romans were perceived to be vulnerable, then there would be raids into the provinces. If these succeeded and went unpunished, then more raids would occur on an increasingly large scale, perhaps eventually prompting full-scale invasions to seize and occupy land. In the years before Julian's appointment as *Caesar* the frontier along the Rhine and Upper Danube had been stripped of many of its garrisons as men were drawn off to fight in the civil wars. Roman weakness was confirmed when barbarian raiders were able to penetrate deep into the settled provinces and come back with plunder and glory. Such successes prompted more and larger attacks, and as no emperor or senior subordinate came to the region with sufficient force and authority to wage full-scale war, these only became more common. Rome was seen to be weak, and the various Germanic war leaders exploited this situation. Julian's task was not simply to restore some order to the frontier defences, but to instil once again a fear of Roman might in the peoples across the Rhine.

The resources with which he was to deal with the situation were by no means lavish. Under Diocletian and Constantine the overall number of men serving in the army appears to have increased significantly, and yet at the same time the size of individual field armies grew smaller. In Julian's day the Roman army was divided into two basic sections, the *limetani* who garrisoned and patrolled the frontiers and the *comitatenses* or field armies. The *comitatenses* have sometimes been seen as mobile reserve, but their origins lay more in successive emperors' desire for protection against internal rivals than in the threat of foreign enemies. Within the army the size of individual units had shrunk, so that the legion of some 5,000 men was no more than a distant memory and most seem to have numbered around 1,000–1,200 men. Auxiliary infantry units were similar in size or perhaps smaller, and cavalry probably somewhere near the 500 mark. Each regiment was commanded by an officer variously known as tribune, prefect or *praepositus*. On campaign many units would be smaller than this. Most units in the field armies were brigaded together in pairs, but this was the highest level of organization and no larger subdivisions within an army were considered necessary. The army of the fourth century was geared towards warfare on a relatively small scale, an impression which Julian's operations in Gaul confirm.

Service in the ranks of the army was compulsory for the sons of soldiers, and in general conditions appear often to have been worse than in the early Principate. Considerable numbers of recruits came from barbarian tribes, including many men from outside the Empire, and it has often been suggested that this barbarization of the army led to a decline in military efficiency. However, the Romans had a long tradition of making successful use of foreign soldiers, and it is hard to find many examples of 'barbarian' soldiers proving any less loyal or effective than troops recruited from the provinces. What is certainly true is that the trend towards recruiting troops locally, already visible in the first and second centuries, had become even more pronounced and that soldiers often displayed a particular loyalty to the region in which they were stationed.[7]

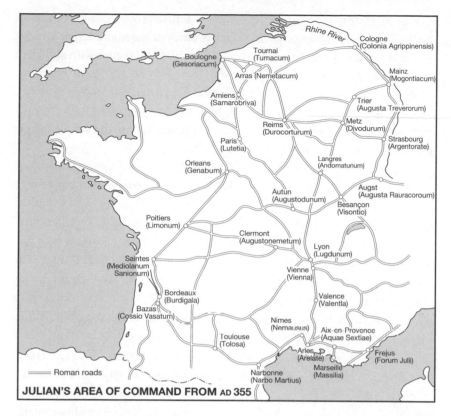

Rhine River

Cologne
(Colonia Agrippinensis)

Boulogne
(Gesoriacum)

Tournai
(Turnacum)

Arras (Nemetacum)

Mainz
(Mogontiacum)

Amiens
(Samarobriva)

Trier
(Augusta Treverorum)

Reims
(Durocorturum)

Metz
(Divodurum)

Paris
(Lutetia)

Strasbourg
(Argentorate)

Orleans
(Genabum)

Langres
(Andomatunum)

Augst
(Augusta Rauracoroum)

Autun
(Augustodunum)

Besançon
(Visontio)

Poitiers
(Limonum)

Clermont
(Augustonemetum)

Lyon
(Lugdunum)

Saintes
(Mediolanum
Sanionum)

Vienne
(Vienna)

Bordeaux
(Burdigala)

Valence
(Valentla)

Bazas
(Cossio Vasatum)

Nimes
(Nemausus)

Aix-en-Provence
(Aquae Sextiae)

Toulouse
(Tolosa)

Arles
(Arelate)

Frejus
(Forum Julii)

Narbonne
(Narbo Martius)

Marseille
(Massilia)

===== Roman roads

JULIAN'S AREA OF COMMAND FROM AD 355

THE FIRST CAMPAIGN, AD 356

By the time Julian reached Gaul it was too late in the year to take the field and he spent the winter at Vienne, gathering intelligence and dealing with administrative matters. In June a report arrived informing him that Augustodunum (Autun) was under attack by a group of Alamanni. Tribal armies lacked skill in siegecraft and had a poor record in taking fortified positions, but in this case the walls were in a state of neglect and only the spirited defence by a group of retired veterans had repulsed them. The Alamanni had instead settled down to a loose blockade of the town, while most of the warriors dispersed to raid the surrounding area. Julian moved immediately to its relief and arrived there on 24 June having encountered no serious opposition.

Summoning his senior officers to a *consilium* to decide how to attack and punish the barbarians, he asked those with local knowledge about the main routes which would lead him eventually to the main town of the Remi (modern-day Rheims), where he had ordered his field army to concentrate and provisions sufficient to feed them for a month to be gathered. Dismissing several alternatives, Julian chose to follow a direct route through heavily wooded country, disdaining the risk of ambush primarily because he was told that the usurper Silvanus had successfully employed the same road. With him he had only a unit of cataphracts – the first such unit of heavy cavalry had been raised by Hadrian, but they later became relatively common, especially in the armies of the eastern provinces – and a regiment of *ballistarii*, who were probably artillerymen, but may just possibly have been equipped with an early type of crossbow. It was not a force especially suited to skirmishing, but at first the Romans did not encounter any raiders and managed to get through the most dangerous stretch of the road without any fighting. As the journey went on, they were attacked by small groups of Alamanni but managed to drive these off, although without inflicting much loss as the cataphracts with their armoured horses were not suited to rapid pursuit. A clear indication of the nervousness of the local population in the face of such widespread raiding was given when the small force reached Tricasa (Troyes) and found the town's gate closed to them. Only after a long and rather undignified debate were the *Caesar* and his men admitted. Following a brief rest, Julian pushed on and joined the main army.

Another *consilium* was held to discuss the situation. Present were Marcellus, the *Magister Equitum* (another title for senior officer in the fourth-century army), and his predecessor Ursicinus, the man responsible for arranging the assassination of Silvanus and who had been ordered to remain till the end of the year to provide additional advice for the young *Caesar*. It was decided to launch an immediate punitive attack on the nearest groups of Alamanni. The attack went in the next day, but under cover of a thick mist the Germans dodged round the Roman column of march and attacked the two legions forming its rearguard. Their battle cries brought some auxiliary units to their aid before they were overwhelmed, but this unexpected near defeat had a deep impact on Julian. The historian Ammianus Marcellinus, at that time an officer on Ursicinus' staff and quite probably with the column, says that it made him 'prudent and cautious' (*providus et cunctator*), which he considered to be amongst the highest virtues of a great commander. The Romans moved against a number of towns taken and sacked by the enemy, although in each case after their success the Germans had dispersed to plunder the surrounding area. Outside Brotomagum (Brumath) a war band stood up to the Romans and Julian fought his first significant action, although it was probably little more than a skirmish. He deployed his troops with both wings advanced, so that it resembled a crescent, and enveloped the Germans. Most seem to have fled before the trap was closed and only a minority were killed or captured. Yet the small victory was enough to overawe the other raiding bands and restore some semblance of order to the area.[8]

Julian then moved north and reoccupied Colonia Agrippinensis. The presence of the Roman army seems to have been enough to persuade the nearest Frankish kings to cease marauding expeditions for the moment and to accept the peace terms imposed by Julian. It was now near the end of the campaigning season and most of the Roman field army dispersed to winter billets. Food may well have been running short and Ammianus mentions that the *Caesar* was especially concerned with arranging for an adequate food supply for the next year's campaigning. Years of raiding and disturbances had disrupted the agriculture of the area and stripped the land bare of many sources of food and fodder. Another major problem was the need to re-establish a proper system of frontier garrisons to deter future incursions. Julian decided to spend the winter at Senonae (Sens). Some deserters went over to the Franks at this point. It is not clear whether these soldiers were Germanic and sympathized with the enemy or whether their desertion was prompted by something else. When Ammianus gives a reason for a soldier deserting it is usually the fear of punishment.

Whatever their motives, the deserters informed the tribes that the *Caesar* had relatively few troops with him. A force of Alamanni promptly attacked Senonae, but were thwarted by the walls which the Romans had hastily repaired. Julian had too few men to sally out and fight in the open, and after a month-long blockade the Germans withdrew, complaining that they had been foolish even to contemplate besieging a town. If surprise or treachery failed to get them within a city's walls, a tribal army would most often run out of food and have to disperse before the defenders were forced to surrender. In the third and fourth centuries many communities which had not felt the need of fortifications in the early Principate acquired walls. Simultaneously the army was putting far more effort into constructing strong ramparts and projecting towers around its bases. Defence was a much higher priority than it had been in earlier centuries.[9]

THE CAMPAIGN AND BATTLE OF ARGENTORATUM (STRASBOURG), AD 357

During the siege of Senonae, Marcellus had conspicuously failed to march to the relief of his commander. Near the end of winter he was replaced by the highly experienced Severus. Ursicinus was also recalled and soon sent to the eastern frontier where war was brewing with Persia. However, as a clear indication of the priority now given to Gaul Constantius had sent from Italy a force of 25,000 men under the command of the *Magister Peditum* Barbatio. The Roman plan was to launch a major offensive against the Alamanni, Julian attacking from the north and Barbatio from the south. Indirect pressure would also be put on the Alamanni by the *Augustus'* own operations from Raetia on the Upper Danube.

Organizing such a major operation took time, and early in the spring a raiding force from one of the Alamannic tribes evaded the Roman troop concentrations and attacked Lugdunum (Lyons). Once again the barbarians were thwarted by the city's fortifications, but they wandered freely around the surrounding lands, burning and looting. Julian responded quickly by forming a force of three cavalry regiments and sending them to cover the three main routes which the raiders were most likely to follow on their return journey. Marauding groups were always more vulnerable as they withdrew, encumbered with their plunder and often overconfident because of their initial success. There were many occasions throughout Roman history when raiders were surprised and massacred as they carelessly carried off their spoils. Often most of the warriors were drunk, and Ammianus recounts one occasion when an entire party were ambushed as they bathed or dyed their hair red in a river.[10]

At first the Roman operation was successful, mopping up with ease any parties of warriors who followed the roads. Only those Germans who abandoned their plunder and took to the wooded country managed to get past the cavalry. However, Barbatio, whose camp was much nearer than Julian's, made no move to support the three cavalry regiments, and in fact one of his officers explicitly ordered these troops not to guard the main road open to the retreating barbarians. In the aftermath of this failure, two of the cavalry tribunes were dismissed – although one reappears shortly afterwards in another command and the second eventually became emperor, so the passage may be mistaken – from the army when blame was falsely placed upon them. It was not a promising start to a campaign which required close co-operation between Julian and Barbatio.

As the main offensive began and the columns advanced against the Alamannic communities which had settled on the west bank of the Rhine, the Romans found that the enemy had in most cases retreated, many to the islands in the river. Progress was slow because the barbarians had constructed numerous barricades of felled trees blocking the main roads and paths, and each of these had to be cleared before the Roman baggage train was able to pass. Julian decided that it was important to attack the Germans hiding on the islands and requested that Barbatio loan him seven of the river barges which he had gathered to be used in the construction of a bridge. The *Magister Peditum* not only refused, but actually ordered the burning of the boats in question. Then, or soon afterwards, he also destroyed a significant part of the grain gathered by Julian to support the army. Ammianus, who describes these incidents, obviously disliked Barbatio almost as much as he admired Julian, but there is no good reason to reject incidents of this sort.

Rome's leaders had always been fiercely competitive, but in late antiquity this competition was bound by fewer constraints than at any other period, including the civil wars of the first century BC. Careers lacked the formal structure and limits of the old *cursus honorum*, and it was possible to reach supreme power either by a sudden leap or by small stages. Since anyone able to win the support of sufficient troops could become emperor, anyone thought capable of this was assumed to harbour such ambitions. Silvanus had probably been a reluctant usurper, but was effectively forced into this bid for power since he was believed to be plotting against the *Augustus* and would most likely have been executed even if he had continued to obey orders. Family connections were no security against suspicion and virtually from the moment of his appointment, Julian had been the target of a whispering campaign designed to throw doubt over his loyalty in the mind of Constantius. Many men rose to power and influence at court by plotting the demise of their superiors, though most in turn fell prey to the machinations of other ambitious men. There was little real security for the leaders of the Late Roman army and state.

Thwarted by Barbatio, Julian was fortunate to capture some German scouts, who revealed under interrogation that the river could be forded in summer. The tribune Bainobaudes, commanding a regiment of auxiliaries called the Cornuti (or 'horned ones', perhaps a reference to a shield device or crest), was ordered to launch a surprise attack. The men are described as light infantry, which probably means that they laid aside the body armour and helmets normally worn in battle for this specific operation. The soldiers were able to wade through the shallower parts of the river and swam through deeper sections, using their shields as floats, and reached an island before the Alamanni were aware of them. In a sudden, vicious attack, the auxiliaries fell upon the Germans and slaughtered all they could find, women, children and the old along with the warriors. This was a raid with murder as the objective, for its purpose was to instil a sense of horror in the other tribes. The context of the operation would anyway have made it difficult to secure captives and take them back to the army. Capturing some boats, the auxiliaries rowed to several other islands, massacring the occupants in the same manner. They then returned to the west bank of the Rhine without suffering any casualties, although most of the moveable plunder they had taken was lost when a boat was swamped. Realizing that the islands were vulnerable, the Alamanni fled to the eastern shore to escape the reach of Rome. Julian busied himself restoring or rebuilding the garrison posts along the river. It was harvest time, and the Romans took the opportunity to gather in the produce of the fields cultivated by the Germans, finding in this way sufficient provisions to stock the granaries of the forts as well as to supply the field army for twenty days.[11]

The Alamanni had suffered a reverse, but a single raid, however appalling its local consequences, was certainly not enough to convince the tribes that Rome had suddenly become invincible once more after years of weakness. A large force of warriors crossed into Gaul and surprised Barbatio's army, routing them and capturing most of their baggage, camp followers and transport animals. Ammianus may have exaggerated the scale of the reverse, but certainly Barbatio was to play no significant part in the remainder of that year's campaigning. Instead he travelled to Constantius' court to intrigue against Julian. A few years later his intrigues would lead to his own execution when the *Augustus* came to believe that he harboured imperial ambitions.

The *Caesar* had more immediate problems on his hands, for seven Alamannic kings had joined together under the overall leadership of two of their number, Chnodomarius and his nephew Serapio, to muster one of the largest tribal armies recorded in the fourth century. Ammianus sets their overall numbers at 35,000 men, led by the kings along with ten royal princes and a large number of other chieftains. As always, it is difficult to know how accurate such a figure is, and whether the Romans or even the Alamanni themselves ever knew precisely how large the force was.

The bulk of the army consisted of those warriors able to equip themselves for battle and fighting in bands with their kinsmen and fellow clansmen. The hard core of the force was provided by the *comites*, the semi-professional fighters attached to the households of the leaders. Chnodomarius is said to have 200 of these well-equipped and highly motivated warriors in his household, but it seems unlikely that any of the less prestigious leaders had so many followers. Tribal armies normally took some time to gather since the individual warriors turned up as their mood dictated, and this force was no exception. Only part of the army was across the Rhine when Julian camped some 21 miles away. The German leaders were accurately informed by a deserter that Julian had little more than 13,000 men at his disposal – probably some 3,000 horse and 10,000 foot – and their numerical advantage, which was probably significant whatever the precise size of their own army, added greatly to their confidence. Further encouragement had been provided by their easy defeat of Barbatio's troops and the knowledge that these were too far away to support the other Roman force.

After advancing to the area around Argentoratum (Strasbourg), they sent envoys to the *Caesar*, instructing him to leave the lands which they had taken by the sword, with the implication that a refusal would mean facing their great host in battle. The Alamanni were treating the Romans just as they would any Germanic tribe whose land they had seized. Such gestures were typical of many of the tribal societies encountered by the Romans throughout the centuries. Julian delayed giving a response to the ambassadors until his troops had completed their current task of repairing an old frontier fort, and then prepared for battle. He was also eager to wait until a large part of the Alamanni had gathered on the west bank of the Rhine, since the defeat of only a small advance guard was unlikely to achieve much in the long term, but he wished to avoid facing their entire strength. This consideration makes it even more difficult to estimate just how many German warriors there were at the subsequent battle.[12]

Julian led his army out of camp at dawn and advanced in a well-ordered column towards the enemy. The infantry were in the centre, flanked by cavalry, which included not just the cataphracts but some horse archers as well as the more conventionally armed horsemen. The entire army was screened by small parties of scouts, probably drawn mainly from the cavalry. By noon they were nearing the enemy, and Julian was inclined to halt and build another camp, allowing the men to rest before giving battle on the following day. When he explained this plan to the soldiers, it provoked a howl of disapproval, the men banging their spear shafts against their shields – a gesture Ammianus says always signified protest, unlike the acclamation of banging shields against knees. Men yelled out begging him to take them against the enemy immediately, declaring that with such a fortunate general they were bound to win. The army's officers were equally keen to fight, arguing that it was better to confront and defeat the Alamanni altogether, rather than have to chase down individual groups if their great army dispersed. Finally a standard-bearer stepped out of the ranks and called on the 'most fortunate of all *Caesars*' to lead them to victory. The army resumed its advance.[13]

Roman commanders were often somewhat theatrical in their dealings with their men, but this incident suggests a very different relationship between general and troops to that in earlier periods. It is just possible that Julian always planned to fight that day, and simply feigned reluctance in front of his enthusiastic soldiers so that their keenness would help them to forget the fatigue of a long march in the heat of late summer. Yet Ammianus certainly does not suggest that this was the case, and such a deception would have been thought entirely praiseworthy in a general and so most certainly not something to suppress. One of the worst things a commander could do was to risk a battle against his better judgement. Caesar would certainly not have chosen to depict himself as being dissuaded by his subordinates from following any planned course of action. The standard-bearer who called out to Julian at first seems similar to centurions and soldiers who are shown addressing Caesar in the *Commentaries*, but it is important to note that the latter were never trying to convince their commander of anything apart from their courage and devotion to him. It is difficult to avoid the conclusion that the soldiers of the fourth century were all too aware of their capacity to dispose of any general and replace him with an alternative of their own choosing, and as a result felt very free to express their opinion.

The Romans pressed on and came to a low ridge not far from the bank of the Rhine. Three German cavalry scouts were seen galloping off to give warning of their approach and a warrior on foot was taken prisoner. He informed the Romans that the Alamanni had been crossing the river for the last three days. Soon their war bands became visible forming a battle line in the distance. Each group was formed in a *cuneus*, a word which most readily translates as 'wedge' and may have meant a vaguely triangular formation – probably caused by the minority of most enthusiastic warriors surging ahead of the remainder – or perhaps simply a narrow but deep column. Ammianus tells us elsewhere that the soldiers' nickname for the *cuneus* was the 'swine's head' (*caput porci*).[14] On their right was an area of broken, marshy ground which included a derelict aqueduct or canal. Probably because of this unsuitable country on their left, the Romans massed all their cavalry on their right wing, apart from 200 men who formed Julian's personal escort. The Alamanni responded by concentrating all of their horsemen opposite their Roman counterparts. It is unclear just how many cavalry the Germans had, but they may well have been relatively few in number and were generally more lightly equipped than their opponents, especially than the cataphracts. The Alamanni followed the tactic encountered by Caesar and described by Tacitus of supporting the horse with groups of agile young warriors on foot. Chnodomarius – who is described as an heroic, indeed almost Homeric figure by Ammianus

– commanded the left of the German army, while Serapio led the right.[15]

As the Romans advanced towards the enemy line, Severus who was in command of the left wing grew suspicious of an ambush from the cover facing him and halted. With their left flank refused, the rest of the Roman army marshalled itself before continuing the advance. The infantry seem to have been deployed in at least two lines. Julian rode around the units addressing each in turn, for Ammianus tells us that it was impossible to be heard by the entire force once it was deployed in battle order (and also notes that a formal speech to an entire army was anyway the preserve of the *Augustus*). Some men he urged on to fight valiantly, but others he begged to restrain their enthusiasm and not surge forward without orders. In the main he repeated the same words to each of the units he rode past. During this long lull, Ammianus tells us that the German infantry sent up a great shout, suggesting that the kings and princes ought to leave the cavalry and dismount to fight with them. It was a sentiment similar to that which had once banned Roman dictators from riding so that they would stay with the phalanx. Chnodomarius was the first to dismount and join them in a gesture reminiscent of Caesar's encounter with the Helvetii in 58 BC or Agricola at Mons Graupius in AD 84. The other leaders quickly followed his example.[16]

As both sides sounded their trumpets the two armies closed into missile range and began to hurl javelins at each other. Then the Germans charged, screaming their battle cry. They closed first with the Roman cavalry and the combat swayed back and forth for some time. Then, while the Roman cataphracts were resting and re-forming, their commander was wounded. At almost the same moment the mount of another man collapsed from fatigue, combined with the weight of the rider and its own armour. These minor events triggered a sudden panic as the entire unit fled. In the confusion most of the rest of the Roman cavalry joined in the rout, some of them streaming towards the Roman infantry. It was a dangerous moment, for if the foot had become infected with the panic the entire flank of the army might have dissolved. In the event the infantry's discipline held firm and they kept their formation as the mass of horsemen bore down on them. Julian had seen the danger and galloped with his bodyguard to rally the fleeing troops, his position marked by his purple *draco* standard, a bronze animal head with an open mouth and something resembling a windsock streaming behind it. It was a type of standard copied from the Danubian peoples in the second century AD and is depicted on Trajan's Column waving over the heads of Dacians and other barbarians.

The sight of his commander shamed one of the cavalry tribunes into stopping and gathering some of his men around him. Ammianus compared Julian's action to an occasion when Sulla stopped his fleeing men by telling them to go and declare that they had left their general fighting alone in Asia. Yet it was very difficult to reassert control over fleeing troops, as even Caesar had found at Dyrrachium. Some cavalrymen formed up again around Julian, and others rallied in the shelter of the heavy infantry, but it seems more than likely that many left the battlefield altogether. Those left may have been shaken, and there is no mention of the cavalry playing much part in the rest of the action. However, nor is there any suggestion that the Alamannic horse were able to threaten the flanks of the Roman infantry, so it is possible that sufficient cavalry had rallied to hold these in check.[17]

All along the main line a fierce combat raged, the air full of showers of javelins and arrows as time after time groups surged into contact and fought hand to hand. In the Roman front line was a brigade of auxiliaries, consisting of the Cornuti and their sister unit the Bracchiati. Ammianus describes these soldiers raising the traditional Germanic battle cry, the *barritus*, which began with a low murmur and gradually built up to a crescendo. Whether these auxiliaries acted in this way because they were themselves German or simply because long years of campaigning against these tribes had taught them that German warriors found this gesture especially intimidating is impossible to say. Soon afterwards two more auxiliary units, the Batavi and the Regni, were fed into the fighting line, presumably on the orders of Julian or one of his senior officers. For a while things stabilized, until a group of the most determined German warriors led by several of their kings in person charged into contact, causing the other war bands to surge forward. Some of the Roman troops gave way, and the barbarians burst through the first line and ran on to attack the troops in reserve.

The main force of this attack fell on the Primani legion in the centre of the second line. These soldiers held firm and gradually began to force the Alamanni back. For a while the German warriors continued to fight with great determination, until their losses grew too heavy and their spirit suddenly collapsed. The whole tribal host gave way and dissolved into flight, their Roman opponents eagerly pursuing them and striking at their backs. As the Alamanni found their escape hindered by the river, Julian became worried that his men might suffer losses by too eagerly following the enemy into the water, and he and his officers galloped around restraining the advancing Romans on the bank of the river. The Romans hurled javelins or shot arrows at the figures trying to swim away. In the initial confusion Chnodomarius managed to slip away, but he was soon found and captured while hiding in a small grove.[18]

Julian had won a major victory in his first substantial battle. As his army withdrew to a hastily laid out camp with makeshift ramparts formed from rows of shields, they found that they lost 243 men and four tribunes killed. Ammianus does not mention how many wounded there were in addition to this. It is claimed that 6,000 corpses of the enemy were counted on the field, and that many others must have died in the pursuit or drowned in the Rhine. As the Roman army celebrated its victory the soldiers began to hail Julian as *Augustus*, prompting the *Caesar* to an immediate rebuke and a public oath declaring that he had no ambitions beyond his current status. There were plenty of courtiers willing to feed Constantius' suspicion of his subordinate, but the *Augustus* was also happy to take personal credit for the defeat of the Alamanni in his official announcement. He is even supposed to have claimed to have been present at the battle, directing the army in person, and that at the end of it the captured Chnodomarius was brought before him instead of to Julian.[19]

In Gaul the *Caesar* was determined to exploit his victory to the full by crossing the Rhine and ravaging the territory of the Alamanni. There was at first some resistance to this from the troops, who felt that the campaign was complete, forcing Julian to persuade them in a speech. Bridging the Rhine, he led a column on a punitive expedition. The Alamanni vacillated in their mood, first seeking peace and then resolving to fight for their homeland, and a tribal army began to mass on the high ground facing the Romans. During the night Julian embarked 800 men in a fleet of small boats and sent them 2.5 miles further up the river, where they disembarked and began raiding and burning the nearest villages. Attack at this unexpected point was enough to draw off the warriors from the heights. The Germans again lost heart, and the Romans met no opposition as they advanced, gathering up the locals' cattle, harvesting their crops, and putting any buildings to the torch.

After 10 miles they came to an area of forest, where a deserter had informed Julian that many warriors were waiting to ambush the invaders. For a while the Romans pressed on, until they saw the main paths blocked with barricades of felled trees – a sure sign that the Germans planned to harass them if they went further. It was now early autumn and the weather was turning cold, so that Julian decided to withdraw rather than risk fighting in unsuitable conditions for only the most modest of potential gains. Instead he moved to the nearby site of a derelict fort originally built by Trajan. The soldiers laboured to restore its fortifications and a garrison was installed and provisioned. This sign that the Romans planned a more permanent presence in their land finally prompted the Alamanni to seek peace, which Julian granted at first for ten months to the three kings who appeared before him.[20]

Fighting seemed over for the year, but as the Roman army made its way back to winter billets one column commanded by Severus unexpectedly encountered some Frankish warriors who were raiding the Roman province. It was later discovered that there were some 600 of these marauders who had concluded that Julian's preoccupation with the Alamanni would prevent him from properly defending other sections of the frontier. Therefore, instead of returning to their homes after a season's raiding, they had decided to establish their base in two abandoned Roman forts and continue their activities throughout the winter months. For fifty-four days in December and January Julian, the *Caesar* in Gaul and second only in status to the emperor Constantius, besieged these Franks until they finally surrendered. To prevent the Germans from escaping across the freezing river, he set up a system whereby soldiers in small boats regularly broke up the ice. This did not prevent news reaching some of their fellow tribesmen, who formed a small army to come to the raiders' relief, but these turned back when they discovered that the surrender had occurred. This operation was carried out competently enough and ended successfully, but the involvement of even a junior emperor in such a small-scale affair is symptomatic of the lower level at which Rome's rulers operated in late antiquity. Throughout his time in Gaul, almost everything Julian did would have been the normal task of a proconsul or propraetor under the Republic, or an imperial legate under the Principate.[21]

MORE OPERATIONS, AD 358–9

Julian spent the remainder of the winter in Lutetia (Paris), dealing with administrative and financial matters. The defeat of the Alamanni had been only partial, and the Romans were aware that most of their tribes and clans were determined to gain vengeance for Argentoratum. Julian had given orders for grain to be gathered to supply the army, but knew that this would not become available until July. The Germans were equally aware of the situation and thus did not expect any major Roman activity before this time. Trusting that they had made this assumption, Julian decided to take the field straight away, feeding his troops with hard-tack biscuit (*bucellatum*) baked from the grain stores of the army's bases. This was a gamble, for if it proved impossible to replenish the fort's granaries then these strongholds, which were normally virtually impregnable to siege, might easily succumb to starvation. When the army moved out, each soldier was provided with a bread ration in this form for twenty days.[22]

Julian's first targets were the Salii, a Frankish people who had settled within the Roman province at Toxiandra, roughly in the area of modern-day Flanders. Before the campaign was under way a deputation arrived from these people, who seem to have been unaware of his intentions. The Frankish ambassadors wanted to be permitted to retain the land they had taken, promising that they would not raid or harass the nearby provincial communities. Julian gave them a deliberately unclear response and followed the envoys' departure with a rapid attack. The Salii were taken completely by surprise and rapidly surrendered, allowing him to impose terms of his own choosing. Following this initial success, the Romans moved against another Germanic people, the Chamavi, who had similarly settled within the province. This time there was some fighting, but the resistance was swiftly overcome and the Germans ordered back to their original home beyond the Rhine.

These victories had come swiftly, and Julian decided that more permanent security could be re-established in the area by repairing and reoccupying three forts along the line of the River Meuse. Garrisons could be provided from the units under his command, but it was more difficult to secure sufficient food to fill the forts' granaries. The army still had seventeen days' worth of biscuit, and Julian ordered them to hand over much of this to the garrisons. This produced uproar, the soldiers once again feeling very free to express disapproval of the general's decision, deriding him as an 'Asiatic' or 'little Greek' in reference to his upbringing. There were still several weeks to go before the harvest would be ripe and most were nervous of campaigning without sufficient food. Ammianus seems to have had considerable sympathy with the soldiers, noting that they were not demanding extra pay or donatives, in spite of the fact that they had not received even their regular salary let alone any bonuses since Julian took command. Constantius had not wanted to give his *Caesar* sufficient funds to win too much loyalty from the army in Gaul.[23]

Ammianus does not tell us specifically what happened after this protest, other than that it was eventually quelled with gentle words, but it is more than possible that the commander backed down. Julian had other problems as well. Severus, his formerly reliable subordinate, was in poor health and would die soon. In his last campaign during 358 he became almost morbidly cautious, so that the column under his command achieved very little. Diplomacy managed to win over one of the most powerful kings of the Alamanni. Another was forced to submit after a punitive expedition laid waste a swathe of his territory. The Romans were guided by a warrior captured by two tribunes sent by Julian explicitly to provide him with a prisoner. At first the marching column was hindered by the familiar barricades blocking the paths, but eventually they were able to penetrate a region the Alamanni had considered safe, prompting the king's capitulation. By this time it was nearing the end of the summer and the Roman army dispersed to its winter billets once more. Julian once again busied himself with administration.[24]

The next year's campaigning again began with a surprise attack on sections of the Alamanni who had refused to submit. In preparation a German-speaking tribune named Hariobaudes had been sent, ostensibly on a diplomatic mission, to gather intelligence about the various leaders' intentions. In addition Julian had secured large amounts of grain from Britain, sufficient both to feed his field army and also to fill the granaries in the forts and the walled towns he intended to restore to a state of defence. Seven of the latter were reoccupied, even the auxiliaries – who usually disdained such tasks as beneath warriors – labouring cheerfully alongside the other troops. Acting on intelligence provided by Hariobaudes, Julian then crossed the Rhine and attacked the Alamanni, most of whom fled, allowing their crops to be burnt or confiscated. By the end of the year virtually all of the Alamannic leaders had submitted. Yet the peace remained tentative, liable to be broken as soon as the Germans once again began to believe that the Romans were weak. When in the winter of 359–60 much of northern Britain was overrun by the Picts and Scots, Julian felt it unwise to risk going to deal with the problem himself. Instead he sent Severus' successor, Lupicinus, with four units of auxiliaries, to restore the situation across the Channel. The size of this force is another indication of the generally small scale of so much of the military activity in the fourth century.[25]

JULIAN AS *AUGUSTUS*, AD 360–363

While Julian was campaigning along the Rhine frontier, Constantius had been fighting on the Danube, but had found his attention being drawn ever more pressingly to the Empire's eastern frontier. In 359 a dispute with Persia – in the third century the Sassanid dynasty of ethnic Persians had overthrown the Arsacid Parthian monarchy – which had long been looming, finally erupted into open war. From the beginning things went badly for the Romans. Needing men, Constantius commanded his *Caesar* to send him four entire auxiliary regiments – the Celtae, Petulantes, Batavi and Heruli

– along with a draft of 300 men from each of his other units. There were rumours that the *Augustus* was almost as concerned to clip the wings of his successful junior colleague as to reinforce the army intended to meet the Persians.

Julian was perplexed by the order. His men were enraged and once again mutinied, refusing to be sent away from their families and relatives, especially as these would be left effectively at the mercy of the Alamanni. Once again they proclaimed Julian as *Augustus*, and this time he accepted, although Ammianus maintains that this was only because he was unable to persuade the soldiers to obey orders and allow him to request that Constantius rescind the order. The 28-year-old was raised on a shield held at shoulder height by some soldiers – the first recorded occasion when a Roman emperor was acclaimed in the traditional Germanic manner of appointing a chieftain. A torque worn around the neck as an award for valour was given by a standard-bearer to provide the new *Augustus* with a diadem. ('This was an improvement on the initial suggestions of one of his wife's necklaces or, still less auspicious, part of a horse's decorative harness.) As he was being paraded through the camp in this way, the 'reluctant' new *Augustus* promised each of the soldiers a substantial bounty in silver and gold for supporting him. Even Ammianus believed that Julian had no real expectation that Constantius would accept him as an equal and share the rule of the Empire.[26]

Rome was once again faced with civil war, but in this case there was comparatively little fighting since Constantius died of natural causes early in 361. The Empire once again had a single master, but his popularity proved fleeting. No longer feeling constrained to feign adherence to the Church, Julian openly professed paganism, alienating the Christians who were by this stage a numerous and powerful group. Even some pagans felt that the decree forbidding Christians to lecture or teach was unfair. Other measures upset groups such as the largely pagan aristocracies of the great eastern cities on whose support he might otherwise have relied. Whatever Julian's intentions, his decisions as emperor betrayed a lack of good sense.

The same could be said of the major expedition which he launched against Persia in 363. For this he mustered an army of some 83,000 men, including a large part of the troops from Gaul who had willingly followed their own *Augustus* to the east, in spite of their earlier reluctance to serve under Constantius. It was the largest Roman army employed against a foreign opponent during the fourth century and it was able to drive deep into enemy territory, defeating all the forces it encountered. Yet Julian failed to force the Persians into a decisive battle and soon faced the inevitable problems of supplying so large a number of men over such great distances. From the beginning of the campaign at least a quarter of his soldiers were occupied in manning and towing the fleet of river boats carrying supplies along the Euphrates.

Julian's behaviour at times suggested a conscious emulation of earlier Roman commanders. Having read that Scipio Aemilianus, Polybius, and a small group of soldiers had cut their way through an enemy-held gateway at Carthage, Julian tried to copy the exploit at the siege of Pirisabora, but he and his party were driven back. Ammianus excused this failure of his hero by explaining that the circumstances in which the original feat had been performed were different. During a reconnaissance of another stronghold at Maozamalcha, Julian and his officers were ambushed by ten Persians, two of whom recognized the emperor from his conspicuous uniform and charged at him. The *Augustus* killed one with his sword, while his body-guards dealt with the other. After Maozamalcha had fallen, Julian publicly emulated Alexander the Great and Scipio Africanus by not harming, or even looking at, a number of extremely beautiful noblewomen who had been captured. Literature had always reinforced the aristocratic ideal of how a great Roman general should behave, but there is a strong sense that Julian came to let a desire to equal great historical commanders dictate too much of his behaviour.[27]

The Romans reached Ctesiphon, having cleared a canal constructed by Trajan and also used by Septimius Severus to bring the supply fleet from the Euphrates to the Tigris. Yet once there, Julian and his officers decided that they were not in a position to take it and so began a withdrawal. Against the advice of his officers, the *Augustus* ordered the transport fleet to be burnt, and instructed the army to march away from the river to retreat through land which the rival armies had not yet traversed. The sight provoked uproar amongst the soldiers, but an order cancelling the original instruction arrived too late to prevent its implementation. In the event it proved easy in the early days of the march to find sufficient fresh water, food and fodder from the lands the Romans were passing through. Soon, however, the Persians reacted and began burning the crops ahead of the enemy column. Julian was given additional cause to regret his rash orders, when he realized belatedly that the destruction of the boats made it impossible for the army to construct a bridge of boats allowing him to cross the Tigris once more and put the river between him and the Persians.

The supply situation now becoming desperate, the army marched on, fighting a number of vicious skirmishes at night with the pursuing Persians.

In one of these Julian galloped out to try to direct the fighting, not even having time to don his armour. He was struck by a javelin which lodged in his side, and fell from his horse. No one was quite sure who had thrown the missile, although Libanius records a rumour that the thrower was Roman, a Christian soldier incensed by Julian's promotion of paganism. The wound proved mortal, and the *Augustus* died in his tent shortly afterwards, his replacement quickly being selected by the army's officers from amongst their own number. With the army in such a precarious position, there was little option save to conclude an ignominious peace with Persia.[28]

In Gaul Julian had proved himself to be a reasonably competent commander in spite of his lack of any military experience before his appointment as *Caesar*. As we have seen, the sort of problems he faced were of the kind routinely dealt with by the provincial governors of earlier periods. By the fourth century only an emperor wielded comparable authority and had the capacity to concentrate sufficient resources to defeat anything more than a few minor barbarian incursions. Julian did something to restore the security of the frontier along the Rhine, although in subsequent years this would prove impossible to maintain without a similarly active military presence in the area. He won a number of successes and suffered no serious defeats, but there is nothing in these campaigns to suggest exceptional talent on his part. Some of his decisions were questionable, and he certainly lacked Scipio's or Julius Caesar's talent for judging the mood of his men.

In the Persian campaign the sheer scale of the operation and the problems inherent in operating deep into enemy territory rather than in a friendly province hugely magnified the consequences of his mistakes and failure to understand his soldiers. Exceptionally large Roman armies did not have a very good record – Cannae and Arausio being the two most famous and disastrous examples – and it seems that forces larger than 40,000 or so men were extremely difficult for a general to control effectively. By the fourth century, when unit sizes had shrunk and the army was geared primarily to warfare at a much lower level, an army of 83,000 men was extremely clumsy. No one, from Julian down, had any experience of handling and supplying such a force. This, combined with the same problems which had helped to prevent Trajan's and Severus' campaigns in the east from producing a permanent defeat of the Parthians, eventually resulted in a humiliating failure. Julian's career is interesting not because of his personal ability as a commander, but for providing a good indication of the circumstances in which Roman generals of the Late Empire performed their task.

CHAPTER 15

ONE OF THE LAST:
BELISARIUS AND THE PERSIANS

Belisarius (AD 505–565)

Belisarius therefore addressed those of his officers who were about him thus: 'It is not my wish to disclose to all what I am thinking. For talk carried about through a camp cannot keep secrets … But seeing that the majority of you are allowing yourselves to act in a most disorderly manner, and that each one wishes to be himself supreme commander in the war, I shall now say among you things about which one ought to keep silence, mentioning, however, first that when many in an army follow independent judgements it is impossible that anything needful be done.'[1]

IN THE FOURTH AND EARLY FIFTH CENTURIES AD THE ROMAN ARMY RETAINED the potential to become a highly effective fighting force. Pitched battles were rarer than they had been during the Principate, for commanders now preferred to defeat an enemy by stealth and manoeuvre without risking such an encounter. Yet when the Romans did choose to fight a battle, they usually won, and at their best Roman armies proved markedly superior to all their opponents, in spite of a few spectacular defeats such as Adrianople in AD 378. The impact of this defeat, where the emperor of the east was killed along with many of his soldiers, has often been exaggerated, and it certainly did not sound the death knell of the army. Military efficiency had always been based on thorough training, and on keeping the troops well motivated, disciplined and properly equipped. At all periods there were occasions when these factors did not apply and the result was often defeat. Maintaining an army in good condition required huge resources of manpower, material and most of all money, as well as the political capacity and will to apply these. This was the essential problem in late antiquity, for while the Romans remained fully aware of how to make the army effective, the circumstances were only rarely conducive to achieving this in practice. Frequent civil wars left emperors weak and insecure, while adding to the economic decline which may in any case have been under way from the late second century. Much of the infrastructure which supported the army – roads, fortified bases supply lines – decayed simply because there was neither the money nor determination from central authority to maintain them. The army was still large and formidable, but it was rarely able to perform at its best and on average its units were of lower quality than those of the earlier professional army.

From the third century onwards Rome was in decline, continued instability nibbling at central government so that a good deal of power came to be dispersed amongst local leaders and it was hard to get anything done at a higher level. Internal weakness resulted in more frequent defeats on the frontiers, which sometimes led to further civil war as emperors were killed or discredited by failure, and some regions decided that the solution to the problem posed by external foes was to create their own emperor. Very gradually Rome's strength grew less, but the sheer size and power of the empire was so great that even by the end of the fourth century she remained much stronger than any of her foreign enemies. The threat posed by the latter was anyway uncoordinated and sporadic, but stretches of frontier perceived to be vulnerable soon became targets for attack.

The presence of an emperor to conduct warfare in a region could, as Julian showed, restore some temporary security, but even when there was more than one emperor these men could not be everywhere simultaneously. Their task was to plug the gaps and hope that these would remain secure for long enough for them to deal with problems elsewhere. If it had been granted a long period of stability without the disruption of internal conflict, then the Empire might still have recovered, but the changed basis of imperial power ensured that this could not happen. Rome declined very slowly and gradually, so that even the final collapse of the western section of the Empire cannot easily be associated with a single cataclysm. Rome itself was sacked by Goths in AD 410, but these Germanic warriors and their leaders were part of the Roman army and the context was more one of civil war than of foreign invasion. The last western emperor, Romulus Augustulus, was deposed in 476, but most of his predecessors had lacked real power and the event itself had little impact on the lives of the wider population. During the fifth century the Empire's western provinces went their own way, like Britain, or were overrun and made into kingdoms by Germanic warlords, many of whom had at some time been in Roman service. In this way groups of Visigoths, Ostrogoths, Franks and Vandals took Spain, Gaul, Italy, Sicily and North Africa.

As the western empire fell to pieces, the eastern section, with its capital at Constantinople and territory embracing the Balkans, Greece, Asia Minor, Egypt and Syria, endured. In many ways it was a more coherent unit than the wider empire had become, and it had more secure natural boundaries to the north. It was a region which a single emperor could effectively rule and, although sometimes these men chose to appoint a co-ruler, the eastern Roman Empire (usually by modern convention referred to as the Byzantine Empire) came once again to possess the political stability which had so long been lacking. By the sixth century it had become rare for an emperor to go on campaign in person, and their willingness to let others command their armies was an indication of greater personal security. Generals' activities were closely watched for any sign of disloyalty, but in most respects the relationship between emperor and field commander had returned to something closer to the conditions of the Principate. Eastern emperors were able to conduct active warfare in more than one theatre simultaneously in a way that had rarely been possible for centuries.

The military resources available had diminished, but were still considerable. In terms of territory the eastern empire was roughly equivalent to its greatest rival, Sassanid Persia, although the Romans – for that was how the Byzantines thought of themselves – were probably wealthier and had a bigger population. The diminished size of their realm to some extent altered Roman emperors' attitude towards the outside world, and there was certainly a tendency to address the Persian king as an equal, or even 'brother'. This was in marked contrast to the diplomacy of earlier centuries, which had always sought to emphasize Rome's vast superiority over other nations. Yet at least some eastern emperors continued to nurse an ambition of a revival of the empire's former power, and during the reign of Justinian (AD 527–65) a concerted attempt was made to reconquer the lost territories around the western Mediterranean. North Africa, Sicily and Italy were all retaken in a series of campaigns, although the gains would prove to be short-lived. One of the most prominent commanders throughout these operations was Belisarius, a man who received his first experience as a general in the wars on the eastern frontier.[2]

BELISARIUS AND THE BATTLE OF DARA, AD 530

Belisarius was one of Justinian's *doryphoroi*, a section of his military house-hold who lived at his expense and were groomed to serve as officers. He was of German extraction, from one of the Danubian provinces, but in cultural terms this probably meant very little. However, he was far more of a professional soldier than the senatorial aristocrats of earlier times, or the academic Julian. In 526 Belisarius and another of the *doryphoroi*, Sittas, were placed in charge of a force sent to raid a region of the Sassanid Empire known as Persarmenia. At first things went well, and the Romans gathered consid-erable plunder, but it was not long before they were confronted by superior Persian forces and defeated. This operation was part of the sporadic hostil-ity along the frontier in the decades following a period of full-scale war between the two powers in 502–6. Then hostilities had opened when the Persian king Kavadh (Cabades in the Roman sources), in need of money and denied a loan or gift by the emperor Anastasius, had launched a sudden plundering expedition into the Roman provinces with a view to making a quick profit. In the end negotiations led to the declaration of seven years' peace, probably accompanied by Roman payments and restrictions against either side's building new fortifications along the border.

The peace proved uneasy, tension increasing still further when in the early 520s Kavadh began to impose the Persian Zoroastrian religion on his Iberian subjects – a move perhaps prompted more by politics than convic-tion, fearing a defection to Rome. The Iberians appealed as fellow Christians for Roman support. Each side was also encouraging its allies to attack the other. A further complication arose when the ageing Kavadh, disliking his oldest son Kaoses, attempted to ensure that he was succeeded by the younger Khusro. Persian ambassadors came to Justinian's uncle, the emperor Justin, asking that he adopt Khusro and so commit himself to ensuring that he suc-ceeded his father. Justin and Justinian were at first elated, until they began to suspect that Kavadh's real aim was to give his son a claim to the Roman throne. Their counter-proposal, a limited adoption of the kind commonly employed for barbarian royalty which would make such a succession impos-sible, was taken as an insult by the Persians. The Romans' fears, like the original proposal itself, reflected the very different relationship between the two powers which prevailed by the sixth century.[3]

Tension continued to grow until a renewal of open warfare seemed inevitable. Campaigns in this area were dominated by the fortresses which allowed the control of the surrounding area. Battles were rare, most of the fighting consisting of raids like the one led by Belisarius, and strongholds provided secure bases from which these could be launched. In 505 the Romans had begun construction of a new fortress at Dara, some 15 miles away from Persian-held Nisibis. Its existence was resented by the Persians after peace had been declared, especially as the Romans gradually increased the forces stationed there. Other moves to construct new frontier strongholds or to concentrate troops near the border were seen as equally provocative. Sometimes, as when the Romans occupied two forts on the Iberian border in about 527, the Persian reaction was enough to force their evacuation. In 528 Belisarius was tasked with building a fort at Minduos, a place which cannot be precisely identified but was evidently not far from Nisibis. This position also proved untenable in the face of a strong enemy reaction, but it may be that this operation was in any case intended to distract the Persians from an ongoing programme of strengthening Dara.

Belisarius' early operations had both ended in failure, but his perceived ability and loyalty ensured that when Justinian became sole emperor on Justin's death in 527 he was granted increasingly senior posts. In 530 he was appointed commander – his title was Master of Soldiers for the East (*Magister Militum per Orientem*) – of one of the five field armies then in existence. With him came his senior clerk (*accessor*) Procopius, who would later write a detailed account of Belisarius' campaigns in his *Wars*. Although 529 had been spent in peace negotiations, Justinian had also been preparing for open war and the newly appointed Belisarius had some 25,000 men concentrated at his base at Dara, a very large army for this period. It is unclear what proportion of this force consisted of cavalry, although it may have been as much as a third. The infantry seem to have been of questionable quality, in part perhaps because the raid-dominated warfare on the eastern frontier gave them far fewer opportunities for seeing active service than their mounted counterparts. Their experience was more often of garrison life and policing duties rather than actual combat.

Throughout his career Belisarius was to rely heavily on his cavalry, rarely trusting units of foot soldiers to fight in any but the most favourable circumstances. At Dara his mounted troops included 1,200 Huns, fighting in their traditional manner as horse archers, and 300 Heruli, a Danubian people who had a particular reputation for ferocity. All of these troops were to prove highly effective in the coming fighting. Another element within the cavalry consisted of Belisarius' own household troops or *bucellarii*. These men lived at their commander's expense, hence their name derived from the military issue hard-tack biscuit, but were bound by an oath of loyalty to the emperor.

It is unclear how many of these men Belisarius had at Dara, although in later years he would have a force of around 1,000 men following him on campaign. They were heavy cavalry, the rider – though probably not the horse – armoured, and equipped with both a spear or two-handed lance and a composite bow. Belisarius' *bucellarii* were especially well trained, even by the standards of such picked troops.[4]

In June an even bigger Persian army advanced against the Romans, the main thrust of a three-pronged attack which was being mounted by Kavadh. It numbered some 40,000 men and was under the command of a man named Peroz or Firuz (Perozes in Greek) who was a member of the Mihran house, an aristocratic family which produced so many Persian commanders that the Romans had come to believe that 'Mihran' was an actual rank. Like the Roman army, its strength lay in its mounted troops for most of the Persian infantry were poorly equipped and badly motivated levies, in most circumstances even less effective than their enemy counterparts. Before the main part of the battle Peroz was reinforced by 10,000 men from the garrison of Nisibis, but these do not appear to have been markedly better troops. The Persian cavalry was almost entirely heavy, consisting of cataphracts with both horse and man heavily armoured. They were armed with bows and generally showed a preference for fighting at a distance, but were also willing to close and fight hand to hand when necessary. Peroz also had the Immortals, named after the royal bodyguard of the king of kings in the days before Alexander had shattered the Persian Empire, as an élite cavalry reserve. It is unclear whether all 10,000 of these men were with the army.[5]

Procopius tells us that the Persians were supremely confident as their army advanced to camp just a few miles from the Roman position. Not only did they significantly outnumber their opponents, but they were buoyed up with the knowledge that they had beaten the Romans in all major engagements fought over recent decades. Peroz sent an envoy ahead instructing Belisarius to have a bath prepared for him in Dara for the following night. Yet in fact he and his subordinate commanders had been shocked by their first sight of the Roman army, for Belisarius had carefully prepared for battle. He had chosen a position no more than a few hundred yards in front of the main gateway in the circuit walls of Dara. With a hill on their left the Roman troops had strengthened their main position with a trench. In the centre there was a straight ditch, at each end of which another ditch ran back at 90 degrees to connect with other straight trenches running parallel with the first. A few crossing places were left in each section, for it would be easier for the Romans to make use of these than for the Persians to find their way

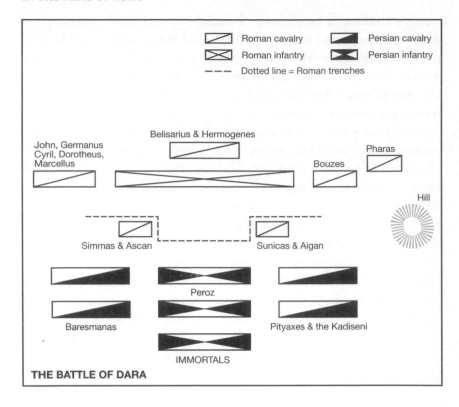

Roman cavalry
Roman infantry
Persian cavalry
Persian infantry
— — — Dotted line = Roman trenches

John, Germanus
Cyril, Dorotheus,
Marcellus

Belisarius & Hermogenes

Bouzes

Pharas

Hill

Simmas & Ascan

Sunicas & Aigan

Peroz

Baresmanas

Pityaxes & the Kadiseni

IMMORTALS

THE BATTLE OF DARA

across in the heat and confusion of battle. Behind the trenches Belisarius formed a line consisting of all of his infantry and probably a small number of cavalry. In reserve was a line entirely composed of cavalry. In front of the ditch, in the angle next to the connecting trenches, were two units each of 600 Huns. Those on the left were led by Sunicas and Aigan, while the group on the right was under the command of Simmas and Ascan. All four of these men were themselves Huns, and also members of Belisarius' household *doryphoroi*. The remainder of the Roman cavalry was divided between the two wings. On the left these were led by Bouzes and Pharas who commanded the Heruli. Five commanders are given for the horse on the right wing, namely John son of Nicetas, Cyril, Marcellus, Germanus and Dorotheus.

The Roman formation was geared to receiving a frontal attack and, with the walls of Dara so close behind them, such an attack was the only viable option open to Peroz if he wished to take the city. No siege could begin until the enemy army had been defeated. Roman soldiers were seen as undisciplined by the Persians, yet the trenches would prevent the bulk of the enemy from being lured forward into open country where Peroz could overwhelm them with his superior numbers. Earlier Roman armies had made use of fieldworks to protect a position – both Sulla and Julius Caesar had on occasion protected their flanks with trenches, ramparts and forts – but there is no real parallel to Belisarius' decision to protect almost his entire frontage in this way. In earlier conflicts such a move would have deterred most enemy commanders from attacking at all, but Peroz had few alternatives. He had been ordered by Kavadh to take Dara and had been given over half of the total number of troops dispatched against Rome to permit him to achieve this. Therefore he would encourage his men before the battle by telling them that the Romans' trenches were an indication of their deep fear of the Persians.[6]

On the first day Peroz was not willing to risk a major attack and for hours the two armies stood facing each other without any aggressive move on either side. Late in the afternoon a group of Persian cavalry advanced alone against the Roman left wing. The most forward Roman squadron pulled back, feigning panic, and managed to lure the Persians into a careless pursuit before turning on them. Seven Persians were killed and the rest fled back to their main lines. This Roman success was a little surprising, for Persian cavalry were normally thought to be too well disciplined to fall for such a ploy. It may be an indication that much of the army was contemptuous of its Roman opponents and so less careful in its manner of fighting. After this there were no more attacks, but a young Persian warrior rode forward and offered to fight any Roman in single combat. Procopius tells us that the challenge was answered by one of the household of Bouzes, a certain Andreas, who was not a soldier but a wrestling instructor and bath attendant of his master. Even so, he was evidently armed and equipped like a cavalryman and in close attendance on Bouzes. Andreas killed the first challenger with disdainful ease and followed this success by defeating a second, more experienced warrior who came forward soon afterwards. His victory produced a great cheer from the ranks of the Roman army. It was late in the day and the Persians soon began to withdraw. As night fell, the Romans marched back to their billets in Dara, cheerfully singing songs of victory.[7]

The next day was spent in an exchange of messages, the Romans trying to persuade the Persians to withdraw and being accused of faithlessness by Peroz, who would later order their letters to him to be fixed to his standard. It was on this day that Peroz received the reinforcement of 10,000 men from Nisibis. Negotiations having failed, on the following morning both commanders addressed their men in the clear expectation that a battle would occur. Belisarius is supposed to have stressed how badly equipped and poorly motivated the enemy foot soldiers were. Both armies deployed, the Persians in two main lines with the infantry in the centre and the cavalry on the wings. Peroz kept the Immortals in reserve, with orders not to move forward until he gave them a signal. He himself took station with the foot in the centre, but it does not seem that these were expected to launch a serious attack and their role was more to pin down the Roman infantry by their presence and to provide shelter behind which the Persian cavalry could rally. The left wing, which included a strong contingent of the wild Kadiseni, was led by Pityaxes, while the right was under Barasmanas. After deploying in this way, the Persians waited for hours without making any move forward. Procopius explains that the Romans were accustomed to eat at noon, whereas the Persians did not take a meal until later in the day, so that Peroz hoped that standing for hours in the hot June sun would weaken the enemy more than his own men. In the meantime the Romans made one alteration to their battle order when Pharas

> came before Belisarius and Hermogenes [the Roman second in command], and said: 'It does not seem to me that I shall do the enemy any great harm if I remain here with my Heruli; but if we conceal ourselves on this slope, and then, when the Persians have begun to fight, if we climb up this hill and suddenly come upon their rear, shooting from behind them, we shall in all probability do the greatest harm.' Thus he spoke, and, since it pleased Belisarius and his staff, he carried out the plan.[8]

Pharas and the Heruli moved to a concealed position on the reverse slope of the hill on the army's left flank.

In the afternoon the battle began with the Persian cavalry launching an attack on both wings. Romans and Persians deluged each other with arrows, but the Persians were shooting into a strong wind which took some of the force from their missiles. Elsewhere Procopius claims that Roman archery was more effective than the Persian method anyway, for the Romans had copied the techniques used by the Huns. As Persian units in the first line of cavalry tired or ran low on ammunition, they were replaced by groups of horsemen from the second line to maintain the pressure. After a while, with many men having shot off all of their ammunition, the horsemen on both sides began to charge into contact. A furious attack by the Kadiseni broke through the Roman left. Seeing the enemy horsemen rushing forward in pursuit of the fleeing Roman horsemen, Sunicas and Aigan led their Huns against the left flank of the breakthrough. Before they came into contact

Pharas had already brought his Heruli round from behind the hill to attack the Kadiseni in the rear. Panic and confusion spread rapidly throughout the Persian right wing. Some of the cavalry were able to find shelter behind the solid ranks of foot soldiers, but most were driven from the field with heavy loss. Procopius claims that 3,000 Persians fell in this stage of the fighting.

As his right dissolved into flight, Peroz switched the weight of his attack to the left wing, sending the Immortals to reinforce the cavalry already there. Seeing this move, Belisarius sent orders to Sunicas and Aigan telling them to move across to join the other Huns. Other cavalry were sent up from the reserve to mass behind the Huns, ready to threaten the flank of any units able to smash through the Roman wing. It is unclear on which side of the trenches these troops were positioned, although the Huns were certainly in front and it is possible that the other units had also crossed by one of the pathways left for this purpose. Barasmanas' men, their attack given new impetus by the Immortals, were able to drive back the Roman cavalry facing them and surged on in pursuit. The Huns then led the attack against the Persians' exposed flank, driving right through the mass of enemy horsemen to cut them off from their own army. Sunicas personally killed Barasmanas' standard-bearer with his spear. Many of the Persian cavalry who had been cut off halted their pursuit and made a desperate attempt to hack their way back to their own lines.

At the same time Barasmanas led a group of Immortals in an effort to recapture his standard. Attacked by Roman cavalry from several directions simultaneously, the Persians had little room to manoeuvre and could not charge without exposing their flank or rear to an enemy. This time Sunicas cut down the Persian general himself and Barasmanas' death robbed his men of any confidence which still remained. Those cavalry able to escape fled, their panic spreading to many of the nearest infantry who dropped shields and weapons and joined in the rout. The Romans are said to have killed a further 5,000 enemy soldiers in this section of the field, but Belisarius and his officers quickly set about restraining their men from pursuing too far, knowing that scattered men on blown horses would be all too vulnerable to counter-attack by even a small number of fresh enemies. The victory he had already achieved was enough. Kavadh's main army had been defeated in a pitched battle and the humiliation was deeply felt by the enemy. Peroz had the gold and pearl encrusted headband which marked his rank taken from him by the king.[9]

LATER CAMPAIGNS

In the next year a force of 15,000 Persians, guided by Arab allies, attacked at an unexpected point further south along the Euphrates, well away from the main campaigning areas over which the rival armies had recently fought. The attack surprised Belisarius, and it took him some time to move his army down to confront the enemy near Callinicum. His intention was to put on a demonstration of force which would be sufficient to make the invaders withdraw without having inflicted too much damage on the population of the province. With him were some 20,000 men, including 2,000 local allies and a considerable number of new levies, for some of the troops who had fought at Dara had been detached to reinforce the frontier garrisons in case Kavadh launched a fresh attack while the main army was further south. The Persians did not become aware of his approach until he was about 14 miles away, and immediately began to retreat, for they too had no particular desire for a battle. Belisarius' decision to shadow them at a distance proved deeply unpopular with both his senior subordinates and the ordinary soldiers, although Procopius notes that no one dared criticize his strategy to his face. On Good Friday, 18 April 531, the Persians had reached Callinicum and were on the edge of a stretch of barren and sparsely populated land leading back to their homeland. If the Roman army followed them into this country they would find it no easier than their enemies to draw food, for there were no significant garrisons in the region.

The thought of entering this land, or alternatively letting the Persians escape, at last provoked a burst of open dissent from the Roman soldiers. Belisarius addressed the army, explaining that there was nothing to be gained by battle when the enemy was already being driven from their lands. He also noted that it was not a good time to fight because on the next day they would all fast in preparation for Easter Sunday and so lack the stamina for a hard battle. The men remained truculent and began to insult him openly, prompting the general to declare that he had only been testing their valour and that he was keen to fight. Procopius suggests that this was a genuine change of heart on his part rather than a ploy to fire up the soldiers' spirits. Like Julian at Argentoratum, Belisarius was forced by his army to fight in conditions he did not actually believe were suitable. In this case, though, his earlier judgement proved wise, for the battle ended in defeat. Lacking the carefully prepared position they had held at Dara, the Roman army proved brittle in the whirling cavalry fight which developed and lost 800 men along with most of the allied soldiers. Belisarius was one of the last to flee, fighting on with his *bucellarii* in an effort to support a detachment of men under Ascan who had been cut off by the enemy, and only pulling back after the latter had been killed.[10]

The defeat was unfortunate, but did not undo the principal gains of Dara. Kavadh's death in the autumn of the same year took some of the momentum out of the Persian war effort for a while and would shortly lead to peace negotiations with Khusro. Belisarius was soon afterwards recalled to Constantinople, for Justinian had decided to send him on an expedition to reconquer North Africa from the Vandals. In spite of the limited resources given to him – he had an army of only 5,000 cavalry, including his *bucellarii* along with a contingent of Huns, and 10,000 infantry – Belisarius landed on the coast in 533 and had defeated the Vandal king Gelimer by the following year. Some of the difficulties he faced would have been familiar to earlier commanders, but others were more symptomatic of just how much the Roman army had changed by the sixth century. Early in the campaign he lost 500 men before it was discovered that the stores of biscuit provided for the army had not been properly made. It was normal for this hard tack to be baked twice, a process that helped to preserve it, but also reduced its weight by about a quarter. Evidently obliged to supply the army with a set weight of biscuit, the official responsible decided to make himself a handsome profit. He declined to pay bakers to prepare the biscuit properly and instead arranged to have the supply crudely heated by placing it in the furnace room of the public baths. The biscuits appeared satisfactory, but retained the original weight of the flour and quickly began to go off. There was nothing new about such an attempt to profit at the expense of the State and of the soldiers on campaign, for at the height of the Second Punic War a company contracted to supply the legions in Spain had been convicted of scuttling decrepit ships in order to claim compensation from the Senate for non-existent cargoes.[11]

Another significant event early in the expedition was the execution of two Hunnic soldiers who had killed a comrade in a drunken brawl. This produced an uproar from the rest of their unit, who felt that a state of intoxication ought to prevent a man from being held responsible for his actions. Many of the other troops also joined in the protest, nervous that their general might acquire a taste for punishing other infractions of discipline in a similarly harsh manner. In this case Belisarius held firm, determined to prevent his men from plundering or otherwise abusing the mass of the population and so alienating those who might otherwise be keen to turn against their Vandal overlords. On the whole he was successful in preventing this, flogging as an object lesson some soldiers who had been caught foraging, and by the standards of the day Belisarius imposed a tight discipline on his men.[12] When Carthage capitulated, he deliberately waited to enter the city in daylight, so that he could keep more of a watch on his men – a measure which Julius Caesar had employed at Massilia during the Civil War.[13] His contingent of Huns claimed that they had been misled over their terms of service when first recruited, and proved of questionable loyalty throughout the campaign. By the end they appear to have been willing to remain with Belisarius or defect to Gelimer depending on who seemed most likely to win. After the defeat of the Vandals at Tricamarum in December 533, the discipline of the entire army broke down as they scattered in pursuit, plundering at will. Procopius describes how the soldiers,

> being extremely poor men, upon suddenly becoming the masters of very great wealth and of women both young and extremely comely, were no longer able to restrain their minds or find any satiety in things they had, but were so intoxicated … that each one wished to take everything with him back to Carthage. And they were going about, not in companies but alone or by twos … And Belisarius, taking note of all this, was at a loss how to handle the situation. But at daybreak he took his stand upon a certain hill near the road, appealing to the discipline which no longer existed and heaping reproaches upon all, soldiers and officers alike.[14]

The very thing Belisarius had feared happening to the army after Dara had occurred after this later victory, though fortunately the Vandals proved incapable of exploiting the Romans' vulnerability. Gradually by his direct pleas and rebukes he was able to bring some organization to the chaos, but even this was at best partial. Not long afterwards one of his best subordinates was mortally wounded in the neck by an arrow fired by a drunken junior officer who had been cheerfully aiming at a bird. Later, after the war seemed complete and he had returned to Constantinople, Belisarius had to be recalled to quell a mutiny amongst his old army.[15]

Yet in spite of such unpleasant episodes the African expedition had proved a great success, and Belisarius was received by Justininian amidst great ceremony. Not only was the tradition of granting victorious commanders triumphal honours revived, but Belisarius was allowed to march in triumph – literally, for he walked on foot rather than riding in a chariot – through Constantinople. Some of the spoils captured in Africa and carried in the procession were recognized as having originally been taken by Titus from the Temple of Jerusalem for his own triumph, and later plundered from Rome by the Vandals. These were sent to the churches in Jerusalem. At the end of the parade both the captive Gelimer (an Arian Christian like all his people, he had spent the day repeatedly muttering 'Vanity of vanities, all is vanity', a quote from the second verse of the Book of Ecclesiastes) and the victorious Belisarius both prostrated themselves before Justininian and the Empress Theodora. There seemed no need for a slave to whisper reminders of his mortality to the Roman general, for it was clear that he remained no more than the emperor's servant.

In 535 Belisarius was sent with a force of just 7,500 men to reclaim Italy and Sicily for the empire. Relations with the Osthrogothic kingdom of Italy had long been good, but had soured in recent years when a faction hostile to Constantinople had come to power. Their activities provided Justinian with a pretext for war, but the success in Africa had anyway encouraged him to seek further adventures in the west. Most of the communities in Sicily welcomed Belisarius and by the end of the year all of the island was under his control. The campaign in Italy proved tougher from the beginning and Naples was only taken after a difficult siege when the Romans discovered the long-forgotten tunnel of an old aqueduct which still led inside the city's walls. In December the citizens of Rome opened their gates to Belisarius, but he and a force of only 5,000 men soon found themselves under siege by the Goths.[16] In one skirmish the Roman commander and 1,000 cavalrymen unexpectedly bumped into a force of tribesmen who had just crossed the Milvian Bridge after the garrison guarding it had either deserted or fled without fighting. Belisarius was soon in the thick of the fighting, and was singled out by the enemy after the deserters amongst them yelled out to attack the man riding the white-faced grey. Procopius tells us that most of the Goths

> began to shoot at Belisarius. And every man among them who laid any claim to valour was immediately possessed with a great eagerness to win honour, and getting as close as possible they kept trying to lay hold of him and in a great fury kept striking with their spears and swords. But Belisarius himself, turning from side to side, kept killing as they came those who encountered him, and he also profited very greatly by the loyalty of his own spearmen and guards in the moment of danger. For they all surrounded him … holding out their shields in defence of both the general and his horse, they not only received the missiles, but also forced back and beat off those who from time to time assailed him. And thus the whole engagement was centred upon the body of one man … But by some chance Belisarius was neither wounded nor hit by a missile on that day …[17]

When the Goths subsequently launched a direct attack on the city walls, the general ordered his men to wait in silence and not to fire their bows until he himself had shot, for he wanted the enemy to come into close range before they were greeted with a barrage of missiles. When the time came, his first arrow managed to hit and kill one of the enemy leaders, his second another warrior. Then, as all of his soldiers fired, Belisarius directed the men nearest to him to aim at the oxen pulling the enemy siege engines. The attack was repulsed.[18]

Roman successes during the siege encouraged a spirit of overconfidence amongst the troops similar to that which had preceded the defeat at Callinicum. Once again Belisarius felt unable to restrain his men's enthusiasm, and decided that since they were determined to fight he would at least ensure that they did so under favourable circumstances. Attempts to launch a surprise attack failed when the Romans' plan was on each occasion revealed to the enemy by deserters. In the end Belisarius led his men out for an open battle, which at first went well for the Romans. However, their initial success, which drove the Goths back in flight, led to confusion as many of the Roman soldiers dispersed to plunder. The Germans rallied, counter-attacked and inflicted a serious defeat on their opponents. Later the siege was finally broken when a carefully prepared surprise attack proved highly successful and permitted reinforcements to enter the city.[19]

Belisarius began to campaign further north in the Italian peninsula and in 539 was joined by another army led by the eunuch Narses. The latter's instructions evidently included keeping a close eye on his colleague to ensure that he had no ambitions which might threaten Justinian. The two men did not co-operate well and for a while this took the momentum out of operations in Italy. Narses was recalled later in the year and Belisarius achieved more successes in Northern Italy until he too was withdrawn in 540 to be sent to the Persian frontier again. The eunuch general returned to take charge in Italy and conducted the operations there with considerable skill, but was faced with a resurgence of Gothic power. Belisarius helped to restore the situation in the east through a campaign of manoeuvre and diplomacy, before returning to Italy in 544. Rome was lost in 546, recaptured in 548 and taken again by the Goths in 550. By this time Narses had returned to replace Belisarius and it was he who completed the conquest of Italy by defeating the Goths at Tadinae in either 551 or 552 and the Franks at Casilinus in 554.[20]

The recovery of Africa, Sicily and Italy were considerable victories, won by commanders given extremely modest resources for their task, but the eastern empire proved unable to hold them in the long term. Belisarius had won a great deal of glory in his campaigns and was much honoured by Justinian, although he was to be given few more opportunities for active service. Emperors in the sixth century were confident enough of their position to allow others to lead their armies in the field, but that did not mean that they were free from all suspicion that generals might attempt to turn against them. Belisarius was briefly recalled to an active command in 559 when barbarian raiders threatened Constantinople itself. In 562 he was accused of treason and imprisoned, and although subsequently released, he lived out his remaining years in bitterness and disappointment, dying in 565.

In some ways Belisarius commanded his army in a style similar to the generals of earlier generations. Although at times he wielded spear, sword or bow in the thick of the fighting, his primary role was to direct the actions of the others, a function he performed by staying behind the fighting line. Yet in so many respects the world and the nature of warfare had changed profoundly by the sixth century. One major difference was in the scale of operations. The 25,000 men mustered at Dara represented an exceptionally large force for the period. The author of a later sixth-century military manual assumed that armies would usually number between 5,000 and 15,000 men, with most being at the lower end of the scale, and it was forces within this range that Belisarius led in Africa and Italy. With the occasional exception on the eastern frontier, none of Rome's opponents fielded armies which made larger forces than this necessary, even if sufficient men could have been found. Cavalry formed a much higher proportion of the total than had been the case with earlier armies and, under Belisarius at least, did the bulk of the fighting. Although armies had shrunk in size, they still operated over large areas. Pitched battles were rare and wars consisted predominantly of skirmishes, raids and sieges.

As the style and level of warfare changed, so did the essential character of the Roman army. Belisarius was held to be a fairly strict commander, and yet the troops under his command were repeatedly guilty of indiscipline, pressuring him into fighting against his better judgement at Callinicum and Rome, and running wild after their success in Africa. Mutiny was nothing new in the Roman army, having been comparatively common even under the Republic, but the truculence and almost routine disobedience of soldiers in the sixth century had rarely, if ever, been matched in the past, even during the confusion of civil wars. The literary ideal of the great commander who imposed strict discipline on slack soldiers no longer features in late antiquity, for much of the army's formal system of regulations and punishment had vanished. Military theory still stressed the importance of keeping soldiers well drilled, but in practice only a small proportion of units – often including the *bucellarii* of a capable leader – came anywhere near this ideal. As armies grew larger by the standards of the day, the probability increased that a significant number of soldiers would prove extremely unreliable. Centuries of making and breaking emperors had left Roman soldiers unwilling to accept tight discipline, and attempts to restrict their behaviour prompted complaints, outright mutiny or desertion.[21]

There is a strongly medieval feel to the campaigns of Belisarius. For almost a thousand years European warfare would be characterized by relatively small armies, often including a fair proportion of infantry levies whose military value was negligible and mercenaries or allies whose loyalty was sometimes uncertain. The most effective troops were usually the well-armed and mounted retainers of kings or noblemen. Warfare was dominated by fortified positions from which raids could be launched, and most of the fighting was small-scale. Sometimes such strongholds would suffer siege, but rarely did pitched battles occur. Even the greatest kingdoms of the period were incapable of supporting military forces which in any way resembled the well-equipped, organized and disciplined Roman army of the Late Republic or Principate. Such an army was simply too expensive, and had anyway often proved, even for Rome, a difficult thing to control. For several centuries the Byzantine army preserved in its ritual and language some traces of the old army, but in most important respects it was a very different institution. In the west the army vanished with the collapse of empire, while in the east it changed into something else. As the old army of the legions disappeared, with it went the *imperator*, the Roman general with his distinctive style of command.

CHAPTER 16

LATER YEARS:
THE LEGACY OF ROMAN GENERALS

'THE PERSONALITY OF THE GENERAL IS INDISPENSABLE, HE IS THE HEAD, HE is the all of an army. The Gauls were not conquered by the Roman legions, but by Caesar.' Napoleon's verdict is unsurprising, since he identified so strongly with the idea of the 'great man' shaping the world around him and saw parallels between his own career and the great figures of antiquity. From the Enlightenment onwards European education, art and culture was dominated by stories of the classical world, and the history of Greece and Rome was often told as a sequence of episodes dominated by one or two individuals – the philosophers, statesmen or generals, such as Socrates and Plato, Pericles and Demosthenes, Philip and Alexander, or many of the Romans we have discussed in the preceding chapters. Ancient biographers like Plutarch concentrated on the character of a subject and how his – always 'his' since the significant characters of antiquity celebrated in the sources were invariably men – virtues led to his successes and how his flaws led to any failures. In an age when learning, combined with the determination to implement its lessons, seemed to offer a way to understand and improve the world, the emphasis on the inner strength of the individual was highly attractive.

For Napoleon his own talent and will – even his star – shaped his rise from obscurity to supreme power in France and permitted the subjugation of almost all of Europe. We may point to other factors which made all this possible – the political chaos of the Revolution creating a vacuum of power at the centre; the introduction of massed conscription which provided him with armies of a size previously unimaginable; the military reformers who laid the foundations for much of the strategy and tactics which would make La Grande Armée so formidable – but acknowledging their importance does not force us to the conclusion that Napoleon's character and talents were irrelevant. He did not create from thin air the *corps d'armée* system which permitted his armies to out manoeuvre more clumsy opponents, or the imperial staff which co-ordinated their movements, but he certainly set his distinctive stamp upon them. The staff in particular was based around him and the written orders dispatched from it worded in his own idiosyncratic way. In a real sense the spirit of Napoleon imbued his army in a way that few of his opponents could match. The warfare of the period was obviously shaped to a great degree by more practical things – sheer numbers of soldiers and the ability to train, move and supply troops with food, clothes, weapons, ammunition, all of which cost a state money – and Napoleon himself remained ever aware of this. Yet this does not alter the fact that the conflicts of those years cannot be understood without some allowance for the personality of the emperor.[1]

In a similar sense there is at least a degree of truth in the claim that it was Caesar who conquered Gaul. As we have seen, there was a strong element of chance leading to Caesar's fighting a Gallic rather than a Dacian war, and his own desire for glory to serve his political ends influenced many of his decisions, most notably to attack Britain. It could be argued that the Roman Republic's drive to expand was bound to lead to the conquest of Gaul at some time, so that if Caesar had not begun this in 58 BC then someone else would have done it later. Yet this would imply an inevitability about the course of history which would remove from human beings any real independence of action. In this scheme underlying trends and pressures – perhaps social, ideological, economic, or conditions created by developments in technology, a rising or declining population, or shifts in climate and changes in the environment – dictate that events must happen, effectively removing the human element from history altogether.

Such a view is extremely difficult to square with observation of the real world, for life is full of conscious and unconscious decisions, all of which have consequences. Furthermore people vary hugely in their reactions and abilities, even when they appear to come from a very similar background and environment. In war, as perhaps in no other activity, the capacity of each actor to influence events is obvious, since the consequences of their decisions and actions tend to be dramatic. If Caesar had not conquered Gaul another Roman commander might have done so at some future time, but he would not have done it in precisely the same way as events occurred between 58 and 50 BC. Caesar's personality, and indeed that of everyone involved on both sides, helped to shape the course of his campaigns, but the man at the top of a hierarchical organization inevitably has more influence than any other single individual. Essentially we have returned to our starting point to say that leaders and generals matter, and that they were and are a significant, if not necessarily decisive, factor in determining the course and outcome of a conflict.

In this book we have looked at a number of conflicts and individuals during centuries of expansion, consolidation, and finally struggle against collapse. Warfare and generals were ever present in Roman history. Rome's rise and fall would surely still have happened even if the fifteen men discussed in this book had died in childhood, as did so many of their contemporaries, or been killed while leading their armies. Yet their careers and victories represented important stages in this process and did much to determine the detail of the way in which this occurred. At various times the appearance of especially talented or determined leaders injected higher levels of purpose and momentum into Roman war-making than was the case in other periods. Men like Marcellus, Fabius Maximus and Scipio Africanus helped Rome to endure Hannibal's onslaught and finally to defeat Carthage. Pompey and Caesar may ultimately have torn the Republic apart, but they also added more territory to the Empire than any other leaders. Augustus publicly justified his new regime through conquest as much as through the claim to have restored internal peace and stability.

War and politics remained inseparably linked since there was no greater service that a leader of the State could perform than to defeat an enemy in war. In late antiquity the old tradition of a mixed civil and military career had been abandoned, and yet even so Belisarius was made consul by a grateful Justinian on his return from Africa. War was frequent in the ancient world and the State needed able men to win its campaigns. In all periods this brought prestige which could be turned to political advantage. The senatorial aristocracy which provided Rome's generals for so many centuries prided itself on the *virtus* which fitted its members for high command, but was never very comfortable with individuals whose martial prowess outshone their peers by too great a margin.

It is instructive at this point to survey the fate of our fifteen subjects. Two were killed in skirmishes – Marcellus by the Carthaginians and Julian perhaps by his own side – and Trajan died of natural causes while on campaign, as did Marius soon after taking Rome. Three were murdered – Sertorius by some of his own officers, Pompey by orders of Ptolemy's courtiers, and Caesar by a conspiracy of senators – and another, Corbulo, was ordered to commit suicide by Nero. Scipio Aemilianus and Germanicus both died amid rumours of poison, Titus unlamented by the brother who succeeded him. Fabius Maximus remained in politics, but the end of his long life was tinged with jealousy for the growing fame of Scipio Africanus. The latter was prematurely forced out of public life into bitter retirement, as in some ways was Belisarius. The last years of Aemilius Paullus were scarred by the opposition he had been forced to overcome in order to celebrate his triumph, and even more by the death of his two sons. In battle Roman commanders directed their troops from just behind the fighting line, a position of some danger. Surviving this and winning great glory brought further perils that were no less real.

AFTER ROME

We must confess Alexander, Caesar, Scipio and Haniball, to be the worthiest and famoust warriors that ever were; notwithstanding, assure your selfe ... they would never have ... conquered Countries so easilie, had they been fortified as Germanie, France, and the Low Countries, with others, have been since their daies.

Even as Sir Roger Williams wrote his *Briefe discourse of Warre* in 1590 and hinted that new developments in warfare – most notably modern fortifications and improved cannon – had lessened the relevance to contemporary commanders of exempla from antiquity, many other military theorists were actively seeking to learn from the Greeks and Romans.[2] This was not entirely new, since Vegetius' late fourth-century *Epitome of Military Science* had been one of the most frequently copied secular manuscripts throughout the Middle Ages. It is difficult to establish the extent to which Vegetius' ideas actually influenced the behaviour of medieval captains on campaign, but he was certainly well thought of by the literate community. Many of his recommendations, for instance avoiding battle except in the most advantageous circumstances, and withdrawing behind well-provisioned fortifications until an invader ran out of food and had to retreat, were certainly characteristic of medieval warfare. However, the leaders who put these into practice may well have based their decisions on experience rather than the advice of a Roman theorist.

By the sixth century Roman warfare had itself become characteristically medieval, with relatively small armies, looser discipline than in earlier years, and a prevalence of raiding and other small-scale operations over larger battles. Medieval kingdoms lacked the wealth, resources and degree of centralization needed to field armies resembling in any way those of Rome at her height. It was not until the late fifteenth and sixteenth centuries that conditions began to change as states became more sophisticated and fielded ever larger armies. Traditional methods of controlling armies proved impractical as numbers of soldiers grew, a problem made worse by the much greater need for order if the new light firearms were to be wielded effectively. Literacy was becoming more widespread, access to books and pamphlets made far easier by the introduction of the printing press. Some ancient authors were rediscovered, and many made more accessible by translation into modern languages. By the late sixteenth and seventeenth centuries leaders like Maurice and William of Nassau in the Netherlands and Gustavus Adolphus in Sweden were consciously trying to turn their armies into forces based on the discipline, organization and tactical system of the Roman legions. In 1616 John Bingham published an English translation of *The Tacticks of Aelian* which included not only diagrams showing pikemen in seventeenth-century dress performing the individual movements, but also a section on how the ancient drills had been adapted for use in the Dutch service. The cover was even more direct, for it depicted Alexander the Great handing over his sword to Maurice of Nassau.

With armies designed after the Roman model – or at least after what the military reformers thought was the Roman model – it is unsurprising that in many ways commanders can be observed acting in a rather Roman way for several centuries. At the head of armies rarely numbering more than 30,000 men moving in close formation, they too could see most of a battlefield. Many of the conditions within which the general operated, and his capacity to control his troops, had not changed – telescopes would improve visibility, but at the same time the clouds of smoke produced by black powder weapons reduced this. Communication was still no faster than the speed of a dispatch rider. The staff who assisted a leader were usually, as in Roman times, drawn from family and friends, comparatively few in number, unspecialized in purpose, and lacking any formal training. It seems doubtful that Caesar or Pompey would have found the battlefield of Gustavus Adolphus or Marlborough so very different from their own experience, or indeed vice versa.

The seventeenth- or eighteenth-century commander was still similarly mobile, moving to a vantage point to observe or riding along behind the line, trying to guess where the next crisis or opportunity would occur and placing himself in the best position to respond. Through personal observation, sending an officer to look on his behalf, and reports sent by his subordinates controlling each section of the line, the general attempted to understand the battle, committing as appropriate the units which, like any Roman leader, he had kept in reserve. At times he might ride forward and lead a charge. Some commanders through temperament or sense of obligation did this more often than others, though most who led in this way would, like Gustavus Adolphus, eventually be seriously wounded or killed. The development of modern artillery ensured that even leaders who remained behind the line were still at far greater risk of injury than their Roman counterparts.

It is easy to find many occasions when seventeenth- or eighteenth-century commanders act in a way strongly reminiscent of Roman leaders – the gesture of grabbing a standard in an effort to rally a fleeing or faltering unit became as much an artistic cliché in this era as it had been a literary motif for the Romans. It was also in reality a practical method of trying to stop routers. It is much harder to say whether they did this because most were well educated in the classics and consciously emulated heroes of the past as Julian the Apostate had done, or whether similar battlefield conditions simply produced similar responses.

Yet in some respects eighteenth-century warfare differed markedly from Roman conflicts. Much of the formality, cautious manoeuvring, and reluctance to risk battle of the eighteenth century has more in common with the tentative campaigns of Alexander's Successors than the ruthless determination with which Rome usually waged war. Another difference was in the relationship between the leader and his soldiers. Military discipline as it developed in the military revolution of the early modern era was shaped by the problem of employing hand-held firearms effectively. Muskets were of limited range – their introduction had not really provided infantry with a weapon any more effective than the bow, but it was much easier to train musketeers than archers. They were also extremely inaccurate and slow to load, so that a single rank of musketeers might easily be overwhelmed by charging enemy (especially cavalry) before they had fired more than one shot. Therefore, methods were devised requiring infantry to deploy in several lines which would fire and load in turn, at first often by moving through the rank ahead before giving fire. Over time, improved methods of loading lowered the number of ranks needed to present a near constant fire on the enemy from as many as ten down to three or two, but these developments if anything diminished accuracy. In the eighteenth century line infantry did not aim (most muskets did not even have a sight), but simply levelled their piece and fired straight forward. The assumption was that a volley from closely packed ranks was bound to inflict damage on a similar formation as long as it was close enough.

Drill was intended to make all the movements of marching in formation and loading a musket mechanical, for unless everyone co-ordinated their actions the result would be confusion and probably many accidental injuries. Discipline was therefore extremely rigid, since the intention was to turn the soldier into an automaton, virtually a 'walking musket'. Although marching in step and keeping formation were important in the Roman army, victory in hand-to-hand combat did not come purely from such tight drills. Initiative and individual aggression were, under the right circumstances, actively encouraged by the Roman military, for often the actions of a few men represented the difference between victory and defeat. One of the Roman general's most important tasks was to act as witness and judge of the behaviour of individual soldiers. The army's tactical system gave the commander a vital role in co-ordinating the units under his command and encouraged him to intervene at a low level if necessary. However, this was never at the expense of discouraging a high degree of initiative in subordinate officers at all levels. The role of legates, tribunes, prefects and centurions was vitally important. One of the reasons why a general could afford to ride up and down the line trying to direct events at what he judged to be the most crucial section of the fighting was his confidence that subordinate officers would act appropriately to control the troops in other sectors of the battlefield.

The Roman aim was to have somebody inspiring and directing the troops at every point – the army commander's authority and prestige gave him the potential to instil more purpose into events than anyone else, but many others were capable and willing to take charge when he was occupied elsewhere. There were unwise subordinates as there were unwise generals, and sometimes acts of initiative by a junior officer made the situation worse or led to defeat (and at Gergovia in 52 BC had provided the army commander with an excuse for failure). Yet on the whole the activities of the general and subordinates complemented each other to give the army far greater flexibility than any of its opponents.

Only in the late eighteenth century did something of this flexibility return to European armies. Through the *corps d'armée* system Napoleon was able to control effectively the strategic movements of armies more than twice the size of anything which had been possible using more traditional methods, or for the Romans. By its nature this required the granting of far more freedom of action to his subordinates and especially the corps commanders. Yet the army was not so large that the emperor was unable to see and be seen by most of his soldiers. On campaign he spent a good deal of time in the saddle, and his formal and informal visits to units usually culminated in the immediate promotion or decoration of individuals. Though only a handful of the soldiers of La Grande Armée ever found the marshal's

baton they supposedly carried in their backpack, enough men had spectacular careers to convince the rest that courage and ability were both noticed
and rewarded. Discipline was important, but not intended to be so tight that
blind obedience stifled all initiative, an ethos that had much in common with
that of the Roman army.

Napoleon's propaganda and rhetoric was markedly classical and particularly Roman – triumphal arches, reliefs showing the triumph of wreathed
victors, eagles as standards and classically inspired helmets for some units.
Napoleon had a wide knowledge of military history, including that of the
ancient world, and listed Caesar amongst the great captains from whose
campaigns much could be learnt about generalship. His order of the day at
Austerlitz – 'Soldiers, I shall in person direct all your battalions; I shall keep
out of range if, with your accustomed bravery, you carry disorder and confusion into the ranks of the enemy; but if the victory is for a moment uncertain, you shall see your Emperor expose himself in the front rank' – could
easily have come from a Roman general. Napoleon was most active before
a battle, bringing about the circumstances in which his army could smash
the enemy, and left much of the tactical handling of the actual fighting to
subordinates. The sheer size of his armies, especially in some of the later
campaigns, encouraged this, making it important for the Imperial
Headquarters to be fairly static and so easy for messengers to locate.

Wellington, who in most cases led smaller forces and had a far less
numerous and efficient staff with which to control them, acted during a
battle in a very Roman style. At Waterloo he was very mobile, riding around
close to the front line, trying always to be at the critical point, issuing orders
and receiving reports wherever he happened to be, and intervening wherever
he thought appropriate, even at times at a very low level – 'Now Maitland,
now is your time!' The British accounts of the battle mention the sudden
appearance of the duke, although his was certainly not a style of leadership
encouraging too much initiative from his juniors.[3]

After Waterloo it became impossible for an army commander to direct a
battle in such a personal way, at least in Europe where the growing power of
the nation state, combined with developments such as railways and telegraphs,
produced armies numbered in hundreds of thousands and eventually in
millions. At the same time improvements in weaponry rendered traditional
close formations suicidal and increased the size of the battlefield. Battles
were now fought over distances that made it impossible for a commander to
observe the entire action in person. Only indirectly could he now lead his
men, and many of the tasks of closely supervising and inspiring the soldiers

as they fought were now left solely in the hands of subordinates. Yet the classics continued to form a central part of education, including the military education provided for young officers in a number of countries, and most military men had some familiarity with the great campaigns of the Greek and Roman past. A direct influence on their behaviour is in most cases difficult to prove, since merely performing an action similar to something once done by Scipio or Pompey may simply provide an indication that good and successful leaders often act in much the same way. Indirect influence, however distant is hard to dispute, for the classical tradition ran so deep in Western culture. The many leaders who modelled themselves on Napoleon, for instance Havelock, McClellan, and even 'Boney' Fuller, were copying a man who had closely associated himself with the great leaders of history.

Military theorists in the post-Waterloo era were as divided as those of the Renaissance over the relevance of Greek and Roman warfare to their theme. Clausewitz saw the formal battles, usually joined through mutual consent, of antiquity as having little in common with modern war. Yet for all his influence on the Prussian and later German military, the study of military history, including that of the ancient past, became established as a vital part of a staff officer's education. In the extreme case of Von Schlieffen, the quest to draw practical lessons from ancient battles reached a level close to obsession. The interest in the past was especially deep in the German army, and it should not be forgotten that in the same period German scholars dominated most fields of study into the ancient world, but they were not alone. The influential French theorist Ardant du Picq took many of his examples from Roman battles because he believed that the ancients were more willing than more modern sources to tell the truth about men's behaviour in battle .[4]

The world has changed since the nineteenth century, and one of the greatest shifts has been the falling from wider consciousness of the classics. Yet it is still not unknown for military writers to seek lessons for the present day from the wars of Rome. In one sense the increased probability that Western armies will fight asymmetric warfare against opponents less sophisticated than themselves, rather than wars against those with similar tactical systems and levels of technology, creates a situation not unlike that faced by Rome. For much of its history the Roman army was better equipped and, even more importantly, far more organized and disciplined than its enemies. In Victorian parlance many Roman campaigns were 'small wars'. Perhaps it is in the way that such operations were conducted, rather than in the famous battles against Carthaginians or Macedonians, that lessons for the present day should be sought.

CHRONOLOGY

BC

753   Traditional date for foundation of Rome by Romulus.

509   Traditional date for expulsion of Rome's last king, Tarquinius Superbus.

396   The Romans introduce pay for their army.

390   Gauls under Brennus rout a Roman army at the River Allia and sack Rome (these events were dated to 387 by Polybius).

295   Romans achieve a great victory over an army of Gauls, Samnites, and Umbrians at Sentinum.

280–275   **War with Pyrrhus**, who had been hired by the Tarentines to fight Rome.

c. 275   Birth of Fabius Maximus.

c. 271   Birth of Marcellus.

264–241   **First Punic War**.

c. 236   Birth of Scipio Africanus.

228   Birth of Aemilius Paullus.

225   Invading Gallic army defeated at Telamon.

222   Marcellus wins right to dedicate *spolia opima* during his consulship.

218–201   **Second Punic War**.

217   Dictatorship of Fabius Maximus.

216   Romans suffer massive defeat at Cannae. A smaller army is ambushed and defeated by Gauls.

214-205   **First Macedonian War**.

213–211   Marcellus takes Syracuse after long siege.

209   Scipio Africanus captures New Carthage. Fabius Maximus recaptures Tarentum.

208   Marcellus killed whilst on reconnaissance.

206   Scipio wins decisive victory in Spanish campaign at Ilipa.

204   Scipio invades Africa.

203   Death of Fabius Maximus.

202	Scipio defeats Hannibal at Zama.
200–196	**Second Macedonian War**.
197	Philip V decisively beaten at Cynoscephalae.
192–189	The **Syrian War** against the Seleucid Antiochus III.
191	Antiochus' invasion of Greece defeated at Thermopylae.
189	Antiochus defeated at Magnesia.
c.184	Death of Scipio Africanus. Birth of Scipio Aemilianus.
172–167	**Third Macedonian War**.
168	Macedonians under Perseus defeated at Pydna.
c.160	Death of Aemilius Paullus.
157	Birth of Marius.
154–138	**Lusitanian War**.
153–151	**Second Celtiberian War**.
149–146	**Third Punic War**.
146	Destruction of Carthage and Corinth.
143–133	**Numantine War**.
139	Viriathus murdered.
137	Roman army under Mancinus is defeated and surrenders to Numantines.
133	Numantia surrenders to Scipio Aemilianus.
129	Death of Scipio Aemilianus.
c.125	Birth of Sertorius.
113	A Roman army under Cn. Papirius Carbo is defeated at Noreia by the migrating tribes, the Cimbri and Teutones.
112–106	**Jugurthine War**.
106	Birth of Pompey.
105	Cimbri and Teutones destroy a large Roman army at Arausio.
102	Marius defeats Teutones at Aquae Sextiae.
101	Marius and Catulus defeat Cimbri at Vercellae.
c.100	Birth of Julius Caesar.
91–88	The **Social War**, the last great rebellion by Rome's Italian allies. The Socii are defeated only after a hard struggle.
88	Sulla marches on Rome when Marius takes the command against Mithridates from him.
86	Death of Marius.
82–72	Sertorius campaigns in Spain.
74–66	Final defeat of Mithridates of Pontus.
73–70	A major slave rebellion led by Spartacus.
67	Pompey given extraordinary command to clear the Mediterranean of pirates, and succeeds in a brief, but highly organised campaign.

66	Pompey given extraordinary command to complete the war with Mithridates.
58–50	Caesar given the provinces of Transalpine and Cisalpine Gaul, and Illyria, which he uses as a base to conquer Gallia Comata.
58	Caesar defeats the migrating Helvetii. Caesar defeats the Germanic king, Ariovistus.
57	Caesar defeats the Belgic tribes, winning the battle of the Sambre.
55	Caesar bridges the Rhine for the first time and leads an expedition to Britain.
54	Caesar crosses the Rhine a second time and leads a larger invasion of Britain.
54–53	First major Gallic rebellion against Caesar.
53	Crassus defeated and killed by Parthians under Surenas at Carrhae.
52	Second major Gallic rebellion led by Vercingetorix.
49–45	Civil War between Caesar and Pompey.
48	Caesar is checked at Dyrrachium, but defeats Pompey at Pharsalus. Pompey flees to Egypt and is murdered. Caesar pursues to Egypt and intervenes in power struggle to place Cleopatra on the throne.
47	Caesar leads swift campaign to defeat Pharnaces, King of the Bosporus, at Zela.
46	Caesar suffers a near defeat at the hands of Labienus at Ruspina in North Africa, but finally defeats Pompeian army at Thapsus.
45	Caesar wins final victory at Munda in Spain.
44–42	Caesar's assassination provokes a further cycle of civil war between the conspirators and Caesar's supporters led by Mark Antony, later joined by Octavian, Caesar's nephew and adopted son.
42	Brutus and Cassius defeated in twin battles of Philippi.
36	Antony launches major offensive against the Parthians, but this bogs down when he fails to take Phraapsa, and he loses many men to disease and starvation in the subsequent retreat.
31	Antony defeated by Octavian in naval battle at Actium. Octavian becomes effectively the sole ruler of the Roman Empire.
29	M. Crassus campaigns successfully in the Balkans, killing the king of the Bastarnae with his own hand, but is denied the right to dedicate the *spolia opima* by Octavian.
27–AD 14	**Principate of Augustus.**
15	German tribes raid into the Roman provinces and defeat Lollius Urbicus. Birth of Germanicus.
12–9	Tiberius conquers Pannonia, whilst his brother, Drusus, campaigns in Germany.
9–7	Tiberius campaigns in Germany.

AD

4–5	Tiberius resumes command in Germany and completes the conquest of a new province extending to the Elbe.
6–9	Massive revolt in Pannonia and Dalmatia. Huge numbers of troops, including cohorts of freed slaves, sent to suppress the rebels, many of whom had previously served as Roman auxiliaries. Tiberius and Germanicus eventually defeat the rebels.

9	German revolt led by Arminius of the Cherusci massacres three legions led by Varus in the Teutoberg Wald.
10–11	Tiberius and Germanicus secure the Rhine frontier and lead brief punitive expeditions against the German tribes.
14	Death of Augustus followed by mutinies of the legions on the Rhine and Danube, which are suppressed by Germanicus and Tiberius' son, Drusus.
14–37	**Principate of Tiberius.**
15	Germanicus leads Rhine armies against the Germans and buries the remains of Varus' army.
16	Germanicus defeats Arminius at Indistaviso, but fails to gain final victory in the conflict and is recalled to Rome.
19	Arminius murdered by rival chieftains. Death of Germanicus.
37–41	**Principate of Gaius** (Caligula).
41–54	**Principate of Claudius.**
41	Birth of Titus.
43	Claudius launches invasion of Britain.
47	Corbulo suppresses the Frisii.
53	Vologaeses I of Parthia occupies Armenia and places his brother Tiridates on the throne.
54–68	**Principate of Nero.**
55	Corbulo given eastern command.
56	Birth of Trajan.
64	Corbulo mounts demonstration of force in Armenia. Following a peace settlement Tiridates receives his crown from Nero.
66–74	The Jewish rebellion.
66	The Syrian governor, Cestius Gallus, leads an expedition to Jerusalem, but is forced to retreat and suffers heavily in the pursuit.
67	Vespasian given command in Jewish War and subdues Galilee. Josephus surrenders to him after the fall of Jotapata. Corbulo forced to commit suicide.
68–69	**Year of Four Emperors.** Nero's death prompts a civil war as the provincial armies nominate their commanders as successor.
70–79	**Principate of Vespasian.**
70	Titus captures Jerusalem after a long siege.
79–81	**Principate of Titus.**
81–96	**Principate of Domitian.**
85	Decebalus, King of Dacia, invades Moesia and inflicts a heavy defeat on its governor.
86	Cornelius Fuscus defeated in Dacia.
88	Another Roman army invades Dacia and defeats Decebalus at Tapae.
96–98	**Principate of Nerva.**
98–117	**Principate of Trajan.**

101–102	**First Dacian War.**
105–106	**Second Dacian War.**. Dacia is annexed as a province.
113–117	Trajan's **Parthian War.**
117–138	**Principate of Hadrian.**
138–161	**Principate of Antoninus Pius.**
161–180	**Principate of Marcus Aurelius.**
324–337	**Reign of Constantine** as undisputed emperor.
332	Birth of Julian.
337	Imperial power divided between Constantine's sons, Constantinus II in the west, Constans in Africa, Italy and Illyricum, and Constantius II in the east.
340	Constantinus killed in civil war with Constans.
355	Julian appointed *Caesar* in the west.
356	Julian campaigns against the Alamanni.
357	Julian defeats the Alamanni in a pitched battle at Strasbourg.
358	Julian campaigns against the Franks.
360–361	Julian proclaimed *Augustus* by his army. Death of Constantius.
363	Julian launches massive Persian offensive.
429	Vandals invade and overrun Africa.
451	Aetius turns back the offensive of Attila's Huns at Chalons (Campus Mauriacus).
469–478	Visigoths overrun Spain.
476	The last emperor of the west, Romulus Augustus, deposed by Odovacer who creates the Ostrogothic kingdom of Italy.
502–506	Anastasian war with Persia. Persians capture Amida, but this is returned to the Romans as part of the peace treaty.
505	Birth of Belisarius.
528	Belisarius defeated at Minduos.
530	Belisarius wins great victory at Dara.
531	Belisarius defeated at Callinicum and removed from the eastern command.
533–534	Belisarius defeats the Vandals in Africa.
535–554	Attempt made to reconquer Italy with armies led by Belisarius and later Narses. Rome captured and recaptured several times.
552	Narses defeats Totila's Ostrogoths at Taginae.
553	Narses wins another victory over the Goths near Mt Vesuvius.
554	Narses defeats an invading army of Franks at Casilinus.
565	Death of Belisarius.

GLOSSARY

ala: (1) Division of Allied troops roughly equivalent in size to a legion (third to second century BC). One such unit supported each legion.
(2) A unit of auxiliary cavalry of similar size to an infantry cohort in the army of the Principate (late C1st to C4th AD).

aquilifer: The standard-bearer who carried the legion's standard (*aquila*), a silver, later gold, statuette of an eagle (C1st BC–3rd AD).

auctoritas: The prestige and influence of a Roman senator. *Auctoritas* was greatly boosted by military achievements.

auxilia (**auxiliaries**): The non-citizen soldiers recruited into the army during the late Republican and Imperial periods. By the third century AD the difference between these and the citizen legions appears to have been minimal.

ballista: A two-armed torsion catapult capable of firing bolts or stones with considerable accuracy. These were built in various sizes and most often used in sieges (C3rd BC–6th AD).

bucellarii: Soldiers paid and supported by a particular commander and forming part of his household. These men were still part of the regular army and supposed to be loyal to the emperor. The name derives from the ration hard-tack biscuit (*bucellatum*) and emphasized the commander's obligation to feed his soldiers (late C4th–6th AD).

cataphract: Heavily armoured cavalryman often riding an armoured horse. The Romans first encountered such warriors in eastern armies, but later made use of them themselves.

centurion: Important grade of officers in the Roman army for most of its history, centurions originally commanded a century of sixty to eighty men. The most senior centurion of a legion was the *primus pilus*, a post of enormous status held only for a single year (C4th BC–3rd AD).

century (*centuria*): The basic sub-unit of the Roman army, the century was commanded by a centurion and usually consisted of sixty, later eighty men (late C4th BC–3rd AD).

carroballista: A version of the **scorpion** mounted on a mule-drawn cart to increase mobility (C1st BC–6th AD).

cohort (*cohors*): By the first century BC the cohort replaced the **maniple** as the basic tactical unit of the legion. Auxiliary infantry were also formed into cohorts. Usually these consisted of six centuries of eighty soldiers with a total strength of 480 (C1st BC – 3rd AD).

comes: Officers of the later Roman army, ranking below the *Magistri Militum* (late C3rd–6th AD).

comitatenses: Units included in the regional forces not tied to specific frontier provinces (C4th–6th AD).

commilito (pl. *commilitones*): Comrade: this familiar form of address was often employed by a Roman general when speaking to his troops, especially at times of civil war.

consul: The year's two consuls were the senior elected magistrates of the Roman Republic, and held command in important campaigns. Sometimes the Senate extended their power after their year of office, in which case they were known as **proconsuls**.

decurion: Cavalry officer who originally commanded ten men. Under the Principate the decurion led a *turma* of about thirty horsemen (C1st–3rd AD).

dictator: In times of extreme crisis a dictator was appointed for a six-month period during which he exercised supreme civil and military power. Later victors in civil wars, such as Sulla and Julius Caesar, used the title as a basis for more permanent power (C5th–1st BC).

dux: Officers of later Roman army (late C3rd–6th AD).

dux (**duces**) **limitis**: Commanders of all troops (*limitanei*) within one of the regions into which the frontier provinces of the later empire was divided (late C3rd–6th AD).

equites singulares: The term used for the bodyguard cavalry attached to the staff of provincial governors under the Principate. These units seem to have been about 500 strong and were recruited from men seconded from the auxiliary *alae* (C1st–3rd AD).

equites singulares augusti: The emperor's own horse guards for the first three centuries of the Principate, these provided an élite cavalry force to support the Praetorian Guard (C1st–3rd AD).

foederati: Allied barbarians obliged to provide military service to the emperor. Usually served in their own units and sometimes under their own commanders who normally held Roman rank (C4th–6th AD).

gladius: A Latin word meaning sword, gladius is conventionally used to describe the *gladius hispaniensis*, the short Spanish sword which was the standard Roman side arm until well into the third century AD. Made from high-quality steel, this weapon could be used for cutting, but was primarily intended for thrusting (C3rd BC–3rd AD).

hastatus (pl. *hastati*): The first line of heavy infantry in the Republican legion, recruited from younger men (late C4th–C2nd BC).

imaginifer: The standard-bearer who carried the *imago*, a standard bearing a bust of the emperor (C1st–3rd AD).

imperium: The power of military command held by magistrates and pro-magistrates during their term of office (C3rd BC–3rd AD).

legatus (pl. *legati*): A subordinate officer who held delegated *imperium* rather than exercising power in his own right. *Legati* were chosen by a magistrate rather than elected (C3rd–1st BC).

　　(1) *legatus augusti pro praetore*. This title was given to the governors of the military provinces under the Principate who commanded as representatives of the emperor (C1st–3rd AD).

　　(2) *legatus legionis*. The title given to legionary commanders under the Principate (C1st–3rd AD).

legion (*legio*): Originally a term meaning 'levy', the legions became the main unit of the Roman army for much of its history. Under the Republic and Principate they were large, predominantly infantry, formations of *c.* 4,000–5,000 men, but by late antiquity most seem to have dwindled to a strength of about 1,000.

limitanei: The grade of troops commanded by the *duces limitis*, the military commanders of the various regions, usually on the frontier, into which the provinces of the later empire were divided (C4th–6th AD).

Magister Militum: Title given to the senior officers of the later imperial army (C4th–6th AD).

Magister Equitum: (1) Second in command to the Republican *dictator*, the Master of Horse traditionally commanded the cavalry, since the dictator was forbidden to ride a horse (C5th–1st BC).
(2) Title given to senior officers of the Later Imperial army, equal in status to *Magistri Peditum* (C4th–6th AD).

Magister Peditum: Title given to senior officers of the Later Imperial army (C4th–6th AD).

maniple (*manipulus*): The basic tactical unit of the Republican legion, the maniple consisted of two centuries (late C4th–C2nd BC).

ovatio (**ovation**): A lesser form of the triumph. In an ovation the general rode through the city on horseback rather than in a chariot (C5th BC–1st AD).

palatini: Units of higher status and prestige than the *comitatenses*, the *palatini* also formed part of the field armies of late antiquity (C4th–6th AD).

pilum (pl. *pila*): The heavy javelin which was the standard equipment of the Roman legionary for much of Rome's history (C3rd BC–3rd AD).

praefectus castrorum: Third in command of a legion during the principate, this was an experienced officer who was usually a former *primus pilus* (C1st–3rd AD).

prefect (*praefectus*): Equestrian commander of an auxiliary cohort or *ala* (C1st–3rd AD).

praetor: Praetors were annually elected magistrates who under the Republic governed the less important provinces and fought Rome's smaller wars.

Praetorian Guard: The military bodyguard of the emperors of the Principate, commanded by tribunes and the whole corps commanded by two Praetorian Prefects. They were disbanded by Constantine in 312 after supporting his rival Maxentius (C1st–4th AD).

princeps (pl. *principes*): The second line of heavy infantry in the Republican legion, recruited from men in the prime of life (late C4th–2nd BC).

quaestor: Magistrates whose duties were primarily financial, quaestors acted as deputies to consular governors and often held subordinate military commands (C3rd–1st BC).

quincunx: The chequerboard formation used by the Republican legion in which the three lines were deployed with wide intervals between the maniples, the gaps being covered by the maniples of the next line (late C4th–2nd BC).

scorpion: The light bolt-shooting *ballista* employed by the Roman army both in the field and in sieges. They possessed a long range, as well as great accuracy and the ability to penetrate any form of armour (C1st BC–6th AD).

signifer: The standard-bearer who carried the standard (*signum*) of the century (C3rd BC–3rd AD).

socii: The Italian allies of the Republic. After the Social War (90–88 BC) and the general extension of citizenship to most of the Italian peninsula the *socii* disappeared and all Italians were recruited into the legions (late C4th–C2nd BC).

spolia opima: The highest honour which a triumphing general could claim was the right to dedicate *spolia opima* in the Temple of Jupiter Optimus Maximus on the Capitol. The right could only be gained by killing the enemy general in single combat and was celebrated on only a handful of occasions.

testudo: The famous tortoise formation in which Roman legionaries overlapped their long shield to provide protection to the front, sides and overhead. It was most often used during assaults on fortifications (C3rd BC–3rd AD).

triarius (pl. *triarii*): The third and senior line of heavy infantry in the Republican legion, recruited from veteran soldiers (late C4th–2nd BC).

tribunus militum (**military tribune**): (1) Six military tribunes were elected or appointed to each Republican legion, one pair of these men holding command at any one time (C3rd–C2nd or C1st BC).
(2) Under the Principate each legion had one senior, senatorial tribune and five equestrians (C1st–3rd AD).

tribune of the plebs (*tribunicia potestas*): Although holding a political office without direct military responsibilities, the ten tribunes of the plebs elected each year were able to legislate on any issue. During the later years of the Republic many ambitious generals, such as Marius and Pompey, enlisted the aid of the tribunate to secure important commands for themselves.

triumph: The great celebration granted by the Senate to a successful general took the form of a procession along the Sacra Via, the ceremonial main road of Rome, displaying the spoils and captives of his victory, and culminated in the ritual execution of the captured enemy leader. The commander rode in a chariot, dressed like the statues of Jupiter, a slave holding a laurel wreath of Victory over his head. The slave was supposed to whisper to the general, reminding him that he was mortal. Under the Principate only members of the imperial family received triumphs, but other commanders were granted the insignia of a triumph (*ornamenta triumphalia*) (C5th BC–4th AD).

turma: The basic sub-unit of the Roman cavalry for much of its history, the *turma* consisted of around thirty men. Under the principate it was commanded by a decurion (late C4th BC–3rd AD).

veles (pl. *velites*): The light infantry of the Republican legion, recruited from the poor or those too young to fight as heavy infantry. It is unclear whether they were identical to or superseded the *rorarii*, another term applied to light infantrymen in the Republican legion (late C4th–2nd BC).

vexillation (*vexillatio*): (1) A detachment operating independently, a vexillation might consist of anything from a few men to several thousand and could be drawn from several units (C1st–3rd AD).
(2) Many cavalry units of the later field armies were known as vexillations. They appear to have been similar in size to the old *alae* (C4th–6th AD).

vexillum: A square flag mounted crosswise on a pole, the *vexillum* was used to mark a general's position and was also the standard carried by a detachment of troops (C1st–3rd AD). A general's *vexillum* seems usually to have been red.

NOTES

Introduction

1 Onasander, *The General* 33. 6 (Loeb translation, slightly modified).

2 On Roman military theory see J. Campbell, 'Teach yourself how to be a general', *Journal of Roman Studies* 77 (1987), pp. 13–29 and K. Gilliver, *The Roman Art of War* (2000); for the factors determining the appointment of commanders contrast E. Birley, *The Roman Army, Papers 1929–1986* (1988), pp. 75–114 and J. Campbell, 'Who were the *viri militares?*', *Journal of Roman Studies* 65 (1975), pp. 11–31.

3 For the generally low opinion of Roman commanders see Maj. Gen. J. Fuller, *Julius Caesar: Man, Soldier and Tyrant* (1965), pp. 74–75; W. Messer, 'Mutiny in the Roman Army of the Republic', *Classical Philology* 15 (1920), pp. 158–175, esp. p. 158; F. Adcock, *The Roman Art of War under the Republic* (1940), p. 101. The elder Moltke's comment that 'In war with its enormous friction even the mediocre is quite an achievement' quoted in M. Van Creveld, *Command in War* (1985), p. 13.

4 For a recent survey of Rome's early history see T. Cornell, *The Beginnings of Rome* (1995).

5 *Iliad* 12. 318–321 (translation R. Lattimore, University of Chicago Press, 1951).

6 The Horiatii and Curiatii, Livy 1. 23–27, Horatius Cocles, 2. 10–11.

7 On Rome's early military organization see Cornell (1995), pp. 173–197; B. D'Agustino, 'Military Organization and Social Structure in Archaic Etruria', in O. Murray and S. Price (eds.), *The Greek City* (Oxford, 1990), pp. 59–82;

E. McCarteney, 'The Military Indebtedness of Early Rome to Etruria', *Memoirs of the American Academy at Rome* 1 (1917), pp. 122–167; M.P. Nilsson, 'The introduction of Hoplite Tactics at Rome', *Journal of Roman Studies* 19 (1929), pp. 1–11; E. Rawson, 'The Literary Sources for the Pre–Marian Roman Army', *Papers of the British School at Rome* 39 (1971), pp. 13–31; L. Rawlings, 'Condottieri and Clansmen: Early Italian Warfare and the State', in K. Hopwood, *Organized Crime in the Ancient World* (Swansea, 2001); and A.M. Snodgrass, 'The Hoplite Reform and History', *Journal of Hellenic Studies* 85 (1965), pp. 110–122.

8 For the role of the commander in Greek armies see E. Wheeler, 'The General as Hoplite', in V. Hanson (ed.), *Hoplites: the Classical Greek Battle Experience* (1991), pp. 121–170.

9 Plutarch *Pyrrhus* 16 (Penguin translation).

10 Livy 10. 26–30, esp. 28; for a discussion of single combat see S. Oakley, 'Single Combat and the Roman Army', *Classical Quarterly* 35 (1985), pp. 392–410.

11 For a discussion of the nature of aristocratic *virtus* see N. Rosenstein, *Imperatores Victi* (1990), esp. pp. 114–151.

12 For the development of the Republican army see L. Keppie, *The Making of the Roman Army* (1984), and E. Gabba, *The Roman Republic, the Army and the Allies* (Oxford, 1976), trans. P.J. Cuff.

13 On the context of command see Van Creveld (1985), pp. 17–57. On the availability of maps and other geographical information in the Roman world see A. Betrand, 'Stumbling through Gaul: Maps, Intelligence, and Caesar's *Bellum Gallicum'*, *The Ancient History Bulletin* 11. 4 (1997), 107–122, C. Nicolet, *Space, geography and politics in the early Roman empire* (1991), and B. Isaac, 'Eusebius and the geography of Roman provinces', in D. Kennedy (ed.), *The Roman army in the east. Journal of Roman Archaeology Supplementary Series* 18 (1996), pp. 153–167.

CHAPTER 1 Fabius and Marcellus

1 Frontinus, *Strategems* 1. 3. 3.

2 For accounts of the opening stages of the Second Punic War see J. Lazenby, *Hannibal's War* (1978), pp. 1–66, A. Goldsworthy, *The Punic Wars* (2000), pp. 143–190.

3 On Punic armies see Goldsworthy (2000), pp. 30–36.

4 Livy 22. 7. 6–14, 8. 2–7, Polybius 3. 87.

5 Plutarch, *Fabius Maximus* 1–5; on his first consulship see S. Dyson, *The Creation of the Roman Frontier* (1985), pp. 95–96.

6 Plutarch, *Fabius Maximus* 5, Livy 22. 9. 7–10. 10.

7 Plutarch, *Fabius Maximus* 4.

8 Polybius 3. 89. 1–90. 6, Livy 22. 12. 1–12, Plutarch, *Fabius Maximus* 5.

9 Plutarch, *Fabius Maximus* 5.

10 Livy 22. 15. 4–10.

11 Livy 22. 13. 1–18. 10, Polybius 3. 90. 7–94. 6, Frontinus, *Strategems* 1. 5. 28.

12 Polybius 3. 100. 1–105. 11, Livy 22. 18. 5–10, 23. 1–30. 10.

13 For a detailed discussion of Cannae see A. Goldsworthy, *Cannae* (2001).

14 Plutarch, *Marcellus* 12 and discussion in Lazenby (1978), pp. 94–95.

15 Plutarch, *Marcellus* 1–3.

16 Plutarch, *Marcellus* 4–7; generals preventing bad omens from discouraging their men, Frontinus, *Strategems* 1. 12. 1–12.

17 Plutarch, *Marcellus* 8.

18 Livy 23. 15. 7–17. 1

19 For an overview of the campaigns in Italy during these years see Goldsworthy (2000), pp. 222–229; Livy 23. 15. 7–16. 1, Plutarch, *Marcellus* 10, *Fabius Maximus* 20; sword and shield of Rome, Plutarch, *Fabius Maximus* 19, *Marcellus* 9.

20 Syracuse: see Goldsworthy (2000),

pp. 260–268, 'Tarentum: see ibid. pp. 229–233, 235–236; Marcellus' death, Livy 27. 26. 7–27. 14, Plutarch, *Marcellus* 29–30, Polybius 10. 32.

CHAPTER 2 Scipio Africanus

1 *Imperator me mater, non bellatorem peperit* – Frontinus, *Stratagems* 4. 7. 4.

2 Livy 26. 19. 3–9, Gellius, *Attic Nights* 6 (7). 1. 6.

3 Polybius 10. 2. 1–5. 10; F. Walbank, *A Historical Commentary on Polybius* 2 (Oxford, 1967), pp. 198–201, who notes that Polybius' story of Scipio being elected to the aedileship in the same year as his brother is incorrect.

4 Polybius 10. 3. 3–6; Pliny *Natural History* 16. 14; Livy 21. 46. 10.

5 Livy 22. 53. 1–13; Frontinus, *Strat.* 4. 7. 39.

6 Livy 222. 61. 14–15; cf. N. Rosenstein, *Imperatores Victi* (1993), pp. 139–140.

7 Livy 26. 18. 1–19. 9; cf. H. Scullard, *Scipio Africanus: Soldier and Politician* (London, 1970), p. 31, J. Lazenby, *Hannibal's War* (Warminster, 1978), and B. Caven, *The Punic Wars* (London, 1980).

8 For earlier campaigns in Spain see A. Goldsworthy, *The Punic Wars* (London, 2000), pp. 246–253.

9 Polybius 10. 6. 1–9. 7; Walbank 2 (1967), pp. 201–2.

10 Polybius 10. 7. 3–5; Walbank 2 (1967), p. 202, cf. Lazenby (1978), p. 134.

11 Polybius 10. 9. 4–7, Livy 26. 42. 1.

12 Polybius 10. 9. 7, Livy 26. 42. 6; Walbank 2 (1967), pp. 204–205.

13 Accounts of the assault, Polybius 10. 9. 8–17. 5, Livy 26. 42. 6–46. 10, Appian *Spanish Wars* 20–22; Walbank 2 (1967), pp. 192–196, 203–217.

14 Polybius 10. 13. 1–4.

15 Sallust, *Bellum Catilinae* 7. 6.

16 Plutarch, *Marcellus* 18, Polybius 8. 37. 1.

17 Polybius 10. 15. 4–5. See also A. Ribera I Lacomba con M. Calvo Galvez, 'La primera evidencia arqueológica de la destrucción de Valentia por Pompeyo', *Journal of Roman Archaeology* 8 (1995), pp. 19–40 for evidence of Roman atrocities, although in this case committed during a civil war. For discussion of Roman plundering see A. Ziolkowski '*Urbs direpta*, or how the Romans sacked cities', in J. Rich and

M. Shipley, *War and Society in the Roman World* (London, 1993), pp. 69–91, although not all his conclusions have been generally accepted.

18 Livy 26. 48. 5–14.

19 Polybius 10. 18. 1–19. 7, Livy 26. 49. 11–50. 14, cf. Plutarch, *Alexander* 21.

20 Polybius 10. 39. 1–40. 12; Livy 27. 17. 1–20. 8, 28. 1. 1–2. 12, 1. 13–4.4.

21 Polybius 11. 20. 1–9, Livy 28. 12. 10–13. 5.

22 Polybius 11. 21. 1–6, Livy 28. 13. 6–10.

23 On the battle in general see Polybius 11. 21. 7–24. 9, Livy 28. 14. 1–15. 11. For discussion of the location of the battle and Scipio's manoeuvre see Lazenby (1978), pp. 147–149, Walbank 2 (1970), pp. 296–304, and Scullard (1970), pp. 88–92.

24 For a more detailed account of the African campaign see Goldsworthy (2000), pp. 286–309.

25 For this period see Scullard (1970), pp. 210–44.

26 Livy 35. 14.

CHAPTER 3 Aemilius Paullus

1 Livy 44. 34.

2 For brief accounts of the First Macedonian War see J. Lazenby, *Hannibal's War* (1978), pp. 157–169, and A. Goldsworthy (2000), pp. 253–260. For a critical view of Rome's motives in the war, see W.V. Harris, *War and Imperialism in Republican Rome 327–70 BC* (1979), pp. 205–208.

3 Livy 31. 6. 1; for the description of the declaration of war see Livy 31. 5. 1–8. 4; and comments in Harris (1979), pp. 212–218, F. Walbank, 'Polybius and Rome's eastern policy', *Journal of Roman Studies* 53 (1963), pp. 1–13, P. Derow, 'Polybius, Rome and the east', *Journal of Roman Studies* 69 (1979), pp. 1–15, and in general J. Rich, *Declaring War in the Roman Republic in the period of Transmarine Expansion. Collection Latomus 149* (1976).

4 The negotiations between Flamininus and Philip V, Polybius 18. 1. 1–12. 5, Livy 32. 32. 1–37. 6; Cynoscephalae, Polybius 18. 18. 1–27. 6, Livy 33. 1. 1–11. 3.

5 The Magnesia campaign, Livy 38. 37–44, Appian, *Syrian Wars* 30–36.

6 On the Galatian campaign, Livy 38. 12–27, 37–41; on the debate over Vulso's actions, Livy

38. 44–50; the Lucius Flamininus scandal, Livy 39. 42–43.

7 For the causes of the war see Livy 42. 5–6, 11–18, 25–26, 29–30, and comments in Harris (1979), pp. 227–233.

8 Size of army, Livy 42. 31; Spurius Ligustinus, Livy 42. 32–35.

9 Perseus' army at start of war, Livy 42. 51. One of the best studies of any Hellenistic army is B. Bar Kochva, *The Seleucid Army* (1976); for equipment see P. Connolly, *Greece and Rome at War* (1981), pp. 64–83.

10 Livy 42. 49. 53, 43. 17–23, 44. 1–16; Cassius Longinus, Livy 43. 1. 4–12.

11 Livy 44. 4. 10 – '*cum Romanus imperator, maior sexaginta annis et praegravis corpore*'.

12 Paullus in Spain, Livy 37. 2. 11, 37. 46. 7–8, 57. 5–6; in Liguria, Livy 40. 18, 25, 28. 7–8, Plutarch *Aemilius Paullus* 6; Paullus' sons, Plutarch, *Aemilius Paullus* 5.

13 Size of army, Livy 44. 21. 5–11.

14 Livy 44. 34. 3.

15 Livy 44. 32. 5–34. 10; see also F. Walbank, *A Historical Commentary on Polybius* 3 (1979), pp. 378–391.

16 Plutarch, *Aemilius Paullus* 15–16, Livy 44. 35; for a detailed discussion of the campaign see N. Hammond, 'The Battle of Pydna', *Journal of Hellenic Studies* 104 (1984), pp. 31–47.

17 Livy 44. 36. 12–14.

18 Hammond (1984), pp. 38–39.

19 Livy 44. 36. 1–4.

20 Livy 44. 37. 5–9, Plutarch, *Aemilius Paullus* 17.

21 Plutarch, *Aemilius Paullus* 17–18, Livy 44. 37. 10–40. 10, Frontinus, *Stratagems*. 2. 3. 20, and Hammond (1984), pp. 44–45.

22 Plutarch, *Aemilius Paullus* 18, and Hammond pp. 45–46.

23 Plutarch, *Aemilius Paullus* 19.

24 Plutarch, *Aemilius Paullus* 20.

25 Plutarch, *Aemilius Paullus* 19.

26 Plutarch, *Aemilius Paullus* 19–22, Livy 44. 41. 1–42. 9.

27 Polybius discussed the relative strengths and weaknesses of the legion and the phalanx, 18. 28. 1–32. 13.

28 Plutarch, *Aemilius Paullus* 21, Livy 44. 44. 1–3

29 Plutarch, *Aemilius Paullus* 30–32, Livy 45. 35. 5–39. 19.

30 Plutarch, *Aemilius Paullus* 32 (translation by R. Waterfield, *Plutarch: Roman Lives* (Oxford 1999)).

31 Plutarch, *Aemilius Paullus* 34 (Oxford translation, 1999).

32 Livy 45. 32. 11.

CHAPTER 4 Scipio Aemilianus

1 Appian, *Spanish Wars* 87.

2 For an account of the Telamon campaign see Polybius 2. 23–31.

3 Livy 34. 9. 1–13, 11. 1–15. 9, Appian, *Spanish Wars* 40.

4 For an analysis of these operations see S. Dyson, *The Creation of the Roman Frontier* (1985), pp. 174–198.

5 Polybius 32. 9. 1–2.

6 On Scipio's character see Polybius 31. 23. 1–30. 4. For Scipio's life and career in general see A. Astin, *Scipio Aemilianus* (1967).

7 Appian, *Spanish Wars* 44–50.

8 Polybius 35. 1. 1–4. 14, with Walbank 3 (1979), pp. 640–648; Appian *Spanish Wars* 49.

9 Lucullus' campaign, see Appian, *Spanish Wars* 50–55, and comments in Dyson (1985), pp. 202–203; on Galba see Appian *Spanish Wars* 58–60.

10 Polybius 35. 5. 1–2.

11 Tribune in Legio IV, Cicero *De Re Publica* 6. 9; for an account of Scipio's role in the Third Punic War see A. Goldsworthy, *The Punic Wars* (2000), pp. 342–356.

12 Appian, *Spanish Wars* 61–75, with Dyson (1985), pp. 206–213.

13 Appian, *Spanish Wars* 76–83, Plutarch, *Tiberius Gracchus* 5–6, with Dyson (1985), pp. 214–217.

14 Appian, *Spanish Wars* 84.

15 Appian, *Spanish Wars* 85.

16 Frontinus, *Strat.* 4. 1. 1, 1. 9.

17 Frontinus, *Strat.* 4. 3. 9.

18 Appian, *Spanish Wars* 86–89.

19 For the siege in general see Appian, *Spanish Wars* 90–98.

20 Frontinus, *Strat.* 4. 7. 27.

21 Appian, *Civil Wars* 19–20.

CHAPTER 5 Marius

1 Plutarch, *Marius* 7 (translation by R. Waterfield, *Plutarch: Roman Lives* (Oxford 1999)).

2 Plutarch, *Marius* 3.

3 Plutarch, *Marius* 2.

4 Plutarch, *Marius* 3 and 13.

5 Plutarch, *Marius* 4–6, Sallust, *Bellum Jugurthinum* 68. 1–7 and G.M. Paul, *A Historical Commentary on Sallust's Bellum Jugurthinum* (1984), pp. 166–171, and R.J. Evans, *Gaius Marius* (1994), pp. 19–60.

6 Sallust, *Bellum Jugurthinum* 27. 1–.36. 4.

7 Sallust, *Bellum Jugurthinum* 44. 1–45. 3.

8 Sallust, *Bellum Jugurthinum* 85. 13–17.

9 Sallust, *Bellum Jugurthinum* 103–114, Frontinus, *Stratagems* 3. 9. 3.

10 For a discussion see L. Keppie, *The Making of the Roman Army* (1984), pp. 57–79, E. Gabba, *Republican Rome: the Army and Allies* (1976), and F. Smith, *Service in the Post-Marian Roman Army* (Manchester, 1958).

11 Sallust, *Bellum Jugurthinum* 87–88, 100, 'more by their sense of shame than punishment', 100. 5.

12 Valerius Maximus 2. 3. 2, Frontinus, *Strat.* 4. 2. 2; on training methods see Vegetius, *Epitoma Rei Militaris* 1. 11–19.

13 Plutarch, *Marius* 13–14, Polybius 6. 37.

14 Plutarch, *Marius* 11, S. Dyson, *The Creation of the Roman Frontier* (1985), pp. 161–164.

15 Appian, *Celtica* 13.

16 Velleius Paterculus 2. 12. 2, Orosius 5. 16. 1–7, Plutarch, *Sertorius* 3.

17 Plutarch, *Marius* 12, Strabo *Geography* 4. 1. 13.

18 Plutarch, *Marius* 14–15, Sulla 4, *Sertorius* 3.

19 Plutarch, *Marius* 15 (Oxford translation by R. Waterfield, 1999).

20 Plutarch, *Marius* 25 (Oxford translation by R. Waterfield, 1999).

21 For a more detailed discussion of combat in this period see A. Goldsworthy, *The Roman Army at War 100 BC – AD 200* (1996), pp. 171–247.

22 Plutarch, *Marius* 15–18, Frontinus *Strat.* 4. 7. 5.

23 Plutarch, *Marius* 17.

24 Plutarch, *Marius* 19; for a discussion of the army's servants see J. Roth, *The Logistics of the*

Roman Army at War, 264 BC – AD 235 (1999), pp. 91–116.

25 Plutarch, *Marius* 20, Frontinus, *Strat.* 2. 9. 1.

26 Plutarch, *Marius* 21–22.

27 Plutarch, *Marius* 23–27.

28 Appian, *Civil Wars* 1. 28–33, Plutarch *Marius* 28–30.

29 Plutarch, *Marius* 33–35, *Sulla* 8–9, Appian *Civil Wars* 1. 55–63.

30 Plutarch, *Marius* 45.

31 Plutarch, *Marius* 33 (Oxford translation by R. Waterfield, 1999).

CHAPTER 6 Sertorius

1 Plutarch, *Sertorius* 10 (Penguin translation).

2 Plutarch, *Sertorius* 3–4, cf. Livy 27. 28. 1–13.

3 Plutarch, *Sertorius* 4–6, Appian *Civil Wars* 1. 71–75.

4 Plutarch, *Sertorius* 7–12, Appian *Civil Wars* 1. 108; cf. S. Dyson, *The Creation of the Roman Frontier* (1985), pp. 227–234. For a useful survey of Sertorius' campaigns see P. Greenhalgh, *Pompey: The Roman Alexander* (1980), pp. 40–57.

5 Plutarch, *Sertorius* 14, Appian, *Civil Wars* 1. 108.

6 Plutarch, *Sertorius* 14; Caesar, *Bellum Civile* 1. 41.

7 Plutarch, *Sertorius* 16, Frontinus, *Stratagems* 1. 10. 1; 4. 7. 6, cf. 1. 10. 2.

8 Frontinus, *Strat.* 1. 11. 13.

9 Plutarch, *Sertorius* 18.

10 cf. G. Castellvi, J. M. Nolla and I. Rodà, 'La identificación de los trofeos de Pompeyo en el Pirineo', *Journal of Roman Archaeology* 8 (1995), pp. 5–18.

11 For the Lauron campaign, see Plutarch, *Sertorius* 18, Frontinus, *Strat.* 2. 5. 31, and Greenhalgh (1980), pp. 46–48.

12 Plutarch, *Sertorius* 18–19 and *Pompey* 19.

13 Plutarch, *Sertorius* 20–22, Appian, *Civil Wars* 110, Sallust, *Histories* 2. 98.

14 Treaty with Mithridates, Plutarch, *Sertorius* 23–24, Appian, *Mithridates* 68.

15 Plutarch, *Sertorius* 22.

16 The final campaigns, Plutarch, *Sertorius* 25–27, Appian, *Civil Wars* 111–115, Greenhalgh (1980), pp. 54–57.

CHAPTER 7 Pompey

1 Pliny, *Natural History* 7. 95 – translation taken from Greenhalgh, *Pompey: the Roman Alexander* (1980) p. 122.

2 For Pompey's life in general see P. Greenhalgh, *Pompey: the Roman Alexander* (1980) and *Pompey: the Republican Prince* (1981).

3 Appian, *Civil Wars* 1. 40, 47, 63–64, 68, Plutarch, *Pompey* 3, Greenhalgh (1980), pp. 1–11.

4 Plutarch, *Pompey* 4.

5 Plutarch, *Pompey* 5–8, Appian, *Civil Wars* 1. 80–81.

6 Plutarch, *Sulla* 29.

7 Appian, *Civil Wars* 1. 95–103, Plutarch, *Pompey* 10–11 and *Sulla* 30–35.

8 Plutarch, *Pompey* 11–12.

9 Plutarch, *Pompey* 14; for Pompey's early commands up to this point see Greenhalgh (1980), pp. 12–29.

10 For the Lepidus affair see Plutarch, *Pompey* 15–16, Appian, *Civil Wars* 1. 105–106, and Greenhalgh (1980), pp. 30–39.

11 A. Ribera i Lacomba con M. Calvo Galvez, 'La primera evidencia arqueológica de la destrucción de Valentia por Pompeyo', *Journal of Roman Archaeology* 8 (1995), pp. 19–40.

12 For the Slave Rebellion see Plutarch, *Crassus* 8–11, Appian, *Civil Wars* 1. 116–121.

13 Greenhalgh (1980), pp. 64–71.

14 Plutarch, *Pompey* 22.

15 The pirate problem and Pompey's appointment, see Appian, *Mithridates* 91–93, Plutarch, *Pompey* 24–25.

16 For a detailed review of the sources for the debate surrounding the *Lex Gabinia* see Greenhalgh (1980), pp. 72–90.

17 The campaign against the pirates, see Appian, *Mith.* 94–96, Plutarch, *Pompey* 26–28.

18 The Metellus affair, Plutarch, *Pompey* 29.

19 Cicero, *de imperio Cnaeo Pompeio* 28, Plutarch, *Pompey* 30–31.

20 For Lucullus' campaigns see Appian, *Mith.* 72–90, Plutarch, *Lucullus* 7–36; Tigranes' comment, Appian, *Mith.* 85.

21 Plutarch, *Pompey* 32; Appian, *Mith.* 97

22 Frontinus, *Sratagems* 2. 5. 33.

23 Appian, *Mith.* 98–101, Dio 36. 45–54, Plutarch, *Pompey* 32, Frontinus, *Strat.* 2. 1. 12; for a discussion of the sources and detailed narrative of the campaign see Greenhalgh (1980), pp.105–114.

24 Plutarch, *Pompey* 33, Appian, *Mith.* 104.

25 Plutarch, *Pompey* 34.

26 Strabo, *Geography* 11. 3. 499–504, Plutarch, *Pompey* 35, Frontinus, *Strat.* 2. 3. 14, Appian, *Mith.* 103.

27 Plutarch, *Pompey* 41–42, Appian, *Mith.* 107–112.

28 For a discussion of Pompey's other operations in the east and his Settlement see Greenhalgh (1980), pp. 120–167.

CHAPTER 8 **Caesar**

1 Suetonius, *Julius Caesar* 60.

2 If only through their contribution to the first page of Asterix comic books.

3 For an introduction to the literature on Caesar's Commentaries see the collection of papers in K. Welch and A. Powell (eds.), *Julius Caesar as Artful Reporter: The War Commentaries as Political Instruments* (1998).

4 For Caesar's life see C. Meier (trans. D. McLintock), *Caesar* (1995), and M. Gelzer (trans. P. Needham), *Caesar: Politician and Statesman* (1985). The incident with the pirates, Suetonius *Julius Caesar* 4.

5 For this period see Meier (1995), pp. 133–189; the incident during the Catilinarian debate is in Plutarch, *Brutus* 5.

6 Meier (1995), pp. 204–223.

7 Caesar, *Bellum Gallicum* 1. 2–5.

8 Numbers, *BG* 1. 29; crossing the Arar 1. 13; Tigurini 1. 7, 12.

9 *BG* 1. 7–8; his army in Gaul see H. Parker, *The Roman Legions* (1928), pp. 48–71.

10 *BG* 1. 8–10.

11 *BG* 1. 11–20.

12 *BG* 1. 21–22.

13 *BG* 1. 52.

14 *BG* 1. 23–26.

15 *BG* 1. 27–29.

16 Size of army, *BG* 1. 31, the total probably including the 24,000 recently arrived Harudes; King and Friend of the Roman People, *BG* 1. 35.

17 The campaign against Ariovistus, *BG* 1. 30–54.

18 *BG* 2. 20.

19 *BG* 2. 25.

20 *BG* 1. 52; the Belgian campaign see *BG* 2. 1–35.

21 Meier (1995), pp. 265–301.

22 Plutarch, *Cato* 51.

23 Suetonius, *Julius Caesar* 47.

24 *BG* 5. 24–58, 6. 1–10, 29–44, Suetonius, *Julius Caesar* 57.

25 *BG* 7. 1–2.

26 *BG* 7. 3–10.

27 On rebellions see A. Goldsworthy, *The Roman Army at War, 100 BC – AD 200* (1996), pp. 79–95.

28 *BG* 7. 11–15.

29 *BG* 7. 16–31.

30 *BG* 7. 47.

31 Operations around Gergovia and involving Labienus, *BG* 7. 32–62.

32 *BG* 7. 66–68.

33 *BG* 7. 69–74.

34 *BG* 7. 75–78.

35 *BG* 7. 79–80.

36 *BG* 7. 88.

37 *BG* 7. 81–89, Plutarch, *Caesar* 27.

CHAPTER 9 **Caesar and Pompey**

1 Cicero, *Letters to Atticus* 7. 3 (Loeb translation).

2 On the build-up to the Civil War see C. Meier, *Caesar* (1995), pp. 330–363; the desire to be first, Plutarch, *Caesar* 12.

3 Appian, *Civil Wars* 2. 34–35, Plutarch, *Caesar* 32.

4 On the early stages of the war see Meier (1995), pp. 364–387; 'stamping his foot', Plutarch, *Pompey* 57, 60.

5 Caesar, *Bellum Civile* 3. 3–5, Plutarch, *Pompey* 63–64, Appian, *Civil Wars* 2. 40, 49–52.

6 Mutiny of *Legio IX*, Appian, *Civil Wars* 2. 47.

7 Caesar, *Bellum Civile* 3. 6–10.

8 Caesar, *BC* 3. 11–30, Appian, *Civil Wars* 2. 50–59, Plutarch, *Caesar* 65.

9 Caesar, *BC* 3. 34, 39–44, Appian, *Civil Wars* 2. 60–61.

10 Caesar, *BC* 3. 45–53, Suetonius, *Julius Caesar* 68. 3–4.

11 Caesar, *BC* 3. 54–56, 58–72, Appian, *Civil Wars* 2. 61–63, Plutarch, *Caesar* 65.

12 Caesar, *BC* 3. 73–76.

13 Caesar, *BC* 3. 77–81, Plutarch, *Caesar* 41.

14 Sources for Pharsalus see Caesar *BC* 3. 82–99, Appian, *Civil Wars* 2. 68–82, Plutarch, *Caesar* 42–47 and *Pompey* 68–72.

15 Plutarch, *Pompey* 73–79, 80 and *Caesar* 48, Appian, *Civil Wars* 2. 83–86, 89–90.

16 For a description of the later campaigns in the Civil War see Meier (1995), pp. 402–413; Caesar and Cleopatra, see Plutarch, *Caesar* 48–49 and Suetonius, *Julius Caesar* 58; Zela, see Plutarch, *Caesar* 50.

17 Caesar, *African War* 82–83.

18 Plutarch, *Caesar* 53.

19 Meier (1995), pp. 414–486.

20 On the army in this period see L. Keppie, *The Making of the Roman Army* (1984), pp. 80–131.

21 Suetonius, *Julius Caesar* 68, cf. Caesar *BC* 1. 39 where he uses a loan from the centurions and tribunes to pay the troops.

22 Suetonius, *Julius Caesar* 67.

23 Suetonius, *Julius Caesar* 65.

24 Suetonius, *Julius Caesar* 57, cf. Plutarch, *Caesar* 17; encouraged men to have decorated equipment, Suetonius, *Julius Caesar* 57.

25 Caesar, *Bellum Gallicum* 1. 42.

26 Scaeva, *BC* 3. 53, *ala Scaevae*, *Corpus Inscriptiones Latinarum* 10. 6011; Crastinus, Appian, *Civil Wars* 82.

27 Appian, *Civil Wars* 2. 47, 92–94, Suetonius, *Julius Caesar* 69–70.

CHAPTER 10 Germanicus

1 Velleius Paterculus, *Roman History* 2. 129. 2.

2 For the rise of Augustus and creation of the Principate see R. Syme, *The Roman Revolution* (1939).

3 Augustus and the soldiers, Suetonius, *Augustus* 25; for the army in this period in general see L. Keppie, *The Making of the Roman Army* (1984), pp. 132–171.

4 For Crassus and the *spolia opima* see Dio 51. 24.

5 Suetonius, *Claudius* 1.

6 Suetonius, *Tiberius* 18–19, Velleius Paterculus, *Roman History* 2. 113. 1–115. 5.

7 Velleius Paterculus, *Roman History* 2. 104. 4.

8 Suetonius, *Caius* 23.

9 See M. Todd, *The Early Germans* (1992); for the strategic position on the Rhine frontier in this period see C. Wells, *The German Policy of Augustus* (1972).

10 On Caesar's presentation of the Gauls see K. Welch and A. Powell (eds.), *Julius Caesar as Artful Reporter: The War Commentaries as Political Instruments* (1998), and especially the papers by Barlow, 'Noble Gauls and their other in Caesar's propaganda', pp. 139–170, and L. Rawlings, 'Caesar's portrayal of the Gauls as warriors', pp. 171–192.

11 Defeat of *V Alaudae* see Dio 54. 20, Velleius Paterculus *Roman History* 2. 106. 1; for the campaigns in general see Wells (1972); Tiberius' decision to divide his army in Pannonia, Velleius Paterculus, *Roman History* 2. 113. 1–2.

12 Velleius Paterculus, *Roman History* 2. 117. 1–119. 5, Dio 56. 18–22.

13 Dio 56. 23–24, Suetonius, *Augustus* 23.

14 Celebration of Germanicus' birthday by a third-century army unit see R. Fink, *Roman Military Records on Papyrus* (1971) No. 117; Suetonius, *Caius* 5, 9.

15 Suetonius, *Augustus* 24–25.

16 Tacitus, *Annals* 1. 16–45, 48–49; 'not a cure, but a disaster', 1. 49.

17 Caesar, *Bellum Gallicum* 8. 3.

18 Tacitus, *Annals* 1. 50–51.

19 For a discussion of Germanic warfare see A. Goldsworthy, *The Roman Army at War 100 BC – AD 200* (1996), pp. 42–53; for the aims and methods of Roman punitive expeditions see ibid. pp. 95–105.

20 Tacitus, *Annals* 1. 55–58.

21 Tactitus, *Annals* 1. 61–2.

22 Tacitus, *Annals* 1. 59–63.

23 Tacitus, *Annals* 1. 63–69.

24 Tacitus, *Annals* 1. 70–71.

25 Tacitus, *Annals* 2. 5–8.

26 Tacitus, *Annals* 2. 9–11.

27 Tacitus, *Annals* 2. 12–13.

28 Tacitus, *Annals* 2. 14.

29 Tacitus, *Annals* 2. 14–18.

30 Tacitus, *Annals* 2. 19–22.

31 Tacitus, *Annals* 2. 23–26.

32 Suetonius, *Caius* 2, 4–6.

33 Tacitus, *Annals* 2. 88.

CHAPTER 11 Corbulo

1 Frontinus, *Stratagems* 4. 7. 2.

2 On the relationship between the princeps and the army see B. Campbell, *The Emperor and the Roman Army, 31 BC–AD 235* (1984).

3 Suetonius, *Augustus* 25. 4. The second tag was actually a quote from Euripides, *Phoenisae* 599 where it is used ironically. Much the same idea is expressed in Appian, *Iberica* 87.

4 For a discussion see D. Potter, 'Emperors, their borders and their neighbours: the scope of imperial *mandata*', in D. Kennedy, *The Roman Army in the Near East. Journal of Roman Archaeology Supplementary Series* 18 (1996), pp. 49–66.

5 *Inscriptiones Latinae Selectae* 986 (translation from Campbell (1984), pp. 359–361).

6 Tacitus, *Annals* 11. 18.

7 Tacitus, *Annals* 11. 19–20.

8 On Parthian armies see A. Goldsworthy, *The Roman Army at War 100 BC – AD 200* (1996), pp. 60–68; on the Parthian state see N. Debevoise, *The Political History of Parthia* (1938), M. Colledge, *The Parthians* (1967); on relations between Rome and Parthia see B. Isaac, *The Limits of Empire* (1992), pp. 19–53, B. Campbell, 'War and Diplomacy: Rome and Parthia, 31 BC–AD 235' in J. Rich and G. Shipley, *War and Society in the Roman World* (1993), pp. 213–240, and D. Kennedy, 'Parthia and Rome: eastern perspectives' in Kennedy (1996), pp. 67–90.

9 Crassus and Carrhae, Plutarch, *Crassus* 17–33.

10 Plutarch, *Antony* 37–51.

11 Tacitus, *Annals* 13. 6–8.

12 Tacitus, *Annals* 13. 9. On recruitment see J. Mann, *Legionary Recruitment and veteran settlement during the Principate* (1983) and P. Brunt, 'Conscription and volunteering in the Roman Imperial Army', *Scripta Classica Israelica* 1 (1974), pp. 90–115.

13 See B. Isaac, *The Limits of Empire* (1992), pp. 24–25 and E. Wheeler, 'The laxity of the Syrian legions', in Kennedy (1996), pp. 229–276.

14 Tacitus, *Annals* 13. 35.

15 Tacitus, *Annals* 13. 3; on the identity of the legions under Corbulo see H. Parker, *The Roman Legions* (1957), p. 133–135.

16 Tacitus, *Annals* 13. 36 and Frontinus, *Strat.* 4. 1. 21 and 28.

17 Tacitus, *Annals* 13. 37–39.

18 Tacitus, *Annals* 13. 39.

19 Tacitus, *Annals* 13. 40–41.

20 Frontinus, *Strat.* 2. 9. 5.

21 Tacitus, *Annals* 14. 23–26.

22 Tacitus, *Annals* 15. 1–3.

23 Tacitus, *Annals* 15. 4–6.

24 Tacitus, *Annals* 15. 7.

25 Tacitus, *Annals* 15. 8–17.

26 Tacitus, *Annals* 15. 18. 24–31.

27 Paulinus, Tacitus, *Annals* 14. 29–39; Agricola, Tacitus, *Agricola passim*; Lucullus, Suetonius, *Domitian* 10.

28 Tacitus, *Annals* 15. 28 on Annius' role in eastern campaign; for the politics behind this alleged plot see M. Griffin, *Nero: the End of a Dynasty* (1984).

CHAPTER 12 – Titus

1 Josephus, *Bellum Judaicum* 5. 59–61 (Loeb translation).

2 A good narrative of the Year of Four Emperors is provided in K. Wellesley, *The Long Year: AD 69* (1989).

3 For Vespasian see B. Levick, *Vespasian* (1999).

4 Josephus, *BJ* 5. 97 (Loeb translation).

5 On Josephus see T. Rajak, *Josephus: The Historian and his Society* (1983), and S. Cohen, *Josephus in Galilee and Rome* (1979). On Judaea in this period see E. Schurer, *The History of the Jewish People in the Age of Jesus Christ*, rev. ed. G. Vermes, F. Millar, M. Black, M. Goodman (Edinburgh, 1973–87), A. Smallwood, *The Jews under Roman Rule* (1976), and M. Avi-Yonah, *The Jews of Palestine* (1976). There is also a good deal of relevance in B. Isaac, *The Limits of Empire* (1992).

6 A good indication of the general ignorance about the nature of Judaism can be gained by reading Tacitus' brief summary of Jewish history which preceded his account of the fall of Jerusalem, *Hisories* 5. 2–13. See also M. Whittaker, *Jews and Christians: Greco-Roman Views* (1984) for a collection of sources describing pagan attitudes.

7 For the Jewish aristocracy in this period see M. Goodman, *The Ruling Class of Judaea: Origins of the Jewish Revolt against Rome, AD 66–70* (1987).

8 For the Cestius Gallus campaign see Josephus, *BJ* 2. 499–555, and also S. Brandon, 'The Defeat of Cestius Gallus in AD 66', *History Today* 20 (1970), pp. 38–46.

9 Tacitus, *Histories* 2. 5.

10 Josephus' surrender, Bell, J., 3. 340–408.

11 Tribunate, Suetonius, *Titus* 4; legatus of *XV Apollinaris* Josephus, *BJ* 3. 64–69; Japha, *BJ* 3. 289–305; Tarichaeae, *BJ* 3. 462–502; Gamala, *BJ* 4. 70–83.

12 *BJ* 5. 44.

13 Titus' forces, *BJ* 5. 40–46, Tacitus, *Histories* 5. 1. On the army in the Jerusalem campaign see A. Goldsworthy, 'Community under Pressure: the army at the Roman siege of Jerusalem', in A. Goldsworthy and I. Haynes, *The Roman Army as a Community in Peace and War. Journal of Roman Archaeology Supplementary Series* 34 (1999), pp. 197–210. The centurion, see E. Dabrowa, *Legio X Fretensis: A Prosopographical Study of its Officers I–III AD. Historia Einzelschriften* 66 (Stuttgart, 1993), No. 19, p. 89, with the review by B. Isaac in *Scripta Classica Israelica* 14 (1995), pp. 169–171. The inscriptions are *Corpus Inscriptiones Latinarum* III. 30, *Inscriptiones Latinae Selectae* 8759a and *L'Aunée Epigraphique* 1923. 83 respectively.

14 Josephus' description of Jerusalem's monuments, *BJ* 5. 136–247.

15 Number of defenders, *BJ* 5. 248–250, and overall population, 6. 420–434, Tacitus, *Histories* 5. 13.

16 *BJ* 5. 47–51.

17 *BJ* 5. 52–66.

18 *BJ* 5. 86–7 (Loeb translation).

19 *BJ* 5. 67–97.

20 *BJ* 5. 98–135.

21 *BJ* 5. 258–274; impact of artillery stones, 3. 245–7; number with each legion Vegetius, *Epitoma Rei Militaris* 2. 25.

22 *BJ* 5. 275–283; incident at Jotapata, 3. 229–232.

23 *BJ* 5. 284–303.

24 *BJ* 5. 310–311 (Loeb translation).

25 *BJ* 5. 304–341, Suetonius, *Titus* 5.

26 *BJ* 5. 346–355, and discussion in Goldsworthy (1999), p. 203.

27 See P. Connolly, *The Jews in the Time of Jesus* (1994), pp. 77, 86.

28 *BJ* 5. 356–360, 460–490.

29 *BJ* 5. 491–511, Dio 65. 5. 4.

30 *BJ* 5. 548–561.

31 *BJ* 5. 522–526, 6. 1–32.

32 *BJ* 6. 33–92, cf. Josephus, *Vita* 361–363.

33 *BJ* 6. 93–5, 118–163.

34 *BJ* 6. 164–192, 220–235.

35 *BJ* 6. 236–266.

36 *BJ* 6. 316–413.

37 *BJ* 7. 5–16 (Loeb translation).

38 Fears over renewal of civil war, Suetonius, *Titus* 5; the triumph, *BJ* 7. 123–157, and Vespasian's comments, Suetonius, *Vespasian* 12; on Vespasian's reign and Titus role see Levick (1999), pp. 79–106, 184–195.

39 Last words, see Suetonius, *Vespasian* 23; funeral, Suetonius, *Vespasian* 19; Titus' unpopularity before his accession and affair with Berenice, Suetonius, *Titus* 6–7.

CHAPTER 13 Trajan

1 Cassius Dio, 68. 18. 2–3 (Loeb translation).

2 On the relationship between the *princeps* and the army see B. Campbell, *The Emperor and the Roman Army 31 BC–AD 235* (1984); for Claudius in Britain see Dio 60. 19. 1–22. 2 and Suetonius, *Claudius* 17.

3 Dio 67. 6. 16, 7. 2–4.

4 For Trajan's background and career in general see J. Bennett, *Trajan: Optimus Princeps* (2nd edn. 2001).

5 Bennett (2001), pp. 11–19.

6 Pliny, *Panegyricus* 15. 1–3.

7 Bennett (2001), pp. 19–26, 42–62.

8 Dio 67. 6. 1 (Loeb translation).

9 For surveys of the meagre sources for the Dacian wars see Bennett (2001), pp. 85–103, S. S. Frere and F. Lepper, *Trajan's Column* (1988), L. Rossi, *Trajan's Column and the Dacian*

Wars (1971), I. Richmond, *Trajan's Army on Trajan's Column* (1982).

10 Head taking on the Column, scenes 57–58, 140, 183–184, 302–303; for a discussion of this phenomenon in the Roman army see A. Goldsworthy, *The Roman Army at War 100 BC–AD 200* (1996), pp. 271–276; writing names on shields, Dio 67. 10. 1; on decorations see V. Maxfield, *The Military Decorations of the Roman Army* (1981).

11 The battle of Tapae and the story of the bandages, Dio 68. 8. 1–2.

12 Finding captured equipment in a fort, Dio 68. 9. 3.

13 Dio 68. 9. 1–2, 4–7.

14 Dio 68. 10. 3–12. 5.

15 Dio 68. 13. 1–6.

16 The Tiberius Claudius Maximus inscription, *L' Année Epigraphique* 1969/70, p. 583 and the comments in M. Speidel, 'The Captor of Decebalus', *Roman Army Studies 1* (1984), pp. 173–187.

17 Trajan's character, see Dio 68. 6. 1–7. 5; on the Parthian war see Dio 68. 17. 1–31. 4, and in general F. Lepper, *Trajan's Parthian War* (1948), and Bennett (2001), pp. 183–204.

18 Hatra, Dio 68. 31. 1–4.

19 Dio 69. 5. 2 (Loeb translation).

20 Dio 69. 9. 2–4 (Loeb translation).

21 *Inscriptiones Latinae Selectae* 2558, cf. Dio 69. 9. 6.

22 *Inscriptiones Latinae Selectae* 2487, 9133–5; for a discussion of these Lambaesis speeches see Campbell (1984), pp. 77–80.

CHAPTER 14 Julian

1 Ammianus Marcellinus 15. 8. 13.

2 Dio 56. 15. 2.

3 Herodian 4. 7. 4–7, 12. 2.

4 The satirist Lucian lampooned the many exaggerated accounts of Verus' behaviour in his *Quomodo Historiae*.

5 The best study of Roman warfare in this period is H. Elton, *Warfare in Roman Europe, AD 350–425* (1996). There are a number of biographies of Julian, notably R. Browning, *The Emperor Julian* (1976), and G. Bowersock, *Julian the Apostate* (1978). For a survey of our principal

source and his times see J. Matthews, *The Roman Empire of Ammianus* (1989).

6 Ammianus Marcellinus 15. 8. 1–17.

7 Loss of Colonia Agrippinensis, Ammianus Marcellinus 15. 8. 19. On the Late Roman army see Elton (1996), K. Dixon and P. Southern, *The Late Roman Army* (1996), and A. Ferrill, *The Fall of the Roman Empire* (1986). On the meagre evidence for unit sizes in this period see T. Coello, *Unit Sizes in the Late Roman Army. British Archaeological Review Series 645* (1996) and W. Treadgold, *Byzantium and its Army, 281–1081* (1995).

8 For the initial operations see Ammianus Marcellinus 16. 2. 1–13; 'prudent and cautious' 16. 2. 11.

9 Ammianus Marcellinus 16. 3. 1–4. 5; on fortifications and the poor preparedness of tribal armies for siege warfare see Elton (1996), pp. 82–86, 155–174.

10 Ammianus Marcellinus 27. 1–2.

11 The early phases of the 357 campaign, see Ammianus Marcellinus 16. 11. 1–15.

12 Army sizes, Ammianus Marcellinus 16. 12. 1–2, 12. 24–26, 12. 60.

13 Ammianus Marcellinus 16. 12. 1–18.

14 On the *cuneus* and its nickname see Ammianus Marcellinus 17. 13. 9, Tacitus, *Germania 6*, and Vegetius, *Epitoma Rei Militaris 3. 17*.

15 Ammianus Marcellinus 16. 12. 19–26.

16 Ammianus Marcellinus 16. 12. 27–35.

17 Ammianus Marcellinus 16. 12. 36–41; note also the comments in H. Delbrück (trans. W.J. Renfroe), *The Barbarian Invasions. History of the Art of War, Volume 2* (1980), pp. 261–268, esp. 263–264 on the practicalities of a commander rallying troops in this way. Delbrück's comments on this battle are, as always, highly interesting, but his belief – almost to the point of obsession – that barbarian warriors were so ferocious that they could only be defeated by greatly superior numbers of soldiers from civilized states does not rest on any evidence and makes many of his conclusions questionable.

18 Ammianus Marcellinus 16. 12. 42–66.

19 The losses, Ammianus Marcellinus 16. 12. 63; Constantius' reaction 16. 12. 67–70.

20 Ammianus Marcellinus 17. 1. 1–14.

21 Ammianus Marcellinus 17. 2. 1–4. In Libanius' account, which is also highly favourable to

Julian it is said that the Franks numbered 1,000, Libanius, *Opera* 18. 70.

22 Ammianus Marcellinus 17. 8. 1–2.

23 Ammianus Marcellinus 17. 8. 3–9.

24 Ammianus Marcellinus 17. 10. 1–10.

25 Ammianus Marcellinus 18. 2. 1–16, 20. 20. 1. 13.

26 Ammianus Marcellinus 20. 4. 1–5. 10.

27 For Pirisabora see Ammianus Marcellinus 24. 2. 15–17; Maozamalcha see 24. 4. 1–5.

28 Ammianus Marcellinus 24. 7. 1–25. 3. 23.

CHAPTER 15 **Belisarius**

1 Procopius, *Wars* 2. 18. 5–6 (Loeb translation).

2 On the Late Roman army in the east see W. Treadgold, *Byzantium and its Army, 281–1081* (1995). For a broad survey of Byzantine warfare see J. Haldon, *The Byzantine Wars* (2001). For the conflict with Persia see G. Greatrex, *Rome and Persia at War, 502–532* (1998).

3 See Greatrex (1998), esp. pp. 120–165; on Belisarius' origins see Procopius, *Wars* 3. 9. 21; the raid in *c.* 526 *Wars* 1. 12. 20–3.

4 Minduos, Procopius, *Wars* 1. 13. 2–5; appointment to command 1. 12. 24; the forces at Dara see 1. 13. 23 and Greatrex (1998), pp. 169, 173, and for a general discussion of the army in this period pp. 31–40.

5 Procopius, *Wars* 1. 13. 23, 1. 14. 1 and discussion in Greatrex (1998), pp. 175–176.

6 Procopius, *Wars* 1. 13. 19–23; for the use of field fortifications by Sulla see Frontinus, *Strategems* 2. 3. 17 and by Caesar see *Bellum Gallicum* 2. 8.

7 Procopius, *Wars* 1. 13. 24–39.

8 Procopius, *Wars* 1. 14. 33 (Loeb translation).

9 For the battle see Procopius, *Wars* 1. 14. 1–55 and the discussions in Greatrex (1998), pp. 171–185 and Haldon (2001), pp. 28–35; for the punishment of Peroz see *Wars* 1. 17. 26–8.

10 Procopius, *Wars* 1. 18. 1–50 with Greatrex (1998), pp. 195–207.

11 Belisarius' recall and appointment to the new command, Procopius, *Wars* 1. 21. 2, 3. 9. 25, 3. 10. 21, 3. 11. 18; size of army 3. 11. 2; the incident with the biscuits, 3. 13. 12–20; fraud during the Second Punic War, Livy 25. 3. 8–4. 11.

12 Procopius, *Wars* 3. 12. 8–22; Belisarius orders flogging of soldiers, 3. 16. 1–8.

13 Caesar *Bellum Civile* 1. 21, 2. 12.

14 Procopius, *Wars* 4. 4. 3–7 (Loeb translation).

15 Procopius, *Wars* 4. 3. 23–4. 25; the later mutiny and campaign against the Moors, 4. 14. 7–15. 49.

16 Procopius, *Wars* 5. 5. 1–7; siege of Naples 5. 8. 5–10. 48; size of force at Rome, 5. 22. 17.

17 Procopius, *Wars* 5. 18. 9–15 (Loeb translation); for the full account of the action 5. 18. 1–29.

18 Procopius, *Wars* 5. 22. 1–10.

19 Procopius, *Wars* 5. 28. 1–29. 50.

20 See C. Fauber, *Narses: the Hammer of the Goths* (1990), Haldon (2001), pp. 35–44, and H. Delbrück (trans. W.J. Renfroe), *The Barbarian Invasions. History of the Art of War, Volume 2* (1980), pp. 339–383.

21 On discipline under the Republic see W. Messer, 'Mutiny in the Roman Army in the Republic', *Classical Philology* 15 (1920), pp. 19–29.

CHAPTER 16 **Later Years**

1 For a discussion of Napoleon's style of command see M. Van Creveld, *Command in War* (1985), pp. 58–102.

2 For Sir Roger Williams see G. Parker, *The Military Revolution* (1988), p. 6.

3 On Wellington in battle see J. Keegan, *The Mask of Command* (1987), pp. 145–154.

4 For a discussion of this period see Creveld (1985), pp. 103–147.

INDEX